Love, Human and Divine:
The Heart of Christian Ethics

MORAL TRADITIONS & MORAL ARGUMENTS / A SERIES

Love, Human and Divine:
The Heart of Christian Ethics

EDWARD COLLINS VACEK, S.J.

GEORGETOWN UNIVERSITY PRESS / WASHINGTON, D.C.

Georgetown University Press, Washington, D.C.
© 1994 by Georgetown University Press. All rights reserved.
Printed in the United States of America
10 9 8 7 6 5 4 3 2 1   1994
THIS VOLUME IS PRINTED ON ACID-FREE OFFSET BOOK PAPER.

Library of Congress Cataloging-in-Publication Data

Vacek, Edward Collins.
    Love, human and divine: the heart of Christian ethics / Edward
Collins Vacek.
        p.   cm.
    Includes bibliographical references and index.
    1. Love--Religious aspects--Christianity.   2. God--Love.   3. God-
-Worship and love.   4. Christian ethics--Catholic authors.
    I. Title.
    BV4639.V25   1994   241'.4--dc20
    ISBN 0-87840-551-8   93-37944

To My Mother and Father
Who Loved Me To Life

Contents

7
Self-love   *239*

8
Philia   *280*

9
Friendship with God   *319*

Editor's Preface

Moral Traditions & Moral Arguments, as a series, presents systematic, scholarly accounts of major themes in Christian ethics in order to critically examine those insights that, perduring through the ages, have shaped and continue to shape Christian lives and communities. These books are intended to provide scholars with a precise understanding of moral traditions as well as an appreciation of their contribution to contemporary life.

Published by the Georgetown University Press, these first two titles inaugurate a series whose complex of careful analyses and broad scope offer books of interest and use to scholars in ethics, theology, religious studies and philosophy. Stephen Pope's *The Evolution of Altruism and the Ordering of Love* and Edward Vacek's *Love, Human and Divine* are an auspicious beginning for an important series of publications which concern the "heart of Christian ethics."

Weston School of Theology   JAMES F. KEENAN, S.J.,ED.

Introduction

You shall love the Lord your God
with your whole heart,
with your whole soul,
with all your mind.
This is the greatest and first commandment.
The second is like it:
You shall love your neighbor as yourself.
On these two commandments the whole law is based,
and the prophets as well. (Mt 22:37–40)[1]

Should we love God? Responsible theologians have said no. Should we love our neighbor? All Christians say yes, but they dispute what it means to do so. Should we love ourselves? Some Christians say it is sinful to do so, while others say it is the basis of virtue. Does the love of God have anything to do with loving our neighbor? Some Christians deny there is any real connection, while others say the two are in practice identical. And what is love? Offhanded answers are many, but extensive investigations are few. These questions introduce the central issues of this book.

I shall argue that the love of God must be the center of Christian life and theology.[2] Since Christians say that "God is love" (1 Jn 4:16) and that the Christian life is summed up in the two great commands (Mt 22:37–40), any hesitation to explore the role of love in ethics would seem peculiar. It is, nevertheless, typical. Love has *not* been central in most Christian ethics and dogmatic theology.[3] As Gérard Gilleman noted thirty years ago, "The very soul of the moral life expressed in the fundamental law of love . . . does not obviously appear to be reflected in our classical treatises on morals."[4] In fact, Catholic theology since the Middle Ages, following the intellectualist strand of Aquinas's thought, has generally emphasized reason.[5] And recent theology has made justice and hope more central than love.[6] Enda McDonagh observes of love that none of the great theologians "have given it the central, architectonic place one might expect. . . . In moral theology [love] received a very skimpy treatment."[7] Similarly,

Garth Hallett comments: "Strange as this assertion may sound after nearly two millennia of Christian emphasis on agape, the Christian norm of neighbor-love offers relatively virgin territory for inquiry."[8]

One reason that contemporary theologians avoid the topic of "love" is its reputation for being a "mushy" term.[9] As Alan Soble notes, "Stores in this country today stock and sell books on love by the millions: fictional, psychological and sociological, upliftingly practical, sentimental, and, with only a few exceptions, mildly to utterly conceptually confused."[10] For similar reasons, Stanley Hauerwas attacks its importance: "If Christianity is primarily an ethic of love I think that it is clearly wrong and ought to be given up."[11] Jules Toner observed that "even those who write best about love devote very little space to considering what love is"; moreover, he says, what they write is so often contradictory.[12] This mushiness, confusion, and contradiction are not inevitable. Rather than avoid the term "love," it is better to give it a thorough analysis. Popular books surely have their place; they motivate, console, and inspire.[13] Poetry and art surely *evoke* the experience of love better than the abstract discourse of philosophy and theology.[14] Nevertheless there is a place for a careful, critical, theological evaluation of love.

Throughout this book, a phenomenological orientation will be evident. I use the term "phenomenological" in the broad sense of close attention to human *experience*.[15] The history of phenomenology shows that an accurate description of experience is a very difficult, if most rewarding enterprise. Toner writes, "As far as any clear and discriminating awareness goes, most of what is in our consciousness is as unknown to us as what is in the unconscious."[16] However, when we carefully and critically probe our experiences, the results often surprise and repay the effort.

I will try to articulate the experience of those who have been formed by Christianity.[17] I do not claim an experience somehow free from all tradition. My reflections are mightily influenced by the Western Christian tradition, as will become evident. At the same time, I do not envision the theological task as simply arranging or exploring the meaning of what has already been said in the tradition.[18] Rather, I dialogue with others who have been formed by the Christian revelation. I appeal to contemporary experience as a criterion of what is true in the tradition, even as that experience is mightily formed and challenged by the tradition.[19] I employ a hermeneutics of "welcome" or "trust" toward both the Christian tradition and my own experience, but I also subject each to a hermeneutics of "suspicion." I will suggest significant modifications to the tradition. In fact, the following pages are devoted to arguing that many of the disparate things that theologians have said about love are inadequate. In the main, however, this book is expository. I present my understanding of Christian love. Something new, I think, must be said.[20]

Since this is a book of theology, I use Christian symbols and I appeal to Christian convictions. I cite biblical passages, not as proof-texts, but rather to indicate that this book swims in the Christian stream.[21] I make few attempts at extended exegesis, though I hope my use of the Scriptures is exegetically sound. Scripture says many things, not all of them consistent. And my reading of commentaries suggests that professional exegetes, in greater and lesser degrees, all engage in eisegesis when it comes to the love commandments.[22] Still, the final appeal I make is not that a given idea can be found in Scripture but that it adequately illumines Christians' experience.

This book spans the fields of spirituality, dogmatics, and ethics. I consider interdisciplinary work desirable, if dangerous. Theologians specialize in separate disciplines for good reasons, not least of which is that few of us can master one field of theology, let alone more than one. Still, moral theologians rightly regret the division that occurred in the Middle Ages between moral theology and spirituality, and recently we have lamented a too great separation between moral theology and dogmatics. I hope to make a modest contribution to the unity of these three theological disciplines.

I should acknowledge at the outset that God's love for us is not "proved" in this book. Does God love us? That is my experience and my hope. It is a hope born of much confirming evidence, but also a hope challenged by considerable contrary evidence. In chapel I have sung "The Lord hears the cry of the poor," knowing full well that outside the door many poor seem to be heard by no one. I have pondered the justice of God, since the "bad guys" frequently seem to win.[23] Without denying this "contrary evidence," I still believe that God loves us. This belief is convincing to me and millions of others, not as a wish-fulfillment, but as an experience, especially in those powerful moments of life when we feel ourselves touched by Someone transcendent. We can never "prove" that any person loves us. Indeed the attempt to prove another's love is usually a sign that the experience of being loved has been lost. But in prayer I and countless other Christians have had some confirmation that God does love us, and we find ourselves loving God. This book testifies to that love relationship.

The central idea of this book is quite simple: (1) God loves us; (2) we love God; (3) we and God form a community; (4) we and God cooperate.

Such a love-schema provides a distinctively *theological* foundation for Christian ethics. That is my goal. This theological foundation will be presented in Chapter 4, which is the heart of the book. Three chapters lead up to that central chapter. In order to understand some of the presuppositions of this love-schema, I examine in Chapter 1 the place of emotion and participation in forming a distinctively Christian ethic. Chapter 2 attempts to analyze the general nature of love. Chapter 3 indicates that we can love not just other individuals but also ourselves, our communities, and our God.

Five chapters follow the central chapter and, I hope, prove its fruitfulness. I distinguish three kinds of love by asking "for the sake of" whom we are loving. We love our beloved for the sake of the beloved (agape), or for our own sake (eros), or for the sake of a "friendship" we share with them (philia). Chapter 5 examines agape which, I hope to show, is mistakenly claimed to be "the" Christian love. Since love for the sake of the self is so often neglected or disparaged, I found it necessary to devote the next two chapters to eros. Chapter 8 treats "friendship" or philia, which I propose is the most complete Christian love, a thesis that at first surprised me. The last chapter briefly explores the meaning of grace as friendship with God.

While writing this book, I found myself changing my mind. I began more allied with the Protestant stress on self-sacrificing agape, and frankly I was appalled by the egocentricity which dominated so much pre-Vatican II Catholic ethics. Over time I rethought my Catholicism and now have a new appreciation for eros. But along the way I discovered philia, which I now think holds pride of place among Christian loves.[24]

I want to give a brief, preemptive response to the likely charge that so much is left out of this book, even much that is directly relevant. My response is to agree. I ask the reader not to assume that what is left out is denied. The topic of Christian love needs to be developed in its Christological, Trinitarian, ecclesiological, and soteriological connections.[25] I acknowledge further that even an adequate theology of love will not of itself solve many other active debates in moral theology.[26] But, as the manuscript expanded beyond expectations, I had to set aside these and other related topics.[27] What the book does not do is enormous. I hope what it does do will serve the Christian community. As Beverly Harrison puts it, what we desperately need today is "a new vision of *both* God *and* humanity, a vision of holiness or godliness and a vision of humanity as co-capacity-in-relationship."[28] That is what I have tried to provide, since "where there is no vision, the people perish" (Prv 29:18).

I want to thank the Society of Jesus, the Association of Theological Schools, the Outboard Marine Company, and Thomas Beeler for grants that made completion of this project possible. I also thank Weston School of Theology for sabbatical time and for the many excellent personnel and resources it made available to me. I particularly want to thank many friends without whose personal support and often considerable editorial help this project could not have been completed, especially Margaret Causey, Lucretia Yaghjian, Tom and Jennifer Beeler, Randy and Anne Sutherland Howard, Maureen Donohue, Howard Gray, John Haughey, Stephen Pope, Julie Bowen, my students, and many Jesuit colleagues who encouraged me while I lived with them in Cambridge, Santa Clara, Berkeley, and Manila. Sometimes they taught me by challenging my pet ideas, more often by teaching me about love.

NOTES

1. All biblical quotations are from *New American Bible* (New York: Kennedy & Sons, 1970). Italics in the quotations are my own.

2. James Gustafson has passionately and rightly chastised theologians for failing to provide a *theocentric* ethic. Gustafson's critics argue, however, that he does not provide a sufficiently Christian understanding of God. See James Gustafson, *Ethics from a Theocentric Perspective* (Chicago: Univ. of Chicago Press, 1981, 1984), 1:236; 2:27–28. For a critique, see Gordon Kaufman, "How is *God* to be Understood in a Theocentric Ethics?" *James Gustafson's Theocentric Ethics*, ed. Harlan Beckley and Charles Swezey (Macon, GA: Mercer, 1988), 30–35; also several essays of *Journal of Religious Ethics* 13 (1985) were devoted to this critique. For an anthropocentric approach to *understanding* God, see Gordon Kaufman, *Theology for a Nuclear Age* (Philadelphia: Westminster Press, 1985), 20, 28; Sallie McFague, *Models of God: Theology for an Ecological, Nuclear Age* (Philadelphia: Fortress, 1987).

3. Daniel Day Williams, *The Spirit and the Forms of Love* (New York: Harper & Row, 1968), 132. Similar neglect is found in philosophy; see Irving Singer, *The Nature of Love* (Chicago: Univ. of Chicago Press, 1987), 1:xi.

4. Gérard Gilleman, S.J., *The Primacy of Charity in Moral Theology* (Westminster, MD: Newman, 1959), xxi.

5. *Summa theologiae* II–II.182.1. This intellectualism is the common understanding of his thought, and it has abundant textual support. See Etienne Gilson, *Moral Values and the Moral Life* (Hamden, CT: Shoe String Press, 1961), 39. The tradition has neglected his other view that human blessedness consists in love, a view that was emphasized by Augustine and by Aquinas's contemporary Franciscan theologians. See the magnificent commentary on Augustine by Oliver O'Donovan, *The Problem of Self-Love in St. Augustine* (New Haven: Yale, 1980); also Jacques Leclercq, *La Philosophie morale de saint Thomas devant la pensée contemporaine* (Paris: Vrin, 1955), 357–61; Gilleman, *Primacy of Charity*, 126–31.

In the footnotes of this book, *ST* refers to *Summa theologiae*. I will generally follow—usually after checking the Latin—the translation by the Fathers of the English Province, *Summa Theologica* (Westminster, MD: Christian Classics, 1948). *Veritate* refers to *De Veritate*; *Caritate* refers to *De Caritate*; *Sententiarum* refers to *Commentum in Libra*

Sententiarum Magistri Petri Lombardi; *Duo Praecepta* refers to "In Duo Praecepta Caritatis et in Decem Legis Praecepta, Expositio."

6. Vincent MacNamara, *Faith and Ethics* (Washington: Georgetown Univ. Press, 1985), 61–62, 64, 146–47, 151. See also George Newlands, *Theology of the Love of God* (Atlanta: John Knox, 1980), 17.

7. Enda McDonagh, "Love," *The New Dictionary of Theology*, ed. Joseph Komonchak et al. (Wilmington: Glazier, 1987), 602.

8. Garth Hallett, *Christian Neighbor-Love* (Washington: Georgetown Univ. Press, 1989), vii.

9. Gustafson, *Ethics from a Theocentric Perspective*, 1:236; 2:88; and "How Does Love Reign?" *Christian Century* 86 (1966): 654–55.

10. Introduction to *Eros, Agape, and Philia*, ed. Alan Soble (New York: Paragon House, 1989), x.

11. Stanley Hauerwas, "Love's Not All You Need," *Cross Currents* (Summer-Fall, 1972): 172.

12. Jules Toner, *The Experience of Love* (Washington: Corpus Instrumentorum, 1968), 8. Toner's book is still one of the very best on love. It is both intellectually exciting to those who pursue his question and extremely dull to those who seek practical advice. Toner's prose is so simple that the considerable difficulties involved in understanding his thought indicate the difficulty of the topic.

13. I do not devote much attention to immature, spurious, pathological, or other nonideal kinds of love, even though it is fear of these distortions that often keeps theologians from giving love its due place. Nor do I discuss in detail particular forms of love such as parental, motherly, teenage, married, or romantic love. The most interesting and practical things said about love often have to do with these matters. Still, in order to be able to intelligently judge what is true or authentic or what is partial or inclusive in these kinds of love, it is useful to reflect on the basic idea of love.

14. Rosemary Haughton, *The Passionate God* (New York: Paulist, 1981), 1–11.

15. I will not, as Aquinas, Tillich, and others try to do, explain love as an ontological feature of all reality.

16. Toner, *The Experience of Love*, 63; see also Karl Rahner, S.J., "Thomas Aquinas on the Incomprehensibility of God," *The Journal of Religion* 58 (Supplement 1978): S117.

17. I do not claim that religio-moral experience cannot, more or less adequately, be interpreted in different frameworks, e.g., those of the other great world religions; see Kaufman, *Theology for a Nuclear Age*, 20–24. To be sure, a deep love for Jesus or for the Church may make little or no sense to non-Christians. The focus of this book—the love of God—will not be available to ethical persons who are nontheists. My goal here is not to argue with them, but only to offer to Christians a plausible interpretation of their own experience. My project is, of course, open to criticism and revision.

18. My goal is a correlational theology; see Paul Tillich, *Systematic Theology* (Chicago: Univ. of Chicago Press, 1967) 1:8–9. Much recent theology, by contrast, both inside and outside of the Catholic Church, holds that theology should be more "intratextual" than correlational; see David Tracy, "The Uneasy Alliance Reconceived," *Theological Studies* 50 (September 1989): 555, and George Lindbeck, *The Nature of Doctrine* (Philadelphia: Westminster, 1984).

19. Francis Schüssler Fiorenza, "Theology: Transcendental or Hermeneutical?" *Horizons* 16 (Fall 1989): 329–41.

20. Alison Jaggar, "Love and Knowledge," *Gender / Body / Knowledge: Feminist Reconstructions of Being and Knowing*, eds. Alison Jaggar and Susan Bordo (New Brunswick: Rutgers Univ., 1989), 161ff.

21. We learn the meaning of Christian love in interaction with the biblical stories, chiefly, the story of Jesus. In learning about love from these stories, however, we need some idea of what love is in order to know, for example, that his death on the cross is an act of love and not a fine form of masochism.

22. Hallett, *Christian Neighbor-Love*, 2, 47–62, 82, indicates six different interpretations of the commandment to love the neighbor; and, in his judgment, the one the New Testament upholds is the one least evident in the standard commentators.

23. History is itself ambiguous and does not clearly prove God's active presence for the good. Until recently, the racist Afrikaners were victorious, against overwhelming odds, in their fight against native South African peoples; they attributed their victory to God's special care for them; see Allister Sparks, *The Mind of South Africa* (New York: Knopf, 1990), 112–15.

24. Gene Outka's *Agape* (New Haven: Yale Univ. Press, 1976) does so many things extremely well, but his emphasis is on Protestants. Though he considers some Catholic authors, what they have to say does not much enter his final conclusion.

25. See Marjorie Suchocki, "Theological Foundations for Ethnic and Gender Diversity in Faculties / or / Excellence and the Motley Crew," *Theological Education* 26 (Spring 1990): 37–41; Stephen J. Duffy, "Our Hearts of Darkness," *Theological Studies* 49 (December 1988): 597ff.

26. Paul Ramsey, *Basic Christian Ethics* (Chicago: Univ. of Chicago Press, 1978), 114–15 passim; John Finnis, *Natural Law and Natural Rights* (Oxford: Clarendon, 1980), 409–10; and Germain Grisez, *The Way of the Lord Jesus* (Chicago: Franciscan Herald Press, 1983), 586–89, each suggest a foundational position somewhat similar to the one I shall present, but on this basis they mount a strong attack against a way of doing ethics I support (see Edward C. Vacek, "Proportionalism: One View of the Debate," *Theological Studies*, 46 [June 1985]: 287–314). William Frankena has masterfully shown that the Christian recommendation of love leads in a great variety of directions in ethics; "Love and Principles in Christian Ethics," *Faith and Philosophy*, ed. Alvin Plantinga (Grand Rapids: Eerdmans, 1964), 203–25. If valid, the basic ideas of this book should be foundational for all Christian theology.

27. At one point, I had a 1,200-page manuscript. I wrote very long chapters on Divine Command Ethics, Natural Law Ethics, Aquinas, Nygren, Outka, and John Paul II. I have included small parts of those essays in this work, but I decided to leave most of it out since it would break the flow of this work.

28. Beverly Harrison, *Making the Connections* (Boston: Beacon Press, 1985), 36.

1

Christian Life

"Where your treasure is, there your heart is also" (Mt 6:21). Our Christian treasure is our relationship with God, and thus our heart's desire is to be with God. When we love God, we receive a new and more vibrant heart from God (Ez 36:26). This book is an extended reflection on the transforming power of love, particularly, love of God. Since our hearts select what counts as valuable to us, I also hope to show how our life-giving relation to God shapes our moral lives.[1]

This first chapter addresses some preliminary considerations. It argues that our love relation with God implies a distinctively Christian moral life. Second, it briefly develops the general structure of emotions since, I will argue, love is an emotion. Third, since love is directed to values, this chapter explores several kinds of values. Finally, since love is a kind of existential participation, it explores the free, historical, and graceful nature of such participation.

DISTINCTIVELY CHRISTIAN LIFE

Over the past three decades, moral theologians have energetically debated the question of whether there is anything distinctive about Christian ethics compared to secular ethics.[2] The answer that frames this entire book is that Christian morality is quite distinctive because a Christian's spirituality is quite distinctive. And a Christian's spirituality is quite distinctive because it originates in and flows from a personal relationship with God and God's people. *What* good Christians are doing, *holistically* taken, is fundamentally different from what good atheists are doing because what Christians are doing is, among other things, cooperating personally with God. Only when "ethics" is restricted to public behaviors does Christian moral life approximate the moral life of nonbelievers. Our love relationship with God makes the difference. Let me explore this difference.

Christian theology reflects on the great deeds of our God, the God of creation, the Yahweh of Israel, the Abba of Jesus, the God whose complete

1

reign we eagerly expect. This story is the secret history of our public history.[3] For Christians, this story forms and transforms both our idea of God and our understanding of our moral lives.[4] Our Christian symbols and images provide interpretative keys by which we can understand the events of our lives. As a result, "ethical reflection is not a function of an ahistorical reason, able to intuit moral absolutes, as the Enlightenment would have it, but a form of reasoning informed by specific historical interpretations of human nature, the world, and the ultimate."[5] These interpretations are, or should be, influenced by our relationship with God, since every great love relation transforms our approach to life.

The primary interpretative key, the Rosetta stone for understanding our history, is Jesus Christ. His nearness to God marks the perfection of being human. Christian saints are those who carry forward this love relationship by "imitating" him in their own unique and creative way. Christian saints are those who follow their Lord, even as they do what he did not do. St. Francis, for example, brought out fresh possibilities of loving God that Jesus did not realize in his lifetime.[6] Each of us can contribute to the fullness of Christian love. The Christian story—the story of God's relationship with creation—continues in us.

In one of the most important New Testament texts on love, St. Paul writes, "The love of God has been poured out in our hearts through the Holy Spirit who has been given us" (Rom 5:5). According to Paul, through this love, we "have been washed, consecrated, justified" (1 Cor 6:11); we have a "new birth and renewal" (Ti 3:5); and we are "created anew" (Gal 6:15). The early Church experienced this new life as transforming. Oddly enough, however, ordinary Catholic moral theology long advanced a natural law ethic that all but forgot this love relationship with God. It appealed to experience, but not this experience. Indeed, it prided itself on proposing an ethic that any reasonable atheist should approve. This ordinary natural law, even though it often cited Thomas Aquinas, did not follow the more explicitly religious strands in his theology. For Aquinas, the religious relation makes a difference: the "end of all human actions and affections is the love of God," and this end measures all our other affections and actions. Most interestingly, for Aquinas, this love is itself *not* to be measured by reason, nor can the exterior acts that flow from it be measured simply by reason.[7] Aquinas is often read for those sections in which he makes right reason the norm. But he also says that the rule of charity, though it builds upon the other virtues, is higher than the rule of the soul which is right reason itself.[8] Put in contemporary language, charity or friendship with God is the ultimate relationship. And this relationship makes a significant difference in what we perceive, value, and prefer, and, consequently, in who we are and what we do.[9]

The neglect of the influence of love for God in our moral lives led to the overestimation of the place of ordinary prudence in the life of a Christian.[10] For Aquinas, the wisdom that is the result of charity is able to "judge rightly by a connaturality" with divine things. Since this connatural wisdom "is more excellent than wisdom as an intellectual virtue, [and] since it attains to God more intimately by a kind of union of the soul with Him, it is able to direct us not only in contemplation, but also in action."[11] In other words, the life of friendship with God, including not only contemplation but also action founded on this love, transforms our moral life. Such is the theme of this book. Christian ethics ought to begin with charity. Unfortunately it too often does not.

This friendship does not give us merely extra motivation for acts already completely intelligible in themselves. The religious relation not only helps us to resee the world; it also adds a new dimension to what our acts mean.[12] If, as I shall later argue, our acts are ways that we cooperate with God, then that cooperation is part of the very meaning of our acts. If I walk through the park with my fiancée, the full meaning of the act—its "what"—is "walking through the park with my friend." I do not perform merely an act of moving my feet, nor an act of walking, nor an act of walking through the park. On this evening, her presence is not an added motive. Without her I would not take this walk, because what I want to do is to walk in the park with her. Without her I could not do the act I want to do. If, however, I had decided to go for a walk alone and if, unbeknownst to me, she also happened to be walking in the park, I would still be taking a solitary walk. Similarly, if atheists de facto are cooperating with God, that cooperation is not what they intend to do. Their actions are not part of a friendship with God that they want to foster. Thus, Christians can perform different acts than atheists: they can consciously act with God.

To make this relationship only an "added motive," as some natural law ethicists would have it,[13] reduces aspects of the objective world to a subjective attitude. Rather, the religious relationship makes a difference in the very meaning of what an agent is doing.[14] For example, Paul condemns sex with a prostitute, not because it would violate human dignity or the nature of the sexual act, but because it would "take Christ's members and make them the members of a prostitute" (1 Cor 6:15; cf. Rom

1:26–27). Paul did not add a Christian motive; he rethought the nature of this act itself when performed by a Christian. In his view, Christ is also involved in the act.

Some Christians have suggested that atheists who seek "the good" or "the fullness of being" or "wholeness" are doing exactly the same as Christians are doing when they love God.[15] Absent from these views, however, is the experience of a personal God. To be sure, the referent may de facto be the same. But just as a stranger's cooperation with a woman who happens to be my mother is not really the same experience as my cooperation with her, so a relation to "Being" or the "good in general" is experientially different from a relation to "my God." Again this religiously decisive and humanly important difference is not just extra motivation. For us believers, it is not enough that our acts affirm the good nor is it enough that, unwittingly, it is God whom we are serving. Rather, the primary act we want to do is to be involved with the God who is involved with us.

This relationship adds new passion and meaning to life. It provides a response to a worrisome question that may be put to natural law ethicists: "How is it that when religious belief and practice are brought into harmony with the reasonable requirements of the secular world, so often they lose their power to attract and to satisfy?" Without this passion and new meaning, the "Church which squares up to modernity loses precisely that 'Dionysian' element which fundamentalism so often preserves."[16] Natural law ethics, to the degree that it brackets our love relationship with God, does lose something powerful. But with this love relation, a new passion is released that can and should lead to an energetic engagement with the world.

An atheist may, of course, discover morally good solutions to a given problem. Atheists, however, cannot see how their actions fit into a life of loving cooperation with God. Jesus' "command to love is not an abstract and general policy that can be separated from the story that this is God working for our redemption."[17] Love for enemies becomes more than an oxymoron and more than an ethical rule when we realize that God loves us even when we are sinners and that we can cooperate with this reconciling love (Rom 5:8; 2 Cor 5:20).

Thus, an atheist *cannot* perform the *same* act as a believer, even if an outside observer cannot tell the difference. Isaiah describes Assyria as God's "rod in anger" sent "against a people under my wrath." Isaiah adds, "But this is not what [Assyria] intends." Isaiah sees that God is acting through Assyria to punish Israel. If the king of Assyria had known he was helping Israel's God, presumably he would have ceased to act. That was not the act he wanted to perform. Will Assyria be rewarded for its (unintended) cooperation with Yahweh? No, "I will punish the utterance of the king of Assyria's proud heart" (Is 10:6–12). God punishes Assyria for the deed *it* was performing, a hostile act against God's people. In sum, our relationship with God contributes to the very content of our actions. Our actions are part of our own individual relationship with God as well as part of our relationship to the Christian community. Unfortunately these relationships have often been neglected in much Catholic ethics, almost as if their significance was nugatory.[18] Rather they are constitutive of the acts we perform.

EMOTIONS AND VALUES

The great eighteenth-century American theologian Jonathan Edwards devoted a lengthy treatise to developing a much neglected thesis: "True religion, in great part, consists in holy affections."[19] A contemporary author, Robert Roberts, makes a similar claim: "Whatever else Christianity may be, it is a set of emotions. It is love of God and neighbor, grief about one's own waywardness, joy in the merciful salvation of our God, gratitude, hope, and peace."[20] The history of Christianity is often told in terms of *orthodoxy*, the truth of doctrines believed; and Christians are frequently evaluated in terms of their *orthopraxy*, the good that they do. But the inner history of Christianity is what we might call its *orthokardia*, the ordered affections that unite us with God, ourselves, other people, and the world. These affections give rise to both doctrine and practice. Ultimately, our perfection as a person is measured strictly according to the degree of development of our loves.

To live a Christian life, it is not sufficient to think about God's revelation, nor is it sufficient to will the deeds required by it. A Christian is one who has felt the love of God and who desires to respond with love. In fact, as Bernard Lonergan argued late in his life, Christian conversion is first a conversion of the heart, not of the mind or the unaffected will.[21] In Scripture, we are exhorted to "experience this love [of Christ] which surpasses all knowledge, so that you may attain to the fullness of God himself" (Eph 3:19). For Paul, neither an intellectual understanding of all truths, nor a determined commitment to serve others suffices: "If I have the gift of prophecy and, with full knowledge, comprehend all mysteries. . . . If I give everything I have to feed the poor . . . but have not love, I gain nothing" (1 Cor 13:2–3). Alan Drengson rightly argues, "It is easy to think that it does not matter what we feel so long as we *act* in the right ways. And this is true as far as the law goes. But how we feel determines how we are spiritually and vice versa."[22]

While I cannot here give a developed treatment of the role of the "emotions," the affective element in our moral and religious lives should be underscored.[23] Western philosophy has emphasized intellect. Christianity likewise has emphasized the intellect in dogma and the will in morality as obedience to God's will. Philosophical and theological anthropology must be expanded to include the emotions.[24] Without in the least denigrating the role of intellect and will in the Christian life, I shall emphasize our emotional life. G. K. Chesterton once observed: "The Madman is not the man who has lost his reason. The Madman is the one who has lost everything except his Reason."[25] A person without emotions would be dead to the value of the world and of God. Emotions are in part cognitions; they apprehend objects as either positively or negatively valuable, as good or evil. Through emotions we become attached to those great goods that inspire our lives, and without them we "become incapable of understanding any moral argument at all."[26]

Without our emotions, the world would be experienced as valueless; diamonds would be no more precious than coal. William James proposed an illuminating thought experiment. "Conceive yourself, if possible, suddenly stripped of all the emotion with which your world now inspires you, and try to imagine it *as it exists*, purely by itself, without your favorable or unfavorable, hopeful or apprehensive comment. It will be almost impossible for you to realize such a condition of negativity and deadness. No one portion of the universe would then have importance beyond another; and the whole collection of its things and series of its events would be without significance, character, expression, or perspective."[27] Those who disparage the emotions fail to realize what would happen if we had no emotions.

Each "object" has value, much as each material object has some color. (These objects need not be outside ourselves. We can feel our own inner life, e.g., be angry that we are so ignorant. Emotional objects can be anything that has some "content" or intelligibility. An "object", thus, might be a person, an aspect of a situation, a relation between two beings, and so forth.) Color or texture are apprehended through sense perception, while natures are grasped through intellection. Value is apprehended through the emotions. Thus, anger, fear, or disgust indicate that some evil has been experienced, while delight, pleasure, or joy indicate some good. The valuable aspects of an object are not simply projections of the subject's needs onto objects. For example, we can appreciate the beauty or liveliness of a rattlesnake, even when we are simultaneously repelled by its dangerousness. Religious values, in particular, are objectively given through the believer's *affective* life.[28] Religious living includes emotional experiences of the holy. The distinguishing feature of religious emotions is that, directly or symbolically, they involve God.[29]

It is important to insist that our affections can attain something true about their objects. That is, they can be objective, revealing what is true. They have "intentionality, transcendence, and meaningfulness."[30] As the intellect is to the "whatness" of an object, so the heart is to its value.[31] Just as we cannot legitimately make the color or the "nature" of an object be whatever we want it to be, so we cannot legitimately make the value of the object be whatever we want.[32] Rather we surrender or submit to the value of an object, letting the object reveal itself to us as it is. Our ability to do so is a hallmark of our mature, spiritual existence. As von Hildebrand wrote, "The capacity to conform ourselves to the important-in-itself is one of the deepest and most fundamental features of the person; it lights up his character as an image of God, a subject, one called to partake as a partner in the dialogue with God."[33]

Our affections are not mere body-states, merely noncognitive aspects of ourselves, having nothing to do (except perhaps a causal relation) with objects. That is, emotions are not merely bodily resonances such as the chill which runs down our spine in the presence of an awesome vista. Rather, our emotions are cognitive acts through which we apprehend values. On the other hand, we do not simply acknowledge that an object has value; we are also moved by such values. Emotions are acts by which we perceive values in reality, and they are acts in which we are enlivened by reality's goodness or repulsed by its evil. Emotions are self-involving; we are affected or changed.[34] If we are not moved by the value of something, but only intellectually attribute a value to it, we are not experiencing the value. We may be employing a memory of a previous emotional experience or applying concepts or rules about the good (that were themselves originally derived from some emotional value apprehension). But if we are not feeling and being moved by the value of the object, we are not presently experiencing an emotion.

Our affections are no more innate than our conceptual knowledge. Though we are by nature inclined to know and to feel, these activities are learned by knowing and feeling specific objects.[35] Our culture invests enormous resources to the education of the intellect. Unfortunately our educational system does not devote as much energy to educating the emotions, and therefore does not sensitize us to the breadth and depth of the realm of values. In fact, traditional schooling probably stifles emotional growth as much as it helps.[36] Like other forms of knowledge, emotions are learned in the endless encounters we have with various objects. We learn what a chair is by seeing and sitting on one or more chairs, and we learn what is beautiful or harmful or holy by interacting with objects that have these qualities. In these interactions, we find ourselves responding to these objects, moving away from or toward them. These responses become internalized habits, i.e., persistent patterns of appreciation or evaluation. Or they are neglected, discounted, and even positively discouraged, so that we become hardened to some values.

Emotions are thus learned in response to particular values.[37] We do not learn emotions apart from valuable objects, any more than we learn thinking without thinking of something real or ideal. We are angry about injustice, or warmed by an act of kindness, or distraught at our failures, or in awe before the majesty of God. Furthermore, specific emotions take on a peculiar character depending on their object. Anger at the cat is different from anger at our little sister. Love for God is different from love for a neighbor, and love for strangers is different from love for a spouse. In the language of phenomenology, our emotions "intend" the specific values of their objects. Some emotions are transient, changing in accord with the flux of objects before us, but other emotions persist, e.g., an anger that lasts for weeks, or a love that lasts for more than a lifetime.

The people who are important to us and the communities we live in modify, direct, and reinforce our emotional experiences, refining them or blunting them. Through its Scriptures, liturgy, and so forth, Christianity provides a definite set of "objects" which educate our affections in quite specific ways. Christianity is a "school of affections." Christian symbols, stories, or rituals evoke particular emotional responses. They thereby form the human heart in distinctive ways. Christian stories and images present model persons who evoke a response in our hearts and thereby help us to get an accurate emotional view of the world.[38] Our disdain for the handicapped or adulterers is corrected by loving the Jesus who heals the deaf and forgives the adulteress (Mk 8:37; Jn 8:11); eventually our disdain withers and we come to appreciate what he saw in them. We develop a specifically Christian set of affections. Thus, like other cultures, the Christian tradition teaches a way of emotionally relating to the world. The traditional practice of contemplating Gospel stories is an invaluable source for educating our emotions. Christians learn to rejoice when the rich sell all and give to the poor. They perceive the genuine goodness in this act, a goodness that may not be apparent in some other ways of life. To be sure, an atheist may also appreciate such goodness. The Christian tradition does not have a monopoly on human values. But the Christian tradition makes it likely that these values will be seen, embraced, and affirmed.

Thus, we do not emotionally apprehend values in a simple, unmediated way. We experience within a tradition. We live out of the Christian tradition which forms us even as we add to it. The criterion for emotional adequacy must be reality or truth, but this truth is mediated by the distinctive way of life of the community and the distinctive way God deals with that community. Obviously, this pattern of relating is not given once for all times, nor is its development one of simple progression. The Bible itself hardly depicts a linear development in how the community responds to God and world or how God relates to the community and the world.[39] The postbiblical Church continues this ever fluctuating, affective relationship.

Like intellectual knowledge, emotions tend to generalize themselves. We know one chair and we get some idea of all chairs. We feel the preciousness of one human being, and we get a feel for the preciousness of all human beings. Like intellectual knowledge, emotions can overgeneralize. We see white swans and we think all swans are white. Similarly, the bad experience we had with a few white persons may become a generalized racism. Thus, there are accurate generalizations and inaccurate generalizations in the intellect, and the same is true in the heart. Furthermore, like our thoughts, our affections make mistakes in appreciating particular objects.

Our emotional apprehension of values can be not only overgeneralized or mistaken, but it can and will always be partial. No situation has but one value; rather it always contains a complex of values.[40] Our emotions will attend to but some of these values, just as our intellect and sensory perception will attend to but some aspects of a situation. We can feel the value of the object as a whole, e.g., the dignity of another person, but we may also become fixated on some partial value, e.g., the ugliness of some facial blemish. Errors occur when some single value or set of values is seized upon to the neglect and detriment of other values. A disordered emotional life usually attends to something true, but only partially true. These value-mistakes lead to distortion and cause harm. Emotions, like everything human, can go wrong. It is not true that emotions are neither right nor wrong.[41] When we inadequately value reality, reality will, in the long run, resist our false valuations, just as it resists our false perceptions and intellections. Sincerity is not a substitute for rightness.[42] But we can over time correct our affective evaluations so that they accord with reality. Just as our intellect can be reeducated, so can our heart. By further contact with reality and further dialogue with fellow human beings and traditions, we learn that our ideas or emotions are askew. Then we have an opportunity to modify our previous ways of intellectually or emotionally relating to the world.

So we learn our emotions—along with their values—roughly the same way we learn everything else. We encounter objects and we respond to them as they affect us. We attend to our experience as carefully as possible, asking what is really given in the emotion and what is imported from other sources. We sort through the many emotions we have in response to a complex situation. We listen to what other individuals and our various communities find noteworthy and preferable. The genuine insights of secular culture can and should also modify or inform us. We are not only ecclesial persons; we are also people who experience in many other relationships, each of which can teach us how to feel well.

Finally, our emotions move us into action. We run from the snake we fear, often without much thought, and we snuggle next to those we love, again often without much thought. Of course, we can and usually do reflect at least somewhat before acting on our emotions. The task of discernment is to sort out the various tendencies moving us to and fro at the moment, in the particular phase of development we are in, and within the whole of our life. Then we consent to one or more of these emotional tendencies.[43] We yield to our fury at the plight of this abused woman, or we bide our time so that in the long run greater justice might be done. The maxim "If it feels good, do it" is in principle valid. This maxim usually is inadequate, however, because we really have not sufficiently felt and sorted through all the values, real and ideal, that are possible for us to act upon. Or the maxim is inadequate because our feelings are themselves distorted. Similar inadequacies are found in the maxims "If you think something is right, then it is right" and "If you have a good reason to do something, then it is good to do it."

Prior to Vatican II, much Catholic ethics focused on actions. Subsequently, there has been in some quarters a laudable shift to consider these acts as part of a whole life. Still, even this approach has tended to neglect the emotions that are requisite to both our actions and a full human life. Without certain affections, we can act generously, but not be generous. And when we have been given something, the requisite response is first a feeling of gratitude, and only derivatively some deed in response.[44] A return gift without the feeling would be an incomplete response. Perhaps every good action can be performed without love. We can help another, even sacrifice our lives, out of pride or for praise. Thus, "the disposition out of which something is done is as much part of the virtue as the intention or the action."[45] Out of the fullness of a good heart flows morally good deeds (Lk 6:45). This is true for individual and social life. As Daniel Maguire observes, "Good social changes are always rooted in affection, though they may find their immediate stimulus in a variety of events. Ideals are the power behind these changes, and ideals are helpless unless enfranchised by affection."[46]

A morality that focuses on deeds overlooks the crucial importance of our affections.[47] The affections are in themselves *morally* valuable, quite apart from whether they lead to any deeds. For example, a man who experiences joy at another's misfortune is not good, even if such perverse pleasure never leads him to actively cause any harm. The New Testament commends emotional attitudes in themselves. As Vincent MacNamara notes, "The insight of the early church that the Christian should live his life in joy (2 Cor. 9:7; Heb. 10:34), in thankfulness (Acts 5:41; Col. 3:17), in humility (John 13:14–15; Phil. 2:3) and without anxiety (Matt. 6:25; 1 Pet. 5:7) may not lead to an observable difference of behaviour but may refer to attitudes and dispositions that are part of Christian virtue (Phil. 4:4–7)."[48]

Christianity, in sum, is a traditioned community that enables us to appreciate the most fundamental goods of human life.[49] It is a community that educates our minds and our hearts to feel the holy presence and activity of God. Our communal life engenders in us affections that give us an especially profound access to this reality. Our community's value-perceptions are not the only true view of reality. But we Christians believe that our perspective is uniquely and richly revealing of the way reality really is.[50]

THE STRUCTURE OF EMOTION

Our language for emotions is unsettled. The etymology of "emotion" indicates a "going out." In contemporary usage, however, persons who are emotional are often thought to be caught up in themselves. Likewise, the meaning of both "passion" and "affection" have flip-flopped. The etymology of these words suggests "being acted upon" or "receptivity." Today we commonly say that "passion" is an internal power that impels persons outside themselves. In one description of love, a contemporary author nicely, if unselfconsciously, illustrates how our language jumbles the perceptive, receptive, and responsive moments of emotion: "Love . . . requires

responding to another out of *being caught up in* the feelings and the meaning of what the other person is experiencing. . . . the other becomes *incor-
porated into my self.* . . . we have to *get out of ourselves* and become
interested in the other. Hospitable love cares enough to *create space in one's
own life* in order to *welcome another in.*"[51] Thus, in describing love as an
emotion, we do well to be aware that emotion words often conceal part of
the structure of the emotions they describe. Emotion language includes
receptive words like being "touched" or "moved" or "affected." But it also
includes extroverted expressions: "he was stuck on her" or "beyond himself with rage" or "charmed out of his shoes." These variations are under-
standable as attempts to name various aspects of the structure of emotion.
In what follows, I sort out four "moments" in the structure of our emotions. And in the next chapter, I shall use this fourfold structure to analyze
the general nature of love.

Emotion is a complex activity: the self (1) as an *openness*-to-good (2)
becomes *conscious of* the value of a specific object, (3) is *affected by* that
valuable object, and (4) *responds to* the object's value.[52] That is, an emotion involves a general openness, a value-perception, a being-affected, and
a value-affirmation or a disvalue-rejection. There is an intelligible, though
not invariant, sequence in the way these four moments develop. Initially,
our general emotional consciousness is alert in varying degrees. We are
"alive" or nearly "dead" in our general sensitivity to creation and the Creator. Or we are keen for the appearance of certain kinds of values, though
numb to other kinds. Secondly, we engage in a particular act of awareness.
Our openness, attentiveness, or sensitivity becomes focused on a particular object, whether that be a lion, a lovely painting, or our Lord. We perceive the goodness of something. (That goodness may be, as I shall shortly
discuss, relative to our own well-being or it may be independent of it.)
Thirdly, we feel ourselves psychologically and perhaps bodily moving
toward or away from the object, or we feel ourselves content to be with it.
That is, we are affected. We experience a change in ourselves, inclining us
to or away from the object, or inclining us to rest in its presence. Fourthly,
we respond to the value of the object, adding our own affirmation or
rejection. We affirm the valuable object in its own right and perhaps foster
its growth, or we reject its evil and perhaps seek to destroy it. The first
moment is a general condition for having a particular emotion. The subsequent three moments form a triadic structure found in particular emotions.

One basic word used for emotions embodies in shifting ways this
fourfold complexity. The word "feeling" originally meant to examine by

touch. This meaning is apt for the complex structure of emotions. First, touch is our primary sense, and as bodily beings we are constantly alert to the touch of material objects. Second and third, whenever we touch something to examine how *it* is, *our body* is also changed. Finally, if what we feel is sufficiently good or bad, we respond by further touching it or by withdrawal, e.g., when we touch a silk scarf or a hot stove. These bodily meanings of feeling as touch tend to be separated in various uses of the word "feeling" for emotions. Thus we may say, "I don't feel anything these days," indicating that our general emotional openness is nearly absent (e.g., depression); or we may say, "I feel nothing toward him," when our feelings toward a particular person or types of persons are blocked. Occasionally, we say, "I can feel the good in him" or "I feel the situation is right," thereby pointing to the perceptive moment of emotion. When, however, someone asks, "How are you feeling?" we point to how we have been affected, not to what it is that we have perceived to be valuable or disvaluable. But when we say, "I feel strongly about . . .," the word "feeling" often refers to our affirming or rejecting response.

Each of these four "moments" of the structure of emotions may vary greatly in intensity, range, and depth. First, there are variations in our general openness or closedness to value. Some people are "very emotional," prone to react to a scraggly flower hidden in the crannied wall; others seem stolid to the point of being *unable* to be moved even by enormous tragedies. Some people *can* love more than others. Second, there are variations in our actual emotional perception of specific goods or values. In an emotion, when the object's value "awakens" us or "grabs our attention," we feel or discover the object's value. Some people, however, are unable, for example, to be awakened by the splendor of a sunset or the misery of a slum. They have eyes, but emotionally see nothing noteworthy. Even if they are sensitive to other kinds of values, these particular values and disvalues do not "speak" to them. They may be able to give an otherwise accurate description of the poverty of a slum, but they have little or no sense of its misery. Thus, one person will feel or emotionally perceive a value, while another will miss that value. The lover, as we shall see, is the one who most can feel new values. Third, there are variations in the ability to *be moved* by objects. That is, there are variations not only in our emotional perceptions of value, but also in how we are affected by what we "see." Some "feel deeply" in the sense that they are greatly moved or affected by what they perceive. For example, when Paul wrote to the Corinthians, he did so "in great sorrow and anguish, with copious tears—not to make you sad but to help you realize the great love I bear you" (2 Cor 2:4). Some can feel a wide range of values, but they are greatly limited in their ability to feel the impact of these values on their lives. Fourth, there are variations in the ability to affectively affirm or negate the value of an object. That is, there are also variations in our response. Some persons readily say their yes or their no to beauty or ugliness, to mystery or injustice; but others are much more hesitant to respond.

Full emotional intentionality is not automatic. The various aspects of this fourfold structure may separate from one another. First, some persons may be relatively closed to all values; they may, however, still freely do good without actually feeling that good. For example, they may act on the conviction—perhaps originally discovered by someone else, and then made into a principle—that human beings are worthy of help.[53] Second, some persons may be closed to most values, but a few kinds of value, e.g., sexual attractiveness or the plight of the poor, may awaken them. These strong values penetrate their slumber and, in so doing, may over time expand their general openness. Third, some feel particular values, e.g., the goodness of another, but, because of fear or bad past experiences, they are not touched or moved by the goodness they experience. Others are readily affected, but this being affected may have little to do with any subsequent response. Theirs may be a "sentimentality" of "being moved" that runs its course largely independently of the object, or the object may open the gateway for emotional flooding which then precludes any response to that object. Some may be so absorbed in the impact of how they are affected that they all but forget the object that affected them. Fourth, still others perceive goodness, are moved by it, but then, e.g., out of habitual pride, are unable to affirm it. Conversely, some persons may perceive and respond to the need of another, but not allow themselves to be touched by the one they help.

The four moments which constitute full emotional intentionality may occur at different times and may follow a variant sequence. For example, at one time we may feelingfully perceive the sacredness of a person and, later, we may be unable to feel that value. We may still respond positively to that person out of a memory of what we once felt. Or, it often happens that we affirm the human dignity of a man who is repulsive to us; we do so out of a sense of socially learned duty toward all persons. But then, in our actions on his behalf, we come to perceive the value we had somewhat dutifully postulated, and subsequently we become quite moved by the unique preciousness of his person. He is no longer a drunken bum but an "immortal diamond." In this latter case, affirmation precedes emotional perception and this perception precedes feeling affected. In other cases, we may feel ourselves touched by, e.g., an act of generosity, and this, in turn, expands our general openness to perceive the world with more friendly eyes. Emotion is a complex activity.

Emotions become more fully human to the degree that we freely consent to each of these four structural moments. These moments are in good part spontaneous and not explicitly chosen. Nevertheless, we can consent to or dissent from these spontaneous, active and passive movements of our self. We thereby make them our own. First, we might freely relish our general openness to the good, or we might bemoan our closedness. Thus, for example, we dislike our insensitivity to the beauty of art, and in consenting to this dislike we ready ourselves for a greater degree of openness. Second, we may sense ourselves invited to see a particular value, and we can then consent to this inclination as part of who we are and want to be. We may experience a glimmer of sacredness in a stranger, and we freely activate ourselves to perceive the full light of God's glory in that stranger. Third, we may feel how a good or an evil affects us, and we can freely accept how we become in the presence of this value. We may relish the warmth we feel in performing a generous deed, or we may refuse to hide from ourselves the guilt we feel for having been stingy. Fourth, when we feel ourselves moving toward affirming the beloved, we may consent to that self-transcendence. We may delight in our ability to unite with God in affirming the world. Thus, each of these spontaneous movements "can be brought to a free decision and in choice can be . . . ratified and transformed into a freely given, fully human" act.[54] In short, we have the freedom to consent to emotion's various moments.

Or we can freely dissent from, resist, or bracket these movements. For example, we may not want to respond to the value we have felt, because we have other involvements or because we are too sinful to be concerned about anyone other than ourselves. We may worry that we are becoming too soft or too vulnerable to the needs of people about us, and so we resolve not to let ourselves be touched. Though these four moments each have their own spontaneity, we can dissociate our self from them, saying, in effect, this is how I am but not how I want to be. Gradually, over time, this dissociation, performed through freedom, will modify these moments. The generous person will become hardened and the kind person will become contemptuous. Through our free consent or dissent, our previous emotional structures are gradually or, on occasion, suddenly modified.

Thus, freedom completes this fourfold structure of emotions. But there are also variations in our exercise of freedom. Some experience the four "moments," but their freedom is too weak to effectively consent to or dissent from these movements. Emotions simply happen in them rather than being what they freely enact as part of their personhood. Their freedom is underdeveloped and thus they may be more controlled by their emotions than self-possessed. On the other hand, some have the freedom to readily integrate these moments into their life. They engage their subjectivity fully in their emotions. For most of us, freedom is exercised with greater and lesser depth and intensity.

People who emphasize deeds or duties often exclude emotions from morality. This exclusion, though wrong, springs from two genuine insights that will be important in our future considerations. First, our acts are moral only to the degree that our freedom is engaged. Second, our emotions are not able to be willed into existence because they are prevoluntary.[55] For example, we cannot make ourselves be angry at something we see as funny. Still, even though we cannot will ourselves to have any particular emotion, this does not mean, as we have just seen, that our emotions are beyond the reach of freedom. We can will to put ourselves in circumstances where certain emotions are likely to arise, and we can somewhat will ourselves to be attentive to features of an object that are likely to evoke that emotion. And, once a particular emotion begins to arise, we can consent to it and thereby reinforce it. We can say yes to the compassion we begin to feel, or we can say no. That is, we decide how we want to be. Just as we judge the emotional responses of others as immature or inappropriate, so we can do the same in ourselves. And then we can be attentive to opportunities for changing ourselves. As Sidney Callahan writes, "When we talk of someone's good character or virtue, we imply that they have shaped and directed their natural involuntary temperament and emotions in certain positive ways."[56] The same is true in judging our own character. The formation and transformation of our emotional life is a major task of our moral development.

CORRELATIVE OBJECTIVE VALUES

I began this chapter by saying that where our treasure is, there our hearts are. That is, there is an essential correlation between our emotions and our values. Each emotion intends one or more values, and each value is experienced only through an emotion. Properly functioning emotions give access to objective values. The last section explored the meaning of emotion. This section explores the correlative values.

Kinds of Value

Our emotions reveal the value that an object has, either its present actual value or the value it can become. But values are of many kinds and can be understood in various ways. Here, after considering a subjectivistic aberration, I look at three types of objective value.[57] First, the aberration. "Being affected" can become detached from the other three moments of an emotion. Then some things are experienced as *merely subjectively satisfying*, as valuable only *because* of the way that we are affected by them. Thus, getting "sweet revenge" or "getting drunk" might be satisfying to us, even if we know that these things are not objectively good. Other things may be objectively good, but we may desire them *only* because they are satisfying to us. For example, we may tell the truth, not because we affirm the value of truth-telling, but only because we would feel uncomfortable in lying. What is sought in such acts is not their intrinsic goodness but only the satisfaction they bring. An object may be "valued" not because it is valuable, but only because of the satisfaction it delivers. This is a form of subjectivism.

Some things, however, are experienced as *important in themselves*. We recognize that they are good in themselves, whether or not they satisfy any need in us.[58] For example, we feel the disvalue of a poor person's hunger. We feel that this hunger in itself is an evil, and likewise that the feeding of the poor is good, something important in itself. We might find that working with poor, starving people offends most of our refined sensibilities, and yet we insist that this work is most worthwhile. This "important in itself" can have a reference to our lives and our practical activity, but— this distinguishes it from the third kind of value—it need not have that reference. It is not that we don't care about starving people in the Sub-Sahara, but this concern, though it really affects us, may not be appropriate to the way we must now carry on our active life. Our response might be a distant, but sincere "Ain't it awful," and then we go on about our lives. In this second type of value, the important in itself appears to us, affects us, and may even lead to a value-response, but we do not ally our lives to the bearers of this kind of value.

The *important in itself to me* is a subset of the above type of value. Some goods are not only experienced to be good in themselves, but also pointedly to bear a relation to our life which we must consent to (or actively resist). We find ourselves moved to ally ourselves to them or to overcome them.[59] We not only experience them as having in themselves a goodness or evilness, but also are moved to allow these values to lay claim on our life. All babies are important, but this baby, my child, is the one that is important to me. This baby is the object of my devotion and responsibility. In our typical loves, it is this sort of value we are concerned with. Still, to say that something is important *to* me is not yet to say whether it is affirmed as good *for* me or affirmed independently of what good it brings to my life.[60] These two possibilities are realized in two different kinds of love, which I will call eros and agape.

Freedom and Bestowal Value

There is an important subset of this last sort of value that has special relevance for our loves. In all loves, the value of the beloved is an "importance in itself to me." Without the "to me" there would be no love. My life would not be bound up with the beloved. Without the "importance in itself," however, there also would be no love. Love is directed to the objective value of the beloved, a value that the beloved really or ideally has.

Here I want to look at a variation on the "important in itself to me." I will call it "*bestowal value.*" It may be found in various acts of love. Among all the valuable objects which are important in themselves and could be important to me, I freely let some have a special importance in my life. While some valuable objects practically demand my response, e.g., the plight of an accident victim lying in the street, many other valuable objects require greater involvement of my freedom before they can become specially important in my life. Biblical examples of bestowal value are God's choice of Israel, the smallest of the nations (Dt 7:7–8), or God's choice of one Jew as "my beloved Son" (Mk 1:11), or God's choice of Mary as the favored handmaid (Lk 1:48). This bestowal value seems to lie outside the usual canons of rationality. Still, it plays such a significant part in human and divine life that we should not ignore it.

Before describing this phenomenon further, I must immediately distinguish this position from a common misunderstanding of all values that are important in themselves. Bestowal value is not a matter of seeing, giving, or positing value where there is none. In our subjectivistic age, a popular notion of value is that it is some importance we *give* to objects that in themselves have no importance. The result is that if one "values" African violets more than African Blacks, then African violets *are* more valuable. That is, no place is given to the "importance in itself." This subjectivistic position is quite foreign to the one I am trying to describe.[61] When I say that we frequently allow some object to have special importance to us, I do not mean to say that we give value to objects which have none. The latter view, as Timothy Jackson notes, might be held by a "Radical Protestantism" or an antifoundationalism: "Instead of recognizing value, we create it *ex nihilo*."[62] Bestowal value is different. Without distorting their importance in themselves and presupposing that importance, we bestow on certain objects the status of being specially important to us.

This distinction is crucial, so let me give three examples. Suppose that I once chose one gold locket out of two that seemed exactly the same. The one I chose is now special to me and becomes more so with time. I would not be satisfied if, after someone stole "my" locket, someone else offered its twin as a replacement. I chose "this" locket. My initial reason for choosing this locket rather than another was arbitrary, but now it has become important to me in a way that the other one has not. As a second example, suppose that my vocation is to work "hands-on" with the poor. In doing this work, I come to love this work. I feel its unique worth. I might acknowledge that working for structural reform is more important in itself than working in a soup kitchen. But I continue to do what has become specially important in itself for me. I know that the reason this work appears special to me is my own long-term involvement in it. I have become changed by this sort of care for the poor. Someday work for structural reform might attract me, but not now. Such experiences are commonplace. An object or activity has a particular preciousness to me, and it has this because of my freedom and history with it.

To take a more extended example: Imagine that the woman I married was a woman quite suitable and attractive to me. She seemed "right for me." Still, speaking abstractly, that is, apart from my history, it is probable that had I waited longer another woman, in another way, would have been "right for me." At some point I decided not to keep my options open, decided not to wait to see if someone "better" would come along. I decided to become more involved with her. I can give many good reasons for my choice, but I can also admit that she became especially precious to me only through my decision to become more involved with her—something that I could have resisted. Her preciousness to me now has arisen in part from my ongoing decision to let her be special to me. I would not go before an impartial forum and say that she is the best woman in the world, but in our marriage I gladly say she is the best.[63] She is especially precious to me in a way that other women are not, because I decided to let her preciousness appear to me and did not decide to let the preciousness of another woman so involve me.

I am calling this value to me which is dependent for its appearance on my free choice "bestowal value." Bestowal value arises through freedom and is developed in history. As Singer writes, "Bestowal value . . . is created by the affirmative relationship *itself*, by the very act of responding favorably, giving an object emotional and pervasive importance."[64] I bring certain objects and not others within my emotional life and give the former particular importance for my life. As my chosen treasure, the beloved objects become part of my own heart. Once again, this value is not some form of "imputed goodness," goodness that the beloved does not really have.

"Bestowal value" accounts for a certain "existentialist" feature of our emotions. William James pointed out in his discussion of "the will to believe" that often only the leap of free decision makes possible the revelation of value. Without the leap of involvement, we will never know the full value of an object. With continued "leaping," the value of one person becomes ever more apparent and the value of another person de facto will be less apparent. Given our finitude, such choices are necessary. As Robert Frost mused: "Two roads diverged in a yellow wood, and sorry I could not travel both and be one traveller. . . . And that has made all the difference." Human freedom makes a difference in this selection of who or what shall be special to us. Human freedom does not merely consent to what is, but also has a creative role in deciding what shall be important to us.[65] Because of human freedom, no quality or set of qualities in an object can guarantee that an emotion will occur or that a particular object will become important to us.

Freedom, however, is not the only factor in determining what will be specially important to us. Since our freedom is always situated, human finitude also plays a part. We have feelings for those whom time and accident bring into our lives. We can imagine billions of people we might love, but in our actual situation comparatively few can be special to us. We "love the one we're with." Had our circumstance been different, e.g., had this person not gotten sick and needed our help or had that person not gone to the same party, our emotional life would be quite different. Within these contingencies, our freedom bestows specialness when we consent to become deeply involved with this or that object.

Bestowal value is a dangerous category, since it opens the door to prejudice and subjectivism. Again, why call attention to this kind of value? The reason is that it seems so much a part of our lives. It clarifies many of the events of our religious tradition and history, since some place needs to be made for the "arbitrary" (at least as far as we can tell) decisions of God.[66] Why did God accept the best offering of Abel, but not of Cain? Why did God choose the Israelites? Why did God's special favor rest on a beloved Son rather than a beloved Daughter? Why did Jesus choose the disciples, who were neither the worst nor the best of men? The Bible is realistic about the arbitrariness of many decisions, "about the scandal of particularity," about the power of freedom to select neither in terms of comparative value nor in terms of equality. Similarly, we can and must freely select among alternative possible goods, commit ourselves to one particular person or thing or way of life, and then let that value take on added importance for our lives.

In brief, though everything has an importance in itself, not everything becomes specially important to us. We have a certain freedom to select which importances we shall allow to become significant and determinative for us. Even for God, whose love is the objective measure of the intrinsic value of all things, some historical realities are more important than others because God has chosen them and freely acted on their behalf. The world God creates contains large dollops of at least apparent arbitrariness. Out of all the creatures of all possible worlds that might have been, the creatures of this world are, to some degree at least, simply the beings that God thus far has "chosen."

EXISTENTIAL PARTICIPATION

In the next chapter I will describe love as an emotional participation in a valuable object. Above I have briefly analyzed the meaning of "emotion" as well as the kind of "value" love intends. Here I examine "participation." The guiding idea is that participation means unity-in-difference, a sharing through which the uniqueness of the parties is enhanced.

Contemporary theologians rightly insist that our reality is radically relational. As Hans Tiefel writes, "Relationships with God and each other . . . constitute who we are. To lose them would be to lose ourselves, for without them we could not be ourselves and might not be."[67] Invoking the image of the trinity, John Mahoney asserts, "As in God, so in his human creatures made in his image, reality is essentially relational. . . . the fullness of personal identity is to be found only as interpersonal identity."[68] Putting this another way, Gordon Kaufman writes, "We are, after all, fundamentally social beings belonging to and constituting each other, not individual atomic egos living by and to ourselves alone."[69] Daniel Day Williams puts the matter in terms of human subjectivity: "The fundamental human craving is to belong, to count in the community of being, to have one's freedom in and with the response of others, to enjoy God as one who makes us members of one society."[70]

Thus, many theologians insist we are relational beings. Our relations, however, come in many forms. Love is the form this book explores, but hatred, force, knowledge, work, etc., are other ways of relating. Personal love is a kind of relationship in which persons share life without losing themselves. I shall use the word "participation" for such a relationship. As contemporary ethicists struggle against individualism and become more aware of the significance of relationships for human life, something like the idea of "participation" becomes both attractive and necessary. In the terse words of James Gustafson, "The human venture is participation."[71]

Participation language is widely, if unreflectively, used in our Christian discourse. We speak of "participating" in the liturgy; we "take part" in a community project; we "share" ourselves "with" another. We have our being "in" God, and God is "within" us. We are in a "covenant" with Yahweh; we are *God's* people and God is *our* God. The New Testament says we are made "through" the Word, and that Word "made his dwelling among us" (Jn 1:3, 14). We abide in Christ and Christ in us (Jn 6:56, 15:5). We "belong to" the Mystical Body, and we "share in" God's life. The Epistles speak of our "living with and in" Christ (Rom 6:8; 2 Tim 3:12) and of Christ "living in" us (Gal 2:20). We are disciples of Jesus, and we share in the body of Christ (1 Cor 10:14). We are "partakers of the divine nature" (2 Pt 1:4) and "have become partners of Christ" (Heb 3:14). And we await the coming of the Kingdom when God will be all in all (1 Cor 15:28). These scriptural themes suggest some form of mutually involving, personal participation; but Scripture does not speculate on the exact meaning of that participation.

The idea of participation has had a long and often obscure history. As a technical term in metaphysics, it has been used to explain the relation between this world and its ultimate ground, a relation which we do not experience but rather deduce from the principles of causality.[72] In an emanationist or pantheistic theory, the relationship between this world and Being is so close that their *difference* tends to be obscured. Individual beings are merely parts of Being. In a deist view, their relationship is so extrinsic that their *unity* is nearly lost. After an original creation there are at most occasional interventions by the deity. These extremes fail to conceptualize adequately either the unity or the difference between God and creation. Classical Catholic metaphysics avoids these extremes; but in its laudable desire to establish a thesis true of all creation, it obscures the distinctive way that persons experientially participate in God. That is, it fails to thematize adequately the kind of unity that *persons* may share. Equally important, it curiously also fails adequately to acknowledge how human beings are different from God. It claims that God possesses in an unrestricted fashion what we dependently "possess in some partial or restricted way."[73] But then, since God possesses (or is) all goodness, human beings have nothing distinctively their own. As Karl Rahner suggests, such a notion wipes out the positive contributions of finite beings and renders these beings superfluous before an infinite God.[74]

Absent from these and indeed most metaphysical presentations of participation has been the biblical sense of *personal* interaction between God and creation. The biblical idea of participation is concerned less with a metaphysical origin and more with an existential relationship. This relationship requires distinctively personal qualities, including (1) history, (2) freedom, and (3) grace. Classical metaphysical approaches, concentrating on what is common to all beings, failed to highlight these three qualities.[75] Human existence was often examined through the lens of Aristotle's four kinds of causes, which were designed to explain the interactions of nonpersonal things. Rahner stretched to the breaking point these traditional categories when he spoke of the effects of the union of God with human beings as "quasi-formal" causality.[76] With this concept, Rahner indicated how one person shapes the form of another without losing its own form. Personal beings can give their own forms or identities without losing themselves. And they can receive the form of another and thereby be enhanced in their own form. The traditional view understood our transformation through grace as the infusion of supernatural principles into a natural being. In much theology, however, this transformation through grace was not an experiential datum, but belonged to the realm of blind faith. Rahner gradually came to see that the presence of God in our lives is inadequately understood in terms of nature and supernature, and he came to assert that our divinely transformed existence can and should be grasped through concrete experience.[77]

Existential or personal participation is a way of being united with "another" which does not diminish, but rather enhances, the distinctiveness of those who are united.[78] Two people playing solitaire side by side presumably are not sharing in an activity. That is, without some sort of unity there is no participation but only two individuals acting independently. At the other extreme, when a woman has her identity only in her husband, she is not sharing life with him. That is, without growth in her uniqueness, there may be fusion but not participation. By contrast, as a friendship grows, the friends become more distinctively themselves; without their friendship there would not be this growth. In a brief formula, this existential form of participation is a *unity-in-difference.*[79] Greater unity promotes greater personal differentiation. Many theories of love founder for failing to observe this basic requirement. For example, they so identify lover and beloved ("another self") that lovers are loving themselves in loving the beloved. Or, on the other hand, they quite frequently insist that lovers must lose themselves if they truly love another.[80]

The importance of this unity-in-difference appears in Christian spirituality. Unity with God and personal perfection grow in direct and not in inverse proportion.[81] At the same time, the more religious consciousness sees creatures as related to God, the more it desacralizes these creatures by seeing that they are not God. Participation in God's kingdom means a move forward to a realm where God will be all in all (1 Cor 15:28), yet each creature will attain its own proper perfection.

History: When persons participate in one another, they create a common history. All participative relations take place in and through a history which the participants create and by which they are created. The identity of tomorrow's participants is formed by their interaction today. This is true for God as well as for human persons.

Classical metaphysics left God simply unchanged in eternity.[82] Creatures metaphysically participated in God, but God did not participate in them. Their history was an imperfection compared to God's immutability. The history created by each creature was only a deficient or incomplete form of the perfection found in God. Therefore the history of the creature made no positive contribution to God. Moreover, the past was often taken as normative, because it represented the design previously established by a perfectly provident God. The future was frequently thought of as at best a return to the golden past, so that any positive creativity was assumed to be impossible. Process theologian Daniel Day Williams offers a different understanding:

> God shares with the creatures the power of his being, allowing them a measure of freedom and spontaneity so that God's temporal interaction with the creatures is a real history of inter-communication and action. What happens in this world makes a difference to God. He responds concretely to every new event by taking it as a datum into a new phase of his own life and adjusting it within the harmony of his vision. What remains fixed for God is the absolute integrity of his aim which looks toward the fullness of life for the whole creation. To move the world toward this fulfillment, God shares in the concreteness of events. . . . We avoid here one of the curious consequences of the Augustinian ontology which is that the world can add nothing to God. . . . As concrete life, God is conscious, personal being.[83]

In this understanding of existential participation, human *history*, religiously viewed, is the ongoing, personal interrelation between God and creation—in individuals and as a whole.[84] This union is progressively created; God and creation move freely toward this union rather than harken back to it.[85] God *will* be all in all. In this Christian, personalist framework, human history is also divine history.[86] The Incarnation means that God chose to be involved in history and that human history—paradigmatically, Jesus' history—affects God. As Lucien Richard argues, "While God transcends history, history is important to him and makes a difference."[87] God shares in our history, and we share in the divine involvement in the world. God's power is not only the metaphysical power of causing beings to exist, but also a personal power to enter into relationship with those beings.

This personal power, as James Nelson argues, is a distinctive kind of "relational power." It includes both being able "to absorb the influence of another without losing the self's own center" as well as "the strength of exerting influence on another." Nelson adds that "the greatest influence often consists in being influenced, in enabling another to make the largest impact on oneself."[88] The ability to receive, and not just the ability to give, is thus a virtue.[89] In and through the love relation between God and humans, each party receives the other and is modified. Something genuinely new, i.e., not originally found either in God or in human beings, arises through love. Each party becomes what it can be through participating in the other. One of God's personal gifts to us is to let us be significant to God's own life. The symbols of the Incarnation and the cross say that we do not live and suffer alone; we share the sufferings of Christ (2 Cor 1:5), and our God lives and suffers with us.[90] In classical metaphysics and much Christian theology, there has been little tolerance for a God who not only gives but also receives, who not only sustains but also shares in history. Accordingly, Christian spirituality encouraged us to give and not receive, to live in but not share the world's history. But, as I hope will become clearer through this book, God's love would be meaningless, if God were unable to be influenced by us.[91]

Freedom: We are free persons and God can be mutually involved with us only with our free cooperation. For revelation to occur, God must freely speak, but we must also freely listen. Thus, the self-disclosure of God takes place only in and through God's freedom *and* ours. The "relational power" of God does not compel our freedom. Rather, God's power as love is the more manifest as it invites and evokes our freedom.[92] We *personally* cooperate with God not whenever we do any good action, but only when our actions are freely performed as ways of acting with God.

We who receive God's self-communication can through freedom become either a personal partner or enemy of God.

By God's choice our free history is also the "free history of God himself in the world."[93] The implication of God's choice is that, when we act freely, our choices are not solely matters of finite goods and human self-determination. Our freedom codetermines, though in a dependent way, the manner and form of God's involvement in the world.[94] To extend the Pauline metaphor, the *head* of the body does not say to the feet, "I do not need you" (1 Cor 12:21). To be sure, without God, we can do nothing. But without our free cooperation, God cannot do what God wants to do through us. As Charles Curran notes, "Put very boldly, God is powerless to intervene directly in human history. . . . The empowering work of God will be mediated by free human beings."[95] Popular theology often takes a view that forgets human freedom, holding that God could do the "same" things without each one of us. But God's personal involvement with us must not be understood in terms of mechanical causality, as if God moves us like physical objects in order to achieve certain results. That is, there must be a mutually free quality to this relationship.[96]

Unlike metaphysical participation, through which God sustains creatures without requiring their free consent, any personal participation between God and humans depends on human freedom.[97] Religious people often imagine that all legitimate power and control rests with God. Thus, they hold that humans are fit only to obey or disobey the absolutely sovereign God or, sometimes, even that humans are but "instruments" in God's hands. Such views neglect the creativity and spontaneity which are essential to our freedom.[98] We *can* resist God's involvement in our *personal* lives, but we can also cooperate with and contribute to an intimate "partnership with God."[99] Without our cooperation, God cannot be involved with creation in the way God wants to be. God wills, therefore, to depend on humans.

Grace: A personal love relationship always has the quality of a gift. It occurs not automatically, but rather must be freely offered and received. None of the participants—whether God or humans—"earn" the love of the other. Each deserves love, but that love must be freely given. Thus, a love relationship is a grace. In a cosmological framework, grace has too often been understood to be a thing given to us, something that we can pray for and, God willing, we might "get." In a personalist framework, grace *is* God's self-gift and our free reception of that gift. Grace is not some added extra that God gives us out of love; it is not some infused supernatural principle; rather, as I shall later argue, it is primordially God's love itself. Our growth in grace is growth in love for God. We experience grace as prior to, concomitant with, and posterior to our own acts. That is, God invites us to abide in a love-covenant that then is the relationship from which, ideally, all our activities flow. We *experience* the transforming power of this relation, for example, in ecstatic moments during which we feel ourselves "uplifted" by God's love.

In understanding this graced relationship, it is important to insist on our dependence on God, even as we claim our own unique contribution to our relationship with God. If we are sensitive to religious experience, we can recognize this dependence. We experience our dependence in the way our own self-transcendence is evoked and embraced by a presence that we cannot and do not produce or control. In experiencing the dark nights of the senses or soul, or in experiencing frailty, loss, or death, we learn that we are a dependent origin of a particular and limited horizon or world. We learn that, without the gracious approach of God, we are left with an empty sense of ultimate meaninglessness. In facing our sinfulness, we learn that we have the one-sided capacity to deny the one relation that finally makes sense out of our lives but not the capacity to one-sidedly bring about this relation. Without this central relationship, our life loses focus and purpose, and we are unable simply to will that everything be "fine."[100] In the words of piety, we learn that by ourselves we are "nothing." We experience the overcoming of this nothingness as grace. With grace, we discover a meaningfulness to our lives that goes beyond intelligibility. As Rahner notes, holding on to only what is graspable or intelligible is sin. In our graced relation, God remains eternally transcendent, but nonetheless invites us into mystery; and we love God, even though we can never fully "know" God.[101] In these experiences of God's absence and presence, God is revealed to be God, the One who is wholly other than us. Yet in these graced moments we also experience God as the One who has freely become involved with us. In these experiences, we discover that God enables us to be profoundly free beings. In brief, we share life with God, but we do so in a way that is free, historical, and graced.

CONCLUSION

In this introductory chapter, I have reflected on the way that our relation with God makes the Christian life distinctive. I have also looked at how our emotions relate us to value and how God and we can participate in one another. These considerations prepare us for a careful examination of the nature of love. To that I now turn.

NOTES

1. Linell Cady, "Relational Love," *Embodied Love*, ed. Paula Cooey et al. (San Francisco: Harper & Row, 1987), 137; see also Patrick Byrne, *"Ressentiment* and the Preferential Option for the Poor," *Theological Studies* 54 (June 1993): 233, 240; Gordon Kaufman, *Theology For a Nuclear Age* (Philadelphia: Westminster, 1985), 26; Richard Gula, S.S., *Reason Informed by Faith* (New York: Paulist, 1989), 49.

2. Charles Curran and Richard McCormick, S.J., eds., *Readings in Moral Theology No. 2: The Distinctiveness of Christian Ethics* (New York: Paulist, 1980); Vincent MacNamara, *Faith and Ethics* (Washington: Georgetown Univ. Press, 1985).

3. Mark Taylor, *God Is Love* (Atlanta: Scholars Press, 1986), 343.

4. Paul Ricoeur, "History as Narrative and Practice," *Philosophy Today* 29 (Fall 1985): 214–15.

5. Cady, "Relational Love," 139.

6. Max Scheler, *The Nature of Sympathy* (Hamden, CT: Shoe String, 1973), 87–88; Kenneth Kirk, *Vision of God* (New York: Harper & Row, 1966), 401.

7. *ST* I–II.64.1–4, II–II.24.7, 27.6, 44.1; *Caritate*, 2; *Sententiarum*, 3.27.3.3.

8. *ST* I–II.65.2, II–II.23.3, 24.1, 27.6. Karl Rahner, S.J., explicitly develops Aquinas's view in "The 'Commandment' of Love in Relation to the Other Commandments," *Theological Investigations* (Baltimore: Helicon, 1966), 5:447–50. For his part, Rahner, who began his life's work with an emphasis on knowledge, eventually came to hold that "The act of personal love for another human being is therefore the all-embracing basic act of man which gives meaning, direction and measure to everything else"; "Reflections on the Unity of the Love of Neighbour and the Love of God," *Theological Investigations* (Baltimore: Helicon, 1969), 6:241.

9. Paul Lauritzen, *Religious Belief and Emotional Transformation* (Lewisburg: Bucknell Univ. Press, 1992), 91–107; Manfred Frings, "Max Scheler," *Philosophy Today* 30 (Spring 1986): 34, 36.

10. Timothy O'Connell, *Principles for a Catholic Morality* (New York: Seabury, 1978), 153, claimed that prudence is more important than love. In his revised edition (San Francisco: Harper & Row, 1990), 211–12, he modulates this claim.

11. *ST* II–II.45.2–4, 28.3, 180.7; *Caritate*, 6.

12. For an enlightening, if distressing, exposition of how different religious frameworks lead to different interpretations of reality and correspondingly to different actions, see Dennis Doyle, "The Meaning of AIDS," *Commonweal* 115 (3 June 1988): 343–46.

13. Bruno Schüller, S.J., *Wholly Human* (Washington: Georgetown Univ. Press, 1986), 15ff, reduces biblical language to "reminders" and "exhortations" of things we independently know we must do. He does not acknowledge how our tradition helps us in the first place to know what is good. More importantly, he does not see that our actions have a richer meaning that the atheist is unable to enact.

14. Timothy Sedgwick, "Revising Anglican Theology," *The Anglican Moral Choice*, ed. Paul Elem (Wilton, CT: Morehouse-Barlow, 1983), 136–37, writes: "What therefore becomes most problematic about the traditional natural law approach to morality is that this approach too easily loses from view the very source of Christian life. It begins with principles which express abstract ends of human life rather than the dynamic call which arises from Christian faith. . . . Responsibility emphasizes the dialogical structure and personal character of life. The moral life is lived in response to the call of God,

neighbor, and all of creation." This is not to say that a religious horizon directly determines the particular decisions that we make. The influence of a horizon is much more indirect; see Thomas Ogletree, *Hospitality to the Stranger* (Philadelphia: Fortress, 1985), 79.

15. William Spohn, S.J., shows the place of these conceptions in the thought of Jonathan Edwards; "Union and Consent with the Great Whole," *The Annual of the Society of Christian Ethics* (1986), 22–23. Thomas Byrnes, "H. Richard Niebuhr's Reconstruction of Jonathan Edward's Moral Theology," *The Annual of the Society of Christian Ethics* (1986), 40, argues that Edwards did not understand God impersonally.

16. Gabriel Daly, "Catholicism and Modernity," *Journal of the American Academy of Religion* 53 (December 1985): 796.

17. Stanley Hauerwas, "Love's Not All You Need," *Cross Currents* (Summer-Fall 1972): 228; also see Hauerwas, "The Demands of a Truthful Story," *Chicago Studies* 21 (April 1982): 59–71.

18. MacNamara, *Faith and Ethics*, 195.

19. Jonathan Edwards, *Religious Affections*, ed. John E. Smith (New Haven: Yale, 1959), 93–124. I use the term "emotion" interchangeably with "affections," "passions," and "feelings" since there is no commonly accepted usage. Jules Toner, *The Experience of Love* (Washington: Corpus, 1968), 66, makes a case for the word "affection" as the most apt word because its current usage tends to hold together the active and passive aspects. "Emotions," however, still seems the commonly used term.

20. Robert Roberts, *Spirituality and Human Emotion* (Grand Rapids: Eerdmans, 1982), 1.

21. Bernard Lonergan, S.J., *Method in Theology* (New York: Seabury, 1972), 106–7; Patrick Byrne, "Ressentiment and the Preferential Option for the Poor," 230–34.

22. Alan Drengson, "Compassion and Transcendence of Duty and Inclination," *Philosophy Today* 25 (Spring 1981): 39.

23. Emotions fall into various types, each with its own structure. I will concentrate on the type that includes love. There are other types of emotions such as anger or joy which are often taken to be primary examples of emotions, but in fact are secondary responses to something already felt through the sort of emotional perception I shall be describing.

24. Robert Doran, S.J., "Jungian Psychology and Christian Spirituality," *Review for Religious* 38 (1979): 508–10; Lauritzen, *Religious Belief and Emotional Transformation*, 30.

25. G. K. Chesterton, *Orthodoxy* (Westport, CT: Greenwood Press, 1974), 32.

26. Charles Taylor, *Sources of the Self* (Cambridge: Harvard Univ. Press, 1989), 73–74; see also Sidney Callahan, *In Good Conscience* (San Francisco: Harper, 1991), 95.

27. William James, *Varieties of Religious Experience* (New Hyde Park, NY: University Books, 1963), 150; James unfortunately goes on to draw subjectivist conclusions from this thought-experiment.

28. Hans Reiner, *Duty and Inclination* (Boston: Nijhoff, 1983), 133–41, 159–61; Peter Spader, "The Primacy of the Heart," *Philosophy Today* 29 (Fall 1985): 223–29.

29. Don Saliers, *The Soul in Paraphrase* (New York: Seabury, 1980), 12–13; Lauritzen, *Religious Belief and Emotional Transformation*, 60.

30. Dietrich von Hildebrand, "The Role of Affectivity in Morality," *Proceedings of the American Catholic Philosophical Association* (1958), 92.

31. Dietrich von Hildebrand, *Ethics* (Chicago: Franciscan Herald, 1953), 217.

32. Reiner, *Duty and Inclination*, 122.

33. Von Hildebrand, *Ethics*, 217, 218, 221.

34. Daniel Maguire, *The Moral Choice* (Garden City: Doubleday, 1978), 287; Ogletree, *Hospitality to the Stranger*, 81; Lauritzen, *Religious Belief and Emotional Transformation*, 40–45.

35. MacNamara, *Faith and Ethics*, 200.

36. Being a feeling, valuing person is different from being able to talk about either feelings or values; cf. Doran, "Jungian Psychology and Christian Spirituality," 504.

37. There are some emotions that seem objectless, e.g., anxiety. These emotions, I think, are nonetheless responses to values, namely, ontological values.

38. For an insightful initial description of how this occurs, see William Spohn, S.J., *What Are They Saying About Scripture and Ethics?* (New York: Paulist, 1984), 106–28; cf. also Callahan, *In Good Conscience*, 205–8.

39. Walter Brueggemann, *The Creative Word* (Philadelphia: Fortress, 1982).

40. Ogletree, *Hospitality to the Stranger*, 81–84.

41. Beverly Harrison, *Making the Connections* (Boston: Beacon Press, 1985), 14, offers, I think, contradictory advice when she tells us that feelings are not "right" or "wrong," and then says that they are "the basic ingredient in our relational transaction with the world." These "basic ingredients" can be appropriate and inappropriate, well formed and ill formed. In that sense, they can be right or wrong. We can have appropriate emotions: lustful attraction is not morally equal to respectful attraction. Behavior is not the only or the most important consideration in the moral life.

42. James Keenan, S.J., *Goodness and Rightness in Thomas Aquinas's* Summa Theologiae (Washington: Georgetown Univ. Press, 1992), 16–17.

43. Margaret Farley, *Personal Commitments* (New York: Harper and Row, 1986), 27.

44. Fred Berger, "Gratitude," *Ethics* 85 (July 1975): 306.

45. MacNamara, *Faith and Ethics*, 99; see also Berger, "Gratitude," 305; Outka, *Agape* (New Haven: Yale Univ. Press, 1972), 128.

46. Maguire, *The Moral Choice*, 300; C. Taylor, *Sources of the Self*, 93.

47. Outka, *Agape*, 129, 143; Oliver O'Donovan, *Resurrection and Moral Order* (Grand Rapids: Eerdmans, 1986), 207–11.

48. MacNamara, *Faith and Ethics*, 100.

49. James Gustafson, *Ethics from a Theocentric Perspective* (Chicago: Univ. of Chicago Press, 1984), 2:62.

50. Peter-Hans Kolvenbach, S.J., "Address to Assembly 1989: Jesuit Ministry in Higher Education," *National Jesuit News* 18 (June 1989) Supplement.

51. Gula, *Reason Informed by Faith*, 179–80 (italics mine). Similarly, Rosemary Haughton, *Passionate God* (New York: Paulist, 1981), 6, argues that love should be passionate, that is, "in motion—strong, wanting, needy, concentrated towards a very deep encounter"; she thereby jumbles the various movements we are describing.

52. Von Hildebrand, *Ethics*, 221–43.

53. Von Hildebrand, "The Role of Affectivity in Morality," 91.

54. Toner, *The Experience of Love*, 96, also 70.

55. Toner, *The Experience of Love*, 67; Callahan, *In Good Conscience*, 109–13.

56. Callahan, *In Good Conscience*, 110, 128–29.

57. The following owes much to Dietrich von Hildebrand's *Ethics*, 79–94.

58. C. Taylor, *Sources of the Self*, 74.

59. Arthur Vella, S.J., *Love Is Acceptance* (Dissertation: Pontifical Gregorian University, 1964), 129.

60. Though in the *Summa Theologiae* Aquinas most commonly describes the good as whatever is good for me, in his early work he significantly qualified this position by asserting that he does *not* mean this position to have a bearing on the *moral* life where the *finis* or goal is central to the moral significance of an act: "Although the loveable for everyone is that which is good for him, it is not necessary that it is loved for this purpose (*propter finem*), namely, that it is good for him. Even friendship may not return to oneself the goods one hopes for another: for we love friends, even if nothing is supposed to come of it for us" (*Sententiarum*, 3.29.1.3). Aquinas would have done well to distinguish the good for me from the good or important to me.

61. Values are, like everything else, relative to a culture in at least two ways: they are known within a cultural context and they have a reality which is felt to conform to, oppose, or be foreign to that context. To say that values are relative to a culture, however, is not to succumb to what is now commonly called "relativism." The addition of the suffix "ism" refers to the position that values are *wholly* made up by a person or culture. Relativism, when referring to a person, is often called subjectivism; when referring to a community, it is called cultural relativism. In either case, the particular value is said to have no objective reality, but to be only *whatever* the individual or culture makes it to be. The object is said to be in itself value-free, and then we impose our values on it. My own position rejects this form of relativism; see Edward Vacek, S.J., "Popular Ethical Subjectivism," *Horizons* 11 (Spring 1984): 50–51.

62. Timothy Jackson, "The Disconsolation of Theology," *Journal of Religious Ethics* 20 (Spring 1992): 7–8.

63. For an extended discussion of this phenomenon, see William Earle, "Transcendental Love," *The Autobiographical Consciousness* (Chicago: Quadrangle Books, 1972), 98–124.

64. Irving Singer, *The Nature of Love* (Chicago: Univ. of Chicago Press, 1987), 1:5, also 1:6–15 and 3:391–401. Singer's notion, however, is not clearly distinct from an arbitrary imputation of value (1:14).

65. The same can, I think, be said of God's love for us. If God's love were simply a necessary and predictable feature of God's own goodness, we would not need to trust God. Cf. Lawrence Thomas, "Trust, Affirmation, and Moral Character," *Identity, Character, and Morality*, eds. Owen Flanagan and Amélie Oksenberg Rorty (Cambridge: MIT Press, 1990), 235–57, especially p. 257.

66. Karl Rahner, S.J., "Thomas Aquinas on the Incomprehensibility of God," *The Journal of Religion* 58 (Supplement 1978): S122, says of God's choices that the "thorn of incomprehensibility (it could have been otherwise; why was and is it for all eternity precisely so and not otherwise?) is not pulled from our hearts." See also Stephen Pope, "Proper and Improper Partiality and the Preferential Option for the Poor," *Theological Studies* 54 (June 1993): 252–54.

67. Hans Tiefel, "Severely Handicapped Newborns," *Questions about the Beginning of Life*, ed. Ed Schneider (Minneapolis: Augsburg, 1985), 161.

68. John Mahoney, S.J., *The Making of Moral Theology* (Oxford: Clarendon, 1987), 319, also 345–46.

69. Kaufman, *Theology for a Nuclear Age*, 59.

70. Daniel Day Williams, *The Spirit and the Forms of Love* (New York: Harper & Row, 1968), 146.

71. Gustafson, *Ethics from a Theocentric Perspective*, 2:13.

72. John Finnis, *Natural Law and Natural Rights* (Oxford: Clarendon, 1982), 399–402; Lourencino Puntel, "Participation," *Encyclopedia of Theology* (New York: Seabury, 1975), 1161.

73. W. Norris Clarke, S.J., "The Meaning of Participation in St. Thomas," *Proceedings of the American Catholic Philosophical Association* (Washington: Catholic Univ. of America,1952), 8; John Dunne, C.S.C., "St. Thomas' Theology of Participation," *Theology Digest* 18 (1957): 487–512.

74. Rahner, "Incomprehensibility of God," S113.

75. Rahner, "The 'Commandment' of Love," 439–59, masterfully interweaves grace, freedom, and history.

76. Karl Rahner, S.J., "Revelation," *Encyclopedia of Theology* (New York: Seabury, 1975), 1467.

77. See Edward Vacek, S.J., "Development within Rahner's Theology," *The Irish Theological Quarterly* 42 (January 1975): 36-49.

78. Teilhard de Chardin puts the matter in evolutionary terms. For him the process is, first, differentiation; second, subjectification or interiorization; and, third, communion, which leads to further differentiation. See John Yungblut, "The Impact of Teilhard's New Mysticism on Spiritual Guidance," and Thomas Berry, "The Ethical Imperative of Our Time," *Teilhard Perspective* 20 (August 1987): 5, 6.

79. Lourencino Puntel, "Participation," *Sacramentum Mundi* (New York: Herder & Herder, 1969), 4:350; Toner, *The Experience of Love*, 194–95.

80. Oliver O'Donovan, *The Problem of Self-Love in St. Augustine* (New Haven: Yale, 1980), 134, 146–47.

81. Karl Rahner, S.J., "Jesus Christ," *Sacramentum Mundi* (New York: Herder & Herder, 1968), 3:206; Toner, *The Experience of Love*, 194–95.

82. O'Donovan, *Problem of Self-Love*, 39, 73.

83. Williams, *Spirit and the Forms of Love*, 109.

84. The metaphysics that underlies this book is a form of process theology. No definitive proof can, I think, be given to show that this or any other metaphysical system is the true system. To my mind, process theology still has not been satisfactorily worked out. Still I think that it gives the best account of the Christian conviction that God is involved with the world. For an introduction to process theology, see John Cobb, Jr., and David Griffin, *Process Theology* (Philadelphia: Westminster, 1976). For a convincing account of how Karl Rahner's theology demands a process theology, but comes up short, see M. Taylor, *God is Love*. For an attractive exploration of the contemporary implications of process theology, see Sallie McFague, *Models of God* (Philadelphia: Fortress, 1987).

85. When Tillich wrote that "love in all its forms is the drive towards the reunion of the separated," he harkened back to some primordial good time when all was in harmony, but, as Tillich knew, such a time never existed; *Love, Power, and Justice* (New York: Oxford, 1954), 27–28.

86. Karl Rahner, S.J., "Love as the Key Virtue," *Sacramentum Mundi* (New York: Herder and Herder, 1970), 6:343.

87.   Lucien Richard, O.M.I., "Toward a Renewed Theology of Creation," *Église et Théologie* 17 (1986): 157.

88.   James Nelson, *The Intimate Connection* (Philadelphia: Westminster, 1988), 102–3; see also, Anne Carr, "'Not a Sparrow Falls'," 36–37, and Charles Curran, "Providence and Responsibility," *Proceedings of the Forty-Fourth Annual Convention of The Catholic Theological Society of America* 44 (1989): 58–59.

89.   Richard McCormick, S.J., *The Critical Calling* (Washington: Georgetown Univ. Press, 1989), 219.

90.   Lucien Richard, O.M.I., "Toward a Renewed Theology of Creation," 158; David Smith, "Suffering, Medicine, and Christian Theology," *Moral Medicine*, eds. Stephen Lammers and Allen Verhey (Grand Rapids: Eerdmans, 1987), 259–60.

91.   Williams, *Spirit and the Forms of Love*, 127.

92.   Margaret Farley, R.S.M., "Fragments for an Ethic of Commitment in Thomas Aquinas," *Journal of Religion* 58 (Supplement 1978): S146; Charles Hartshorne, "Scientific and Religious Aspects of Bioethics," *Theology and Bioethics*, ed. Earl Shelp (Boston: Reidel, 1985), 28.

93.   Karl Rahner, S.J., "Man (Anthropology)," *Sacramentum Mundi* (New York: Herder & Herder, 1969), 3:366; see also Richard, "Toward a Renewed Theology of Creation," 160.

94.   Anne Carr, "'Not a Sparrow Falls'," 37.

95.   Curran, "Providence and Responsibility," 59.

96.   Williams, *Spirit and the Forms of Love*, 119.

97.   Williams, *Spirit and the Forms of Love*, 128.

98.   Edward Vacek, S.J., "Catholic 'Natural Law' and Reproductive Ethics," *Journal of Medicine and Philosophy* 17 (1992): 329–46. For the way that Barth vacillates on this point, see Edward Collins Vacek, S.J., "John Paul II and Cooperation with God," *The Annual of the Society of Christian Ethics* (1990), 81–108.

99.   Rahner, "Man (Anthropology)," 365–66.

100.   See Edward Vacek, "Towards a Phenomenology of Love Lost," *Journal of Phenomenological Psychology* 20 (Spring 1989): 1–19.

101.   Rahner, "Incomprehensibility of God," S117, S123, S125.

2

Nature of Love

Now I will show you the way which surpasses all the others. . . . if I give everything I have to feed the poor and hand over my body to be burned, but have not love, I gain nothing. . . . There are in the end three things that last: faith, hope, and love, and the greatest of these is love. (1 Cor 13:1–13)

Although love has been a gold mine for literature and religion, it has seldom been explored with conceptual thoroughness or rigor.[1] Most philosophical and theological writing, when it speaks of "love," does not analyze what love is, but rather assumes it has an evident meaning. Jules Toner does not greatly exaggerate when he says that the West has seen no more than a half dozen serious studies of the nature of love.[2] The topic of love is so familiar that most people think they have read extensively on the subject, much as they feel they have read the works of Freud because his ideas are so widespread. Perhaps love is too precious, soft, or intimate to be subjected to hard scrutiny. Wordsworth may be right that we "murder to dissect." If so, such is the fate of doing theological or philosophical analysis. Still, some service may be rendered to the Church by a careful, phenomenological analysis.

In this chapter I describe love in its most general features. If successful, such a general description will be analogously true of both God's love and ours. It will also be analogously true of our loves for a wide variety of objects: God, self, other human beings, and the rest of creation.[3] In subsequent chapters, I further specify this general love into three types: agape, eros, and philia. Before doing so, I want first to discover the unity in the meaning of love.[4] Put most formally, *love is an affective, affirming participation in the goodness of a being (or Being)*. Woven into this description are two strands. Any theory of love has to account for our experiences of wanting to be with or have those we love, and delighting when we do so. Love unites. A theory of love also must account for our experiences of wanting the best for the beloved. Love is affirming and, to the extent that the beloved is open to fuller value, love is directed to the enhancement of the beloved. Love tends to union, but it also has an uplifting power. Our love relationships generally include both moments of rest and moments of wanting the best.

COMMON MISUNDERSTANDINGS OF LOVE

Love is a complex emotion that normally occurs in association with many other acts. Its essence can easily be confused with what *accompanies* it or is its *consequence*. I begin by paring away some of these associated acts. Love is frequently confused with beneficence or benevolence, with striving, yearning, and desire, or with various feeling-states, identification, and certain related emotions. It is further confused with preference, choice, value judgments, various illusions, or a bond of interests. I look here at each of these misunderstandings.

Beneficence and benevolence: Paul says, "Do everything with love" (1 Cor 16:14). He was aware that we can do good things, including the works of justice, without love (1 Cor 13:1–3; Col 3:14). Thus, love should not be equated with beneficence, that is, doing good deeds (sometimes called "loving deeds"). It should also not be equated with benevolence, which is a disposition to do such good works.[5] Since we can do the right thing for many different reasons, or even do it by accident, not every "loving deed" is done from love. For example, a teacher might work very hard to help her students, but her primary motive might be to obtain an increase in salary. It is even possible that she might despise her students, yet, knowing that her advancement is dependent on their progress, she wants their good. That is, she can be beneficent and benevolent toward her students, without loving them. She "takes care of" them without "caring about" them.[6]

Beneficence and benevolence often lack the emotional quality that essentially belongs to love.[7] One can always ask the open questions, "Why are you doing good?" or "Why do you want the other's good?" It seems intelligible to answer with an emotionally flat "Because I need the job" or "Because it is my duty." When the answer is "Because I love her," that very answer reveals that love is the *origin* of beneficence and benevolence, not identical with them.

Thus "caretaking" is derivative from love, not identical with it.[8] In fact, there are times when we love others quite apart from caring for their needs. Indeed, we can love a sunset, our deceased parents, or a statue without being able to do anything for them.[9] We can also love people whom we decide not to help, e.g., so that they can learn to do for themselves, and we can love people even when we are unable to help, e.g., if we are paralyzed. Further, if love meant taking care of other's needs, we would no longer be able to love them once their needs were fulfilled.[10] Certainly, love moves us to care for the other when the other is in need. Tired feet and an aching back may be symptoms of love, but they are not synonyms for it. Herein lies the basis for common illusions: some people think that they love others simply because they have done so much for them or invested so much energy on them; others think they are loved because so much money or time has been spent on them.[11] None of this is necessarily love.

Striving, yearning, and desire: Love is not essentially a kind of striving after the beloved, since love has its quiescent moments when we are just happily present with those we love. Striving implies some goal that we want to achieve. Love does not have goals unless it discovers some good that needs to be realized. What goal does a mother strive for when she lovingly looks at her sleeping child?[12] Martha scurried about to serve Jesus, but Mary chose the better part by simply sitting by his side (Lk 10:41). Love, of course, wants the well-being of the beloved, but some of the perfection we want for others lies outside of anything we can strive for. The deepest human perfections cannot be directly willed into existence even in ourselves and a fortiori in another. To strive to "make" another love God or appreciate classical music would be to usurp the other's freedom.[13]

Romantic yearning for the beloved is a consequence of love and not love itself. When we are incompletely united with the beloved, we yearn to be more completely united with the beloved. The union of love is both "the source as well as the goal of man's yearning."[14] Personal love for another is also distinct from needing or desiring the other. Naturalists often reduce love to a desire for the satisfaction of some need such as sexual release. Love's movement is entirely different. Yearning and desires cease when their goal or object is attained, but love does not die.[15] The romance of the engagement may end, but love does not end with the marriage ceremony.[16] In its quiet moments, when desires and yearning have been satisfied, love continues on. It is alive in the presence of the beloved. Unlike striving, yearning, or desire, love remains strong and even increases the more it has attained its object. It illumines ever more "the object's initially hidden value."[17]

Joy, delight, and pleasure: Particular acts of love are normally accompanied by joy, delight, and pleasure. Love is usually increased, not diminished by the presence of these accompanying feeling-states. Still, these accompanying feeling-states are not the phenomenon of love itself. It is common to confuse love with the pleasant bodily and psychological feeling-states that the lover experiences while loving. People who argue against "emotionalism" and in favor of an emotionally neutral beneficence frequently want to separate love from the transience of this "feeling good."

Love perdures, however great the variations in our feeling-states. In our imperfect world, one who loves will necessarily suffer. If love were simply an abundance of pleasant feelings, it would disappear when it required suffering; but love does not do this. We can be sad in love, as when a parent loses a child. Less benignly, we can be delighted when the person we hate suffers a loss. So love does not consist in joy or delight.[18] Various pleasurable states, which are resonances in the lover's bodily, psychic, or spiritual self, usually accompany love. They may be part of an experience of love, but they are not identical with it.[19]

Identification: Another frequent mistake is to describe love as a form of identification or fusion with the beloved. For example, it sometimes happens that when a mother literally identifies with her child, she experiences the child's suffering not "as if" it were her own, but as really her own, sometimes feeling the child's pain in her own body. Some initial identification is a necessary prelude to love, but in love the distinctness of lover and beloved is preserved and accentuated.[20] A husband wholly absorbed in his wife is not loving, however consumed his life may be in self-sacrificing service. Those who identify romantically with another often end up hating that other in a desperate attempt to restore their independence.[21] Mere identification is not the same as love.

As we saw at the end of Chapter 1, existential participation means unity-in-*difference*. If God is all and we are nothing, no genuine love for God is possible. Similarly, if God is, as some write, our inmost self or our own depths, then love for God is simply loving ourselves. That is, such theories identify the lover and the beloved, making affirmation of the other nothing more than self-affirmation. True love of another, by contrast, enhances the distinctive character of both the lover and the beloved.[22] Even in genuine self-love, some sort of distinction is present. We affirm not only our actual selves, but also ourselves in our own authentic, ideal possibilities. Self-love is not a matter of importing some external standard of goodness to hold over against our actual self, but rather the affirmation of the real self in its movement toward what it is not yet. In love for ourselves, we become ever more aware not only of our own present goodness, but also of our incompleteness—we are not yet what we shall be.

Shared feelings: Love is sometimes mistaken for the sharing of feelings, such as in sympathy, empathy, or compassion. We often share a similar reaction to some object or event, or we enter into the emotions of another, e.g., feeling with them the loss of their child. Love commonly allows us to share the feelings of others, but love is not the same as sharing of feelings. We can share with another a common anger or hatred toward some object, without loving that other. For example, the statement that "the enemy of my enemy is my friend" does not point to love. We can share another's feelings of spite or envy, but we are not loving that person when we do so. Moreover, love has a wider range of objects than sympathy, empathy, and compassion. We can share feelings only with beings that feel; love is not limited to feeling beings. That is, we can love a painting or a sunset, or we can love our dog even when we do not particularly share any feelings with our pet. We can feel great love for a person in a coma. Love is directed not simply to feeling beings, but to any being.[23] There will be, to be sure, a tendency towards a certain consonance of affections with the one that we love. This is crucial for our relation to God as well as to other persons. But the consonance that is love "must not be confused with the affective harmony which can follow on love: the harmony of desires, joys, fears, sorrows, and so on."[24]

Preference and choice: Love should also not be confused with preference. We can love a painting, even if there is no other painting to compare with it. We can love one person even if there is another person we prefer. Love is not a exclusive choice between two objects. Divorces often spring from confusion on this point. No one should have to answer, without further qualification, the question, "Do you love him or me?"[25] While God should be preferred to fellow human beings, this does not mean that we should love God and not human beings. Similarly, a preferential option for the poor does not or should not mean no love for the rich. Preferring can be done for many reasons, only one of which is love. The poor can be preferred out of a sense of resentment against the rich.[26] Preferring is not love itself. We can prefer taking out the garbage to studying, though we love neither.

God's love is often described as an election. And love is often described as a choice.[27] It is clear that some sort of freedom must be present for a personal love to develop. Still, one can ask the open question, why was this or that person elected or chosen? And the answer may be "out of love," but it might be for other reasons. Depending on our purposes, we chose one person because she is a good accountant, another because we love him, and a third because we hate him. The fact that we elect or choose one person does not mean that we do not love another. Hurt feelings often needlessly arise from this mistake. Thus, choice is not identical with love.

Value judgments and respect: Sometimes authors explain that love is a kind of value judgment.[28] Others hold that love is respect or regard based on a judgment of equal humanity.[29] These views reverse the actual dynamics of our experience. We do not first size up the beloved, approve this and that characteristic, and then conclude that the object is lovable. Nor do we first judge that a person possesses some generic value common to all human beings, and then love that person. Rather we first love the whole being and then come to see its admirable qualities, including whatever value it holds analogously with other like beings. We do not say, "She's intelligent, gentle, and beautiful, and therefore I love her," but, rather, "I love her, and she's so intelligent, gentle, and beautiful." We don't say, "He's a human being, and therefore I love him." In fact, the dignity of "humanity" is first discovered in love for a particular individual, and only then is the importance of respect for all human beings seen. Love precedes rather than follows such value *judgments.*[30]

Love is not a reasoned process, though it is not unreasonable. Often we cannot give clear reasons for our love, and the reasons we adduce are never really sufficient to justify love's intensity or particularity. The beloved is reason enough. As William Luijpen puts it, "I love you because you are lovable, but you are lovable because you are who you are."[31] That is, the beloved's whole value is the starting place. As long as our attitudes remain focused on the criteria of acceptable qualities or generic values, there may be approval, admiration, or respect, but not yet love. A lover often dispenses with "proper standards" and thus looks like a renegade or fool to outsiders.[32]

Standards of value are themselves taken from objects already loved. Just as much conversation is sedimented speech, whose content derives from previous fresh insights and discoveries, so also standards of beauty and goodness are sediments from previous loves. These standards lack the freshness of an active love, and they leave out the uniqueness of the beloved. An active and alive love seizes on the individual core value of the beloved, and this core can never be completely captured in any set of universal judgments.[33] Still, love is not unreasonable. *Le coeur a ses raisons que la raison ne connait pas.* Love brings forth its *own* evidence which reason, working from what has already been discovered in previous loves, can only subsequently attempt to incorporate. Love by its very nature is ever focused on the mystery of the beloved; reason runs the risk of judging what is novel and unique by the standard case or by what has become conventional wisdom. Love-informed reason can come to see qualities of goodness that have not yet been conceptualized; reason-informed love is challenged to overcome the partialities that arise from devotion to a particular beloved.

Alienation and transference: Love should be directed to the goodness of the beloved. Not uncommonly, a spurious love arises from self-hatred or an inability to be alone. Some seek the company of others because they flee facing themselves. Others are helpful to people because, out of their own alienation, they feel they don't deserve anything good, but rather deserve to be subordinated to others. It is not necessary to love one's self before one can love others, but genuine love for others does not spring from self-hate.

Similarly, love is not genuine if it is "due to being attracted to something in the beloved object that is similar to an earlier loved object."[34] In these instances of "transference," one is controlled by past patterns. One is insensitive to the appeal of the new beloved's difference.[35] These supposed loves represent a failure to transcend ourselves and to move toward loving the other in its own right.

Bond of interests: Finally, love should not be mistaken for a bond of interests. Those who love must turn their face toward the one they love, not merely outward to some common goal.[36] Friendship love is commonly misdescribed as simply the sharing of an interest such as a project or hobby.[37] Academic colleagues have common interests, but that does not prevent them from disliking one another. And persons can have a bond of interests in evil actions just as much as in good, but this is not love. There is unity among thieves. A contract represents a bond of interests, but often no love is lost in such working agreements. Thus, marital love is erroneously understood as a contract to secure mutual interests. When one loves, one does not first make an agreement nor does one agree to love for a period of time. Love is prior to any agreements, and it endures even beyond the death of the beloved. To be sure, we can stop loving, but while we are loving we cannot put temporal limits on our love.

We cannot seriously say, "I love you for a week."[38] "There is no limit to love's forbearance, to its trust, its hope, its power to endure. Love never fails" (1 Cor 13:7–8).

In this section, we have seen how love is different from a variety of feelings, attitudes, illusions, and behaviors. Various actions, states, and emotions will usually be present in our loving; some will always be present. But love is something more. What love is, is the task of the rest of this chapter. In philosophical and theological literature, love is called many, many things: "union, presence, co-existence, adherence, affirmation, concern, relating positively, benevolence, taking responsibility for someone, concern for someone, giving of self,"[39] availability, actively leaning toward, acceptance, reverence, respect, openness, equal regard, selflessness, self-forgetfulness, desire, joy, and so forth. I will try to account for the insights of these terms. In saying what love is not, I have been presupposing at least some understanding of what love is. As an emotion, love has a complex, fourfold structure (Chapter 1). I begin with our general openness to love, and then, in later sections, I will develop how we perceive value, are moved by it, and respond.

ACTIVE READINESS

Every human being is in varying degrees and ways in a state of openness or active readiness for experiencing value. Just as the eyes must be open in order to see, so the heart must be open in order to feel the goodness of the beloved. Indeed, we are made for love. At peak openness, we may feel "full of love," even though we have not yet encountered a specific beloved. Love's spontaneous and overflowing quality is clearest at such times. In ordinary periods, we are ready to love if some sufficiently suitable object attracts us. On bleaker days, it takes something very attractive to arouse our love.

Although love is sometimes identified with this general "openness," this readiness is not yet "real love."[40] We can open our eyes all day long, but we do not see until some visible object is present. This readiness is rather the general condition necessary for encountering an object that specifies it into a love for a particular being (or for God). It is not, however, merely an unexperienced universal "condition of the possibility" for love. Rather, we can experience that we are more or less open. We can compare our present openness to what we once felt. We can compare our present openness to that of others whose sensibilities are more refined and acute than our own. We can also feel how we are open to certain kinds of values, e.g., religious, but not to others, e.g., athletic. And in feeling our sensitivity to a certain kind of value, e.g., beauty, we can be aware there is so much more about beauty we cannot appreciate. We can feel how we are open to a particular kind of value when it is found in one object, but are closed to feeling that same value in other objects.

Thus we humans are not simply a *tabula rasa*. Rather we are to greater and lesser degrees actively ready to encounter the good. And we can increase or decrease in this readiness or openness. We can become cold-hearted, almost unable to be touched. Or we may be ever alert like those newly fallen in love. Saints are sensitive to the slightest approach of God, and they are ready to love every human being, including those who seem to others unattractive.

Thus, who we are, that is, what kind of person we have become, makes a difference in what we *can* love. To say that each person is different from others is in good part to say that each has a different *ordo amoris*. In a word, concrete, historical persons have different abilities to love. This is not merely to say that they love different objects or persons but rather that their *structure* of love is distinctive. Their "descriptive" or actual *ordo amoris* is the present structure of their ability to love. This complex structure may itself have a unity which then constitutes their fundamental direction or orientation in life. This structure will be in harmony or disharmony with God's action in their lives. The "normative" *ordo amoris*, by contrast, is the structure of the ability to love that individual persons should have at their stage of development, in accord with the vocation they have from God.[41]

Our actual or descriptive *ordo amoris*, on the one hand, is itself a structure formed by our previous loves; on the other hand, it selects the range or type of objects we will tend toward.[42] This *ordo amoris* is not fixed. It may expand to include ever more nuanced, higher, and more spiritual values; or it may contract to focus more on lower values. In this expansion or contraction, we create a morally perfect or empty self.[43] Some persons develop an expansive heart that is able to appreciate what is good in almost everyone or everything, and other persons' hearts are pinched, unable without difficulty to appreciate the goodness of others. In this expansion or contraction, people draw near to or they separate themselves from God.

INTENTIONAL MOVEMENT

We are not just more or less open and ready to love; we also love definite objects. In discussing particular acts of love, I will use the notion of "intentionality." In the language of phenomenology, consciousness is always "intentional," that is, it is (1) someone's (2) consciousness *of* (3) something. Subject and object or, in personal relations, subject and subject, are essentially related in and through the conscious act. Romeo does not just love; he loves Juliet. Subject, object, and conscious act require one another. There is no beloved without a lover who loves. There is no lover without a beloved who is loved. And there is no love without both a lover and a beloved.

Changes in any one element of the subject-act-object unity involve modifications in the other two. Differences in the object make a difference in the love we can have. Thus, our love for God is a different kind of love than our love for a cat or a chocolate bar or an infant. Differences in the kind of love may make a difference in what we encounter in the beloved: different aspects of Mary appear when Mike loves her "erotically" rather than "agapically." And differences in the lover make a difference in the kind of love: God's love for us is different from our spouse's or cat's love. Thus, a change in one element of the lover-love-beloved unity modifies the others.

Though these claims are perhaps obvious, they are often ignored in theology and elsewhere. First, *love* is frequently discussed as if it did not vary with its particular beloved. Erich Fromm claimed that love is an attitude which knows no difference in its object, and so he concluded that if we love one person we love all human beings and that if we do not love everyone then we do not love anyone.[44] Here love floats free of particular objects. Similarly Günther Bornkamm, Paul Ramsey, Oliver O'Donovan, and others argue that love of God and love of neighbor are the same, since love is love no matter what its object.[45] Using the same word "love" obscures great differences in *experience*. If we experience the same love for our pet rock as for our husband or for our God, something is greatly amiss.

Second, there are *different kinds* of love. Some authors, such as utilitarians and teleologists, mistakenly say that whether we love others for their own sake or for our sake is not crucial, because in either case both the neighbor and we are enhanced. But the type of love we have makes a difference, even if the "results" seem the same. And, in fact, the results in the personal realm are never the same. If we love the world for our own sake, we become a different person than if we love it for its own sake. And in each case, the world shows a different face to us. Other authors mistakenly insist that there is only one kind of love. For example, they say that all love is really self-love, or they say that agape is the only real love, or, again, they say that any love that is not mutual is not love.[46] Furthermore, motherly love, brotherly love, divine love, and the like are different kinds of love. Not only are their subjects different, but the quality of each is different.

Third, *objects* make a difference in the love we have. Love for our husband can be deeper and richer than our love for a stone could ever be, and this spousal love will be different again from love for another man. Those who identify love of God and love of neighbor fail to appreciate how the different "object" modifies the kind of love that is appropriate and possible for each. We may say that we worship our wife and we worship God; but if we mean that literally, we can be sure we do not worship God. Similarly, our love for Jesus is different from our love for Mary or Peter. As we shall see, Christians frequently ignore this point when they say that agape is independent of any qualities in its object.

Fourth, *subjects* make a difference in love. God and people love differently. And each human being loves differently. Because we all have different identities shaped by different genetic, psychological, and personal histories, each of us loves differently. We need only recall two people who love us to realize that who the lover is makes a difference in the concrete love we receive. Moreover, we also become different in the way we respond to each person who loves us.

With the above as background, I will use this triadic structure of "subject," "consciousness-of," and "object" through the rest of this chapter to consider particular acts of love. I begin by looking at *love's* perceptivity. Then I shall consider how the *lover* is modified and next how the *beloved* is modified through love. I will conclude by discussing the relation of freedom to love.

AFFECTIVE PERCEPTION OF HIGHER VALUE

Love is not simply an undetermined openness to good. It also requires an encounter of the lover with the beloved. Emotional activity relates us to the "value" of the object. Love is an emotional cognition directed toward the whole value of the beloved.[47] We love the beloved in all its goodness, that is, in all the good that it is and can be. Hence, love is directed to the fullness of value possible to the beloved. In general terms, *love is an emotional, affirming participation in the dynamic tendency of an object to realize its fullness.* If we can assume that the dynamism of all beings and God is open to further (at least extrinsic) fullness, then love is directed to the realization of the beloved's fullest value.

The first role of concrete acts of love is to bring value to consciousness. Through love, the goodness of the beloved comes to appearance. All emotions point to values or disvalues, but love moves beyond any given values toward new values and beyond any partial goodness toward more of the whole. While love may begin with a present value, it contains a pre-sentiment of greater goodness.[48] We penetrate ever more into the good-ness of the beloved, and the beloved's uniqueness is given with greater clarity and power.[49] Love is an intentional act related primarily to the beloved's core goodness; since this core suffuses the other values of the beloved, love thereby shows them to have a greater worth than their worth as separate qualities. In this way, love is the explorer ship that takes us into the "more" or the mystery of each being.[50] The lover enters this mystery, uncertain whether the higher value of the beloved has simply not yet been seen or whether it is there only as a potential still to be realized. As a con-sequence, "love always has an historical context. The 'not yet' is always an element in the experience of love, the future which has certain ineluctable features and yet which in its concreteness is unknown."[51]

When one loves, it is the whole beloved and not simply some known or unknown, realized or unrealized aspect that one loves. Romeo loves Juliet not for the values he knows she possesses nor for some values she may someday realize; rather he loves her for all the real and potential goodness she is. He need not determine in advance whether the goodness he feels in her is actual or only potential. Nor does he have any complete idea of her total, final value. Love is not directed to some already known or decided higher value but to the object's fullness, whatever that might be. Love's movement, then, is not like that of a father who plots his child's entire life before the child is even born.

Love implies a directedness only toward whatever is proper to the full-ness of the beloved. It is a journey into the unknown, toward values that become clearer only in its movement. The full value of the object is always more than what is presently given. The lover senses a horizon of value—we might call it an aura of mystery—lying in and behind every value that he or she already knows. This horizon of higher value may include new values or it may be a new depth in the values already felt. Thus, love always includes a sense of expectation and hope, and love grounds a trust that exceeds legitimate inferences from past experience. At the religious level, love intimates that reality is an inexhaustible fullness to which we can entrust ourselves.[52]

Objectivity

Our love reveals the objective value of the beloved. It reveals the value that is already actual, as well as the ideal value that can become real in the beloved. Love does not project onto the beloved something that does not belong (really or ideally) to the beloved. The thesis that love illuminates the value of the beloved stands in stark contrast to the aphorism that love is blind. Far from being blind, authentic love is essential to complete objectivity. Full objectivity is made possible only by a loving devotion to the object.[53] Theology would be crippled without the access to God that love gives. Theology would be reduced to blind speculation, to rational inferences from biblical texts or Church decrees, and so on. The so-called blindness of love occurs rather when the self is dominated by a drive for power or sex or some other interest that distorts values in subordinating the object to its own purposes. But this is not love. The one who loves overcomes such distortions.[54]

Thus, instead of being blind, love is the "root of all authentic objectivity, in morality as well as in knowledge."[55] Love is like justice in rendering to the beloved what is its due since it corresponds to the beloved as it is and can be. It is "called forth and measured by the reality of the one loved."[56] The value of the beloved *claims* our acknowledgment.[57] Of course, love can go astray. It can be "more or less truthful when it is true, more or less adequate to its object. . . . In short, affective affirmation can be in accord or partially in discord with the concrete reality of the loved one."[58] That is, love can be mistaken, partial, or inadequate, but so can knowledge and volition. And just as we try to correct knowledge through further efforts at knowing, and just as we sometimes can rectify one volition by another, so we try to correct love gone awry through further acts of love. In that way, love moves from a mistaken, incomplete, or otherwise inadequate apprehension of the value of the beloved to a more complete emotional comprehension of the beloved's goodness. What we move toward is "a love as richly and delicately detailed in its structure as is the total reality of the beloved."[59]

Objectivity should not be understood to require "disinterestedness." Love and purely intellectual activity should not be contrasted as biased self-interest versus objective disinterest. There are many kinds of interest. We should distinguish between the interest motivated, say, by selfishness, and the interest springing from love for an object. We need not divest ourselves of all interests in order to be objective. Although love is not merely the subjective act of being more attentive, it is true that greater alertness and interest are its consequences.[60] Even intellectual activity springs from interest. The heightened interest of a genius stems from a strong, passionate love and leads to far greater objectivity than is possible to one who aspires to a value-free neutrality.[61] To paraphrase Wordsworth, works of genius are love reflected upon in tranquillity.

In reality, those who eschew love in favor of pure reason restrict themselves to a programmatic blindness. The seasoned lover sees the same deficiencies in the object that the rationalist sees.[62] The lover, however, also sees what the cold, gray eyes of the detached observer can never see. Only one who loves can penetrate to the value of the unique center of the beloved, a value core that permeates all other values and thus relativizes without obscuring these deficiencies. The loving disciple, not the "neutral" historian or biblical scholar, is the one who knows Jesus, the Christ. The disciple has an evidence that is not available to those who confine themselves within the strict canons of reason or academic study.[63]

Knowing and Loving

Henri Bergson and Max Scheler argued that love precedes knowledge.[64] By contrast, most authors hold that knowledge precedes emotion. Aquinas, for example, accepted Augustine's dictum that no one can love what he or she does not know; hence "love demands some apprehension of the good that is loved." Aquinas's point does not seem surprising; in fact, to most it has seemed self-evident. But Aquinas rightly qualifies this axiom. Only "some apprehension" is required. One need only know some small aspect of the beloved, or know the beloved only in a vague, general way; from there one can move toward a perfect love. While rationalists might hold that we can only love to the degree that we know, Aquinas observed that great love is not dependent on great intellectual refinement. Reason functions well when it analyzes and synthesizes, but love is not dependent on these uses of reason. In our moral decisions, love can, by the connaturality it creates, illumine our path where, if we relied solely on reason, we would otherwise be uncertain as to what to do.[65] Lovers can know better than the learned what to do.

Thus, Aquinas noted that a thing can be "loved more perfectly than it is known."[66] We can feelingfully apprehend the great value of the beloved even if we cannot give an intelligible account or defense of our apprehension. We can love God with our whole heart, even though we have a very limited intellectual knowledge of God. Because God is and always will remain incomprehensible, at some point in our relation with God we must leave off trying to know God and simply let ourselves be in love with God.[67]

When we fall in love, our perspective is changed and only then will certain forms of new knowledge follow. "Our love reveals to us values we had not appreciated," and subsequently we may intellectually investigate what our heart has discovered.[68] We typically grow in knowledge or achieve some project only when there is some good we love.[69] In our various relationships, there is usually a *perichoresis* of loving, knowing, and willing. Love often leads to knowledge, and knowledge to love. Love often leads to the practical engagement of our will on behalf of a beloved, and this praxis commonly leads to further knowledge and love.

Real and Ideal Value

Since love is a conscious movement toward the beloved's higher or fuller value, it risks the pitfalls of projection or false idealization. Such distortions are a failure of participation, a failure to realize "unity-in-*difference*." Since love precedes any question of whether the beloved's higher value is actual or still needs to be realized, love is not conditional in the sense of demanding that the object first achieve some particular value before we love it. Speaking in the language of grace, no one has to make herself or himself lovable before she or he can be loved. Jesus did not say to Magdalene, "Change your life, and then I will love you." Rather, he looked to her with love, and change became possible. Still, to love an object as it is does not mean to leave it as it is, for such acquiescence would deprive both love and the beloved of their dynamisms. Rather, to love the goodness of the beloved includes *its* ideal good. The goodness of the beloved is always both partially realized and partially to be achieved. Love invites the beloved to "become that which you are."[70]

It is wrong to identify love with "working to improve" the object. Teachers, social workers, even parents sometimes make this mistake. To be sure, our love desires improvement for the object. But this desire can pervert love if it turns into a superficial attitude that is concerned only with "correct" behavior or public "approval." The newlywed can turn into a nag. We feel demeaned and let down if we discover that the encouraging remarks of a "friend" were really motivated by a moralistic desire to change us. This manipulative attitude violates love's nature. Rather, love continuously renews a standing invitation to the beloved that it reveal itself and become ever more valuable.[71]

Over time our love illumines ever more the ideal essence of the beloved. In particular, with persons, we begin perhaps with only a few actions or expressive gestures, and through them we grasp intuitively the direction of development required by the person's normative *ordo amoris*. The person's unique essence is, of course, not fully given in a few actions, but from them a perceptive heart can sketch the first lines of the beloved's identity.[72] This sketch can be mistaken. Human love is no more infallible than any other form of human knowing, though it also need not be seen as more fallible. When it is accurate, love uncovers the unique value of another's life. As Max Scheler wrote,

The more deeply we penetrate into a man through an understanding cognition guided by personal love, the more unsubstitutable, irreplaceable, nonexchangeable, individual, and unique does he become for us. So much the more do the various "wrappings" that are there fall from his individual personal center. These "wrappings" refer to the more or less social "self" of the man, the general bondage to similar drives, needs of life, and passions, as well as to the idols of language that hide from us the individual nuances of experience insofar as they allow us to apply the same words and signs to them.[73]

An understanding of the beloved's uniqueness is not readily found outside a loving intentionality. A scientific attitude accepts only what is recurring and measurable, thereby missing love's attention to the unique. A practical attitude looks for the replicable and the manipulable. An impartial attitude, which some theologians say characterizes agape, sees and respects the basic dignity of the beloved, but refuses to enter into the uniqueness of the beloved. A lover, however, always has some sense of the unique value of the beloved. Thus, love includes more than "a merely abstract recognition of another's subjectivity." And it goes beyond simply respecting the rights and liberties of others.[74] Our love inclines us to affirm the realization of the beloved's unique essence and destiny. The beloved is invited to grow in the direction of the ideal image which our love unveils, an image taken from the beloved in the first place. A sense of repose in what the person has already attained is accompanied by an invitation and a hope for what is yet to be realized.[75]

We have seen that love illumines the objective goodness of the beloved. We now turn to the changes in the subject. Developments in the lover, though more obvious than those in the beloved, are nonetheless difficult to articulate. We look at some salient changes in the subject that are involved in the lover's becoming aware of and attracted to the objective value of the beloved.

RECEPTION OF GOODNESS

Love has a receptive, self-modifying aspect. The lover is changed by the beloved. This receptivity is ignored or denied by those who absolutize autonomy or self-control. Thus, "Love is often defined by theologians as 'active good-will'. . . . Christian love [is portrayed] as totally outgoing, having no element of responsiveness to the qualities of the loved one."[76] Christian writers often belittle "falling in love" or "being in love." They emphasize that love is hard work, and they put the stress on actions that we can initiate and control. Nevertheless, as an emotion, love has a moment of receptivity. The experiences of "falling in love" or "being in love" highlight something that is found in all love.

Actively Being Affected

In love, the goodness of the object catches our attention and appeals to us, and we are changed or "affected" by that goodness.[77] For Aquinas, the good is seen as a kind of force or power that attracts us and causes us to be conformed or inclined to it. We are, so to speak, captured or captivated by the beloved's good. For Aquinas, therefore, love is a "passion," a being acted-upon. Love involves receptivity to the good. Love then leads to desire for the good if it is absent and to joy when the good is present.[78]

Thus, the verb "love" points not just to its object; it also signals a change in the subject. When we say "I love you," in part we mean something like "you make such a difference in my life that I would not be the same person without you." That is, we acknowledge that we are changed by the one we love. People often have difficulty saying "I love you" because such a statement indicates not only an affirmation of the other, but also an admission that who they are is now dependent on the beloved. They have been and want to continue to be changed by the other. Thus, to say "I love you" is, in part, to accept being affected. In situations of conflict between two loved objects, we decide not simply who will be winner of our active energies; we also decide about ourselves, about which beloved will have more influence, at least for the moment, in our affections.[79] This is not to say that we can love others only insofar as they are good for us. Rather, as Karl Rahner says, love "wills the other subject as permanently other. But at the same time the subject grasps and affirms the significance of the other for itself and refers it to itself."[80] For example, we rejoice at the success of a friend, even when her achievement does not help our own lives, perhaps even when her success entails some loss for us.[81] It is her success, but she is important to us, and so we are happy.

Thus, the lover is not an unmoved mover. Hence, speaking of God as both loving and as unchangeable seems contradictory.[82] We humans, at least, are so constituted that we are or can be moved by the presence of the good, whether it is the "important-in-itself" or the "merely satisfying." We are, however, not merely passive. Rather, we are actively receptive. Our receptivity parallels the functioning of our bodily sensation. Consider three examples from touch, hearing, and sight. To be touched means simultaneously to touch. Being touched requires some concomitant activity on our part. Second, listening to music requires some degree of active listening. Our ears are "tuned" to the music, a point that becomes clear if the music unexpectedly ends. Third, when looking at a painting, our active gaze is in fact "led" by the flow of lines and colors and through them is "drawn" into the scene. In these examples, the object of our senses moves us, but it is given to an actively receiving sense. Similarly, the beloved's good moves us and our love is an active receptivity to that good. For this reason, language about being "touched" or "stirred" or "drawn" by the beloved is apt.

The more personal language of "invitation," "call," or "appeal" is also apt for love's receptivity. For example, at times our deepest yearning for ultimate meaning is experienced as itself a response to a prior invitation or, in biblical terminology, a call from God. We would not seek God, if God had not already found us. We would not yearn if we had not already experienced God. That is, our hearts are already touched by Mystery, and we feel drawn to fuller union with that Mystery. Paul Tillich captures both the receptive and active aspects of religious experience when he describes how the mind is *grasped* by an Ultimate *Concern* and when he speaks of "the pure *receptivity* of cognitive reason in an *ecstatic* experience."[83] At other times in our life when we doubt the reality of God, our hearts still feel drawn to what at the time seems only to be an untrue and empty ideal, namely, the ultimate meaningfulness and holiness of Being. When belief returns, we realize that this ideal which seemed to draw us into dark nothingness was all along real Mystery. In this vein, Rahner describes how our initial active readiness and our self-transcendence toward an infinite and potentially empty horizon are themselves both evoked and answered by God.[84]

Perceptive and Receptive

This moment of being affected retains a reference to the valued object that affects us. For Aquinas and others, "the passive moment of love is a necessary condition of the possibility of the active moment of love." The lover is "impressed," that is, changed by the beloved, even as "this change evokes in him an affective bent and tendency towards the beloved."[85] For Scheler and others, however, love is in the first place a perceptive activity which then is the condition for the receptive moment. Both the active and receptive moments of love have, I think, their foundation in experience, and neither necessarily precedes the other. However, each may be experienced with different saliencies. Consider three analogies from ordinary sensory experience: first, we are looking for a friend at a crowded airport; then we see the one we seek, and we feel both pleasure and relief. We see our friend because we are looking. A second example: we are working at our desk when suddenly the blare of a fire engine captures our attention. We were not listening for fire engines, but the siren forces itself on us. A third example: when we reach out to touch the texture of a face or a piece of wood, the experience is usually both expected and surprising. We expect the wood to be rough, but not rough in this way, or the face to be smooth, but not so delicately soft. These three types of experiences have analogies in the experience of love. With someone we already love, we look for and reassuringly find their goodness. While we are among strangers, we may suddenly be captivated by a slight gesture that promises to reveal more. And with acquaintances, we expect them to be good and lovable human beings, but often we are surprised by their unique goodness.

Thus, the active value-perceptivity of love is a moment that may, but need not, precede its receptivity. Ideally, these second and third moments of love's structure are both present and are as if one act. But, as I argued in Chapter 1, such unity is not always given. Both moments, moreover, are essential if love is to be fully an emotion. Most of our loves flow in an undulating stream of both activity and receptivity. On the one hand, as Toner writes, "Love involves passivity and spontaneous activity. The beloved calls and the lover answers from his own inner power of love."[86] On the other hand, however, sometimes the lover seeks and the beloved answers. More generally, our *ordo amoris* is such that we are open to reality's goodness and reality is such that it is inviting us.

In an act of love, we not only feel the beloved's goodness, but let it move us by its importance. The most ecstatic love is the most receptive. The reality of the one we passionately love calls forth and intensely codetermines our being. This receiving may be called a form of self-emptying if by that we mean that our accustomed world is now changed by the presence of the beloved.[87] We take the beloved into account in a way that prior to receiving the beloved we did not.

Aquinas's phenomenology of love, i.e., his account of the experience of love, nicely displays love's perceptive and receptive moments. When we love people, he observes, we are thinking *of them* and at the same time they are *on our minds*. We are not satisfied with a surface knowledge of their goodness, but want to penetrate ever more into their core value. At the same time, we are affected: "In the beloved's presence, the lover delights in him or in the good things about him. . . . Delight arises from a feeling for the beloved that is rooted deep within oneself. This is why we often speak of love as 'intimate'."[88] Not only do we, as it were, live *in our beloved's* life, but there is a change in our inner selves, and in this sense the beloved is *in us*. In loving another, we are fulfilled. In this sense, we now need the beloved, for without the beloved we cannot be as complete.

This being-affected, again, is not without reference to the beloved. Authors often ignore or denigrate "feelings," holding that they are merely aspects of ourselves with no essential connection to the beloved. They are said to be bodily states, much like a headache or chills running up our spine. Rather, Aquinas properly sees that these feelings or ways of being affected bear an essential reference to the beloved. Our delight is in the beloved. This delight is our inner, resonant response to being affected by the goodness of the beloved. And since love is directed to the whole of the beloved, this receptivity includes not just what is pleasant but also what is painful. The beloved becomes one of our reasons for laughing and crying, living and dying. The loss of the beloved becomes loss to our own selves.[89] Aquinas rightly saw that the life of the beloved becomes part of the lover's own identity. Love increases as the beloved becomes ever more rooted in us.[90] In the paradoxical language of love, the "beloved" to whom I *go out* becomes "intimately" *mine*. That is, love is directed to the beloved and yet it deeply affects one's own self. We "dwell" in the beloved, and the beloved dwells in us.[91]

Dante made the same point with two neologisms: When I love, I "in-you" me and I "in-me" you. Augustine beautifully captures the way love enables us to live in another while the other lives in us when he spoke of the death of his dearest friend: "My life was a horror to me, because I would not live as but a half. . . . I feared to die, lest he whom I had loved so much should wholly die."[92] Similarly, St. Paul sends Onesimus back to Philemon with the words, "It is he I am sending to you—and that means I am sending back my heart!" (Philemon 12)

Absence of Feeling

What then can be said about the common situation when we don't "feel any love"? This lack of feeling usually refers to the receptive moment of love. We can note several reasons for not feeling love. First, the love may in fact be gone. We may have become insensitive to the value of those we once loved, and they no longer make a difference to our lives. Second, although they still affect us, other emotions may dominate our consciousness, e.g., anger at them or at others. Third, we may be freely resisting or bracketing these feelings, for example, when we are trying to assert our independence. Fourth, we may still love them, but the receptive aspects may have become rather "quiet" or taken for granted. We feel right or fulfilled in being for and with the beloved, but these feelings do not occupy our attention. Perhaps only when the beloved is gone do we recognize that a peaceful joy had all along been a quiet but important part of our normal consciousness. Fifth, love may continue on in a deficient or incomplete mode.[93] The perception of the beloved's value may persist only as a memory of how we were once attracted by him or her. Or we can still perceive the beloved's value, but we may be too stressed or tired to feel the resonance of that goodness in ourselves.

In spite of the absence of feeling affected, love may in fact be present in a "superactual" or habitual form. That is, love is not a wholly new love every time we encounter the beloved. Today's love is one with yesterday's. It persists even when it is not explicitly or fully actualized toward the beloved.[94] Just as we know many things even when we are not thinking of them, so too we love the beloved even when our consciousness is not fully directed to them. Sometimes we try to recall something we know and yet are not able to remember. In such cases, we know and we don't know. The knowledge is there, but it will not take a conscious form. We cannot will or force it to come to consciousness. Something similar happens in love. And, just as aridity in prayer does not mean the absence of all prayer, so when the "feeling" of love is absent, love may still be real though incomplete. Acting out of a "superactual" love, we at times go through "dry" periods. We act out of the memory or the knowledge *that* we love someone, all the while feeling nothing, yet still hoping that the love will again take its complete form. To be sure, someday we may "wake up" after years of beneficence or cohabitation and realize that the love is really gone. We hope rather that we will discover that this love has grown underground, sending its roots deep into our soul. These considerations are important because authors on love frequently declare that, since love can go on without any longer experiencing attraction to the unique value of the beloved, i.e., without feeling affected and without feeling ecstatic, these feelings have nothing to do with the essence of love. Thus, they say, love is not an emotion.[95] One should, however, not define love by its deficient forms.

I have described three moments of love's structure. First, our openness to being varies in accord with our history. Second, we become aware of the objectively real and ideal goodness of the beloved. Third, we are actively affected or moved by a particular beloved. Now I turn to consider love's affirming response.

AFFIRMING RESPONSE

From a phenomenological perspective, love affects both the subject and the object, the lover and the beloved. We have considered how the lover is affected. Let us now consider changes in the object. At first glance, it would seem that love does not change the object: the object stays the same whether or not we love it; rather, in love we change, because we take a new attitude toward the object. The question is this: Does love bring about any changes in the beloved? When we say, "These mountains have been special ever since the Indians began to pray here," or "This velveteen rabbit is made precious by a child's love," are we speaking simply about changes in our attitudes? The answer to this question depends on whether we take an outsider, third-party view or whether we try to respond from within the experience of love. From a commonsense perspective, love in itself changes nothing. It changes things only when it becomes "loving deeds." From a phenomenological perspective, however, love is itself very creative.

Creativity

This creativity is stressed by Scheler: "Love is the tendency or, as it may be, the act that seeks to lead everything in the direction of the perfection of value proper to it and succeeds, when no obstacles are present. Thus we determined the essence of love as an uplifting and constructive action in and over the world."[96] When understood from within the experience, love appears creative; it creates new values. This should be understood carefully. Love brings about the *presence* of values relative to the lover. That is, values become available to explicit feeling, preference, and choice insofar as love brings about their appearance. Their existence relative to these acts, not their real existence, is the first thing "created" by love.[97] Through love we come to "see," and what was not there for us comes to appearance.

The values created by love are not, however, projected onto the object; otherwise they would be mere illusions. Rather, they are already in the ideal value image of the object but have not yet been felt until love reveals them. Love's creativity, therefore, should not be confused with "idealizing" the beloved. Such "idealization" usually reflects an inability to free ourselves from our own ideas and preoccupations. Rather, love enables us to see the depth of value in the object. On the social plane love acts as the fountainhead of a culture's values.[98] The world is endlessly surprising and rich to those who love.

Love is a relationship between two or more beings (except in cases of self-love) that aims at enhancing the beloved in at least some aspect of its greater being. This "greater being" need not be envisioned beforehand in concrete and specifically determined ways. Rather, love's creativity intends this greater being without first comprehending it. It is a "movement-toward" the not yet realized value. Just as we can remember relations without recalling the terms related, e.g., "I am hungry for something but I don't know what it is," so it is possible for the act of love to intend that which is not yet known. As a creative movement, love is not bound to what actually already exists.[99] When an artist is stirred to create, she is drawn by an object which does not yet exist and which, without her, will not exist, yet whose distinctive nature she must respect even as she works to discover it and draw it into being. She loves the "to-become-real" object, and in that love she then acts to give it reality. The primordial and foundational instance of this love is God's love for creation. Human love, of course, is dependent on many conditions, and these conditions can and do hinder love's effectiveness in realizing the beloved's greater being. Still, this love tends toward creativity, even when it is unable to bring about the realization of the greater goodness it is directed toward.[100]

Love is affirmation. The affirmative (*ad-firmare*: "to give firmness to" or "to strengthen") nature of love clarifies love's power to change its object. Love is not solely a warm approval of what is already present. The movement of love joins the object in its dynamism toward fullness.[101] Love "entails a willing of the beloved, a being with and a being for the beloved."[102] Love's affirmation means "intentionally" sharing and promoting the beloved's *own* tendency to realize its perfection and ward off whatever would cause its destruction, including any self-destructive tendencies. Love is often defined as "concern," "care," or "taking responsibility for." These definitions suggest how our love fosters the goodness of the beloved by uniting ourselves with its own tendency toward fullness. Most of us have, I presume, found ourselves strengthened when someone who loves us comes just to be with us. In such moments, we experience support for living our own lives. Those who love us ally themselves with us. They join their free spiritual center to our lives and commit themselves to be with us.[103] Unlike a judge who assesses merit or fault, but leaves the case when it is resolved, love involves the lover in the life of the beloved.[104] Immanuel Kant argued that we cannot be responsible for the perfection of others since their own personal perfection is a matter solely of their own freedom.[105] This position is a half truth. All persons must take final responsibility for themselves. Still, because of the nature of love, we can and should cooperate with their own freedom, resisting their tendencies to evil (Ez 33:8), and affirming them in their own growth toward fullness.

Originally, God's affirmation moves an essence from idea to reality. Our love participates in and continues this divine affirmation. As Luijpen writes, the beloved's "appeal to me means that he invites me to affirm his subjectivity, to offer him a possibility to *exist*, to consent to his freedom, to accept, support and share in his freedom. My 'yes' to his appeal is known as *love*."[106] By cooperating, where possible and appropriate, with the direction of the beloved's growth toward perfection, our love assists the beloved in achieving higher goodness. In so doing, our love is able to cooperate with God's creative and transforming love.[107]

Redemption of Creation

Thus far in this section we have seen that love is not a calculating will to improve but rather an emotional act that progressively illumines the real and ideal goodness of the beloved and then affirms (and often practically assists) the beloved in realizing its full value. If the beloved is a person, this affirmation may take place, for example, through helpful deeds, through encouragement, through evoking a return love, through mirroring back to the beloved his or her own actual goodness, or through offering to the beloved a vision of his or her ideal possibilities.

Because love is perceptive, we may see what the beloved does not see. The popular claim that people always know what is best for themselves is surely mistaken. Persons who hate themselves often come to discover and love their goodness through responsive coloving with the one who loves them. Zacchaeus came to love what Jesus loved in him. When we love, we make it possible for those we love to be transformed and ultimately to achieve that salvation toward which God's love is beckoning them. When we colove with God's love, we effectively cooperate with God in redeeming the world.[108]

In the affirmation of the beloved's own development, the higher value streams forth of itself from the beloved and not as if it is manufactured by the activity of the lover.[109] Real change in the object brought about by love's affirmation is possible, however, only if the object is open to growth. This openness is clearest in free beings. But what can we say about objects of nature that are not so obviously open to the lover's affirmation? For an answer, we might turn to the mystics.[110] Francis so loved nature that natural objects *became* "brother" and "sister" to him. His love also enabled him to see that God's love of the world was transforming the material world into God's body. Scheler takes from Augustine an explanation of these changes in the object:

> The increasing fullness in the givenness of the object with increasing love and interest is for Augustine not merely an activity of the knowing subject who penetrates into the already present object, but is at the same time a responsive answer of the object itself: a "self-giving," a

"self-revelation" and "opening" of the object, i.e., a genuine *self-revelation* of the object. It is "love's question," as it were, to which the world "answers" insofar as it opens itself and *therein first comes to its full being and value.*[111]

This is a redemptive process wherein a loved object is freed from its closed and separated existence. The world opens itself when one loves it and thereby moves toward its fullest destiny, which is to be in relation to human beings and to God. Human labor spiritualizes matter by giving it a special place in human life; Christian love redeems it by giving it a special place in our relation to God.[112]

We saw above that love is not simply beneficence or service. Still, love's creativity can include a beneficence that is truly helpful. In his younger years, Aquinas remarkably described the affective conversion that leads to *service*:

> Through love the lover becomes one with the beloved, and the beloved is made the form of the lover. . . . Everyone . . . acts according to the exigencies of its form, which is the principle of action and the rule of deeds. . . . The lover . . . inclines through love to acting according to the exigencies of the beloved; and such acting is most delightful, as if befitting its own form. . . . it behooves the lover to serve the beloved to a degree that is regulated by the ends of the beloved.[113]

Love is not essentially focused on the need, self-expression, or fulfillment of the lover. The beneficent lover does not stand outside a relationship, offering merely gifts or service. Rather, the lover so receives the beloved that the beloved's own "form" becomes a principle of the lover's own life and action. Just as we naturally act in fidelity to our own form or identity, so as lovers we act in fidelity to the form or identity of the beloved, which has become part of our own identity. As lovers we have been "transformed," and so we "naturally" act in accord with this new form. Love thereby leads us to act in accord with what is fitting to the beloved. The "rule" of love is the beloved's identity.[114] This transformation is called grace when it is God that we love. When we love God, God's form or dynamism becomes part of our own dynamism and therefore normative for our action. The same, analogously, is also true of God's love for us.

Love also has the task of resisting all that leads to decline in value of the beloved. Love, therefore, can mean opposing particular qualities, deeds, and expressions when these are not consonant with the beloved's ideal essence.[115] Love is not permissive, not open to the beloved's caprice.[116] As a lover of humanity, God is angered by everything that oppresses people, everything that is disordered in the world. As a lover of our selves, God opposes the ways we destroy ourselves through sin. God's love resists and, where possible, overcomes evil. It resists oppression, but this resistance is in the service of enabling people to live. God's love promotes those structures that promote human flourishing, and it works against those structures that denigrate it.

For Christians the paradigmatic case of love's redeeming power occurred, of course, in Jesus. Jesus was one who freed others for a new way of life. In so loving, he met opposition (Jn 11:47–50). Albert Nolan puts it well:

> We are introduced to a man who began the process of liberating the poor from their sufferings by healing the sick, dispelling the fear of demons, encouraging the weak and powerless, teaching people to share what they had and doing so himself. Moreover, he confronted the system, ignored its purity regulations, argued with the upholders of the system, led a demonstration by riding into Jerusalem on a donkey, staged a sit-in in the Temple courtyard and drove out the traders and money changers with a whip, was confronted by the authorities, went into hiding, was betrayed by an informer called Judas, was arrested, interrogated, beaten, mocked, put on trial, sentenced to death and finally tortured to death on a Roman instrument of repression.[117]

Jesus loved, and so he resisted evil, even to the point of being crucified by the system he opposed. God's love includes judgment against all that prevents its fulfillment. Sometimes God's love "is experienced not only as peaceful creativeness but as violent breakthrough," overcoming blockages and bringing to birth new realities.[118] As Tillich noted, "The strange work of love is to destroy what is against love. . . . Love in order to exercise its proper works, namely charity and forgiveness, must provide for a place on which this can be done, through its strange work of judging and punishing."[119] Thus, love is not all peace and harmony; sometimes it brings division (Mt 10:34–38). In a world that is finite and particularly in a world that is sinful, the progress that love promotes may be attained only at considerable cost.

This process is genuinely creative. The full redemptive process does not merely overcome evil. It also does not merely help beings to attain some ideal God set for them, but they subsequently lost, at the dawn of creation. That is, redemption, broadly conceived, is not simply recovery and restoration. It is also a sanctifying transformation. Redeemed objects do not simply strive toward realizing an idea that eternally preexists them. In understanding redemption as simply recovery and restoration—an understanding that draws more from reason's orientation toward the universal and eternal than from love's movement to the higher value—nothing truly new or creative occurs. Restoration does not bring forth something new but only reproduces according to a pregiven type.[120] Rather, love is truly creative.

Love's creativity both affirms what already is and suggests that the very essence of the object is apt for as yet unimagined possibilities, above all, the possibility of fulfilling its inexhaustible destiny of being fully in relation to God.[121] Something new comes to be in the redemptive movement of love. Through divine love, all objects are not merely what they are in themselves; they also have the further potential to be elevated into a holy relationship with human beings and ultimately with God.

Range of Objects

Love is not restricted to certain kinds of objects. It is a movement able to intend any object that bears values. In particular, love for persons is not limited to either self or others.[122] Two errors should be mentioned here. The first is to reduce love of others to a subtle form of self-love. For example, some argue that all love is merely a way to increase one's own happiness or gain salvation. This reduction, of course, makes a sham of real love of others for their own sakes. Unfortunately, following one strand of Aquinas's theology, many pre-Vatican II moral manuals tended to reduce other-love to self-love.[123] The second error is to deny that one can or should love oneself and to attempt to love only others.[124] Christians, especially in the Protestant traditions, frequently speak as if the only worthwhile love is a love for others. Some allow self-love, but only as a way of keeping the beast alive so it can love others for yet another day. Even when this turn to others is not a flight from one's self, it is a denigration or neglect of one's own God-given value. A lack of self-love is ultimately un-Christian. It is a refusal to cooperate with God's love for us.[125]

Love should not be restricted to individual persons. We can love a community of persons, and in two senses: we can love the whole group and we can love individuals *as* members of that group. We can, for example, love a family, and we can love persons because we love their family.[126] It is also a mistake to limit love's objects to human beings. We can love all sorts of nonhuman objects such as pets and paintings. Our emotional affirmation of a symphony or a sunset is not merely a projection of human needs onto the universe. We can love such objects for their own sakes.[127] Finally, we can love God, though what that means will have to be more extensively examined since it has been denied or neglected by many theologians.

Love's objects, thus, are not limited to superior, inferior, or equal beings. The Platonic tradition of love typically held that one legitimately can love only what is more valuable than oneself. This theory implied that God cannot love at all since there is no being superior in value.[128] Some Christians reverse this ancient tradition and proclaim that true love must be directed to inferiors (at least among human beings). In this view, the very essence of God is to move toward sinners and the disenfranchised; human beings become like God by loving only those who are poor, weak, or marginalized.[129] Both of these positions are one-sided. Love is open to the weak and to the strong. Love is directed to the positive values in the beloved, whether the beloved is poor and suffering or rich and exalted. God can love God, something that God could not do if God loved only the inferior. And we can love God, every human being, and all other creatures.[130]

In this section I asked the question, Does love bring about any changes in the beloved? In the first place, love brings to appearance the mystery of value of the beloved. Secondly, love makes us willing to foster and promote by word, deed, or any other means, the development of the beloved. More generally, love is an affirmation that confirms the beloved's own ideal possibilities. Ultimately, Christian love brings the created world into the redemptive order of being related to God.

LOVE AND FREEDOM

In the first chapter, we saw that we do not have the freedom to directly will any of the four moments of love we have now discussed in this chapter. We do have, however, the freedom to integrate these moments into our life-histories, making them our own, as well as the freedom to resist them and thereby dissociate ourselves from them. In this last section of this chapter, I discuss another side of the interplay between love and freedom. I want to focus on how love frees us.

Self-transcendence as Freedom from Determinism

We human beings have tendencies or "drives" for sex, power, or nourishment that form a loosely integrated system of needs and satisfactions.

These drives, responding to our environment, select the kinds of objects we initially relate to but do not determine the nature of love or the particular objects we shall love. Drives push out in all directions, seeking their own satisfaction.[131] But the human spirit can and does go through and beyond these stimulating drives, just as it utilizes but passes beyond our socialization.

Because of these drives and this inculturation, we tend to love those closest to us, while neglecting other, perhaps more valuable or needy, persons. An American is more likely to love his child than to love the Queen of England or a thousand people starving in Pakistan. Our drives tend to limit us to those who satisfy our basic needs. For similar reasons, we are more attracted to the comely, powerful, or rich than to the ugly, infirm, or impoverished.[132] This selective bias of the drives and of culture is overcome by the unrestricted movement of spiritual love.

Because of our freedom, our love is not limited by our bodily drives and needs. We are essentially different from other animals because of the quasi independence of our spirits from our vital functions and from the spatio-temporal particularity to which these functions otherwise limit us.[133] Through spiritual love we also gradually free ourselves from the psychosocial conditioning of class, tradition, and culture and from prejudices that belong to the everyday consciousness.[134] Spiritual love, of course, does not eliminate or act completely apart from our bodiliness or social environment. Still, spiritual love is authentically itself only when it is not controlled by sensual desire, infatuation, or cultural prejudice.[135]

Love has the power to go beyond our drives' initiating stimuli and to outlast them. Love has the power to see beyond the culturally favored. Lovers thereby transcend themselves and participate in an objective world, ultimately in God.[136] As Scheler writes,

> If we have only once experienced how one feature which is worthy of love emerges next to another—whether in the same object or another—or how another feature of still higher value emerges over and above one we had taken till now as the "highest" in a particular value-region, then we have learned the essence of progress or penetration into this realm. Then we can see that this realm cannot have precise boundaries . . . Love loves and in loving always looks beyond what it has in hand and possesses. The drive-impulse which arouses it may tire out; love itself does not tire out. This *sursum corda* which is the essence of love may take on fundamentally different forms at different heights of the value regions. . . . A love that is essentially infi-

nite—however much it is broken, bound, and particularized by the specific organization of its bearer—demands for its fulfillment an *infinite* good.[137]

Once we have experienced the unrestricted nature of love, then we understand how anything that stops this expansive movement diminishes self-transcendence and therefore our spirit.[138] Love moves beyond such limitations and thereby we become ever more spontaneous and free.[139] Without this freedom, human beings would slide back into being merely animals. Human beings walk on a bridge, in transition between the animal sphere and God.[140] Love keeps us moving on this bridge.

The unrestricted nature of love means that it is "measureless." We can acquit many of life's duties, but we have never loved enough. We cannot remain content with the love that we have, without denying love's intrinsic movement. In Rahner's judgment, "If someone were to refuse point blank any willingness and any attempt to love God more than he does now, then in such a case there would no longer be any love at all."[141] We need an ethics that encourages us to aspire to greatness, an ethics that promotes a magnanimity of heart, and an ethics that gives us the courage to risk. Making the infinity of love's quest central to the moral life provides such an ethic.[142]

Self-transcendence as Liberating Expansion

When we freely consent to love's movement, we develop our own individuality. We go beyond our previous integrations to a (partially) new self.[143] In describing love, Aquinas says that a certain "melting of the heart" takes place wherein lovers both become what they love and take into themselves what they love. In Aquinas's metaphysics, of course, a being exists in itself and not in another; it doesn't melt into another; it doesn't become something substantially other than itself. But when Aquinas inquired phenomenologically into the experience of love, he discovered that affectively we really do exist in another and that the other exists in us. As we go out of ourselves, we are inwardly transformed by that to which we extend ourselves. Again, in a metaphysics of substance, it does not make sense to say, as Aquinas does, that one loses one's self, that one's self is divided, that one's limits are removed, that one is outside of one's self, or that one's solid "substance" melts into a liquid.[144] Rather, Aquinas is phenomenologically describing love's self-transforming self-transcendence. He describes love's *kenosis*, in which we do not cling to our form but take on the form of another (Phil 2:7). He also describes love as "ecstasy" in which the lover leaves *aseity*, is "separated from himself," and exists within the beloved. Our love for God means that our solid isolation is melted and we take on God's form. As Aquinas frequently says, "If we love God, we are made divine."[145] I would add: If God loves us, God is made human.

Love expands our lives by enabling us to participate ever more in the world.[146] Through love we are united with the world. *Homo est quodam-modo omnia.* All being becomes progressively ours through this participatory love.[147] Our personal history advances, not primarily through anxiety before death and not necessarily through a dialectic of negations and self-overcoming, but above all through the complex act of an actively receptive, ecstatically affirming love of the world and God.[148] Analogously, through love God participates in history. "God includes all of reality within Godself. God is the all-inclusive subject of love, for God constitutes Godself in loving relations to all other individuals."[149]

Love is usually experienced not as loss but as self-fulfilling liberation because the appeal of the beloved releases a new enactment of our power to love.[150] We transcend ourselves, and this fulfilling expansion opens up new possibilities for further fulfillment.[151] That is, the more we love, the more we are *able* to love. Those who use their gifts receive more gifts (Lk 19:26). A new energy is released into our conscious life when we experience this new and fuller way to be. Since we are dependent on the beloved for the enactment of this love, our expanded capacity is also experienced as a grace, as something that we cannot produce simply out of our own selves, but which, when we consent, enriches our very core. Love "is not the emanation of a nature but the free bestowal of a person, who possesses himself, who can therefore refuse himself, whose surrender therefore is always a wonder and a grace."[152]

When we freely love, we also experience liberation because we let the beloved's real and ideal goodness displace our egocentricity or everyday world. Our fascination with our own goodness is broken; our fearful preoccupation with self-protection is overcome; our fixation with some particular object is loosened. In a word, we are freed from our narrowness. That is, we freely consent to allowing our self to be partially defined by the beloved and its needs or fulfillments. Part of the way we define our lives becomes what the beloved is and requires.

Many Christian authors describe this process exclusively in somber tones: "This decentering of self is no harmonious and simple process. The other, while essential to my own personhood, is a threat to my self-integration. This conflictual situation is not simply the result of original sin. . . . The personal encounter with the 'Other', far from being simply the occasion for my self-integration, involves an unsettling decentering of my being which opens me to plurality, indeed infinity."[153] To be sure, we must struggle against our self-centeredness and we must die to our self-ishness. Though love often requires just such painful progress, the anthropology behind such demands can be needlessly one-sided. We are not just set in our ways, not just selfish sinners. Growth need not be painful. The expansion that comes through love often is enlivening and joyful. In our consent to the beloved, we experience a "liberation from the confines of individual life, from the prison of affective solipsism."[154] Being released from prison can be a joy. Knowledge sometimes makes a bloody entrance, but at other times its arrival is pure delight. Similarly, when we love, and especially when we are "in love," we are often exhilarated. When we are with our beloved—whether that beloved is God, a spouse, or our own selves—we experience the "lightness of being." Time spent with our beloved in the Dionysian realm of play, fantasy, passion, or mystery or in the Apollonian realm of constructive work is experienced as a joyful liberation.[155]

Particularly when we experience a profound love, our lives become reorganized in dramatic and exciting ways. When we "fall in love" with God, other things gain or lose their importance to us depending on how they stand in relation to God. A sort of crystallization occurs: things that were once unimportant now become important because of their relation to God. New things are evaluated by how they promote or diminish our relationship with God. In William James's colorful language,

> What brings such changes about is the way in which emotional excitement alters. Things hot and vital to us today are cold tomorrow. It is as if seen from the hot parts of the field that the other parts appear to us, and from these hot parts personal desire and volition make their sallies. They are in short the centers of our dynamic energy. . . . the focus of excitement and heat . . . may come to lie permanently within a certain system; and then, if the change be a religious one, we call it a *conversion*.[156]

In a religious conversion, all things become important or "hot" to the degree they are related to God or help us to relate to God. Our love for God liberates us from all limited horizons and allows us to see all in terms of ultimate Mystery.

In this section, we have seen that love frees the lover. First, the lover participates in the beloved and thereby fulfills and further expands itself;

second, the subject becomes increasingly free from physical, biological, psychological, and social determinisms and thereby opens out onto the infinite. Love makes us free.

CONCLUSION

In sum, love is an actively receptive movement of the heart that creatively enhances the value of both the lover and the beloved through a union that affirms their respective dynamisms. Where there is love, there is greater vitality, richer beauty, deeper ideas, stronger fidelity, more profound religion. The world, for the lover, is endlessly overflowing, constantly surprising. Love's eyes see the unique and the special in the beloved. Love's heart beats with the dynamism of the beloved and affirms the beloved for what it is and for what it can become. Love's hands reach out to help the beloved in need and to resist its errant tendencies. Love's prayer joins God's own love and redeems the world by enfleshing God's own participation in the world. The perfection of the universe will be reached when God is in all and all is in God.[157] Love is the dynamism for fulfilling this ultimate goal.

NOTES

1. This chapter is a complete revision of my essay, "Scheler's Phenomenology of Love," *Journal of Religion* 62 (April 1982): 156–77. I made these ideas my own and developed them in Edward Vacek, S.J., "Toward a Phenomenology of Love Lost," *Journal of Phenomenological Psychology* 20 (Spring 1989): 1–19. Here I develop them further.

2. Jules Toner, *The Experience of Love* (Washington: Corpus Instrumentorum, 1968), 8.

3. Because I shall argue that one can love God, one's self, animals, things, nations, etc., I am forced to use rather impersonal language. I shall write "objects" or "beloved" or "it" where authors conventionally write "others" or "him" or "her."

4. Paul Tillich, *Love, Power, and Justice* (New York: Oxford, 1954), 28.

5. Jacques Leclercq, *La Philosophie morale de saint Thomas devant la pensée contemporaine* (Paris: Vrin, 1955), 297; Toner, *The Experience of Love*, 181; Oliver O'Donovan, *The Problem of Self-Love in St. Augustine* (New Haven: Yale Univ. Press, 1980), 5, 34. Cf. Germain Grisez, *Way of the Lord Jesus* (Chicago: Franciscan Herald, 1983), 576–77.

6. William Earle, *The Autobiographical Consciousness* (Chicago: Quadrangle, 1972), 113; Stephen Pope, "Proper and Improper Partiality and the Preferential Option for the Poor," *Theological Studies* 54 (June 1993): 258, 262.

7. Max Scheler, *The Nature of Sympathy* (Hamden, CT: Shoe String Press, 1973), 140, 149, 195; Max Scheler, *Genius des Krieges und der deutsche Krieg* (Leipzig: Weisen, 1917), 84; Max Scheler, *Ressentiment* (New York: Schocken Books, 1972), 118–

19; Max Scheler, *On the Eternal in Man* (Hamden, CT: Shoe String Press, 1972), 367. Alan Drengson, "Compassion and Transcendence of Duty and Inclination," *Philosophy Today* (Spring 1981): 34–36; Arthur Vella, S.J., *Love Is Acceptance* (Dissertation: Pontifical Gregorian University, 1964), 126–29. We might also recall here that John Stuart Mill, awakened by romantic poetry, reacted against the Utilitarian ideal of maximal happiness, because it was compatible with a lack of real love for others; see Irving Singer, *The Nature of Love* (Chicago: Univ. of Chicago Press, 1987), 2:485.

8. Toner, *The Experience of Love*, 80; Enda McDonagh, "Love," *New Dictionary of Theology*, ed. Joseph Komonchak et al. (Wilmington: Glazier, 1987), 608–9.

9. Scheler, *Sympathy*, 140–41; Scheler, *Genius des Krieges*, 86–87; Scheler, *Ressentiment*, 92–93.

10. Toner, *The Experience of Love*, 79.

11. Scheler, *Sympathy*, 160–61.

12. Max Scheler, *Formalism in Ethics and a Non-Formal Ethics of Value* (Evanston: Northwestern Univ. Press, 1973), 225–26, 337, 343–44, 507–8; Scheler, *Eternal*, 367–68; Scheler, *Sympathy*, 141, 163–64; Max Scheler, "The Meaning of Suffering," *Centennial Essays*, ed. Manfred Frings (The Hague: Martinus Nijhoff, 1974), 161–62.

13. Scheler, *Sympathy*, 14–41, 150; also Max Scheler, *Schriften zur Soziologie and Weltanschauungslehre* (Bern: Francke, 1963), 84; Scheler, *Ressentiment*, 87.

14. Toner, *The Experience of Love*, 115.

15. Max Scheler, *Selected Philosophical Essays* (Evanston: Northwestern Univ. Press, 1973), 112–14; Scheler, *Soziologie*, 84; Scheler, *Sympathy*, 114, 180–209; Scheler, *Ressentiment*, 117–18, 181. Toner, *The Experience of Love*, 20–21, 72–80, makes similar points, though he tends to think of desire as directed to something that we want for a beloved. See also Margaret Farley, *Personal Commitments* (New York: Harper & Row, 1986), 28–29.

16. Irving Singer, *Nature of Love*, 3:378; also Scheler, *Sympathy*, 116, 141, 150, 187; Scheler, *Soziologie*, 84, 86, 94; Scheler, *Ressentiment*, 87, 181; Scheler, *Essays*, 113.

17. Scheler, *Sympathy*, 141; Daniel Day Williams, *The Spirit and the Forms of Love* (New York: Harper & Row, 1968), 138.

18. Toner, *The Experience of Love*, 35–37, 81–86.

19. Scheler, *Sympathy*, 14–41, 147–48, 153; Scheler, *Essays*, 120–21, 128–30; Scheler, "Suffering," 134–35, 154–55; Scheler, *Ressentiment*, 189; Toner, *The Experience of Love*, 86.

20. Scheler, *Sympathy*, 22, 26–27, 68–71, 78, 120.

21. Scheler, *Sympathy*, 26–27, 44, 70; Scheler, *Essays*, 94.

22. Scheler, *Sympathy*, 62–76, 78, 122–23; Scheler, *Eternal*, 195–96, 228–29; Scheler, *Soziologie*, 86.

23. Max Scheler, *Frühe Schriften* (Bern: Francke, 1971), 400; Scheler, *Formalism*, 261; Scheler, *Ressentiment*, 116–17; Scheler, *Sympathy*, 66, 67–68, 99, 140–43, 150.

24. Toner, *The Experience of Love*, 122.

25. Scheler, *Formalism*, 87–88, 261; Scheler, *Sympathy*, 148, 152–54; Max Scheler, *Schriften aus dem Nachlass: I* (Bern: Francke, 1957), 1:273; Max Scheler, *Schriften aus dem Nachlass: II*, ed. Manfred Frings (Bern: Francke, 1979), 2:192.

26. Patrick Byrne, "*Ressentiment* and the Preferential Option for the Poor," *Theological Studies* 54 (June 1993): 229.

27. Williams, *Spirit and Forms*, 19.

28. Robert Solomon, *The Passions* (Garden City: Anchor, 1977), 185–92.

29. Gene Outka, *Agape* (New Haven: Yale Univ. Press, 1976), 12–13.

30. Scheler, *Nachlass*, 1:234, 273; Scheler, *Sympathy*, 148–50, 166–67.

31. William Luijpen, *Existential Phenomenology* (Pittsburgh: Duquesne, 1968), 321.

32. William Earle, *Autobiographical Consciousness*, 118, 123.

33. Robert Nozick, "Love's Bond," *The Philosophy of (Erotic) Love*, ed. Robert Solomon (Lawrence, KS: University Press of Kansas, 1991), 427; Scheler, *Formalism*, 488; Scheler, *Nachlass*, 1:273; Scheler, *Sympathy*, 149–50, 166–67.

34. Scheler, *Sympathy*, 160–61.

35. Luijpen, *Existential Phenomenology*, 312.

36. Toner, *The Experience of Love*, 188; also Karl Rahner, S.J., "Theos in the New Testament," *Theological Investigations* (New York: Crossroad, 1982), 1:123.

37. James Hanigan, *As I Have Loved You* (New York: Paulist, 1986), 146; C. S. Lewis, *The Four Loves* (New York: Harcourt Brace Jovanovich, 1960), 91, 96–97; cf. Rahner, "Theos in the New Testament," 123.

38. Roger Scruton, *Sexual Desire* (New York: Free Press, 1986), 231; Scheler, *Formalism*, 91–92; Scheler, *Sympathy*, 161; Scheler, *Essays*, 43, 80; Scheler, *Nachlass*, 1:40–41, 159; Max Scheler, *Die Ursachen des Deutschenhasses* (Leipzig: Wolff, 1917), 21.

39. Toner, *The Experience of Love*, 42.

40. Erich Fromm, *Art of Loving* (New York: Harper & Brothers, 1956), 46.

41. Scheler, *Essays*, 99–110, 116–18; Scheler, *Formalism*, 385–86, 515; Scheler, *Nachlass*, 1:132, 264; Max Scheler, *Philosophical Perspectives* (Boston: Beacon, 1958), 32–33.

42. Scheler, *Essays*, 101–2; Scheler, *Soziologie*, 95–96; Scheler, *Nachlass*, 1:223–25, 262, 264, 272–74; Scheler, *Formalism*, 574–76; Scheler, *Perspectives*, 32, 38; Scheler, *Sympathy*, 167–68.

43. Scheler, *Späte Schriften* (Bern: Francke, 1976), 274, 297; Scheler, *Formalism*, 515, 537; Scheler, *Nachlass*, 1:238–39; Scheler, *Sympathy*, 163, 165.

44. Fromm, *Art of Loving*, 46. He adds (p. 60) that if we can love *only* others and not ourselves then we do not love others. Apart from the contradiction involved in that claim, it is also experientially false. Fortunately, in his more concrete analyses, Fromm does not follow his own theory. Similarly, others such as John Gallagher, C.S.B., *The Basis For Christian Ethics* (New York: Paulist, 1985), 93, insist that "genuine love for man opens out on love of all," with the implication that if two people deeply and exclusively loved one another or perhaps even if some persons loved humans but have no feeling for tadpoles, they would not be genuinely loving.

45. Günther Bornkamm, *Jesus of Nazareth* (New York: Harper & Brothers, 1960), 110–11; Paul Ramsey, *Nine Modern Moralists* (Englewood Cliffs: Prentice-Hall, 1962), 146; O'Donovan, *Problem of Self-Love*, 12–13.

46. Paul Ramsey, *Basic Christian Ethics* (Chicago: Univ. of Chicago Press, 1978), 301.

47. Scheler, *Perspectives*, 10–11; Scheler, *Eternal*, 184–88, 282–83; Scheler, *Formalism*, 265, 374; Scheler, *Nachlass*, 1:39, 190–91; Scheler, *Nachlass*, 2:243.

48. Scheler, *Sympathy*, 141–42, 148–49, 153; Scheler, *Formalism*, 256–58, 261.

49. Martin D'Arcy, S.J., *The Mind and Heart of Love* (New York: Henry Holt, 1947), 218.

50. Henri Bergson, *Two Sources of Morality* (New York: Holt, 1935), 43; Scheler, *Sympathy*, 92, 152–54, 192; Max Scheler, *Krieg und Aufbau* (Leipzig: Weisen, 1916), 11; Scheler, *Formalism*, 261; Scheler, *Nachlass*, 1:82, 234.

51. Williams, *Spirit and Forms*, 115.

52. Scheler, *Sympathy*, 141, 148, 154–59, 192; Scheler, *Nachlass*, 1:133, 234; Scheler, *Essays*, 112–14, 116; Scheler, *Formalism*, 261.

53. Luijpen, *Existential Phenomenology*, 326.

54. Scheler, *Eternal*, 74, 95–97, 298, 390; Scheler, *Nachlass*, 1:192, 324–27; Scheler, *Perspectives*, 20–21, 40, 116; Max Scheler, "Metaphysics and Art," in *Centennial Essays*, 109; Scheler, *Nachlass*, 2:244.

55. Scheler, *Genius*, 85.

56. Margaret Farley, R.S.M., "New Patterns of Relationship," *Theological Studies* 36 (December 1975): 632, 643; Farley, *Personal Commitments*, 82.

57. Outka, *Agape*, 161; Evelyn Eaton Whitehead and James Whitehead, *Marrying Well* (Garden City: Doubleday, 1981), 241.

58. Toner, *The Experience of Love*, 155, 158.

59. Ibid., 159, 161.

60. Scheler, *Sympathy*, 71, 157–58; Scheler, *Soziologie*, 96–97.

61. Scheler, *Nachlass*, 1:321–23, 329; Scheler, *Essays*, 125, 127, 130; Scheler, *Soziologie*, 94–95; Scheler, *Eternal*, 311; Bergson, *Two Sources of Morality*, 37–38.

62. Luijpen, *Existential Phenomenology*, 321.

63. Toner, *The Experience of Love*, 187; Scheler, *Sympathy*, 149–50, 160, 166–68; Scheler, *Formalism*, 488, 491; Scheler, *Perspectives*, 20–21.

64. Bergson, *Two Sources of Morality*, 35–39.

65. *ST* I–II.27.2; *Duo Praecepta*, 98b; James Keenan, S.J., *Goodness and Rightness in Thomas Aquinas's* Summa Theologiae (Washington: Georgetown Univ. Press, 1992), 121.

66. *ST* I–II.27.2.

67. Karl Rahner, S.J., "Thomas Aquinas on the Incomprehensibility of God," *The Journal of Religion* 58 (Supplement 1978): S124–25; Karl Rahner, S.J., "The Concept of Mystery in Catholic Theology," *Theological Investigations* (Baltimore: Helicon, 1966), 4:43.

68. Bernard Lonergan, S.J., *Method in Theology* (New York: Herder & Herder, 1972), 122–23.

69. Scheler, *Ressentiment*, 132; Scheler, *Späte Schriften*, 257; Scheler, *Eternal*, 88–89; Scheler, *Nachlass*, 1:264.

70. Scheler, *Sympathy*, 128, 141, 154, 157–59; Scheler, *Soziologie*, 84; Scheler, *Ressentiment*, 93; Scheler, *Nachlass*, 1:234.

71. Scheler, *Soziologie*, 84; Scheler, *Sympathy*, 113, 152–53, 157–59; Scheler, *Essays*, 109–10; Scheler, "Suffering," 131–34.

72. Scheler, *Essays*, 104, 107–8; Scheler, *Sympathy*, 122–23, 154, 160, 166–67; Scheler, *Formalism*, 477, 485, 488, 491; Scheler, *Nachlass*, 1:234.

73. Scheler, *Sympathy*, 121.

74. Robert Johann, *The Meaning of Love* (Westminster, MD: Newman, 1955), 34–36.

75. Scheler, *Essays*, 113–14; Scheler, *Formalism*, 488, 491; Scheler, *Sympathy*, 128, 168.

76. John Cobb and David Griffin, *Process Theology* (Philadelphia: Westminster, 1976), 46.

77. Vella, *Love Is Acceptance*, 100–139. Also, Margaret Farley, R.S.M., "Fragments for an Ethic of Commitment in Thomas Aquinas," *Journal of Religion*, 58 (Supplement 1978): 135–59; Farley, *Personal Commitments*, 31–32; Toner, *The Experience of Love*, 95–109.

78. *ST* I–II.23.4, 26.1. Other terms besides "passion" which Aquinas uses are not wholly clear and have been the subject of much discussion. These include love as "complacency in good," "participation," "connaturality," or "affective union." See *ST* I–II.23.4, 25.2, 28.1.

79. Toner, *The Experience of Love*, 98–99.

80. Karl Rahner, S.J., "Love as the Key Virtue," *Sacramentum Mundi* (New York: Herder and Herder, 1970), 6:340.

81. Toner, *The Experience of Love*, 134.

82. Williams, *Spirit and Forms*, 127–28.

83. Paul Tillich, *Systematic Theology* (Chicago: Univ. of Chicago Press, 1967), 1:112, 114 (my emphasis).

84. Rahner, "Concept of Mystery," 4:48–60.

85. Vella, *Love Is Acceptance*, 122; Mark Taylor, *God is Love* (Atlanta: Scholars Press, 1986), 293. For an excellent article on the complexities involved in Aquinas's thought, see Frederick Crowe, S.J., "Complacency and Concern in the Thought of St. Thomas," *Theological Studies* 20 (March, June, August 1959), 1–39, 198–230, 343–95.

86. Toner, *The Experience of Love*, 95–96.

87. Farley, "New Patterns of Relationship," 639.

88. *ST* I–II.28.2; also I.20.1.

89. See my "Love Lost," 1–19.

90. *ST* II–II.24.4–9; *Sententiarum*, 3.29.1.8.

91. *ST* I–II.28.2; also I.20.1.

92. *The Confessions of St. Augustine*, trans. John Ryan (Garden City: Image Books, 1960), 4, 6; 100.

93. Bergson, *Two Sources of Morality*, 41, held that this pattern underlies ordinary morality.

94. Dietrich von Hildebrand, *Ethics* (Chicago: Franciscan Herald, 1953), 241–43.

95. Ramsey, *Basic Christian Ethics*, 100. Victor Furnish, *Love Command in the New Testament* (New York: Abingdon, 1972), 202, 208, insists that New Testament love is a command that demands the will, not the emotions. But then, like so many others who take this position, he goes on to say that the whole person, including acts of emotion, must be involved.

96. Scheler, *Essays*, 109. Also see Scheler, *Soziologie*, 92; Scheler, "Suffering," 132; Scheler, *Sympathy*, 123–24, 161; Scheler, *Nachlass*, 2:190, 193.

97. Scheler, *Sympathy*, 113, 154; Scheler, *Formalism*, 261; Scheler, *Nachlass*, 1:127–28, 234, 307, 321–22.

98. Scheler, *Sympathy*, 154–61, Scheler, *Formalism*, 261; Scheler, *Soziologie*, 96; Scheler, *Genius*, 85; Scheler, *Nachlass*, 1:306–7, 321–22; Scheler, *Perspectives*, 20–21; Scheler, *Späte Schriften*, 294.

99. Williams, *Spirit and Forms*, 14, describes a "kind of double vision" in love: on the one hand, love lives in the enjoyment of fulfillment; and, on the other hand, love

"realizes itself in the suffering of the Not-Yet." It seems to me that love need not include "suffering"; rather there can be a creative and therefore joy-filled movement toward the not-yet.

100. Toner, *The Experience of Love*, 153–54.

101. Luijpen, *Existential Phenomenology*, 316–17; Scheler, *Eternal*, 229; Scheler, *Essays*, 109–10; Scheler, *Sympathy*, 153; Scheler, *Soziologie*, 81; Scheler, *Späte Schriften*, 277; Scheler, *Nachlass*, 2:190; Toner, *The Experience of Love*, 141–64.

102. Farley, "Commitment in Thomas Aquinas," S145.

103. Von Hildebrand, *Ethics*, 324.

104. Toner, *The Experience of Love*, 52–53.

105. Immanuel Kant, *Metaphysical Principles of Virtue* (New York: Bobbs-Merrill, 1964), 44. See also Wolfgang Nikolaus, "Eros und Agape," *Zeitschrift für evangelische Ethik* 30 (1986): 411.

106. Luijpen, *Existential Phenomenology*, 315.

107. Scheler, *Essays*, 109–12; Scheler, *Soziologie*, 92; Scheler, *Eternal*, 226–27, 304, 312, 448; Scheler, *Genius*, 84; Scheler, *Krieg*, 8; Scheler, *Nachlass*, 1:192–93, 273; Scheler, *Nachlass*, 2:193, 203.

108. Scheler, *Sympathy*, 70–71, 127–28, 160, 164; Scheler, *Essays*, 99, 106–7, 111–13; Scheler, *Formalism*, 488, 490–91; Scheler, *Soziologie*, 89, 92–93; Scheler, *Genius*, 84; Scheler, "Suffering," 162.

109. Scheler, *Nachlass*, 1:322; Scheler, *Soziologie*, 93, 96–97; Scheler, *Sympathy*, 87–91, 157; Scheler, "Suffering," 154.

110. Louis Dupré, "The Christian Experience of Mystical Union," *Journal of Religion* 69 (January 1989): 11.

111. Scheler, *Soziologie*, 96–97; see also Leon Kass, *Toward a More Natural Science* (New York: Free Press, 1985), 274. For parallels in the thought of Paul Tillich, see Alexander Irwin, *Eros Toward the World* (Minneapolis: Fortress, 1991), 86.

112. Scheler, *Nachlass*, 1:192–93, 322; Scheler, *Eternal*, 302–4; Scheler, *Späte Schriften*, 272; Scheler, *Soziologie*, 280–83.

113. *Sententiarum*, 3.27.1.1; but see 3.29.1.1; also *ST* I.20.1, I–II.28.2.

114. Ramsey, *Basic Christian Ethics*, 78, holds a similar position when he writes that the "needs of the neighbor are the rule of love." Still, Aquinas has the better formulation since, on Ramsey's terms, we could not love our neighbors if their needs were filled.

115. Scheler, *Eternal*, 196, 367; Scheler, *Sympathy*, 70, 122, 149–50, 152–53, 166–67; Scheler, *Nachlass*, 1:273; Scheler, *Essays*, 107–8; Scheler, *Ressentiment*, 109; Scheler, "Suffering," 129–30, 160, 162.

116. Luijpen, *Existential Phenomenology*, 316–17.

117. Albert Nolan, *God in South Africa* (Grand Rapids: Eerdmans, 1988), 130.

118. Rosemary Haughton, *The Passionate God* (New York: Paulist, 1981), 36.

119. Tillich, *Love, Power, and Justice*, 49.

120. Scheler, *Soziologie*, 80, 82–87, 92, 95–96; Scheler, *Eternal*, 73–74; Scheler, *Essays*, 132–33; Scheler, *Sympathy*, 82–83, 110–13; Scheler, *Ressentiment*, 84–86.

121. Scheler, *Späte Schriften*, 289; Scheler, *Sympathy*, 157. Through 1922, Scheler held the Augustinian position that God "loves and contemplates the goals and essential ideas of all things before they are created" (*Essays*, 110). At the same time, he held that love brought about not merely a change in appearance of a thing, but a growth in its essence (*Nachlass*, 1:322). In his last writings he resolved this tension by rejecting the

thesis that God has a prevision of essences of real beings. Rather, God knows them only as they are formed in history (*Späte Schriften*, 289; *Nachlass*, 2:121, 206, 246, 257, 260).

122.   Scheler, *Sympathy*, 70, 148, 150, 162–63, 196–270; Scheler, *Ressentiment*, 94–95, 124–25; Scheler, *Frühe Schriften*, 400.

123.   *ST* II–II.30.2.

124.   John Macmurray, *Persons in Relation* (Atlantic Highlands: Humanities Press, 1983), 94–95.

125.   Scheler, *Ressentiment*, 94–97, 124–26, 131; Scheler, *Sympathy*, 69–71, 151–52; Scheler, *Essays*, 120–22; Scheler, *Soziologie*, 86.

126.   Scheler, *Sympathy*, 101, 142–43, 151–52, 194.

127.   Scheler, *Sympathy*, 154–56, 165.

128.   Scheler, *Ressentiment*, 84–85; Scheler, *Soziologie*, 83–88.

129.   Scheler, *Ressentiment*, 84–88; Scheler, *Soziologie*, 88, 93.

130.   Scheler, *Sympathy*, 144, 154–56, 162, 164; Scheler, *Soziologie*, 90; Scheler, *Ressentiment*, 91.

131.   Scheler, *Sympathy*, 187–88; Scheler, *Nachlass*, 1:97, 118, 159; Scheler, *Essays*, 112–14; Scheler, *Formalism*, 538.

132.   Scheler, *Sympathy*, 187–92; Scheler, *Essays*, 112.

133.   Scheler, *Nachlass*, 1:237, 306–7, 324–25; Scheler, *Nachlass*, 2:243; Scheler, *Ressentiment*, 84, 134–35; Scheler, *Essays*, 106–7, 109–10; Scheler, *Soziologie*, 90; Scheler, *Späte Schriften*, 272–74; Scheler, *Perspectives*, 7, 25, 29, 40. For Scheler's view of how the spiritual and biological sides of being human have been related in six different Western typologies, see Edward Vacek, S.J., "Max Scheler's Anthropology," *Philosophy Today* 23 (Fall 1979): 238–48.

134.   Vella, *Love Is Acceptance*, 120; Scheler, *Eternal*, 375; Scheler, *Sympathy*, 152, 160; Scheler, *Soziologie*, 90; Scheler, *Essays*, 106.

135.   Scheler, *Nachlass*, 1:114, 306–7, 324; Scheler, *Späte Schriften*, 277.

136.   Scheler, *Späte Schriften*, 277; Scheler, *Sympathy*, 192.

137.   Scheler, *Essays*, 112–14.

138.   Scheler, *Essays*, 110, 114–16; Scheler, *Sympathy*, 157–58, 160, 167.

139.   Scheler, *Ressentiment*, 91, 93, 97–103; Scheler, *Sympathy*, 144.

140.   Max Scheler, *Vom Umsturz der Werte* (Bern: Francke, 1972), 186, 189–95; Scheler, *Späte Schriften*, 274, 294, 297; Scheler, *Nachlass*, 1:65–69; Scheler, *Genius*, 273, 275; Scheler, *Formalism*, 288–92.

141.   Karl Rahner, S.J., "The 'Commandment' of Love in Relation to the Other Commandments," *Theological Investigations* (Baltimore: Helicon, 1966), 5:451–52; Keenan, *Goodness and Rightness*, 130–32, 139.

142.   Paul Wadell, C.P., *Friendship and the Moral Life* (Notre Dame: Univ. of Notre Dame Press, 1989), 13.

143.   Edward Vacek, S.J., "Personal Growth and the 'Ordo Amoris,'" *Listening* 21 (Fall 1986): 197–209; Luijpen, *Existential Phenomenology*, 314.

144.   *ST* I–II.28.6; *Sententiarum*, 3.27.1.1.

145.   *ST* I–II.28.3, 110.1–2, 111.1, 111.5; II–II.8.4; *Duo Praecepta*, 98a; *Sententiarum*, 3.27.2.1; *Veritate*, 27.1.

146.   Sidney Callahan, *In Good Conscience* (San Francisco: Harper, 1991), 132; Scheler, *Sympathy*, 152, 160, 167, 192, 255–56; Scheler, *Genius*, 65, 85, 120; Scheler, *Perspectives*, 40; Scheler, *Essays*, 110; Scheler, *Späte Schriften*, 266, 277.

147. Scheler, *Perspectives*, 20–21, 40; Scheler, *Sympathy*, 156; Scheler, *Nachlass*, 1:192, 320–21, 325, 327; Scheler, *Eternal*, 73, 196; Max Scheler, *Die Wissensformen und die Gesellschaft* (Bern: Francke, 1960), 204–5.

148. Scheler, *Umsturz*, 186–87; Scheler, *Eternal*, 96, 227, 375–76; Max Scheler, *Man's Place in Nature* (New York: Noonday Press, 1973), 55; Scheler, *Essays*, 109, 114; Scheler, *Nachlass*, 1:192–96; Scheler, *Späte Schriften*, 271–74, 294.

149. M. Taylor, *God is Love*, 345, 357.

150. Toner, *The Experience of Love*, 97.

151. Farley, "New Patterns of Relationship," 639; Toner, *The Experience of Love*, 98.

152. Rahner, "Theos in the New Testament," 123.

153. Lucien Richard, O.M.I., "Toward a Renewed Theology of Creation," *Église et Théologie* 17 (1986): 168. Richard ascribes this decentering to human finitude, but I think it is essential to anyone's love, including God's.

154. Toner, *The Experience of Love*, 98.

155. Earle, *The Autobiographical Consciousness*, 120, 123.

156. William James, "The Divided Self and Conversion," *Conversion*, ed. Walter Conn (New York: Alba, 1978), 124. See also Rosemary Haughton, *Transformation of Man* (Springfield, IL: Templegate, 1967), 32–34.

157. As Scheler rethought his ideas of God, he developed what I think is a bipolar evolutionary panentheism. See my dissertation, Edward Vacek, S.J., "Anthropological Foundations of Scheler's Ethics of Love" (Northwestern University, 1978), chap. 8, and Edward Vacek, S.J., "Max Scheler's Anthropology," 238-48. Love became the source of growth even in God. Our love for God and God's love for us implies growth in each (*Nachlass*, 2:193, 203, 265).

3

Participative Love

I am the vine and you are the branches. He who lives in me and I in him will produce abundantly. (Jn 15:5)

We are enmeshed in a variety of personal and institutional relationships.[1] Our love is not restricted to one-on-one human relationships. Rather, a well-lived life will include love for ourselves, for our multiple communities, and, above all, for God.[2] In this chapter, I will discuss four forms of existential participation: (1) intra-individual, especially the integration of our faith life; (2) interpersonal, particularly discipleship to Christ; (3) person to group, including the Church; and (4) human to our God. I concentrate on the fourth of these relationships. In each of the four, love means union in and through difference. In each of the four loves, either unity or difference has been slighted by theologians.

INTRA-INDIVIDUAL

Integration

Self-love is a matter of how we relate to our own selves. We can and must freely participate in our own lives. That is, we are responsible for integrating our "parts" (which include bodily parts, biological processes, behavioral habits, intellectual abilities, moral virtues, and so on) into a whole life well lived. Some theologians have argued that self-love is impossible because there is no "other" to unite with. They fail to recognize the enormous differentiation within a person that must be brought into a unity.

A person's overall life surpasses in importance these various "parts." Indeed, at times some aspects of a person may have to be sacrificed for the sake of the whole.[3] These "parts" are, of course, multiple in kind and function. For present purposes, I will divide them roughly into prepersonal and personal sides of our self. Our *prepersonal* dynamisms include the physical, biological, and "psychological" dimensions of our lives that we share, in a distinctive and analogous way, with other animals. The activities of these dimensions typically function outside human freedom, for example, our heart, our digestion, or some neurosis. I can do without some but not all of these "parts." Each day many of my cells die, and my identity is not seriously threatened. I can live in paralyzing terror of snakes or have a neurotic fear of rejection, and I am still human. Though I must have some minimal level of bodily and psychological activities, I can still be a person without their full functioning.

One central task of our lives is to integrate these diverse, semiautonomous "parts" into a coherent unity. Integration does not mean that we impose order "from on high." Rather, a more cooperative ordering of these "parts" is required, affirming their own proper dynamism insofar as they contribute to our life as a whole person. Love for our bodies includes respecting their own biological laws. Through proper nutrition, medicine, and mental hygiene we foster the body's dynamisms so as to live healthy lives. Similarly our psychological life contains much that is outside the direct influence of our freedom. We are a plurality of often ambivalent, conflicting, and unresolved psychological tendencies, some of which we struggle against and some of which we simply accept. Many of these tendencies, however, we can love; we affirm them and allow them to be taken up into the dignity of our personal life.

These prepersonal dynamisms are not, in general, antithetical to our personal life. In fact, as biologists, sociobiologists, and psychologists point out, much of our proclivity for living healthy individual lives and for social cooperation arises precisely from these prepersonal tendencies of our selves.[4] The institution of marriage, for example, arises in part from our sexual drive to mate and bear children. These tendencies relate us well or badly to the world. William Luijpen well observes,

> A pre-personal subject, then, is at work "underneath" the *personal* subject. . . . The human body has already concluded a "pact" with the world before the personal subject accomplishes his personal history, and this pact is not made superfluous in any personal history. . . . The pact between body and world is also the "place" of many psychical disturbances. . . . they are a breach between body and world, usually on an affective level, and this breach cannot be restored by a personal intellectual effort or a personal decision of will: the breach is filled when the body, aided by psychotherapeutic means, again opens itself to the world and to other subjects.[5]

We also perform various *personal* acts, e.g., intellectual acts, virtuous deeds, and religious affections. These belong to the spiritual and religio-metaphysical dimensions of our selves. These personal acts enable us to function intelligently in this world. Through these personal acts, we are able to know and appreciate the objects of this world in themselves, and we are able to choose freely among them. Through them, we also have that sense of absoluteness that anchors and motivates our moral decisions. Through them, we have an intuition of Being as the ground and horizon of beings. And through them, we seek the ultimate meaning of life.[6] We need not, of course, have any particular thoughts or affections nor any special metaphysical or religious experiences in order to be human. Still, without some exercise of these personal acts, we lack in basic humanity.

Our "personal" acts can transcend the limits of our "prepersonal" dynamisms, but at least in this life we can never wholly do without the prepersonal aspects of our being. Like the prepersonal dynamisms, these spiritual and religious dynamisms must also be integrated into a coherent life-pattern. For example, the desire to understand the world scientifically can, if not integrated with other sorts of spiritual acts, lead to a seriously distorted life.

Needless to say, freedom's task of integration is never fully achieved in this life. The various "parts" of our lives each have their own characteristic ways of acting, and the task of integration is to bring them into cooperation for the good of the "whole" person. When they are not, i.e., when they subvert the growth of the integrated whole, our self is disordered. Ideally all prepersonal and personal dimensions of our selves (physical, biological, psychological, spiritual, and religious) participate in our overall life-pattern and fundamental option.[7] Through them we accumulate a history of experiences; and these too must also be integrated into our lives. Childhood, adolescence, young adulthood each present their own distinctive challenges and tasks, successes and failures; these abide in us in an integrated or isolated manner.[8]

We must integrate our various dynamisms into a coherent and developing self. We can do so as an act of love for ourselves. Needless to say, there is no automatic harmony or development. Needless to say, too, we can lose our self in the process, subordinating our own larger life-goals to some particular good. For example, our pursuit of money as a means both to survive and to enjoy life's pleasures can in fact become so preoccupying that we risk even life and pleasure, not to mention more spiritual goals, for the sake of money. Each aspect of our selves can grow like so many cancer cells to destroy our integrity. At its best, however, our free self integrates our various dynamisms into our overall tendency to grow toward full humanity.

Life of Faith

Self-love includes the intrapersonal integration of our religious acts. Our specifically religious acts do not float high above the prepersonal dimensions of our selves. They have their prepersonal foundations. These prepersonal tendencies appear, for example, in the comfort we find while smelling incense or fingering a rosary. They appear in that dogged and blind adherence to our childhood faith that characterizes most of us from time to time. Acting out of these prepersonal attachments is not only easier than free, personal believing; it often provides a solid bulwark against the vicissitudes and vagaries of thought and culture. Our unreflected childhood traditions sustain us in times of uncertainty or challenges, sometimes properly and sometimes against true growth in our relation to God.[9] The old maxim of religious life, "Keep the rule and the rule will keep you," had psychological if not religious truth. The religious faith of humans necessarily has its mindless or prerational elements, and most of us can be glad we were imbued with the faith as a child, long before we experienced its truth or made any rational assessment of its claims. A certain "mindless" going along with received traditions will always be part of our lives. Only rationalists think they have understood and decided everything important for their lives. Those who have an exaggerated idea of freedom reject these prepersonal aspects of themselves. Those with more modest self-understanding can learn to embrace and love these aspects.

Thus, part of our self-acceptance involves accepting these prepersonal dimensions of our faith. Still, this is not enough for adult religious living. We must also reflect on the givens of our tradition, understand them, critique them, and personally consent to them or dissent from them. Though the tradition already lives in us, it must be lived freely and ever more fully as our own personal belief. Gradually we must make our "inherited" love of God the fundamental act of our being. That is, we must allow our adult love of God to inform all our other acts, and we must integrate our religious history with all our other activities.

INTERPERSONAL LOVE

Individual to Individual

One form of loving participation occurs *within* a person. A second form takes place between individuals. Through love we share in the life of another person. We share in the loves and hates, hopes and fears, aspirations and limits that contribute to the identity of another person.[10] All that we have said in Chapter 2 could be repeated here.

Love between individuals demonstrates most clearly the truth of Pierre Teilhard de Chardin's two correlative maxims: "to be is to unite" and "union differentiates."[11] We live to belong, but in belonging we become truly distinct. When we love another person, we affirm the other objectively, and that means in all his or her difference; at the same time and in the same act, we realize ourselves as different from the beloved.[12] In contrast to infatuated love or "emotional identification,"[13] genuine love leads us to distinguish ourselves from the other. The worries of some earlier existentialist authors thus were misguided. A love relation *frees* and *individuates* rather than leads to a loss of freedom. In fact, the fear of "losing" oneself keeps a person from seeing the genuine new possibilities that only a love union can open up. In this sense we cannot fully become ourselves without loving others, for only in loving others are these new ways of being ourselves opened up.

Love for others means that we bear some responsibility for their moral lives. This point is disputed. Many people claim that we are not at all responsible for the behavior of others. Even more people would argue that we have no responsibility for their *moral* life. A person's moral life, they claim, is the domain of a person's freedom, an arena where others dare not tread. They point out that no one, not even God, can make decisions for another person; otherwise, the decision would not be that person's decision. Further, no one, not even God, can exercise another's freedom. Thus, no one, not even God, can make another become morally good. Hence we are not responsible for another's moral life. These arguments are true enough as far as they go.

Nevertheless, we do have *some* responsibility for others. Perhaps most obvious, we have a responsibility to create conditions that encourage their free and right decisions. If, for example, poverty is the seedbed of crime and if we can do something to alleviate others' poverty, then we help their moral life by eliminating conditions that lead to immorality. Furthermore we can encourage and support them and their efforts. And we can resist their bad choices.

A less obvious but no less important source of our responsibility for others derives from an important, if seldom noted, feature of interpersonal love. When we are loved, we have a prevoluntary tendency to return love to those who love us.[14] We can refuse this return of love, of course, but our refusal goes against this natural tendency to return love.[15] When we consent to this return, we consent to a union with the one who has loved us. When Magdalene accepts being loved by Jesus and returns his love, then to the degree she is united with him, she "can" no longer sin.

An important ethical thesis follows. We all potentially have some responsibility for other persons' lack of love, since it is possible that, had we loved them better, our love for them might have invited their return love and thus fostered a growth in their *ability* to love. Our love and their response would have changed their *ordo amoris*. Since we rarely or never love people as much as they could be loved, we therefore usually share some responsibility for their moral goodness or badness.[16]

When, however, our love is generously given and responded to, it becomes the lifeblood of a moral solidarity of persons between us. With every act of love performed, a community of love grows. Persons who have been loved become more able to love still others; persons who have been denied love are malnourished in their ability to love. Thus, love builds, and a lack of love destroys, communion among persons.[17] Full human community is not the starting point of history, but its destiny.[18] The complete reign of God is fostered or retarded by our love or lack of love. Thus, the effects of love are, paradoxically, both the increased independence of the lover and "the solidary membership and true co-responsibility of all souls to God."[19]

Discipleship

In Christianity, interpersonal participation takes the special form of discipleship. We Christians take on the mind and heart of Jesus (1 Cor 2:16). In a word, we become disciples. As a result, we approach the world differently. To the degree appropriate to our vocation, we see the world through Jesus' eyes and with his heart; we strive to carry out the redemptive activities that occupied his life and still occupy him in the present world. As St. John wrote, "Our relation to this world is just like his" (1 Jn 4:17, 2:5–6).

Evangelical language is appropriate here. We develop a personal relation with our Lord and Savior: we are those "who love our Lord Jesus Christ with unfailing love" (Eph 6:24).[20] As disciples we are dependent on Christ: "I am the vine, you are the branches." As disciples we carry on his work: "He who lives in me and I in him will produce abundantly" (Jn 15:4). Christ's present activity in part depends on us. Even in his lifetime Jesus could do only a few miracles in Nazareth because he needed the faith of the people in order to be effective (Mk 6:5). As Bernard Cooke comments, Christ does not carry on his saving work "as an isolated historical individual. Rather, his saving work is carried on in relation to others and through their cooperation, i.e., their discipleship."[21]

Discipleship is essential to the Christian way of being religious. "None of us lives as his own master and none of us dies as his own master.

While we live we are responsible to the Lord, and when we die we die as his servants. Both in life and in death we are the Lord's" (Rom 14:7–8). We grow as disciples by loving our Lord more. Contemplative prayer draws us into an ever closer relation with Jesus Christ. That relationship, not any "reasonable" theology, motivates the "excesses" of St. Ignatius's "third degree of humility," wherein the disciple prefers to suffer and be abused as a way of being like Jesus (if only God's will permits). That is, the disciple wants to share in Jesus' life to the full.[22] As Paul writes, "Your attitude must be that of Christ. . . . he emptied himself" (Phil 2:5–7).

This sharing of life as disciples is not simply a matter of imitating some model, however noble or divine.[23] Rather, it is sharing in the life of one we love. Imbued with the mind and heart of Christ, we still have our own minds and hearts. Participation means unity in difference. Our own vocations become ever more differentiated the more we are involved with Christ. Paul follows his famous line "The life I live now is not my own; Christ is living in me" with "I still live my human life" and then he explains, "It is a life of faith in the Son of God who loved me and gave himself for me" (Gal 2:20). Like the great saints, we must do what the historical Jesus could *not* do. We are to make up what is lacking in the sufferings (and successes) of Jesus (Col 1:24). We are to do *greater* things than he did (Jn 14:12).

GROUP PARTICIPATION

Individuals in Groups

Individuals love not only other individuals. They also, in varying ways, love groups.[24] They love humanity, their nation, the Rotary Club, or their family. They freely and affectionately act for and on behalf of such groups.[25] In one New Testament passage, the Jewish elders commended the centurion whose servant was ill, saying to Jesus, "He deserves this favor from you . . . because he loves our people" (Lk 7:5). The centurion's service implied that Jesus, though never individually helped by this centurion, had a responsibility as a member of the Jewish race to respond with a favor.

It is a common mistake to say that we can love only individuals because there is really no such thing as a group. The opposite, though less frequent mistake, is the totalitarian solution. Only the group is worthy of love, and love for individuals is seen as an aberration, a distraction, or, at best, a derivative act. In the first case, there is an inability to see and affirm supraindividual unities; in the second, an inability to see and affirm differences between a group and its members. The group has a reality beyond that of any individual member or all members taken collectively.[26] The group can continue in existence, even though all present members die or depart. The group, however, is dependent on the existence of at least some individuals. For example, without some citizens, there is no nation. The identity of a group is not a mere convention, not simply a way of thinking in which we gather individual people under some nominal rubric. Groups have their own identities and function according to their own inner laws; for example, a state but not an ethnic group must occupy some specific geographical territory.

I will discuss three kinds of groups: the prepersonal, the associational, and the corporate.[27] The first two often pass as counterfeits for the third. The first lacks freedom and therefore its unity is not properly a form of existential participation. The second incorporates freedom, but fails to achieve a communion of persons. The third is a genuine form of existential participation.

Prepersonal belonging: The clearest form of the prepersonal group is the union that occurs in mass behavior. It is found as herd behavior among animals and as "crowd" behavior among humans. In it, individuals lose their independence. For example, ordinarily decent and considerate people have trampled to death fellow human beings in the shared hysteria of a soccer match. The group acts much like a herd, with members blindly moving along with the pack. A sort of mass mood infects the group, robbing individuals of their own freedom. Everyone is engaged, but no one may be personally guilty. Another example: sometimes anti-Catholic bigots standing alongside the roadside during a papal visit have acknowledged feeling an impulse to cheer him as he passed; they had to resist a prepersonal, crowd love.

Another and quite fundamental form of this prepersonal participation is the relation that we have to nature. However much our self-transcendence as persons may enable us to go beyond our "natural environment," we belong to the world of "nature." As James Gustafson remarks, "Man (individual persons, communities, and species) is a participant in the patterns and processes of interdependence of life in the world."[28] This belonging is prior to our choice. We are material beings, part of the material world; we are animals, part of the animal world. In Teilhard's words, "However autonomous our soul, it is indebted to an inheritance worked upon from all sides—before ever it came into being—by the totality of the energies of the earth."[29] We can prepersonally (as well as personally) love this bond we have with nature, and it is a belonging that we ignore at our peril. We belong to it as part of our sanctification, for this realm of nature ultimately is destined to be filled with Christ's life (Eph 1:10, 23).

Association: The second type of bonding might be called a *voluntary association.* In it, individuals freely join one another in order to promote their own individual interests.[30] This form is personal; indeed rationality is supremely prized. But individuals cooperate only as individuals; they give their loyalty to the association only insofar as it promotes their individual interests in the short or long term. The association does not have any reality over and above its members. A business deal may serve as an example. Within the constraints of their contracts, individuals are free to leave or dissolve a business association at any time that it does not promote their own interests.

The members of voluntary associations are, in the words of William Spohn, "self-sufficient free agents who deal with each other as strangers, not as members of communities with committed roles. The lawsuit rather than the family discussion becomes the paradigm for settling differences."[31] This view of society which has dominated much recent ethics wrongly holds that the voluntary association is the basic form of human gathering. In a voluntary association, what unites the members is not mutual involvement of whole persons, but the reciprocal fostering of self-interest. What distinguishes one individual from another is important not in and for itself, but only insofar as it promotes or detracts from their respective projects or self-interest. "The paradigm of market relations, of exchange, involves putting one's own interests first. It involves the assertion that one knows one's own interests best. . . . It involves reducing complex relationships into terms that can be made equivalent."[32]

Corporate person: The third type of group is a personal group or "corporate person."[33] It possesses a real identity that binds together its members. At least some of its members must be mature persons who freely maintain and support the corporate person. A nation, a family, and a friendship are examples of this kind of group participation. It is not just that Tom loves Jennifer and Jennifer loves Tom. Rather they also relish the relationship that binds them; they make sacrifices for it; they make their decisions with an eye to the relationship itself. Their relationship gives them a reason to do things together that as individuals neither might take the time to do. That is, the individuals belong to one another in a unity or "whole" that comprehends them.

"Corporate persons" have an identity over and beyond that of the individual members, even though they are embodied in those members and could not be without them. For example, the United States endures in its new members long after its founding mothers and fathers have been buried. We can love corporate persons. This love is not the same as love for each of the individuals who are members of the group. Indeed, we often love the group without loving all the individuals of the group. We also can love individual persons because of their membership in a group. On the other hand, since no one's identity is wholly exhausted by being a member, we can love individuals, yet not love any groups they belong to.

The members freely receive from the group, and the group may rightfully ask from its members. Still, there will be no strict quid pro quo between the corporate person and the individual interests of the members. A group, e.g., a family or nation, that demanded nothing from its members would be denying its own reality. But the group also sacrifices for its members. In limited cases, e.g., a marriage with an abusive husband or a nation facing a vastly superior military force, the corporate person may have to disband in order to save its members. In a corporate person, the normative pattern is one of mutual dependence of individual and group. Love for the group may require self-sacrifice. This arises not because the self is obliterated in the group, but rather because members so affirm the group that they freely yield to its good. More commonly, without exploiting the group for their own self-interest, members rightly draw upon the common good of the group.

Difficult ethical questions then arise concerning when the individual should be subordinated to the interests of the group, or the group to the interests of the individual. It seems clear that generally the group should function on behalf of the individuals, but what that means in specific decisions cannot be sharply delineated. Thus, a country ought to protect its least well-off members, and this can mean expecting sacrifices from the commonweal. At times, however, a country can ask some of its members to risk their lives or well-being for the sake of the whole. Still, a group must not make inordinate claims on its members. We cannot become human without community, but no human community can claim us absolutely.[34]

Participation in groups includes mutual, though distinctive, responsibilities.[35] The group is dependent on the free engagement and commitment of at least some individuals, and the adult members have responsibilities for the life of the whole, responsibilities they would not have if they were not members. The group is concerned about the actions of its individual members because it is affected by those actions. Jews use an expression which means to be "shamed before the gentiles," the experience all feel whenever one of their members becomes notorious.[36] Similarly, individual members are affected by the actions of their group, and, thus, individual members rightly are concerned about policy decisions of their group. Collective responsibility even for the sins of one's ancestors arises from belonging to the same group they belonged to. For example, Americans collectively share some responsibility for the enslavement of African-Americans.

Even in those groups that we have freely joined, membership involves certain involuntary constraints and demands. As George Wilson writes, "The result of a membership is that *my subjectivity is altered.* . . . I remain free. But as a result of the membership my freedom comes into play, not on a field which is a *tabula rasa*, but on a field upon which some lines have been drawn."[37] Our membership in a family structures our freedom differently than our membership in the state.[38] Maura Ryan nicely remarks on the obligations that flow from participating in a family:

> One of the things that family life can teach us is that we are born into some obligations, and some are born to us, and life includes the acceptance of those kinds of indissoluble and predefined obligations as well as the ones we freely incur. The involuntary quality of kinship can also teach us how to accept others as intimately connected to us, even when they fail to live up to our standards or when they do not possess the physical or personal qualities most attractive to us.[39]

What she says of a family is analogously true of any corporate person.

The group has an identity that it legitimately strives to protect and foster. For example, a murderer is punished not only for harming another individual, but also for harming the whole society. As a reality, the group has, within limits, an obligation to love itself by preserving itself; and in so doing it generally serves its members. Hence, a corporate person rightly tends to preserve its own power (though it does so wrongly when it frustrates the larger purposes for which it exists). Needless to say, corporate persons, like individuals, become dysfunctional, no longer serving their members or no longer serving a valuable function in the world. In these cases, the group can be disbanded or even forcibly changed, occasionally through revolution.

We can love the groups we belong to. That is, "we integrate ourselves into a community and its best hopes. We forge loyalties that bind us, willingly, to this group."[40] Since we all belong to many groups, conflicting loyalties inevitably arise. The strength and intensity of these different claims will vary at different moments of our life. It is our task to weigh the importance and legitimacy of these claims.[41]

Body of Christ

One especially important group for Christians is, of course, the Church. The Church is a corporate person with Christ as its head. Church members participate in the corporate person of the Church. Christians are baptized into Christ (Rom 6:3). They are baptized into the Church and therefore into the life of its head. Thus, Christ is living in them (Gal 2:20). Paul hears a voice, "Saul, why are you persecuting me?" And when Paul, who had been persecuting the Church, inquires who this "me" is, the reply is that it is Jesus (Acts 9:4–5). Jesus was united with the community that Saul persecuted, even though Jesus was different from it. Similarly, the individual members of the community that Paul persecuted were members of the community itself, but they were not identical with it. In brief, these members participated in the community, and this community shared in Christ's life:[42] "So too we, though many, are one body in Christ and individually members one of another" (Rom 12:4). Jesus' love continued to live in the community and in its members. Hence the persecution of these members of this community was in this sense a persecution of Jesus.

Since the Church is not identical with its members, the Church cannot usurp their own distinctive vocations (Rom 12:4).[43] Indeed, the Church not only necessarily must include great diversity within itself, it will also foster that diversity (1 Cor 12:12–31). Since individual Christians are members of the Church, they will of course accept the received identity of the Church (1 Jn 1:3). Since they are not the Church itself, they cannot make the Church whatever they want it to be. But since they participate in the Church, they must take responsibility for the ongoing formation of the Church's ever-developing identity. Both conformism and schism are failures in love. If genuine participation is present, there will be unity in difference between Christ and his Church and between the Church and its members. If genuine participation is not present, fanaticism, self-denigration, or totalitarianism results.

The participative relation between the whole Church and its members is complex. The Church as a whole is an "object" worthy of love. The Church is not a voluntary association, nor is it a prepersonal herd or mass group, however much it at times resembles and incorporates aspects of these. The individual can offer his or her life in service of the greater good of the Church, and the Church finds part of its meaning in serving its members. Being a member of the Church is constitutive of the identity of its members, and all members share in the grace of the whole. Individuals are affected by the reputation as well as by the advance or decline in the spiritual life of the Church.

The Church as a whole is modified by the actions of individuals. "If one member suffers, all the members suffer with it; if one member is honored, all the members share its joy" (1 Cor 12:26). The body of Christ is affected by the sins as well as the graces of its members (1 Cor 6:15–20). Thus, on the one hand, the Church should love its members. That is, it should unite its destiny with theirs and aim at their enhancement. Communities rightly have a special love for "their own."[44] On the other hand, members should unite their destiny with the Church and direct themselves to its enhancement. Each does so to the degree appropriate to the nature of the Church and appropriate to the individual vocations of the members. Individuals rightly give and receive in different ways, but "even those members of the body which seem less important are in fact indispensable" (1 Cor 12:22).

Communities are not isolated entities. They can and must address other groups. That is, one "corporate person" interacts with other "corporate persons." Thus, the Church can and should participate in other groups and thereby influence their identity. These groups also influence the Church, as when the soul of a nation imparts to a regional Church a distinctive language and temper. The Church must participate in the world. In so doing, it modifies the world even as it is modified by the world. It thereby realizes and enhances its own distinctive identity. The earthly Church cannot exist and grow without engaging the rest of the world. The Church should recognize a boundary between itself and the surrounding society, not in order to withdraw from the world, but only so that its interaction with society may be consonant with its own identity. Like other groups, the Church will both confirm and contradict the present world. Stating matters in its own religious language, the Church will sometimes act in a priestly way, sometimes in a prophetic way.[45]

Nonetheless, the Church's first responsibility as a corporate body is to turn to Jesus Christ and his Abba and unite itself with them. Since the relation between the Church and Christ is genuinely one of participation, the Church must recognize that it is not Christ. The difference between Christ and the Church was forgotten when, in pre-Vatican II days, the Catholic Church claimed for itself complete sinlessness. Still, the unity between Christ and the Church means that it is called to a sinless holiness. It is invited to share in Christ's own life. As a consequence of its union with Christ, the Church legitimately forgives sin or blesses, but it does so by praying that the Spirit forgive and consecrate in and through it. Similarly, individual members are neither Christ nor the Church; but because they too are participants, they also have their own mission to forgive and consecrate in and through the Spirit.

The above three forms of specifically Christian participation find their foundation in the fourth: a share in God's life. The first form of participation, religious integrity, lives on in ritual and tradition, but these owe their origin to a personal relation with God and should lead back to it. Similarly, the second form, discipleship, is dependent on Jesus, but he points to the one he called Abba. True disciples of Christ are related to his God (Mt 10:40). Thirdly, membership in the Church is membership in a group whose central identity is formed by God's grace and whose most basic act is to love God in return. This brings us to our next consideration. The fourth form of Christian participation proclaims "One God and Father of all, who is over all, and works through all, and is in all" (Eph 4:6).

CHRISTIAN GOD

The heart of Christian life is the relation of Ground and grounded, of Being and beings, of God and creation, of Jesus' Abba and redeemed covenant partners. This form of participation is essential to understanding the religious dimensions of our lives. It is, however, most obscure and problematic. An existential theory of participation implies not only that we depend on God, but also that God is changed by uniting with us. The two major questions this section addresses are: Does God's love for us affect God? and Can we make a contribution to God's activity?

Understanding God's covenanting love is the Judaeo-Christian key to understanding both God and the unity of God's acts.[46] "The doctrines of creation, redemption, incarnation, grace, and last things all express the one truth that God is essentially love of others. No one doctrine establishes, for the first time, that God is love. All portray the one love of God for the creatures."[47] Who then is our God, and what is God doing? Any attempt to provide a complete answer might be reduced to saying that, first, God is God and, second, God's acts are as numerous as the events of God's and the universe's histories.[48] Gustafson lays out some general features between the simplicity of the first response and the unending complexity of the second:

The Bible tells us of a God who is transcendent and a God who is immanent, a God who acts in history and a God who is nature's God, a God whose kingdom is to come and a God who has been ordering the creation from its inception, a jealous God and a friendly God, a God who creates and redeems and a God who judges and destroys, a God who is a commander and lawgiver and a God who liberates, a God who speaks and a God beyond gods who is mysterious and silent, a profoundly moral God before whom humans are guilty and a profoundly compassionate God who creates new possibilities in reconciliation, a God to whom we can cry for comfort and a God who is indifferent to our private ills, a God of justice and war and a God of peace, a God who is feared and a God who is loved and adored, a God who is the ground of security and a God who undercuts most of the grounds of security on which we depend.[49]

A Related God

Dogmatic theology commonly holds that God is not *really* related to creation.[50] The relationship is said to be wholly on our side, not on God's.[51] The Bible does not think in such terms. Rather a *mutually* involving and binding covenant is important to both testaments.[52] Though there are different covenants (e.g., Gen 6:18; 8:21–22; 15:8), the central covenant of the Hebrew Bible is the one made at Sinai (Ex 19:1–8). The promise of this covenant is renewed through Israel's history: "I will be your God and you will be my people" (Jer 31:31; Ex 11:20; Hos 2:25). The people understand their identity in terms of Yahweh, *and vice versa.* After Israel's defection and exile, the promise of mutual commitment is made again: "Behold, I will gather them together from all the lands. . . . They shall be my people, and I will be their God. . . . I will make with them an eternal covenant, never to cease doing good to them. . . . I will take delight in doing good to them. . . . with all my heart and soul" (Jer 32:37–41). They will wholeheartedly belong to God who belongs to them (Jer 24:7).

There are, of course, many images to depict God's way of belonging. Three favorites are God as a solicitous king (Ps 44:5–9, 47:8–9; Is 52:7), as husband (Hos 2:16–21), and as father (Ex 4:22; Dt 1:31, 8:5, 32:6, 32:19; Ps 103:13; Is 43:6, 63:16; Mal 2:10). In the New Testament, God as father becomes central and God's kingship transmutes into the reign of God. Thus, the disciples pray, "Our Father in heaven. . . . your kingdom come" (Mt 6:9–10). God is for Jesus "my father" (Mt 15:13) and Jesus is the "beloved son" (Mt 17:5). Our relation to God is that of children: "We are God's offspring" (Acts 17:29). These three images of king, husband, and father embody a relational tension. On the one hand, a relation of superiority and inferiority prevails. The king is not a representative of the people, but stands over and sometimes against them. Husbands were understood to be superior to their wives; and fathers are superior to their children. On the other hand, there is an intimacy in each of these relations, most vividly in the familial relationships.

Too often Christian theology has misunderstood this relationship and preferred to think of God as efficient cause and the world as an effect outside of God. "This view cannot capture the uniquely personal and mutually participatory relation between God and the spiritual creature affirmed in the Christian doctrine of grace."[53] Existential participation is a free, historical, graced relation between persons. That is, the God-world relation needs to be conceived not simply along lines of efficient causality, but also in personal categories, in which God's own self is communicated to creation. God is involved in creation in such a way that creation is, as Karl Rahner argues, part of God's own history.[54] God responds to the world in accord with our free responses (Jn 14:21–23; 16:27). God, who has decided to become involved through love with creation, has, so to speak, compromised God's absolute *aseity.* "God has surrendered his triumphant self-sufficiency and brought about his own need."[55] In the Scriptures, it is taken for granted that God changes in response to human activity. After witnessing human sin, God regrets God's own decision to create human beings and decides to wipe them off the face of the earth (Gen 6:5–7). God regrets the decision to make Saul king (1 Sm 15:11). God casts off Israel "in an outburst of wrath," but then repents and decides that "with great tenderness I will take you back" (Is 54:7; Jer 26:19). God's action responds to the good or bad action of Israel (Jer 18:5–10). And Israel appeals to God as its father whose zealous care, pity, and mercy will save the nation (Is 63:15–16).

God is really related to the world. As Paul Tillich writes, "The divine-human relation, and therefore God as well as man within this relation, changes with the stages of the history of revelation and with the stages of every personal development."[56] Though God could be imagined to be beneficent without becoming personally involved, God cannot love without such involvement. The "Lord of history" is not simply our way of referring to a God who in fact has no real relation to history. The problem, as Langdon Gilkey notes, is that "if God does not change and so is out of relation to changing actuality, then he can only 'know' the world as 'possible,' i.e., through his original and eternal idea of it—and not in its actuality. . . . That such a metaphysical position denies or at best makes unintelligible the biblical view of God as dynamically related to history in preservation, grace, judgment and promise . . . is evident."[57] Thus, it is not sufficient to say that God eternally knows the essences of finite beings, and that therefore God need not change when these beings become real. For reality is something over and beyond essences. Let us imagine a woman who dreams of her future child, and let us imagine that her dreams of the child's future life are perfectly accurate. Would we then say that she undergoes no change when her child is born? No, the reality of the child makes a real difference to her. She becomes the mother not of an idea, but of a real child. Something analogous is true of the God who says, "I will be your God and you will be my people." Accordingly, Tillich writes, "God participates in everything that is; he has community with it; he shares in its destiny."[58]

Thus, creation and redemption represent a further determination in God. By God's own choice, God really becomes a creator. As Rahner writes, "The primary phenomenon given by faith is precisely the self-emptying of God, his becoming, the kenosis and genesis of God himself. He can become insofar as, in establishing the other which comes from him, he himself *becomes* what has come from him. . . . because he truly wants to have the other as his own, he constitutes it in its genuine real-ity."[59] Particularly in the Incarnation, God *becomes* human.

The relation between God and ourselves is mutual and—what is more surprising—mutually perfecting: "Yet if we love one another, God dwells in us, and his love is brought to perfection in us" (1 Jn 4:12), and further, "Our love is brought to perfection . . . for our relation to this world is just like his"(1 Jn 4:17). God's love becomes complete in our love, and we become complete in acting as God does to overcome sin and to love God's people (1 Jn 4:11). Commenting on John's remarkable line that *God's* own love comes to perfection in us, Raymond Brown says, "The author dares to make divine indwelling . . . dependent on and expressed by our loving one another. . . . The objection that God's love, since it comes from Him, must already be perfect independently of human beings is based on a philosophical conception of God quite for-eign to Johannine thought. . . . His love is not *perfectly* what it should be until it begets children in His image who themselves love."[60]

As is well known, many contemporary theologians do not have the philosophical problem with God's dependence that Brown alludes to.[61] As John Stacer writes, "Immutability is a perfection only on the level of core identity. Immutability would be an imperfection on the level of living operations such as knowing, loving, and deciding."[62] God changes in response to us, as Walter Kern argues: "God's anger with sin, his joy at men's goodness, would not merely be ways of speaking of effects brought about in sinful or good men, but would be a real activity in God himself. . . . man and the world, as creatures, belong to God . . . without which God would not be what he is, that is, he who thus loves man and the world. . . . God does not change in his being as it is for himself, but in his being for 'the other'."[63] Teilhard well expresses our role in Christ's own fulfillment: "It is through the collaboration which he stimulates in us that Christ, starting from *all* created things, is consummated and attains his plenitude."[64]

Unity-in-Difference

The love relation between God and ourselves is one of existential participation. This love, to be true, must safeguard the *proper way of being* for both the Ground and grounded. God is not one being among beings, simply like us in all things but sin. God is not a human being writ large, no matter how large. The experience of ontological contingency (Why is there something and not nothing? Indeed, why am I?) and the experience of grace (Even when I seem to initiate love, I find upon closer reflection that I am first invited) reveal that our being is originated and dependent. God's Being is in everything, without being either the sum of all things nor one thing more. We experience God as the divine, unfathomable Depth of things, as the Horizon beyond all horizons, and as the No-thing (the negating and inviting ultimate) whose presence keeps us from being satisfied with every thing. God is not one more categorical object to be loved along with a thousand other things.[65] Rather God is God, the Ground of all that we know and love as well as the Ground of our knowing and loving. God truly becomes the Creator through the created, but it should never be forgotten that the Creator is "dependent" on creatures in an entirely different sense than the creatures are dependent on the Creator. Finite beings absolutely cannot exist without God; God cannot exist only relatively, e.g., as Creator, without creatures.

When the proper way of being for creature and God is preserved, the creature does not disappear in the Ground, as occurs in pantheism; nor does the Ground disappear in the grounded, as in atheism, agnosticism, and naturalism.[66] Rather, the relation between God and creation has well been called panentheism: literally, all is in God but also implying that God is in all (Eph 4:6). Panentheism tries to mediate between a traditional theism and pantheism. Traditional theism asserts that God is in no way dependent on human beings, while humans are in every way dependent on God. Pantheism rejects a wholly independent creator and asserts that all is God.[67] Pantheism and traditional theism succeed in their rejection of extremes. They fail because they do not preserve both the unity and the difference between God and creation. God and creation should not be identified, but neither should they be severed. Rather they are bound in a unity-in-difference which God initiates and with which humans cooperate. Thus, by God's initiative, both God and creatures become what they are through the other. Each grows, though in different ways, in like and not in inverse proportion through the relation. And since humans are essentially free, God is genuinely creative of human personhood only insofar as the self God creates is also freely "created" by itself.

Although God is really involved with creation, God also transcends creation. While there has been much salutary discussion of the inviting, sustaining, and embracing nearness of God, the abysmal and even horrifying aspect of the *mysterium tremendum* of God should not be neglected.[68] That is, the transcendence of God should not be forgotten. Our encounters with God are but momentary shooting stars in God's endlessness. Our knowledge and our love of God may grow indefinitely, but complete intelligibility is beyond our capacity since God is permanently the Incomprehensible One.[69] We should wonder at the stars we see, but we should not forget the endlessness of space. The Ultimate who is near is always also the One who is utterly beyond creation. Indeed, the closer the unity we have with God, the more the difference between God and us becomes apparent. God seems easy to understand and readily available to those who are not deeply involved with God.

Human finitude and importance: As created, redeemed, and sanctified, we owe all that we are to God's initiative and sustenance.[70] Deep humility is therefore called for on our part, both because our finitude can never comprehend God and because our sinfulness regularly tries to manipulate God.[71] However much we entertain ourselves with thoughts of our dignity, importance, and even "infinite value," we cannot forever put off the obvious reflection that we are not necessary in the world, that most of creation could get along quite well without us. We live off a heritage that we did not invent, and we modify it only ever so slightly. Even if we could make ourselves to be almost perfect in our kind, we know that our kind is very limited. The advantage of the genius who knows "everything" over the mentally retarded person who knows "nothing" is quickly erased by an embolism or a bullet. When our name appears in the obituary column, almost all of some six billion people will never notice. So we must not exaggerate our importance. We are very finite beings.[72]

When, then, I argue later that we cooperate with God, I do not intend to imply that our contribution is anything but very, very small. The briefest reflection on our place even within the material universe should convince us that we are but very minute cooperators. All the more then, our cooperation with God is that of people who are absolutely dependent. "Neither he who plants nor he who waters is of any special account, only God who gives the growth. . . . We are God's co-workers" (1 Cor 3:7–9). We can and should rejoice in the second half of Paul's claim, but we should never forget the first half. The ontological difference between ourselves and God should never be obscured.

But neither should we forget our own reality and dignity. This too is a not uncommon mistake in Christian literature. Theologians commonly deny to us any kind of independence and assert that our worth has nothing to do with ourselves. Love for God does not require that we empty the self of all its dignity or its self-love. Purity of heart is not synonymous with absence of a heart. God should be the focal point of our lives, but the God we love is our God, One who loves us, not one who is in competition with us and can be supreme only if we are reduced to nothing. Though the mystic sometimes speaks of the loss of self or of the loss of self-consciousness, "he or she certainly appears to enter the ecstasy in full awareness and, afterward, to remember it well enough to write clearly about it."[73] In other words, the self is present even in the mystical experience. We are not God, but then again we are not nothing. As we have seen, Paul, who is often quoted for saying "Not I, but Christ lives in me," first says "I live" and then follows with "I still live my life" (Gal 2:20). That Paul is not speaking literally of a loss of self seems clear from a parallel Pauline claim: "It is not I who do it, but sin which dwells in me" (Rom 7:17). Something other than the denial of self is intended in these passages. These passages emphasize the one with "whom/what" we participate, not the absence of the self. Rather, God cannot be our Creator, Redeemer, and Sanctifier without us human beings, and therefore there is a kind of mutual implication between God and humanity.[74] God cannot be what God wants to be, namely, our Redeemer, unless and until we hear and accept God's self-revelation and self-communication.

It is commonly said that it is sinful to try to become like God. This is false, at least as far as spiritual loving is concerned. We have "become sharers of the divine nature" (2 Pt 1:4). In loving others, we "become" them, but we do not usurp their proper identity, nor do we lose our finitude and selfhood as persons. When we love God, we share God's life; this is not a "transgression" of our limits, but a response to God's invitation. In fact, we are sinful when we refuse to become like God. Sinful transgression occurs when we fail to realize that we are what we are through God (and others) or when we forget we are not identical with that in which we participate. We share in God's life and activity, but we are not God.[75] Those who lack an adequate theory of participation will falsely judge that the desire to share in God's life must involve either the attempt to usurp God's prerogatives or the loss of self. Rather, even as we share in the Infinite, we remain finite. We transgress our limits when we act as if we were God and not merely as participants in God.

Theologians have long argued about what is the basic sin.[76] Some hold that pride is the chief sin, and they admonish us against domination, self-creation, or striving to be independent. Others hold that self-effacement is the basic sin, and they warn us against submissiveness, allowing ourselves to be defined by others, or having no identity apart from our roles or relations. The idea of participation I have proposed points beyond these positions. Domination—even domination by God—represents a failure in love. On the other hand, human autonomy is not sufficient. Our love for God and God's love for us lead not to the loss of self, but to a fuller self.

Similarly, the relation between God and humans has been badly conceived. Judith Plaskow criticizes Tillich for proposing an ontological monism in which religious persons aspire to unity with God, she thinks, because this unity leaves no place for one's own selfhood or for commitment to the further development of the world.[77] The opposite concern appears in the passionate protest of Max Scheler against classical theism's serenely independent God:

> When I ask within the theistic system: "Why am I living?", there is only one recurring final answer: for yourself, for yourself, for yourself! for *that* so-called eternal "blessedness." . . . But I can live only for something that is *more* than myself and beyond me. I must be able to *live* "for" this being, and I cannot do that for a being that is eternally already perfect, good, wise *and* almighty! This idea always throws me back on *my own self!* Rather, to live "for" God can only mean *in God*, with God, *to struggle and overcome*—insofar as in my power—for God's self-realization in the process of the world. . . . A human being is the being in which and through which the ultimate Ground grasps and as Divinity realizes itself. . . . I miss the unity, the zeal, and the worth of this goal in theism.[78]

Scheler protests that if nothing we do can really affect God, then, for practical beings like ourselves, our lives will become anthropocentric. We want to be united with and contribute to something larger than ourselves, but theism says that in relation to God nothing we can do makes a difference. So we end up doing good only for ourselves because—according to classical theism—we cannot do any good for God. Our own self-fulfillment becomes our highest, realizable goal.

I have steered clear of these problems by insisting that love-as-participation is a union that differentiates. The value and individuality of each participant is enhanced, not diminished, in love. Therefore, living for God is concomitant with growing individuality and uniqueness in both God and ourselves. As Rahner writes, "By the fact that a person finds God, that he falls, as it were, into the absolute, infinite and incomprehensible abyss of all being, he himself is not consumed into universality, but rather he becomes for the first time someone absolutely unique . . . he has a unique relation to God in which this God is *his* God, and not just a universal salvation which is equally valid for all."[79]

Mutual growth: As we have seen, the parental image for God has been common in Christianity: "I will dwell with them and walk among them. I will be their God and they shall be my people. . . . I will welcome you and be a father to you, and you will be my sons and daughters, says the Lord Almighty" (2 Cor 6:16–17). This image is apt for God's love. Parental love is (or can be) initially an act of love for a not-yet-existing being. Parents commit themselves to bringing into existence a being which, when real, will not and ought not wholly conform to their own designs but which will fulfill itself in unforeseeable ways through its freedom. Through their love parents unite themselves with the evolving destiny of their offspring in the direction of what befits the child and not merely what would suit themselves. Such is their love for their "creation," and such is God's love for God's creation. God's love is initially a love whose "object" is not yet, yet can be. What is "not yet" is brought into being and its very realization is an increase in value. God's love then continues to foster the distinct and quasi-independent being it has created. As Karl Barth wrote, "God is indeed the basis of all reality. But He is not the only reality. As Creator and Redeemer He loves a reality which is different from Himself, which depends upon Him, yet which is not merely a reflection nor the sum of His powers and thoughts, but which has in face of Him an independent and distinctive nature and is the subject of its own history, participating in its own perfection and subjected to its own weakness."[80] We have our own reality that is originated by God but then enables us to be original.

God's love for creation also brings about an enrichment in God. The Ground does not emanate, losing itself in history and then striving to return to itself, as in some forms of neo-Platonic thought.[81] Rather the Creator creates and thereby takes on a new relation to that which did not exist. On God's side, creation is not a loss, but a gain. Similarly, God redeems and sanctifies us, and thereby God enters into a further relation with us. That is, "the self-sufficient God willed in a free act of love to need a world which is his own history."[82] When we pray "Thy kingdom come, Thy will be done," we are not just praying, as Augustine would have it, for our own good.[83]

An array of dialectical statements follow from understanding the God-human relation as a form of participation. Let me list some: God is free to create, but the Creator is bound to that which God creates. God's identity is united with history, but not wholly identified with history. Human beings can share God's life, without becoming identical with God. In fact, human beings ultimately lose their own identities if they do not join their identities with God. God is supremely powerful, but God cannot force human freedom. Humans have an autonomy vis à vis God, but their freedom depends on God. God remains who God is, even as God becomes related to creatures and is thereby changed. Before God our value is as nothing, and before God we are exalted in dignity. God "has" all, but God does not have our freedom and therefore our selves before we give them to God. God "gets" our selves only by first "giving" God's self. Our relation to God makes a difference to God, even as God creates the difference between God and ourselves.[84] All this makes sense in a theory of participation: as love unites, it differentiates.

God Acts

The God who is related to us is a God who acts. We know *who* God is by what God does. I want to name some of these acts, at least in a general way. My long-term purpose in naming some of God's acts is to indicate ways that we can cooperate with God. I group these acts in a traditional clustering: God creates, saves, and sanctifies; and I add a somewhat novel element: God lives in transcendence.[85] Though, for analytic purposes, I distinguish these four, they should not be kept separate. For example, creation, whose locus classicus is in Genesis, is also depicted in a redemptive form in Isaiah 51:9 and Psalm 89:11–12. Similarly, Paul nicely mixes the creation, redemption, and sanctification: "This means that if anyone is in Christ, he is a new creation. The old order has passed away; now all is new. All this has been done by God, who has reconciled us to himself through Christ and has given us the ministry of reconciliation. . . . so that in him we might become the very holiness of God" (2 Cor 5:17–21).

God creates and sustains: God's love manifests itself, in the first place, as the power that lets us exist. As Tillich writes, "God is the power of being in everything that is, transcending every special power infinitely but acting at the same time as its creative ground."[86] In the realm of earthly causality, we can explain our existence as the "product" of our parents, our own efforts at health care, and the presence of a sustaining environment. But we also recognize that our own existence and the existence of all finite beings are in themselves both implausible and without an explanation. We exist, but we are not our own Ground.[87]

God's primordial covenantal love begins by creating and sustaining the world. "The Lord is true God. . . . who made the earth by his power, established the world by his wisdom, and stretched out the heavens by his skill" (Jer 10:10–12). In the Bible's preevolutionary view, God not only created in general, but God also created specific types of creatures, particularly animals and human beings (Gen 1:21, 27). God works like a laborer to fashion creatures (Gen 2:19–22). God carries on this activity, opening up rivers, planting trees, and giving breath to the people of the world (Is 41:18, 42:5). God's act of creation continues both in nature when God renews the face of the earth each spring (Ps 104:30) and in the human community where God has "called forth the generations since the beginning" (Is 41:4). Most importantly, God creates a people (Is 43:1, 15, 44:24).

For Christian life and Christian ethics, a focus on the original pattern created by God is not sufficient. God's creativity brings order into chaos, but the order that exists is by no means an infallible guide for us.[88] God wants to create new things that were not present in the original creation. That is, from the way things were and are, one cannot infer that this is the way they should be. "Remember not the events of the past. . . . See I am doing something new. Now it springs forth, do you not perceive it?" (Is 43:18–19, 65:17–25) The past, the first act of God's creation, needs to be open to the future. In other words, God's original design is not strictly normative if it is true that "the first heaven and the first earth have disappeared" and that "See I am making all things new" (Rv 21:15). Our own cooperative choices will correspond to God's original creation, but also to the new creation God is bringing about.[89]

God saves and sanctifies: God's salvific activity encompasses a variety of acts. God judges, preserves, liberates, forgives, restores, and reunites. Creation is still marred by a lack of freedom and an abundance of sin, deterioration, or alienation,[90] and God judges these evils (Is 9:6; 1 Cor 5:13). Israel has been from its youth a burden to be carried, but God will carry it to safety (Is 46:3–4). God's redemptive activity presupposes that something is wrong in creation and that God must still struggle against evil. God's reign is not yet achieved, and its victory will come about only in an uncertain future.[91]

The central act of the Hebrew Bible is God's liberation of Israel in the Exodus (Mi 6:4); God frees the people from their bondage (Dt 13:6). In itself, this act occurs not through a revolution or a restructuring of given society, as liberation theologies sometimes suggest, but by a release from slavery in Egypt and a flight to a new land. Redemption, however, is not a one-time act; rather, God redeems the Jews in order to make them a people with a history (2 Sm 7:23). Because of God's everlasting love, God again rescues the people from exile (Jer 31:3). Israel cannot save itself; only God enables it to overcome its enemies and be restored (Dt 9:5–6; Jer 31:4). Testifying that God continues to overcome sickness, sin, and death, Israel sings "The Lord is our savior" (Ps 130:8; Is 38:1–2, 16–17, 20). In the New Testament, it is Christ who redeems us from sickness, sin, death, and the "power" of darkness (Acts 5:31; Col 1:13–14). Jesus heals, and the goal of his healing is the forgiveness of sins and the restoration of relationships (Mt 9:1–8; 2 Cor 5:19; Eph 2:11–22). This redeeming activity not only restores creation to past wholeness but it also creates something new (Lk 6:6–10; Jn 11:26, 44).

Redemption is directed to a new covenantal relation with God.[92] Christian life is not a one-time event, but a process of sanctification or growth in holiness within communal life. Like Jesus, we are consecrated to God (Jn 17:17). Reconciled by Christ, we are "fellow citizens of the saints and members of the household of God"; we "form a building," a "temple, to become a dwelling place for God in the Spirit" (Eph 2:19–22; 1 Tim 3:14); and we are "a chosen race, a royal priesthood, a holy nation, a people he claims for his own" (1 Pt 2:9–10). We are exhorted: "Become holy yourselves in every aspect of your conduct, after the likeness of the Holy One who called you" (1 Pt 1:15–16). God continues to sanctify us.

God lives in transcendence: The God who creates, redeems, and sanctifies us also is the incomprehensible One who lives in transcendence.

Of course, transcendence is not a separate act of God. Rather it is an otherness that belongs to all God's acts. Even when we say that God is near, we must also say that God "dwells in unapproachable light, whom no human being has ever seen or can see" (1 Tm 6:15–16; Jn 1:18). On this topic perhaps we should simply say: Whereof we cannot speak, we ought to keep silence. Still, God's transcendence has implications for our cooperative activity, and so I must try to say something.

God's utter otherness is expressed in spatial metaphors: "Since the earth was founded [God] sits enthroned above the vault of the earth, and its inhabitants are like grasshoppers. . . . [God] makes the rulers of the earth as nothing" (Is 40:22–23). Before this God, fear and trembling are appropriate (Ex 20:18); and those who try to approach in an unauthorized way are destroyed by God (Lv 10:1–2; 1 Chr 13:9–10). God's awesome otherness is colorfully portrayed: "The frame of the door shook and the house was filled with smoke." Isaiah reacts, "Woe is me, I am doomed!" (Is 6:4–5). Though humans can keep the ways of God (2 Sm 22:22), there is another sense in which "as high as the heavens are above the earth, so high are my ways above your ways and my thoughts above your thoughts" (Is 55:8–9). Though God can be intimate and deal face to face with Moses (Ex 33:11–12), God also insists, "My face you cannot see, for no man sees me and still lives" (Ex 33:20–23; also 21:24). The cross symbolizes the fact that our God is not simply gracious but is also "aweful." We must all eventually surrender ourselves to something beyond this world, whether to empty absurdity or, as Christians say, to something real, but wholly beyond our personal good.[93] This tension between revelation and concealment, graciousness and awesomeness, immanence and transcendence, should be preserved.

These descriptions indicate something important: our God, who is near and for us, is also utterly distant and lives apart from us. God loves this world, but God also stands beyond and against this creation. Rudolf Otto is the twentieth-century thinker best known for trying to understand God's transcendent holiness.[94] Though his position is only half the truth—he pays insufficient attention to the immanent and life-giving presence of God—he well discusses the experience of God as one of a distancing awe, fear, and trembling. Something mysterious and transcendent about God remains after the immanent, affirming activity of God has been described. Making a related point, Reinhold Niebuhr warned "that the whole of modern culture tries too desperately to contain the ultimate within the fragmentary tasks and possibilities of history."[95] Thus, we should not limit God to God's immanent activity in our world.

We Cooperate

God's ongoing activity as Creator, Savior, and Sanctifier happens in and through us. We human beings can *cooperate with the ongoing activity of God.*[96] In fact, God's creative, salvific, and sanctifying activity cannot be complete without our cooperation. Our creativity cooperates with God's creativity, and without our cooperation the world will not be as God wants it to become. Without Mary—given what we know from contemporary biology—the Christ would not have been the Jesus of history. Similarly, the very meaning of personal salvation requires that no one can be saved without freely cooperating in that salvation.[97] We must choose to be involved with God who is creating, saving, and sanctifying the world. We human beings are not simply passive recipients of God's saving power. We cooperate in God's saving act.

In Israel, the judges and early kings continued God's activity: "The Lord raised up judges to deliver them. . . . he would be with the judge and save them from the power of their enemies" (Jgs 2:16–18; 2 Sm 9:16). Though the Lord hears the cry of the poor (Ps 86.1, 109:31; Jb 5:15; Jas 2:5), still the people must discharge God's predilection for the poor (Dt 15:11; 2 Cor 8:9). The very work of Christ continues in our own sufferings: "In my own flesh I fill up what is lacking in the sufferings of Christ for the sake of his body, the church" (Col 1:24). Peter continues Jesus' ministry when he heals the cripple (Acts 3:7–8), and Christians carry out God's activity of forgiving sins (Jn 20:22–23). In brief, God "has entrusted the message of reconciliation to us" (2 Cor 5:20, 7:10; also 2 Thes 2:14; 1 Cor 15:1–2; Acts 13:32). We are saved by saving others (Jas 5:20).

Similarly, our sanctification is a gradual process to which we contribute by our own consent to God's action in our lives. We are to be eager to "grow unto salvation" (1 Pt 2:2). We train ourselves in godly disciplines and do good deeds (1 Tm 4:7–8; Jas 2:22). We work out our salvation with fear and trembling (Phil 2:12). God inspires our desires and our own efforts (Phil 2:13) to follow the path to holiness: "Be imitators of God as his dear children. Follow the way of love, even as Christ loved you" (Eph 5:1–3). Thus, in Scripture, "the creature is a real co-performer in this humano-divine drama of history."[98]

We are not only liberated from evil; we are liberated for life. Among the many aspects of life, one frequently neglected aspect is the way freedom often manifests itself in enjoyment, delight, and playfulness. Admittedly, the biblical God is not very playful.[99] And Christianity has unfortunately given little encouragement to pleasure and play; often it has frowned on such activity; only rarely has it given a theological justification for it.[100] Still, those who are in love do delight and play, and Christians are in love. The comic is essential in a well-lived life.[101] Human life needs not only Hamlet, but also Falstaff. We can live in the sheer joy of spontaneous expressiveness; we can and should (if an oxymoron is permitted) live playfully. We can and should indulge in some of life's pleasures. In short, we can live with the freedom of children. Without such playfulness, Evans notes, "traditional morality goes sour. The virtues of dutifulness and rational control and sense of destiny and altruism and subordination of the body and mature realism all become vices, more destructive than creative in human life."[102] The process thinkers are right that God suffers with us; but God also plays with us, and we can play with God. God enjoys creation, and so can we. We can join that part of the mystical tradition that encounters God in "sheer vitality."[103]

Participating in transcendence: Finally, we can lovingly share in God's otherness since love, as we have seen, is not limited to the known. There is something profoundly Christian about other-worldliness. Though this aspect of Christianity has a long and respected history in Christian spirituality, it has been ignored in recent years. This other-worldly element has traditionally been expressed in the practice of asceticism, one of whose goals was to "free" us from being wholly this-worldly.[104] As Robert Doran writes, "We must acknowledge the small door that leads beyond the self and onto the other-worldly dimensions of the incomprehensibility of God."[105]

I propose that in ascetical acts we affirm and thereby participate in God's transcendence. Practices such as fasting or self-denial are usually understood as ways of repenting for sin, training ourselves in self-discipline, or making sacrifices for the sake of greater service. But these practices are also ways in which we affirm and unite with the God who is beyond this good creation. A sense of detachment that ignores prudent provision for one's own world-oriented self flows from this vision.[106] Bishop Kenneth Kirk remarks:

> The other-worldly and the this-worldly seem to have equal claims both upon theological statement and upon Christian behavior. But at least the thought of a transcendence of God over His creation, so infinite that in comparison all creation is as nothing, represents one factor in the Christian revelation as to which there can be no question. It

is to this factor that asceticism, or world-flight, in all its varied forms, has borne consistent witness.[107]

Detachment and renunciation have a permanent place in the Christian life, both for the individual and for the whole community.[108] This sort of renunciation distinguishes Christianity from secular humanism, naturalism, and pantheism, which can make no sense out of it. The limitation or denial of the three great goods of possessions, marriage, and autonomy, which are the focus of religious vows, give witness to the transcendence of God.[109] God is to be affirmed and adhered to even when doing so brings about no earthly good, or even when it may bring about some forms of earthly harm. The death of at least some martyrs brought about no obvious earthly good; indeed it may have only reinforced iniquity in the lives of their persecutors. But the martyrs witnessed to the God who is beyond life in this world. Jesus ended his rich and productive ministry "too soon" in his life. The cross stands as a symbol of all that relativizes, even by denying, worldly good in favor of the transcendence of God.

Still, while holding fast to an affirmation of the awesome otherness of God, we should, with Karl Rahner, add that this otherness is not the only or final word:

> A person who opens himself to his transcendental experience of the holy mystery at all has the experience that this mystery is not only an infinitely distant horizon, a remote judgment which judges from a distance his consciousness and his world of persons and things, it is not only something mysterious which frightens him away and back into the narrow confines of his everyday world. He experiences rather that this holy mystery is also a hidden closeness, a forgiving intimacy, his real home, that it is a love which shares itself, something familiar which he can approach and turn to from the estrangement of his own perilous and empty life.[110]

Mutual Cooperation

God is Lord of history. But since history is also dependent on our cooperative actions, God is dependent on our own contribution to history. That history is also really ours. The Jewish tradition well asserts that in our relationship with God we too can modify God's involvement in history (Gn 18:22–33). Four points must be kept in mind. What is needed is an understanding of our relation to God in which our own personal initiative and genuine contribution to God's activity in world history is not eliminated.[111] We cannot simply transfer our own often agonizing decisions and responsibilities to God.[112] Second, what is needed is an understanding of God that does not make the divine a secondary cause alongside of other secondary causes, perhaps with its own special, intraworldly rights and prerogatives.[113] God is the Ground of all creation, not a secondary cause in the world or a competitor with creatures.[114] Third, God must be understood in personal terms and not simply as "Cause," even Primary Cause. God's activity must be seen in a way that does not deny but rather invites human freedom. Fourth, as a person involved with history, God must be understood to be affected or changed by free human action.

Religious literature often has exalted God at expense of the human. In the past, the tendency was to say that God is the sole author of all that is good and we are the sole authors of all that is evil. The psalmist recounts "the deeds you did in . . . days of old: how with your own hand you rooted out the nations and planted them. . . . For not with their own sword did they conquer the land, nor did their own arm make them victorious, but it was your arm and your right hand and the light of your countenance, in your love for them" (Ps 43:1–4). As a prayer of praise, this is marvelous. As an example of humility before God, it is worthy. But as a complete theological statement it is false. Rather, in these battles the Israelites put "to the sword all living creatures in the city: men and women, young and old, as well as oxen, sheep and asses" (Jos 6:21). Without God they could not be victorious, but without their efforts there would have been no victory.

One should be suspicious of claims such as "following Christ implies death to self" or our personal desires should be "destroyed."[115] Serving God from the heart would be impossible if our self were dead or our personal desires destroyed. The ideal is not, as Meister Eckhart's metaphor would have it, to become completely empty like the air so that God's light can fill it.[116] The traditional claim that we should conform ourselves to God's will surely makes a valid point, but not if it means that we don't have an independent will and our own distinctive desires. God respects that difference; otherwise God does not love *us*. God does not simply love a (deficient) image or reflection of the divine self, but real persons who are other than God's self. Similarly, we should be wary of Germain Grisez's assertion: "Participation in the divine nature is not a human act. Therefore, Christian love itself is not a human act."[117] If our love is not a human act, it is not our love. As Rahner argues, "Both man's independence and his derivation from God are simultaneously given. . . . Total origin from God in every respect, and independent freedom" are two facts which cannot be inferred from one another, but which must be simultaneously held.[118] We cannot do what God can do, but only we can do what we can do. Thus, "the finite is not sacrificed to the infinite; rather, the finite and the infinite exist in complementarity."[119] We should put an end to using common expressions like "what one is doing is not one's own work but God's"[120] or God works *in nobis sine nobis.*[121] Past theology has often been blinded by fears of Pelagianism. Theology can acknowledge that human beings can take a dependent initiative with respect to God.[122] Jesus encourages us to knock and knock again; then God will answer (Lk 11:5–13).

Irreplaceable human contribution: It is obvious to Christians that Jesus is irreplaceable in God's scheme of salvation. What should also be asserted is that we too are irreplaceable—not, of course, for the whole of salvation, but for those aspects of it that can only be accomplished by us. No one else—not Christ nor his Abba—can do what we can do. As Roger Haight notes, "What we do not do to further the kingdom of God will not be done."[123] God can raise up other prophets, writers, wives. But just as a second wife cannot replace a first, so also another prophet cannot replace our own prophetic witness. The second wife may in many ways be a better wife, but she cannot be wifely in the way that the first woman was. To think that one woman could be replaced by another is to fall prey to abstractions: a wife is a wife. One never marries that abstraction; one marries an individual woman; and her individuality makes an enormous difference. Similarly, the contribution that each of us makes to justice or peace is irreplaceable. It is not an empty tautology to assert that without me God cannot do what God does through me.[124] Jesus encouraged his disciples to pray that the harvest master "send out laborers to gather his harvest" (Mt 9:38). Without these laborers, the harvest will not be reaped. In the struggle for justice, our role is irreplaceable: "Auschwitz has taught us that God will not, perhaps even cannot, effect the full redemption . . . unless human beings assume their appointed role of co-creators."[125] God can do other and better things through someone else, but God cannot act without me when it comes to those sorts of things that only I can do, chief of which is that only I can love as I love.

To the extent that we focus simply on the material results of our actions, to that extent it may be a matter of indifference who produces the result. It makes little difference in our assessment of the quality of a dress whether a woman or a man, a white or brown person, sat at the machine that sewed the dress. But we do care about who loves us, for each person's love is very different. And since we experience that God loves us through distinctly different persons, who they are is irreplaceable in mediating God's love.

Theanthropy: The basic theological vision of this book is at once theocentric and dependently anthropocentric. As Pope John Paul II has written, "The more the church's mission is centered upon man—the more it is, so to speak anthropocentric—the more it must be confirmed and actualized theocentrically."[126] I will call this vision "theanthropy."[127] God and human beings cooperate, but they act in different sorts of ways. In this perspective, God is not an outsider who intermittently intervenes. Nor is God simply the Primary Cause, acting on a different plane of being. Aquinas's distinction of primary and secondary causality solves the problem of border disputes between God and humans, and it allows them to cooperate, each in their own way.[128] But this way of describing our experience is still too cosmological. Whatever its metaphysical adequacy, it does not yet account for personal participation between God and ourselves. A personalist account also differs from Gordon Kaufman's God who, at times, seems to be simply the evolutionary process.[129] Similarly inadequate is Gustafson's theocentrism, which at times seems to picture God as an almost animal-like power that enables and makes demands upon us.[130]

I propose rather that God is preeminently a personal God who can and does love. Because God loves us, theocentrism must be replaced by a *theanthropocentrism.* Humans are called into a love partnership with this God. God, human beings, and their covenantal relation are central. "God has irrevocably bound Godself to humanity" and thus God needs us for what God will be and do in human history.[131] Accordingly, we must "take responsibility for the world."[132] In God's own way, God is the Lord of history, but we in our human way are also lords of history. Each of us is a "real partner of God."[133] Thus Mark Taylor writes,

> The qualitative difference between the absolute future and our present unjust world order demands that action be taken to create a more just and human innerworldly future. This is a human task, one that God Godself will not accomplish since . . . God does not intervene into the world process in such a fashion. . . . On the other hand, even though the task of creating a more just innerworldly future is a wholly human task and responsibility, nevertheless, it is God as the absolute future, as self-communicating love, that empowers us to create this new innerworldly future.[134]

"Theanthropic" ethics shares the concern of those who are theocentrists. Its first question is not an anthropocentric one: "What is my duty?" or "What do I have to do in order to be fully human and save my soul?"[135] Rather it asks, "Who is my God and what is God doing?" But since God's being and activity is love, then God's own being and activity is directed to and affected by us (though not solely to and by us). Asking about God leads to asking about our own freedom and distinctive identity because God has embraced these.

One traditional answer to the question, "Why did God make me?" has been "Man was created to praise, reverence, and serve God, and by this means to save his soul." The first half of this formula seems to suggest that God's primary purpose in creating us is God's own self-glorification, not our benefit. The second half is open to the reading that our worship of God is simply a "means" to our own self-fulfillment. Neither of these positions nor their addition seems adequate. One (admittedly awkward) revision might read, "God made us so as to love us and to invite us to know, love, and serve God and within this relation to do our part in God's act of saving the world including ourselves."

CONCLUSION

In this chapter, I have developed some implications of the concept of existential participation. I described this unity-in-difference as present in our relationship with ourselves, our neighbors, various social groups, and above all with God. God is our personal Ground who is bent upon our flourishing. God did not and does not bring about salvation without human cooperation. Jesus' death and God's resurrection of him manifested and realized their mutual union. The rhythm of God's love for Jesus, Jesus' response, and the unity that arises in these two loves, plus the salvific works of the reign of God that flow from this union, constitute the paradigm for our own moral and religious lives: God loves us; we accept that gift, and in return offer the gift of ourselves to God; God accepts our gift; we form a community of love with God; and we thereby can cooperate with God in the redemption of the world. In the next chapter, I shall extensively develop this paradigm.

NOTES

1. Claudia Card, "Gender and Moral Luck," *Identity, Character, and Morality,* eds. Owen Flanagan and Amélie Oksenberg Rorty (Cambridge: MIT Press, 1990), 211–13.

2. Paul Wadell, C.P., *Friendship and the Moral Life* (Notre Dame: Univ. of Notre Dame Press, 1989), 48–49.

3. Lisa Sowle Cahill, "A 'Natural Law' Reconsideration of Euthanasia," *Moral Medicine*, eds. Stephen Lammers and Allen Verhey (Grand Rapids: Eerdmans, 1987), 445–53. Karl Rahner, S.J., "The 'Commandment' of Love in Relation to the Other Commandments," *Theological Investigations* (Baltimore: Helicon, 1966), 5:439–59, develops this part-whole relation between the moral virtues and love.

4. This point is argued at length in Stephen Pope, *The Evolution of Altruism and the Ordering of Love* (Georgetown Univ. Press, 1994).

5. William Luijpen, *Existential Phenomenology* (Pittsburgh: Duquesne Univ. Press, 1969), 61. Some affections—the ones discussed by Luijpen—belong to the prepersonal dimensions, some to the personal dimensions.

6. Rahner, "The 'Commandment' of Love," 442–43.

7. Rahner, "The 'Commandment' of Love," 448–49.

8. Evelyn Eaton Whitehead and James Whitehead, *Marrying Well* (Garden City: Doubleday, 1983), 378–79.

9. Professor Harvey Cox once confessed, "I am a Baptist by birth, by inertia, and by conviction, in descending order of strength." He was only being more honest with himself than most of us.

10. See Edward Vacek, S.J., "Towards a Phenomenology of Love Lost," *Journal of Phenomenological Psychology* 20 (Spring 1989): 3–6; Edward Vacek, S.J., "Personal Development and the 'Ordo Amoris'," *Listening* 21 (Winter 1987): 197–209; also Max Scheler, "The Ordo Amoris," *Selected Philosophical Essays* (Evanston: Northwestern Univ. Press, 1973), 110–11.

11. Pierre Teilhard de Chardin, *Phenomenon of Man* (New York: Harper & Row, 1965), 262; cf. also Paul Tillich, *Systematic Theology* (Chicago: Univ. of Chicago Press, 1967), 2:65.

12. Jules Toner, *The Experience of Love* (Washington: Corpus Books, 1968), 134.

13. Max Scheler, *The Nature of Sympathy* (Hamden, CT: Shoe String Press, 1973), 18–19, 40–41.

14. In this sense, Rahner is correct to say, "Love is dialogal." Karl Rahner, S.J., "Love as the Key Virtue," *Sacramentum Mundi* (New York: Herder and Herder, 1970), 6:343. He overstates the point, however, when he insists that a response of return love from the beloved must be given, or else our love for them is not true or valid.

15. Max Scheler, *Formalism in Ethics and a Non-Formal Ethics of Value* (Evanston: Northwestern Univ. Press, 1973), 535–38; Scheler, *Sympathy*, 102, 159, 164–65; Max Scheler, *Schriften aus dem Nachlass: I* (Bern: Francke, 1957), 1:201; Max Scheler, *Schriften zur Soziologie and Weltanschauungslehre* (Bern: Francke, 1963), 90.

16. Edward Vacek, S.J., "Contemporary Ethics and Scheler's Phenomenology of Community," *Philosophy Today* 35 (Summer 1991): 170–74.

17. Scheler, *Sympathy*, 144, 164–65; Scheler, *Formalism*, 536–38; Max Scheler, *On the Eternal in Man* (Hamden, CT: Shoe String Press, 1972), 448; Max Scheler, *Ressentiment* (New York: Schocken Books, 1972), 106–8.

18. Linell Cady, "Relational Love," *Embodied Love*, ed. Paula Cooey et al. (San Francisco: Harper & Row, 1987), 143. Scheler similarly envisions the end of history: "The great invisible *solidarity of all living beings* with one another in All-Life, of all spirits in the eternal Spirit, and, at the same time, the *solidarity of the world process with the fate*

of the becoming of its highest ground and the solidarity of this ground with the world process"; Max Scheler, *Philosophical Perspectives* (Boston: Beacon Press, 1958), 105, 115.

19.   Scheler, *Eternal*, 382; Scheler, *Sympathy*, 70–71; Scheler, *Ressentiment*, 106–7; Max Scheler, *Schriften aus dem Nachlass: II*, ed. Manfred Frings (Bern: Francke, 1979), 2:193, 201, 262–63.

20.   Patricia Schoelles, S.S.J., "Discipleship and Social Ethics," *Annual of Society of Christian Ethics* (1989), 188–89.

21.   Bernard Cooke, "Non-Patriarchal Salvation," *Horizons* 10 (Spring 1983): 27.

22.   *Spiritual Exercises of St. Ignatius*, trans. Louis Puhl, S.J. (Westminster, MD: Newman, 1959), no. 167, p. 69; Jon Sobrino, S.J., *Christology at the Crossroads* (London: SCM Press, 1978), 403–4.

23.   Sobrino, *Christology*, 132–33, 389–90.

24.   Sandra Schneiders, I.H.M., *New Wineskins* (New York: Paulist, 1986), 28–33.

25.   William Werpehowski, "'Agape' and Special Relations," *Love Commandments*, eds. Edmund Santurri and William Werpehowski (Washington: Georgetown Univ. Press, 1992), 148–52.

26.   For a review of some of the debate over the question of the reality of groups, see James Donahue, "Ethics and Institutions," *Religious Studies Review* 17 (January 1991): 24–32. According to Jacques Leclercq, *La Philosophie morale de saint Thomas devant la pensée contemporaine* (Paris: Vrin, 1955), 308–9, Aquinas held that the community is "more divine" than the individual members of the community. Aquinas unfortunately also sometimes held (p. 332) that "the person is completely ordered to the good of the community of which s/he is a part."

27.   For further development, see Vacek, "Contemporary Ethics and Scheler's Phenomenology," 161–74.

28.   James Gustafson, *Ethics from a Theocentric Perspective* (Chicago: Univ. of Chicago Press, 1984), 2:145 (all in italics in the original).

29.   Pierre Teilhard de Chardin, *The Divine Milieu* (San Francisco: Harper & Row, 1968), 59, also 77.

30.   Stephen Rowntree, S.J., "Johnny Loves Mary Forever: What Therapy Doesn't Know about Love," *Beyond Individualism*, ed. Don Gelpi, S.J. (Notre Dame: Univ. of Notre Dame Press, 1989), 33–34; Charles Taylor, *Sources of the Self* (Cambridge: Harvard Univ. Press, 1989), 193–94.

31.   William Spohn, S.J., *What Are They Saying About Scripture and Ethics?* (New York: Paulist, 1984), 97.

32.   Joan Tronto, "Women and Caring," *Gender / Body / Knowledge*, ed. Alison Jaggar and Susan Bordo (New Brunswick: Rutgers Univ., 1989), 178–79; C. Taylor, *Sources of the Self*, 106.

33.   This organic metaphor properly highlights the unity of the group with its members. But it has a serious drawback. When an arm is cut from the body, the arm dies; but when persons leave their group, their lives may be diminished, but they do not die. At least in contemporary life, their lives may appreciably improve, as when a young adult leaves home to join other communities. Cf. Paul Tillich, *Love, Power, and Justice* (New York: Oxford, 1954), 92. Aquinas frequently fell into the trap of subordinating the individual to the group through organic metaphor; *ST* I.60.5, II–II.26.3; *Sententiarum*, 3.29.1.3.

34.   George B. Wilson, S.J., "Where Do We Belong?" *Studies in the Spirituality of Jesuits* 21 (January 1989): 9–10.

35. Joseph Allen, "The Inclusive Covenant and Special Covenants," *Selected Papers* (American Society of Christian Ethics, 1979), 96–102.

36. Willard Gaylin, *Feelings* (New York: Harper & Row, 1979), 59.

37. Wilson, "Where Do We Belong?" 7.

38. Allen, "Inclusive Covenant and Special Covenants," 114.

39. Maura Ryan, "The Argument for Unlimited Procreative Liberty," *Hastings Center Report* 20 (July/August 1990): 10.

40. James Whitehead and Evelyn Eaton Whitehead, "Obedience and Adult Faith," *Review for Religious* 49 (May/June 1990): 397.

41. Wilson, "Where Do We Belong?" 13.

42. John Mahoney, S.J., *The Making of Moral Theology* (Oxford: Clarendon, 1987), 343–45.

43. Oliver O'Donovan, *Resurrection and Moral Order* (Grand Rapids: Eerdmans, 1986), 167–69.

44. Lawrence Blum, "Vocation, Friendship, and Community," in *Identity, Character, and Morality*, 191.

45. Schoelles, "Discipleship and Social Ethics," 192–93, 196.

46. For a splendid account of covenant, see Margaret Farley, *Personal Commitments* (New York: Harper & Row, 1986), 113–35. See also Edward Vacek, S. J., "God's Action and Ours," *Emmanuel* (September 1984): 370–77. This covenantal ideal includes more than human beings; see James Gustafson, *The Contribution of Theology to Medical Ethics* (Milwaukee: Marquette, 1975), 31–33.

47. Mark Taylor, *God is Love* (Atlanta: Scholars Press, 1986), 390.

48. I shall concentrate on the acts of God. The attributes of God are the conditions of these acts. Thus, for example, God's infinity is nowhere named in the Scriptures; indeed, infinity has only relatively recently been attributed to God by an ecumenical council; see Leo Sweeney, S.J., "Presidential Address," *Proceedings of the American Catholic Philosophical Association* 55 (1981), 8.

49. Gustafson, *Ethics from a Theocentric Perspective*, 2:35.

50. Linell Cady, "Relational Love," 144.

51. Aquinas tried to hold two positions, one stemming from his Christian heritage and the other from Aristotelian metaphysics. On the one side, Aquinas held that names like Savior and Lord "signify the action of God, which is His essence. . . . God was not Lord until He had a creature subject to Himself." On the other, Aquinas held that these "relations applied to God temporally are in God only in our idea," that is, they have reality only "according to our mode of thinking" (*ST* I.13.7). I do not think these positions are compatible. Similar problems occur when Aquinas describes charity as a *mutual friendship* (*ST* II–II.23.1), but then fails to carry through the idea, and instead describes love for God as a kind of agape (*ST* II–II.23.6) or more commonly as a creaturely eros (*ST* II–II.23.7).

52. Louis Newman, "The Quality of Mercy," *Journal of Religious Ethics* 125 (Fall 1987): 167; William Werpehowski, "The Pathos and Promise of Christian Ethics," *Horizons* 12 (1985): 285–86.

53. M. Taylor, *God is Love*, 154. Taylor presents an unusually profound analysis of the problems addressed in this section. He rightly points out an internal tension, even contradiction, in the thought of Karl Rahner; through the help of process theology he points a way beyond these contradictions.

54. Karl Rahner, S.J., *Foundations of Christian Faith* (New York: Seabury, 1978), 222–23.

55. Lucien Richard, O.M.I., "Toward a Renewed Theology of Creation," *Église et Théologie* 17 (1986): 155.

56. Tillich, *Systematic Theology*, 1:61.

57. Langdon Gilkey, *Reaping the Whirlwind* (New York: Crossroad, 1976), 432; see also Enda McDonagh, "Love," *New Dictionary of Theology*, ed. Joseph Komonchak et al. (Wilmington: Glazier, 1987), 609.

58. Tillich, *Systematic Theology*, 1:245.

59. Rahner, *Foundations of Christian Faith*, 221–22.

60. Raymond Brown, *The Epistles of John* (Garden City: Doubleday, 1982), 555.

61. Alfred North Whitehead, *Process and Reality* (New York: Harper Torchbooks: 1957), 523–33. For a presentation of God as related, see Mary T. Rattigan, "The Concept of God in Process Thought," *Irish Theological Quarterly* 49 (Fall 1982): 206–15. For a critique, see Illtyd Trethowan, "The Significance of Process Theology," *Religious Studies* 19 (September 1983): 311–22; Robert Neville, *Creativity and God* (New York: Crossroad, 1980).

62. John Stacer, S.J., "Divine Reverence for Us," *Theological Studies* 44 (September 1983): 446; whether an immutable core may be so separated from living operations is questionable.

63. Walter Kern, "God-World Relationship," *Sacramentum Mundi* (New York: Herder & Herder, 1968), 2:405–6.

64. Teilhard de Chardin, *The Divine Milieu*, 62.

65. Karl Rahner, S.J., "Virtue," *Encyclopedia of Theology* (New York: Seabury, 1975), 1802; Rahner, *Foundations of Christian Faith*, 105.

66. Cady, "Relational Love," 144–46, in her attempt to avoid a patriarchal God tends to fall into naturalism. God is, she writes, "a symbol for the directional, integrative processes in life."

67. John Cobb, "The World and God," *Process Theology*, ed. Ewert Cousins (New York: Paulist, 1971), 165.

68. Rudolf Otto, *Idea of the Holy* (New York: Oxford Univ. Press, 1977), 12–33.

69. Karl Rahner, S.J., "Thomas Aquinas on the Incomprehensibility of God," *The Journal of Religion* 58 (Supplement 1978): S124–25.

70. John Pawlikowski, "Worship after the Holocaust," *Worship* 58 (July 1984): 326.

71. Gustafson, *Ethics from a Theocentric Perspective*, 2:319–20; Rahner, "Incomprehensibility of God," S107.

72. Carol Christ, "Reverence for Life," *Embodied Love*, ed. Paula Cooey et al. (San Francisco: Harper & Row, 1987), 51–64.

73. Louis Dupré, "The Christian Experience of Mystical Union," *Journal of Religion* 69 (January 1989): 4. Dupré also speaks (p. 6) of becoming "nothing" and of a "total displacement of the original center of meaning." These two are, I think, different. The latter is more acceptable.

74. Neville, *Creativity and God*, 82; Beverly Wildung Harrison, *Our Right To Choose* (Boston: Beacon, 1983), 112.

75. Compare Germain Grisez, *The Way of the Lord Jesus* (Chicago: Franciscan Herald Press, 1983), 582–83, who says of Christians, "They are God."

76.   Judith Plaskow, *Sex, Sin and Grace* (New York: Univ. Press of America, 1980), 172. From my limited experience, the distribution of typical sins does not very clearly follow the sexual lines that Plaskow sees.

77.   Plaskow, *Sex, Sin and Grace*, 109–10. This is not really fair to Tillich (*Systematic Theology* 1:245), who argues that God is the origin of both participation and individuation. For similar views see Rahner, *Foundations of Christian Faith*, 62–64.

78.   Max Scheler, *Schriften aus dem Nachlass: III* (Bonn: Bouvier Verlag Herbert Grundmann, 1987), 3:218–19.

79.   Rahner, *Foundations of Christian Faith*, 308–9.

80.   Karl Barth, *Church Dogmatics* 3/4 (Edinburgh: T. & T. Clark, 1961), 365.

81.   Leclercq, *Philosophie morale de saint Thomas*, 330, shows that the metaphysical law that all things return to their source is manifestly false.

82.   Rahner, "Virtue," 1802. See also Carol Jean Vale, S.S.J., "Teilhard de Chardin: Ontogenesis vs. Ontology," *Theological Studies* 53 (June 1992): 330–35; Henri Bergson, *Two Sources of Morality* (New York: Holt, 1935), 232–33, 243; Neville, *Creativity and God,* 83.

83.   Oliver O'Donovan, *The Problem of Self-Love in St. Augustine* (New Haven: Yale Univ. Press, 1980), 39–40.

84.   For a different view of participation, see Rahner, *Foundations of Christian Faith*, 78. For Rahner, the difference between God and humans is not created, but is God's own self; *Encyclopedia of Theology* (New York: Seabury, 1975), 1467. For myself, this difference comes to be through the relation; the relation arises at God's initiative.

85.   Roger Haight, S.J., "The Point of Trinitarian Theology," *Toronto Journal of Theology* 4 (Spring 1988): 198–200, reduces all three of these to salvific activity, and he seems to have little place for an unknowable otherness in God.

86.   Tillich, *Love, Power, and Justice*, 110–11.

87.   I am not implying a proof for the existence of God. As Rahner suggests, "Man is the question for which there is no answer." Affirming God's ineradicable incomprehensibility, Rahner suggests that the typical proofs for the existence of God are inadequate, since we cannot distinguish between the ultimately incomprehensible and the ultimately unintelligible. God is *not* for us the "intelligible simply in and through itself" which—at pain of otherwise falling into a regression into infinity—makes intelligible finite intelligibilities. Rather, the question of intelligibility must be given up and one loves, that is, one must "let himself fall into this incomprehensibility as into his true fulfillment." See Rahner, "Thomas Aquinas on the Incomprehensibility of God," S117, S123.

88.   In the Bible, contrary to the presentation of much natural law, the animals are not all oriented to human fulfillment, nor at times even their own fulfillment (Jb 38: 26–27, 39:9–18).

89.   It is one of the anomalies of Christian history that natural law theories have appealed to the doctrine of creation, i.e., God's making something new, to forbid any novelty and to support the status quo. That is, God was said to have created a permanent inviolable order which human beings must not change.

90.   For a survey of the biblical account of sin, see Piet Schoonenberg, S.J., *Man and Sin* (Notre Dame: Univ. of Notre Dame Press, 1965).

91.   Anne Carr, "'Not a Sparrow Falls'," *Proceedings of the Forty-Fourth Annual Convention of The Catholic Theological Society of America* 44 (1989), 32. The issue of theodicy cannot be raised here. God is working to overcome evil and bring about good. The

questions raised by Job remain, of course. And just as God does not really answer Job, but only puts him in his place, so I shall not attempt to answer such questions here, but only accept my bafflement before this conundrum.

92. This redemption is biblically understood in many ways, e.g., sacrifice, ransom, penal suffering, victory over evil powers. Many of these obscure an understanding of redemption as an act of God's love. See Daniel Day Williams, *The Spirit and the Forms of Love* (New York: Harper & Row, 1968), 39–40.

93. Otto, *Idea of the Holy*, 32.

94. Otto, *Idea of the Holy*, 12–33.

95. Reinhold Niebuhr, *Reinhold Niebuhr: His Religious, Social and Political Thought*, eds. Charles Kegley and Robert Bretall (New York: Macmillan, 1956), 442. Relevant here also is Tillich's comment: "If the holy is completely identified with the clean, and if the demonic element is completely rejected, then the holy approximates the secular. Moral law replaces the *tremendum* and *fascinosum* of holiness. The holy loses its depth, its mystery, its numinous character"; Tillich, *Systematic Theology*, 1:217.

96. Gustafson, *The Contribution of Theology*, 39; see also Edward Vacek, S.J., "John Paul II and Cooperation with God," *Annual of Society of Christian Ethics* (1990), 81–108.

97. Tad Dunne, S.J. "Trinity and History," *Theological Studies* 45 (March 1984): 149–50.

98. Karl Rahner, S.J., "Theos in the New Testament," *Theological Investigations* (New York: Crossroad, 1982), 1:110–11.

99. John Cobb, Jr., and David Griffin, *Process Theology* (Philadelphia: Westminster, 1976), 54–57. God seldom if ever is said to play (Zep 3:17–18), though there are some playful scenes including God (e.g., Gn 18). McKenzie "defends" the fact that Christ never laughs by saying no one in the New Testament ever laughs; John L. McKenzie, "Laughter," *Dictionary of the Bible* (London: Chapman, 1965).

100. For a (wrong, I think) claim that any attention to one's own pleasure is an evil love of self, see Jacques Croteau, O.M.I., "Le bel amour de soi," *Science et esprit* 38 (October 1986): 367–70.

101. Diane Yeager, "'Can't You See that I'm Dancing?' The Counterpoint of the Serious and the Ludic in the Life Well-Lived," *The Annual of the Society of Christian Ethics* (Waterloo, Ontario, 1984), 193–220.

102. Donald Evans, "Comedy and Morality," *The Annual of the Society of Christian Ethics* (Waterloo, Ontario, 1984), 222–24.

103. Evans, "Comedy and Morality," 223. See also, Edward Vacek, S.J., "Max Scheler's Anthropology," *Philosophy Today* 23 (Fall 1979): 245–47.

104. This affirmation of God's transcendence should be distinguished from a denial of the value of this world. In the pre–Vatican II Roman *Sacramentary* the post-communion prayer for the second Sunday of Advent unfortunately used to ask God to teach us "to despise the things of this earth" and "to love the things of heaven." The new *Sacramentary* for the same week improves this prayer when it asks God to teach us "to judge wisely the things of earth" and to "grant us in this life the good things that lead to the everlasting life you prepare for us."

105. Robert Doran, S.J., "Jungian Psychology and Christian Spirituality," *Review for Religious* 38 (1979): 865.

106. Vincent MacNamara, *Faith and Ethics* (Washington: Georgetown Univ. Press, 1985), 127–29.

107. Kenneth Kirk, *Vision of God* (New York: Harper & Row, 1966), 469–70.

108. Teilhard de Chardin, *The Divine Milieu*, 70–101.

109. Karl Rahner, S.J., "Reflections on a Theology of Renunciation," *Theological Investigations* (New York: Crossroad, 1982), 3:47–57.

110. Rahner, *Foundations of Christian Faith*, 131.

111. Matthias Neuman and Jesse Nash, "Authority, Obedience, and Personal Initiative in a Pluralistic Church," *Spirituality Today* 32 (September and December 1980): 218–36, 336–45. William Lynch, S.J., *Images of Hope* (Notre Dame: Univ. of Notre Dame Press, 1965), 156, colorfully describes the human component in the relation to God: "A concept of [God] that would be a greater compliment to God is that he is more truly God to the degree that he communicates his own autonomy to everything. . . . we can well imagine God exulting when man comes through with a wish of his own. And we can imagine him thinking: look at it go."

112. Richard McCormick, S.J., *The Critical Calling* (Washington: Georgetown Univ. Press, 1989), 213.

113. Carr, "'Not a Sparrow Falls'," 20–21; Josef Fuchs, S.J., "Das Gottesbild und die Moral innerweltlichen Handelns," *Stimmen der Zeit* 202 (1984): 373–82; McCormick, *The Critical Calling*, 213–14; M. Taylor, *God is Love*, 358.

114. Rahner, *Foundations of Christian Faith*, 86–89.

115. Gérard Gilleman, S.J., *The Primacy of Charity in Moral Theology* (Westminster, MD: Newman, 1959), 201–2. If the self that must die is only the sinful self, then the claim is rather obvious, though misleading.

116. Waldo Beach and Richard Niebuhr, *Christian Ethics* (New York: John Wiley & Son, 1973), 182, 193–94.

117. Grisez, *The Way of the Lord Jesus*, 601, (all in bold print); cf. James Keenan, S.J., *Goodness and Rightness in Thomas Aquinas's* Summa Theologiae (Georgetown Univ. Press, 1992), 142. The problem with this way of stating the divine-human relationship is that it makes us merely tubes or empty containers. We must preserve the unity-in-difference of participation. Charity is both God's act and our act.

118. Karl Rahner, "Grace and Freedom," *Encyclopedia of Theology* (New York: Crossroad, 1975), 601. Unlike Rahner who roots the divine-human difference in God, Gerry Heard, *Mystical and Ethical Experience* (Macon, GA: Mercer, 1985), 37, roots this difference in our sinfulness.

119. Marjorie Suchocki, "Openness and Mutuality in Process Thought," *Feminism and Process Thought*, ed. Sheila Greeve Dvaney (New York: Mellen Press, 1981), 70, 75.

120. Doran, "Jungian Psychology and Christian Spirituality," 503.

121. Peter Lombard's *Sentences*, cited by Otto Hermann Pesch, "The Theology of Virtue and the Theological Virtues," *Changing Values and Virtues*, eds. Dietmar Mieth and Jacques Pohier (Edinburgh: Clark, 1987), 83.

122. Gerald May, *Will and Spirit* (San Francisco: Harper & Row, 1982), 6, 234. May is convinced, however, that "the self-determined use of personal will almost inevitably leads to willfulness" (p. 259).

123. Roger Haight, S.J., "Foundational Issues in Jesuit Spirituality," *Studies in the Spirituality of Jesuits* 19 (September 1987): 35.

124. In this book, I do not try to explain how God acts through us. Avery Dulles, S.J., "Faith, Church, and God," *Theological Studies* 45 (September 1984): 549, makes this suggestion: "God who is present in every part of His creation, could gently direct mundane causes from within, somewhat as the mind directs the body in which it dwells. The success of God's activity would depend upon, without being determined by, the proper functioning of innerworldly agencies. Breakdowns at the lower levels could explain sin and evil, but higher achievements would be attributable to the divine influence." Similar claims are found in Richard, "Toward a Renewed Theology of Creation," 162.

125. Pawlikowski, "Worship after the Holocaust," 325. Pawlikowski's formulation in another essay ("Christian Ethics and the Holocaust," *Theological Studies* 49 [December 1988]: 656–57) seems to rely too one-sidedly on human beings: "Humanity must learn to save itself from future instances of holocaust, nuclear or otherwise. . . . Perhaps because of the freedom [God] has granted humanity He cannot do it." This position rightly affirms the distinctive role of human beings. But the issue is not mainly one of freedom. The issue is that God is—to use classical language—the Primary Cause, and hence God will not act as a secondary cause. But as Primary Cause, God can save us.

126. John Paul II, "Dives in Misericordia" (Boston: Daughters of St. Paul, 1980), no. 1; for an elaboration of his views, see Edward Vacek, S.J., "John Paul II and Cooperation with God," *Annual of Society of Christian Ethics* (1990), 81.

127. I adapt this phrase from Haight, "Foundational Issues in Jesuit Spirituality," 41. I do not find Haight's presentation fully convincing, however, because it draws exclusive lines between God and humans even as in other places it unites them. Thus he says (p. 33) that what is at stake in a decision "is not God's will but my will." Both are at stake. Haight denies that God has a specific will for history, but he seems to confuse this with divine determinism or predestination. He seems to hold that if a decision is mine, it cannot be God's, and vice versa. The point of this chapter on participation is to overcome that form of dichotomous thinking. Love allows for a unity-in-difference.

128. Mahoney, *The Making of Moral Theology,* 247.

129. Kaufman seems to hold that God is the "complex configuration of factors, powers, and processes (physical, vital, and historical)" or "this whole grand cosmic evolutional movement"; Gordon Kaufman, *Theology for a Nuclear Age* (Philadelphia: Westminster Press, 1985), 42, 44.

130. Gustafson, *Ethics from a Theocentric Perspective,* 2:269–70, says that animals have purposes but not intentions; and God, unlike human beings, likewise has purposes but not intentions. If Gustafson is correct in eschewing love language for humans and God—and the harshness of the world unfortunately gives abundant evidence for that position—then the present book is fundamentally mistaken; but then, I assume, so is Christianity, which describes God as one who so loved us that God sent the divine "Son" to share in our life.

131. Kaufman, *Theology for a Nuclear Age,* 45. How this position squares with Kaufman's more naturalistic understandings of God need not be explored here.

132. Sallie McFague, *Models of God* (Philadelphia: Fortress, 1987), 134.

133. Karl Rahner, S.J., "The Experiment with Man," *Moral Medicine,* ed. Stephen Lammers and Allen Verhey (Grand Rapids: Eerdmans, 1987), 232.

134. M. Taylor, *God is Love,* 400.

135. Bernard Häring, *The Law of Christ* (Westminster, MD: Newman, 1963), 1:35, 39–41, rightly argues against anthropocentrism. Kaufman, in *Theology For a Nuclear Age*, seems to take an anthropocentric position: "A supreme test . . . of the Christian symbols . . . is their capacity to provide insight and guidance in our situation today" (p. 28), and "Devotion to God and service to God are devotion and service to that which truly gives us our humanity" (p. 37).

4

Love of God as Foundation of Moral Life

Jesus replied: "This is the first: 'Hear, O Israel! The Lord our God is Lord alone! Therefore you shall love the Lord your God with all your heart, with all your soul, with all your mind, and with all your strength.' This is the second: 'You shall love your neighbor as yourself'. There is no other commandment greater than these." (Mk 12:29–31)

This chapter deals with the heart of Christian life. It addresses the original question that prompted this book. The question is simple: What is the relation between love of God and love of neighbor? That question raised two other questions: First, what is love?—a question that led to the previous three chapters; second, how can the disparate and conflicting things Christians say about love be organized?—a question that leads to the following four chapters. For this chapter, the primary question is: What does it mean to say God loves us and we love God? Oddly, all these questions—so central to Christianity—are seldom reflected upon in depth.

Traditionally Christians have claimed that yes, God loves us—that is why God creates and redeems us—but that no, God does not love us if that means that we make a difference to God, since God can in no way be affected by us. As to the second part, can we love God? Again a yes and a no were given. Yes, we should devote our lives to God's purposes, or even yes, we are metaphysically necessitated to love God; but no, we creatures can do nothing for God, or no, we sinners cannot really share divine life, or no, any love for God is God's action in us, not really ours.[1]

A frequently heard claim is that God loves us and *therefore* we should love our neighbor. The "therefore" is not obvious.[2] Often the first of the two great commandments is collapsed into the second. Paul makes little mention of the first commandment; in fact he says that the whole law is summed up in love of neighbor (Rom 13:10; Gal 5:14). And many of our contemporaries have, upon reflection, concluded that no intelligible meaning can be given to the phrase "loving God." They urge us to concentrate on "loving our neighbor," a task, they say, that is more than enough to occupy us.[3] Dan Maguire offers a variation on this approach:

"There can be no vertical love between us and God; we can only get to God horizontally through love of people."[4] Are these authors correct?

We can give these issues a twist: Why is it a sin against *God* that I do not love my *neighbor*? When David violated Bathsheba and had Uriah killed, he cried out, "I have sinned against God and you" (2 Sm 13:13). Contemporary Jewish theologians distinguish sins against my neighbor from sins against God; one does not need to ask God's forgiveness for the former, but only for the latter. It is clear how David harmed his fellow human beings, but how did he sin against God? Likewise, Christian theologians too seldom clarify why I must ask God's forgiveness for sins against my neighbor or—even more difficult—against myself.[5] Would it not make more sense to ask forgiveness solely from my neighbor or from myself? And, when I am reconciled to my neighbor, am I thereby reconciled to God, needing no recourse to sacramental confession or any other prayer to God for forgiveness? Conversely, when, through the sacrament of reconciliation, I become reconciled to God, do I also need to ask forgiveness from the specific person I have offended? In brief, what is the connection between God and neighbor and self?

In this chapter, I develop at length a simple schema: (1) God affirms us; (2) God receives us; (3) we accept God's love; (4) we affirm God; (5) God forms community with us; (6) we cooperate with God in loving God and the world; and finally (7) we grow in a limited coresponsibility with God. In short, this chapter examines the connection between grace and the moral life: "How can and ought we, who have been loved by God, live?"

GOD LOVES US

"God is love" (1 Jn 4:16). What does it mean to say that God loves us? We have many commonplace expressions for this noncommonplace miracle: God gives God's self to us; God accepts us; God offers a share in divine life; God shares our life; God communicates God's self to us; God opens God's self to us. While these and similar expressions are familiar, it is not clear what they mean nor whether they are consistent with one another. Some of the expressions are out-going, others indicate receiving. This is not surprising after what we have seen in Chapter 2 about the nature of love. Love has both an out-going affirming moment and a receptive moment.

I shall first treat God's affirmation and then God's reception of us. By "us" I mean both the community and every individual. From a Hebraic viewpoint, God's creative and providential activity is usually seen to be directed primarily to the people (Ps 100:3).[6] Social grace is prominent. But, particularly in the New Testament, God's grace can be given to individuals quite apart from their closest relationships (Lk 12:52–53, 18:29). Dramatically put, some will be chosen at the end time, while others will be left weeping in the fields (Mt 24:40). Thus, what is said below about "us" can and should be understood to be said, *mutatis mutandis,* about individuals, communities, and even the cosmos.[7]

God's Affirming Love

In Chapter 3, I described at some length the *central acts of God.* God's love for us is engaged when God acts as our Creator and Sustainer, and as our Redeemer and Sanctifier. All that was said there should be recalled here as contributing to the present discussion of God's affirming love. Here I want to focus on *our experience of receiving* God's love. I do so as a way of further clarifying the meaning of God's love for us. Love, we have seen, is an act of emotional participation that creatively affirms the beloved. In what sense is this true of God's love? I have argued that love in its active aspects is a form of self-transcendence directed (1) to union with a beloved (and therefore is not simply self-affirmation or self-expression) and (2) to the enhancement of the beloved. The second derives from the first. I want to make the same point here by proceeding in reverse order. I shall discuss two ways that we are enhanced, and I shall show how they point to the union God has with us. In brief the gift of our own life and the gifts of the material goods of creation point to a third gift: God's gift of self.[8] Since the first two kinds of gifts are in themselves highly ambiguous, they are not in themselves a conclusive proof of God's love. The full meaning of these gifts presupposes rather than proves God's love for us.

Our existence: We Christians typically give thanks to God for our lives. God's affirmation transforms the bare idea of us into a reality. That is, God creates us. God not only gives us existence, but also situates us with specific parents, culture, nation, and so forth. Our reality essentially includes a particular biological, psychological, cultural, and religious life. We are born within genetic, cultural, and religious traditions that long antedate our birth. Though we may and eventually ought to chose both our bodily life and these life-giving traditions, they give us an identity that is not of our own choice. They are given to us. We can destroy these gifts, e.g., through suicide or unbelief, but we meet them as already present in us.

To see our life as a genuine enhancement, we must see it as *good.* When we are given something that we deem evil, we do not experience *it* as a gift, though sometimes we are willing to overlook the "gift" and focus on the good intentions of the giver. Unfortunately, existence is not unambiguously good. It was not an atheist, but the author of 1 Peter 1:24–25, who quoted Isaiah 40:8 to make the point that "all mankind is grass, and the glory of men is like the flower of the field. The grass withers, the flower wilts." Most people are grateful to be alive, but some people are unhappy they exist. To some contemplating suicide, life seems a curse, not a gift. Similarly, the genetic, cultural, and religious traditions we have received are not unambiguously good. For example, those who reject the "gift of faith" sometimes do so because this "gift" seems more a suffocating prison than life-giving fresh air.

Furthermore, the fact that we have a good life does not necessarily imply that it was given to us as a gift of love. Sadly, many human beings are conceived by "mistake," and the pregnancy and subsequent birth owe more to biological processes and social forces than any desire someone had to give a gift. One non-Christian view of God is that God necessarily creates, i.e., God creates not out of love but out of a necessity of God's own being. It is thinkable that the Creator created us *not* because the Creator wanted to love *us*, but as an overflow of divine goodness or even out of an arbitrary whim. It has even been imagined that the Creator is a malevolent god who created us because our existence makes possible greater suffering or evil. After Auschwitz, some suggest, the evidence favors a perverse god who created us able to experience some love, laughter, and pleasure so that isolation, misery, and pain are all the more cruel. Human life is ambiguous enough that no definitive refutation can be made of these alternative views. The fact that we are alive, even the fact that we experience our life as good, does not prove God's love. Nothing outside of the experience of love itself can "prove" love.

We Christians, of course, understand our existence, broadly conceived, as an act of God's creative goodness whereby we advance from nonbeing into being. We experience contingency to mean that, out of a myriad of possible persons, we have been and are chosen to exist and to grow (Col 3:12). We experience our lives as fundamentally good and destined for fullness, not frustration. We experience our various traditions as positively formative contributions to our identity. In brief, we experience God as a gracious Creator, even if also as an awe-evoking Abyss.[9] Even when we experience sundry evils and limitations, including death, we trust that these losses and threats and defeats will not be finally victorious, but will "somehow" open up new, perhaps wholly unsuspected possibilities for life.[10] "Hope springs eternal." We experience this hope as arising in us from something beyond ourselves and this world since neither we nor this world give sufficient reason for that hope. Thus, in appreciating our very lives, we experience God's loving affirmation.

To speak of our existence as a good gift, then, is itself an interpretation of faith. This is a bold interpretation, not fully supported by just looking at our lives apart from God. We confidently interpret our lives as truly good for us only because we come to see that the final meaning of goodness is to be in a love relation with God. Like two human beings in love, we are confident that we have all that we finally need if only we are with our beloved. Unlike the love between two human beings, our confidence is anchored in a love partner who cannot be destroyed by the many contingencies and tragedies of human life.

Sustaining world: Christians typically give thanks not only for their existence, but also for the world that sustains them. Our lives are constantly nourished and enriched by a vast array of goods. We have a world that can satisfy our needs for air, light, food, drink. We have a world that offers scope for intellectual curiosity and an exercise of our talents. Through the process of evolution, we have evolved as creatures who find this world a home. We Christians see this sustaining world as the way that God sustains us. We thank God for sun and sea, for wine and wool. We also can and do thank God for all the things we have made with our minds and hands, since we include these human products among the ways that God sustains us.

Still, two questions, parallel to those about our existence, can be asked. The first question is whether this sustaining creation is really *good?* If not, it is not really a gift. Some Christians optimistically argue that, since God looked at all God had made and found it good (Gn 1:31), then all things are good for us (cf. 1 Cor 6:12). Others more soberly see evidence that leads them to hold that things are on the whole not for our good; they say we don't need the second law of thermodynamics to realize that over time all things fall apart and we don't need Darwinian theory to tell us that this is a hostile world. Still others hold that the world has no overall meaning; rather, it begrudgingly yields to us only what we make of it. Karl Rahner wisely warns Christians against a glib affirmation of God's goodness in giving us this world: "We cannot now speak of God's love for us as though we were addressing men who have repressed all their experiences of the absurd and are so comfortably well-balanced that they find it very instructive to be told that the world is on the whole very well ordered and governed by a God of love."[11] In fact, the case can be made that atheism, Manicheanism, or polytheism (with its friendly and unfriendly gods) each quite plausibly fit our experience of this mixed bag we call our world.[12]

We Christians can admit that, viewed from *outside* our love relation with God, our explanations of the problems of absurdity and evil may seem highly contrived. To those who pride themselves on being "hard realists," all our attempts at theodicy will seem nothing more than the rank refusal to face the obvious. What the outsiders fail to see is that the "fact" of God's love is not really a "conclusion" we draw after examining all the evidence of good and evil. Rather, it is more a primal conviction, born in certain individually and communally experienced encounters with God, that then serves as the interpretive key for all other positive and negative experiences. Having experienced God's love, we are convinced that the world is God's good gift. We are also convinced that, somehow, new possibilities will be forthcoming even from the evils we experience. That is, we are confident that God's love somehow will find a way to bring good, perhaps of a different kind, out of darkness and evil. We are like Job: no matter how bad things get, we still trust that our redeemer lives (Jb 19:25). We trust that this world, for all its evils, is not a bad joke.[13]

A second question is whether the world's sustaining goods really are given to us *out of love* for us. The fact that, so to speak, something good and useful has plopped into our backyard does not necessarily imply that someone loves us. Many atheists are "grateful" for life's goods, without being grateful to anyone. Some people would prefer to do as much as possible without these goods if enjoying them created obligations, in particular, the obligation to serve God. Thus, the world's goods seem to many to be here by sheer accident, while others fear that these goods are the way God secures our servitude. Even theists have imagined that God established a good material world, not out of love for us, but for some other reason, e.g., so as to enjoy the drama of human interaction or to create an object of beauty or just as a form of play. Nevertheless, we Christians do see this world as God's sustaining gift. It is our prior experience of God's love that gives us reason for doing so. I turn now to that experience of God's love which is presupposed for seeing both our existence and the goods of the world as gifts of God's love.

Union with God: Does God love us? We Christians believe God does. We may rely on the testimony of Scripture, tradition, or our present community for this belief. This testimony, however, seems itself to be a reflection on both individual and communal experiences of God's love. If we are not only to understand but also authentically believe this testimony, we must ourselves have some experience of that to which these witnesses point. That is, we must experience God's love for our own selves. Since our own experiences of God's love frequently occur during prayerful reflection on the goodness of our existence and of the material world, I have begun with these two gifts. Now I turn to the experience of being loved itself.

Theology in the past commonly held that God created us, but that God could (and, before Christ, did) withhold God's gift of self to us.[14] Recent Catholic theology, however, has argued that the only God we know, the Christian God, creates and sustains us in order to unite with us. God cannot love *us* if we do not exist. Thus, God creates and sustains us in order to give God's own self to us.

What does it mean to give one's self? What does it mean for persons to give, not some good thing to represent themselves, but their very own selves? Indeed, is the latter even possible? Rahner writes, "It is decisive for an understanding of God's self-communication to man to grasp that the giver in his own being is the gift."[15] Though Rahner's phrase "self-communication" is oft repeated, its exact meaning is seldom made clear by either Rahner or others who use this phrase. The gift of one's self is different from the two kinds of gifts I have discussed. Parents may "give" their children new life, but not give themselves. Someone may be unable to give us any of the world's goods, but still love us very much.

A gift of one's self, love, is the act of uniting one's self with the beloved. When someone gives himself or herself to us, we become aware that we do not live our lives alone. We may resist his or her presence in our lives or we may welcome it, but it is now a given inviting some response. When we are aware that the someone who has united with us is that Someone who is the source of the universe, then we experience this presence as God's love. We feel we belong to One to whom the universe belongs; and at the same time, we have the experience that this One has chosen to belong to us. We experience that all our activities, to the degree that they are good, are ways of embodying the goodness of this divine Presence. God is experienced not as an outsider who does good things for us, but as one who shares life with us. Such is God's love for us.

God's love means that God transcends God's *aseity* and enters our life. God unites God's own self with our self and thereby makes God's own self available to us. The God who is Being, Life, Power, Light, and Love enables us to be, to be alive, to be effective, to know, and to love. In exercising these acts, we can, if we are sensitive, experience ourselves both as original sources of these activities and, at the same time, as united to and drawing from an Ultimate Source whose very nature is these acts. In exercising these acts, we develop in depth our distinctive selves, even as we sense that whatever depth we have itself opens out into and belongs to unfathomable Mystery. We feel ennobled, but we sense that our glory springs from the fact that God is united with and active in us. God says to each of us, "You are my beloved son [or daughter]. On you my favor rests" (Lk 3:22). Affirmed as a member of God's family, we rejoice that we belong to the divine. We are created, sustained, redeemed, and sanctified because God is with us. These experiences reflect the active, affirming aspects of God's love for us.

God's Receiving Love

Love is not only an affirmation. Love also means receiving the beloved into one's self, i.e., being affected. God's love of us implies that we make a difference to God. When one embraces, one is also touched. As Walter Brueggemann puts it, our God is

> the God who embraces. It is central to covenant that this One cannot embrace without being transformed by the ones who are embraced. There is no immunity for God here; embracing a partner is not an afterthought, but is definitional for God. . . . The conventional God of the catechisms makes all his caring moves *after* everything is settled and there is nothing at stake for the Strong One. But here it is affirmed that not everything is settled in advance. Very much is at stake for God; his godhood is recharacterized and redecided in company with and in the presence of the mixed multitude. That is the deep issue in covenant.[16]

Love not only means that I will live on behalf of your life, but also that I will be affected by your successes and failures. It not only means that I will so act as to increase your life, but also that your good becomes part of my own life. By God's own "bestowal," we become not just intrinsically valuable, but also important to God. Love creates a "need" for the beloved. God is motivated not only by God's own goodness, but also by that which God has created, sustained, and graced. God repeatedly says to Israel and to us, I will be your God and you will be *my* people. God is *interested* in us, not like a baseball statistician but more like a player-coach. As Lucien Richard notes, "God cannot be understood as alone significant to the world. The world and human history are also significant to God."[17]

God's sharing in our life includes empathy and compassion for us (Is 63:15).[18] God moves beyond detached self-containment and becomes vulnerable in taking on our vulnerability. God suffers with us.[19] God becomes concerned for our humanity with all its troubles and finitude (Phil 2:5). Otherwise it is only anthropomorphic exaggeration to say that God *loves* the world. As Michael Gilligan writes,

> The mainstream of Christian theology has not adequately accounted for the receptivity of God in his relations of love with his creatures, that if God is not open to being affected by his creatures as well as to effecting them, much of Christian piety as well as the teaching of Scripture must be reduced to mere metaphor. For God's goodness to correspond to the Christian image of perfect love, his experience must be able to be determined by the lives of finite beings as well as they are determined by his. And such a relation of reciprocal love requires that the creatures be . . . able to be sources of novelty and surprise to which God can respond in joy and . . . sorrow and even anger, in a manner analogous to that described in Scripture.[20]

God does not solely love God's own self. Rather God loves *us*, and that means that who we are and what we do make a *difference* to God. God's being and action are modified by us and our actions.[21]

Love for persons, we saw in Chapter 2, means not only affirming the beloved but also, at the same time, receiving the beloved as a focus for one's own heart and mind. We have seen that for Aquinas love means an ecstasy in which our own hearts are melted and the being or form of the beloved becomes a principle or form for the lover's own self. Again, love means not only I "in-you" me but also I "in-me" you. Margaret Farley rightly observes, "Love testifies to the reception of the beloved in the life of the one loving, and by commitment the one who loves yields to the beloved a new claim on his or her love. Such 'yielding' is indeed a surrender, at once eminently active and yet passive. By it one places oneself by one's own action into a relationship whereby one will be acted upon as well as act. One will be claimed, called, at the disposal of another."[22] Most people might agree that our love for God should be like this. But if God loves us, the same is analogously true of God. Otherwise, I suggest, God does not love us.

Unity-in-Distinction

Love is a form of participation, a unity-in-difference. God does not lose divinity in uniting with Jesus' humanity, and Jesus does not lose his humanity in his union with the divine. Similarly, when God gives God's self to us, God does not lose God's self. The oft-repeated gospel maxim that in losing ourselves we gain ourselves (e.g., Lk 9:24), though it refers to disciples, also reveals something about God. When God gives God's own self, God gains a new self. God "belongs" to more than just God. God becomes related to us, bent upon our flourishing, especially that flourishing that is a friendship with God. The act of creation not only brings into reality something outside of God; it is also an act of self-determination in which the One who was not eternally our creator *becomes* our creator.[23] God's act of love modifies God's self to be lover-of-us.

God's acceptance of us does not, of course, entail that God approve of us wholly as we are. It does not mean denying our sinfulness. God loves us even as God judges us. Because of love, God is interested in overcoming the discordance between ourselves and God.[24] Overcoming discordance and living in communion, however, should not be understood as eliminating the difference between God and us. If God loves us, God affirms and enables our own dependent autonomy. God wants us to be free, and that means to determine our own lives. God's love does not take away our responsibility nor abolish our own unique dynamism. Rather, it accentuates both. God wants us to freely do our part to overcome our alienation from God, and that means no merely forensic forgiveness is sufficient.

Two alternatives should be avoided. Theologians often write that Christians are "those who seek to do their Lord's will rather than their own."[25] On the other hand, Aquinas surprisingly argued that, in the actual details of our lives, we should *not* live in strict conformity with the will of God.[26] He gives the example of a woman who should love her children with a partiality that God does not have since God loves all in terms of the common good or since God has greater love for better persons. The truth, an adequate theory of existential participation insists, lies in neither of these claims. Rather, when allowance has been made for the fact that God is not another finite creature and that therefore God's will is of a different sort, then both God's will and our own will have their respective contributions to make to every decision we make. Because God's love affirms *us*, we can and should exercise our own will. We do not have exclusive alternatives: either God's will or our own. Out of love for us, God wills what we properly will. God affirms our authentic freedom.[27]

Still, Aquinas's separation of our legitimate will from God's has a point. God is the God of the universe and the God of the whole human race, not simply our God. God's love for us will appear faithless if it is taken to mean that God will always promote our own good regardless of the cost to others or regardless of the natural laws of the world. Rather, God's faithfulness means, negatively, that God will not reject us even if God cannot support our further flourishing on earth; and, positively, it means that no matter what our fate God will cherish us. The relation between God and ourselves will often not be for our own immediate or long-term earthly good. The cross did not promote Jesus' earthly life. The death of a small child is not obviously good for the child. Suffering often "does not build up and develop its victims; it corrupts, corrodes and destroys them."[28] What is essential is only that God and we human beings participate in one another, whether in life's goods or ills, whether in living or dying. God's love for us, as for Jesus, assures us that God will not finally deny us, but it does not assure us that we will not have to sacrifice, suffer, or die a tragic death.

The Bible does not hide these harsh realities. Rahner soberly counsels: "There must be a deep solidarity with a world in torment before one dares speak of the love of God."[29] In Farley's brutally frank words: "God does not always do the deeds that are expected, even when they are desperately needed. . . . God appears not only as one who does not fulfill what is promised but as one who abandons, uses, excludes, conspires against, defeats, hands over to be raped and killed."[30] God's love is powerful, but it does not always promote our earthly flourishing. In this sense it may well be true: we may be more faithful to the individual purposes of God than God can be to ours. Many Jews at Auschwitz were faithful to God, even when God and most of the rest of the human race appeared to have abandoned them.[31] God's identity is not wholly bound up with promoting our well-being. God's promise is that God will be with us, loving us, but not loving only us. God's promise is also to be with us as we struggle with the evils that are not from God's hand. Even if we are defeated in this struggle God is still with us, and that is more than enough.

WE LOVE GOD

We cannot win God's love by our works, but God also cannot win or command our love simply by doing good things for us or even by offering God's own self. Our free reception and consent is necessary. We must be willing to dwell in God and live ecstatically in and for God. This self-transcendence, however, is initiated, enabled, and directed by God's prior love for us. Put in terms of familiar quotations, Pascal's "We would not seek you, Lord, if you had not first found us" is a more adequate starting point than the popularly cited "Our hearts are restless until they rest in Thee."[32]

We Accept God's Love

When God loves us, then, in Tillich's language, we must accept that we are accepted.[33] Admitting our dependence, finitude, and sinfulness, but also our goodness, we feelingfully accept that we "matter to Someone," that our simplest and most complex strivings toward the good and evil make a difference not only to ourselves but to God. We can refuse to accept all this. We can intellectually acknowledge God's self-offer, but not allow it to emotionally touch us. We can allow it to make some difference, as long as it does not require us to make any major changes in our affections. Or we can acknowledge, affirm, and consent to it, and thereby be transformed. We can emotionally accept that "we belong to God" (1 Jn 4:6). We can accept that, because God unites with us and accepts us, *our lives and actions are no longer merely our own.* To speak with a maternal metaphor, we consent to eat for two.[34] We accept the responsibility of our own place in God's life.[35]

We who receive God's self-gift must embrace it for what it is, namely, a free Person; therefore we cannot dispose of this gift as if it were something that we possess. If we try to turn this gift into a thing, we not only act blasphemously, but we also lose the gift, since personhood, above all, divine Personhood, is lost when it is treated as something at our disposal. Rather, we yield to God the power to personally influence us. God's self-offer is a call to our freedom, a call to determine our identities as persons who are related to God.[36] Accepting God's love means a transformation of our self, a readjustment in which our emotions, beliefs, and actions are reoriented around a new focus,[37] namely, God and our relation to God. We can resist God's initiative and our dependence, or we can accept the presence of God as codeterminative of who we are. This acceptance transforms and enlarges our capacity to receive.[38] If we are open to fully accepting God's self-gift, we find that we grow in ways unimaginable outside our relation with the Ultimate of our lives.

There has been a tendency, found in some Protestant thought, to insist that we should accept that we are accepted in spite of the fact that we are wholly unacceptable. A Catholic view, which I share, holds that we should accept that we are accepted, even if at present all we can feel is that we are unacceptable. The Catholic view is that God does indeed find something worthy of love, and we can too. Since love is essentially related to the good, accepting that we are loved means acknowledging that God sees value in us.[39] Not all who are loved can emotionally accept that they are loved. To do so would be to admit that they have an intrinsically valuable self, and their self-hate rejects this. At the very least, we must accept God's love for us as one creature or human being among many, much as each person in a large gathering may feel honored when some dignitary graces the group with a visit. More personally, we can experience God's love as *for our unique self.*

Full acceptance of God's love requires not just acknowledging God's goodness, but also being genuinely affected by God's gift.[40] An emotional acceptance of being loved is essential to a full Christian life. Aquinas rightly insists that being loved is less important than loving.[41] Still, those authors who recommend complete "selflessness" render difficult or impossible an experience of God's love for us. The experience of being loved should be gladly welcomed and savored; it should not immediately be converted into a duty or power to love others. Rather, empowerment for service typically derives from letting ourselves feel loved and therefore good. As John Stacer writes, "Our human sense of worth is amplified by being mirrored back to us through the divine cherishing." As an overflow of a sense of our goodness we are enabled to love. Because of God's love for us, we are freed both to accept who we are and to transcend ourselves and be generous toward others. "We experience our best selves in the presence" of God's love.[42] We feel uplifted by the enlivening presence of Someone pure and good. We feel challenged to change when we see how our imperfection and sin keeps us apart from the One we most want to be near. Accepting God's love undergirds our self-confidence, openness, and sense of responsibility. Ann Belford Ulanov describes this experience at length: it is

> an experience of our own particular I-ness made possible, supported, caught up in something greater than ourselves. We feel our I-ness in touch with what is, what matters at the heart of things; we feel united around a core. We know ourselves linked up with a greater being, one which is endless and unfathomable, so that we cannot define it but can only walk around it, telling of it. A feeling of spaciousness pervades, of circulating life and breath, indeed of something breathing into and through our own breath, making us feel alive in body, mind, heart. The dualities of subject and object are softened, made unimportant. We live in an other and that other lives in and through us, yet a sense of self relating to other—not becoming other—persists vibrantly. A joyous sense of being alive and living creatively exists. . . . Henceforth we do not do good works or act helpful but rather live,

one with another, in the presence of this live center that holds us all together and in being. . . . Our motivation for the good thus differs radically from good works done out of guilt, fear, aggrandizement, or urges to power. Theology describes this experience as grace.[43]

This grace is our "justification" or "righteousness." This experience of being loved offers an alternative to extrinsic or forensic views of salvation. To be saved is to accept that we make a difference to God. To be saved is to yield to the uplifting power of being loved. To be saved is to feel unworthy of love, yet also to feel important in the eyes and heart of the one Person who finally matters. To be saved is "participation, reunion overcoming the powers of estrangement."[44] To be saved is to be liberated from the constrictedness of our lives.[45] It is to let go of our typical and cherished ways of interpreting ourselves and our world; it is to cease trying to prove or justify ourselves; it is to step outside the security and approval gained by acting in accord with law.[46] To experience salvation is to accept Another's affirmation of ourselves and our world, an affirmation that is not contingent on our success in negotiating the trials and triumphs of life.

Once again, let it be added, this salvation is not merely individual. God saves Israel, the Church, the world. That is, God can and does love "corporate persons." The universal Church or a local church can feel blessed and uplifted by God's love. God is felt to be with them as a community. The members of the group can accept that they live not simply in themselves nor simply in their relations to other groups. Rather, as a group they live in relation to God. Then the group too no longer needs to be preoccupied with itself, with "turf questions." It can be moved beyond its own tendencies to exclusivism or self-preserving structural rigidity. It can even dare to lose its life for the sake of others.

Accepting that we are beloved daughters and sons of God brings freedom. In allowing ourselves to feel loved and therefore affirmed by God, we no longer have to anxiously protect ourselves against rejection. We can let go because even if we fail in our efforts, even if we are crushed by fate or by our enemies, or even if some of our decisions are wrong, still we are loved by God. The acceptance of being accepted means that, like the prodigal son, we know we always have a Parent waiting to embrace us (Lk 15:11–32).

To be saved is, of course, something that we cannot do for ourselves. But the reason we cannot is not simply our own helplessness. Rather we cannot accomplish our salvation because we cannot make another love us.

We are dependent on God's first loving us. On the other hand, since our salvation is a personal relationship, God cannot save us without our consent. God saves us through us. Albert Nolan puts it well: "To say that salvation is both God's responsibility and ours does not mean that salvation comes partly from God and partly from us. . . . salvation comes totally from God and totally from human beings."[47]

We accept God's *love which is active in us* in diverse ways. God's love for us is *experienced* as *judgment* insofar as we emotionally acknowledge that we are living in discordance with One who is pure and good. It is experienced as *justification* insofar as we accept this love and are converted to want to live in relation to God. It is experienced as *sanctifying* insofar as we consent to being drawn into ever closer union with God. It is experienced as *actual* grace—inviting, challenging, and enabling us—insofar as we accept being moved to actively transform ourselves and our world. And it is experienced as *beatifying* insofar as we relish the concordance of our lives with God. The completion of a covenant with God requires our return love, and to that I now turn.[48]

We Affirm God

When we accept that we are accepted by God, we feel more intensely both our distance from God and a new sense of our goodness and wholeness. Furthermore, the conditions are set for our response. It is logically possible for God to love and take responsibility for the beloved and thereby be modified by it without, however, allowing the beloved to freely respond in kind. This is the case with the material world. Such is not the case with us. God wants us to respond and to do so in an analogously person-to-person way.[49] We are invited to love God in return. In so doing we follow Christ who gave himself as "an offering to God" (Eph 5:2).

It is also possible for us, upon learning of the love God has for the world, to say, "So what?" What sort of "logic of the heart" leads us to love those who love us and to love what they love? Our earlier phenomenological investigation indicated that we are predisposed to love those who love us. There is a prevoluntary movement of our own spirit to unite with those who have united with us. We accept their union with us, and we are inclined to consent to its life-giving affirmation. To be sure, we can resist or reject this movement, just as we can reverse our bodily predisposition to walk forward rather than backward. Thus, we are disposed to respond in love to God, even though we can resist this tendency. God's love invites and enables but does not, because it cannot, force a response. God's invitation continues even if we refuse to respond, since the nature of love is to love forever. But, feeling loved, we can respond affirmatively. We can offer ourselves to God. Feeling that we already belong to God, we can consent to and affirm this belonging. We can transcend ourselves and our finite lives and unite with the divine dynamism and destiny.

What does it mean to say, "We love God"? The answer is not easy. Indeed many accounts deny, remain silent, or speak only vaguely about our act of love for God. Gene Outka says that "love for God cannot be part of the content of agape as an ethical principle, since in relation to God the agent has nothing whatever to do."[50] He adds, "Much Protestant literature reflects misgivings about direct love for God and transposes it altogether to neighbor-love."[51] Matters are not much improved in traditional Catholic ethics. Germain Grisez writes, "The commandment to love is the demand to keep the commandments. . . . There is no special and separate act of loving God."[52] Thomas Higgins anemically explains that love for God means, first, that we must not hate God; second, that we must obey God's laws; and third, that we must occasionally make "explicit acts of love."[53] The Bible too is rather silent:

> Apart from the summary of the law, there is not more than a single reference (Luke 11.42) in the Synoptic account of Jesus' teaching to man's love for God. In the rest of the NT the "love of God" nearly but not quite always means God's love for men. In I John 5.3, love for God is expressly identified with the keeping of his commandments (cf. John 14.15, 21); and Paul in Gal. 5.14 and Rom. 13.10 calls love of neighbour the *fulfillment* of the law. . . . What is harder to find in the NT is any expression of love towards God which recalls the 'thirst' of the Psalmists (Pss. 42 and 63).[54]

One strand of Catholicism pursued the Psalmists' path with a passion. This thirst, however, meant that we love God simply for our sakes. God is our supreme good, so to speak, the world's deepest and most thirst-quenching fountain: we love God only because thereby our desire is satisfied. It was against this view that Anders Nygren vigorously protested. James Gustafson's theocentric ethics continues that polemic today and, like Nygren, he too has little to say about our love for God.

One reason for the tradition's hesitancy to encourage love for God is an understanding of love as beneficence. When love means doing good for the beloved, and when it was not clear how we can do good for God, theologians instead recommended contemplation of the eternal ideas or greater attention to creation.[55] While I think we can do something for

God (and not simply for creatures), there is a more obvious and basic meaning of love for God. It means, not that we do good for God, but that we love God. We affectively unite ourselves with God. As lovers of God, we rest in God.[56] But we do not only rest. In love there is movement of our mind and heart and will into the core of God. We do so in such a way that the being and goodness of God becomes ever more real to us.[57] Love means that we constantly move toward ever greater penetration into the mystery of God: our gods are always too small. And loving God also means we contribute to the fuller realization of God's own relational being and goodness.

I have described *God's* love for us as a going out and a receiving, an *affirming union and acceptance. Our* response to God is one of *acceptance and affirming union*, active reception and out-going response. God's gifts to us can and should evoke from us not only expressions of gratitude, but also and in the first place an attraction to the giver of these gifts, an attraction to the inviting mystery that is God. The gift of God's own self evokes in us a desire to be with God. As Aquinas says, "In the beloved's presence, the lover delights in him or in the good things about him."[58]

The appropriate response to God's love for us is not simply respect. We can respect God's superiority to ourselves, even as we distance ourselves further from the "Infinite One." As Rudolf Otto showed, a sense of distance, awe, and "aghastness" is an appropriate response to God's majesty.[59] However, this is not in itself a response of love. We would do well to respect a devil's power, and a devil in turn would do well to respect God's power; but respect is not a response of love responding to love. To be sure, we respect those we love, but love's intimacy tends to dissolve respect's distance. Respect emphasizes difference[60] and is but a component of love's unity-in-difference.

The proper response to God's love for us is not simply respect but a return love. Our response is to unite with and affirm God's dynamism. By loving God, we become responsible for not frustrating God's history-involved dynamism and responsible for aiding wherever possible that dynamism in achieving its own ends. We try to live in such a way that the God who loves us (i.e., shares responsibility for our growth and consents to be affected by us) is fulfilled, not frustrated. As lovers of God, we take on, in our own limited way, God's own concerns. Ignatius in the third week of his *Spiritual Exercises* says we should have compassion for our Lord, and John Paul II makes the same claim.[61] They affirm the lover's heart; they know that the God who in Jesus once shared our suffering still shares our sufferings. In joining ourselves with God, uniting our heart with God's heart, we feel with the God who suffers with us. More broadly, we share as widely as we can in all the affections of God's heart.

In the existential order there is a change in our being when we love God. As Aquinas says, love "is that union or nexus or transformation by which the lover is transformed into the beloved, and is in a manner changed into him," i.e., into God, in the case of "charity."[62] Our own dynamism is not confined to itself but also shares in the dynamism of the divine. Through knowledge and affection, we dwell more completely in ourselves and yet ecstatically in God. We begin to ally ourselves, to the extent humanly possible, with God's loves and hates. We come to love and hate, in our finite and differentiated way, what God loves and hates and in accord with the preferential order of God's loves and hates. Our conscience, as Josef Ratzinger notes, "expresses the thought of a kind of co-knowledge of man with God."[63] In being in love with God, our old patterns give way to a new way of looking at life. Being in love with God "dismantles and abolishes the horizon in which our knowing and choosing went on and it sets up a new horizon in which the love of God will transvalue our values and the eyes of that love will transform our knowing."[64]

Before concluding this section, however, I must add a recurring corrective. There is wisdom in the reticence of the Bible and of the tradition to speak much of our love for God. This God is not a being alongside other beings, but rather the One in whom we live and move and have our being (Acts 17:28). We love God, not a "product of man's genius and art" (Acts 17:29). We love One who is Mystery and transcends all creation. To say that we take responsibility for God's own life is not to imply that God could not care for God's own self. Rather it is to say that God invites and enables us to share God's own life. Our love for God is for the God who remains the origin and sustainer and redeemer of our lives.

COOPERATIVE FRIENDSHIP WITH GOD

A brief summary of the three points made thus far: first, when God loves us, God creates, sustains, and unites with us, and we make a difference to God. Second, we accept God's love for us and we take responsibility for living a life that is relevant to God. Third, when we love God, we affectively affirm God's own self. All this happens within the differences appropriate to Creator-creature relations.

God Forms Community With Us

Out of love for us, God offers to live in covenant with us. This covenant is not a philanthropic relation.[65] Philanthropists benefit humanity, and often do so quite generously, without, however, necessarily getting involved with those whom they help. Our covenant with God is also not a "voluntary association" wherein relatively equal parties negotiate over an issue or service, quite apart from any "personal relation" to one another. In a covenant, the relationship itself is an important good to be promoted and increased. Commenting on the Bible's marital imagery for covenant (Jer 2:2–3:5; Hos 2; Acts 17:26–27; and Eph 5:25–27), Robert Adams notes,

> God's love for us is surely seen as involving a desire for certain relationships between God and us, for their own sakes and not merely as good for us. . . . No doubt it would be possible to interpret all this on the hypothesis that God desires to be related to us only because it is good for us. But I think that is implausible. The Bible depicts a God who seems at least as interested in divine-human relationships as in human happiness *per se*. But if such fellowship is desired for its own sake by God, God's desire is self-concerned inasmuch as the object of the desire involves him as essentially as it involves us. And would we have it any otherwise? Let him who would rather be the object of benevolence than of love cast the first stone.[66]

It is possible for each of two beings to love the other without any mutuality. Each might not know of the other's love or, while knowing, might still be indifferent to the other's love. It is not so with the Christian God. God is involved by the relationship. Grisez puts it well: "Divine love transforms created persons into partners in communion who are related to the divine person much as the divine persons are related to one another. . . . the very constitution of God includes us."[67] What is true in the classical thesis of divine immutability is that God's love does not cease if no response is forthcoming. God does not hate sinners. What is false in it is that it changes God's love into disinterested philanthropy. Rather God is the one "who bears our burdens" and saves us (Ps 68:20).

Aquinas insists that our friendship with God goes beyond benevolence. It requires "a certain mutual return of love, together with mutual communion," a flowering friendship in which life and interests are shared.[68] By God's choice, God's ongoing involvement in history has become dependent on our free cooperation. "This human freedom and obligation to let God become the saving, transforming God of humanity reveals the creative character of humanity's loving response. In love human beings let God be the God he would be for humanity."[69] According to classical mysticism, our "love changes God Himself."[70] While God is always transcendent, God also is one who is involved in history. And the increase of worldly value that we bring about makes a difference to the history-bound God. We have a covenant responsibility to God and for God. As John Paul II writes, we are "partners of the absolute."[71] Again, this partnership is not that of two independent, coequal selves, but rather the partnership or friendship that is possible between a personal Ground and a personal grounded. Through mutually involving love, God and we form a community.[72]

This community we share with God has its *shared world*, that is, its own set of mutually known and loved "objects."[73] This shared "world" is objective and in principle includes what God knows and loves insofar as this is able to be comprehended by us, i.e., within the limits of our uniqueness and finitude. We are, if not *capax infiniti*, at least *capax indefiniti*.[74] In the we-subjectivity between God and us, we can know something of what God knows, therefore know objectively, and love something of what God loves, therefore love wisely, and will some of what God wills, therefore will religiously. In short, we live not just in our "world" but also in the "world" that God and we share.

We Cooperate With God—Christian Ethics

What is the connection between God's gift of self and our moral life? Let me begin with some inadequate connections. Suppose a child were to say to her parents, "I love you so much, and so you should obey me." Or suppose a parent were to exclaim, "I gave you life, so throughout your lifetime you must pursue the goals I have set for you." These sorts of statements seem strange, but they parallel claims sometimes heard: "God loves us and *therefore* we must obey God." "God gives us life and *therefore* we should follow the nature that God has set for us." God's *self*-communication does not easily translate into a set of commandments or plans about how we ought to live. God's love does not straightforwardly ground either a divine command ethic or a natural law ethic.

Should we obey those who love us? The opposite seems more appropriate. The devotion of others to us does not of itself require that we obey them. Their devotion ordinarily means that they will serve us. They will seek our good, perhaps do our will or follow the patterns that we freely set. We love God and therefore we affirm God's will, but this is not the same as obeying God's will. In fact, if love required obedience, God should be more inclined to obey our will, since God loves us more than we love God. Accordingly, God's love for us and our love for God essentially leads to mutual affirmation, not one-sided obedience. When we give ourselves to another, it would be wholly inappropriate for that other to say, "Well, since now you are mine, I can do with you as I will." Unfortunately, when people attracted to religion consider giving themselves to God, they often fear that God will react just this way. Rather, God's love for us affirms our freedom, and our love for God should expand that freedom. This freedom, of course, is not license. It is the ability we have to seek, create, form, and commit ourselves and our world in accord with our relation to God.

Secondly, Christian morality is also not simply a matter of following or fulfilling our nature. Natural law ethics commonly does not give our personal relation to God a central place.[75] Natural law often understands itself to be an autonomous ethic, containing nothing specifically different from an ethics in which God has no place. Thus, what is most important in our Christian life is eliminated or marginalized, namely, our relation to God. Rather, in a religious ethic, we should not be oriented simply to fulfilling ourselves. As covenantal partners, we no longer live simply for ourselves, but also for and with God. Human beings can strive to fulfill their natures simply out of love of self. They can try to be virtuous or respectful of others *because* it is fulfilling for them to do so. This fulfillment is not yet love for God. Writing to Philemon, Paul sends Onesimus, whom he describes as "my heart." He asks for gracious treatment of Onesimus. He appeals not to Philemon's virtue nor to Onesimus's dignity, but to the relation that he, Paul, has with Onesimus: "If then you regard me as a partner, welcome him as you would me" (Phlm 12, 17–18). So it is with us who are God's partners. When we deal well with ourselves, one another, or the rest of creation, we treat these creatures not just for themselves but also as God's beloveds.

Thus, Christian ethics is not at bottom a matter of obeying God nor a matter of fulfilling our natures. Christian ethics must begin with God's love for us and it must keep this love central. Friends do not ask us for obedience or that we live our lives in accord with their plans for us. Friends also do not ask us just to "be who we are." Rather, friends ask that who they are make a difference to who we are; they ask to be a part of who we are and what we do. They ask for communion. Fidelity to that communion requires sharing life with them, and this sharing is the new moral context for all we are and do. Sharing life with God is a radically new context.

In acting morally, we Christians cooperate with the God who acted in Jesus and is still acting: "It is the Father who lives in me accomplishing his works. . . . the man who has faith in me will do the works I do, and greater far than these" (Jn 14:10–12). God's love is operating in us. To love God is to cooperate with what God wants to do in and through us. Our Christian moral life begins with God's care for us; it becomes our care for God; and it expands to caring for what God cares for.[76] As Pierre Teilhard de Chardin writes, "In action, I adhere to the creative power of God; I coincide with it; I become not only its instrument but its living extension."[77] This process is the foundation of a distinctively Christian ethics.

The first principle of Christian ethics is *not* "do good and avoid evil" but rather "love God" or "be with, be for, and cooperate with God." We begin with our experienced relation to God, not with a relation to the good. Needless to say, one can still ask the philosopher's open question "But is it good to be with and cooperate with God?" This question tries to show that the criteria of good and evil are prior to questions of relationships. The philosopher argues that if cooperating with God were not good, then we should not do it.[78] The point is logically correct; but making it is to begin with an abstraction, that is, to begin with a principle that is itself derived from experience. I have argued above that we derive our notion of good and evil from what we love and that, hence, our relationships are prior to our criteria for the good. We do not first set up criteria for the good friend and then discover such a person. Rather, we love or hate persons, and in those experiences, especially of falling in love, we discover (new) meanings for good and bad. Every human relationship, at least if it has any depth, modifies our understanding not only of what are the available goods, but also of the meaning of good and evil themselves. For Christians the final decisive criterion of the good is what is discovered while being in relation to God. We Christians reflect within our relation to God, and therein we discover the good. That relationship is not simply an answer to the question of the highest good. That relationship defines and redefines what shall count as good.

We pray, "Thy will be done on earth as it is in heaven." In so doing, we acknowledge that our actions should be united with God's activity. This does not mean that we thereby lose our initiative or freedom. Since God is acting through us, God must act through our freedom. We make our own unique contribution to this cooperation. We are not literally "instruments" of God. God's own creative and liberating purpose will be achieved only through our efforts.[79] Bernard of Clairvaux well writes, "What was begun by grace alone, is completed by grace and free choice together, in such a way that they contribute to each new achievement not singly but jointly; not by turns, but simultaneously. . . . Each does the whole work, according to its peculiar contribution."[80] God's greatness does not extinguish the contribution that we alone can make. As we saw in the last chapter, God cannot act as a secondary cause because God is not a secondary cause. We are not actors on a stage, playing out as best we can a prewritten script. Rather, we are more like improvisational artists, who, in response to a powerfully engaging audience, develop an original scene with our imagination and creativity.

To recapitulate in one sentence, the main point for ethical activity is: "We are God's co-workers" (1 Cor 3:9). The religiously ethical person or deed is one that cooperates with God and with what God is doing in the world.[81] Thus it was for Jesus: "I am in the Father and the Father is in me. . . . it is the Father who lives in me accomplishing his works" (Jn 14:10). Jesus' "thoughts were directed not in the first instance to what man ought to do and in the second place to what aid he might receive from God in doing what he ought to do, but rather toward what God was doing and what man ought to do in the light of God's doing."[82] So it should be for us. Needless to say, since God is involved in a near infinity of unilateral, mutual, and multilateral relationships and activities, we are charged only with our tiny share of carrying out the activity of God. "It is one and the same Spirit who produces all these gifts, distributing to each as he wills" (1 Cor 12:11). Thus, our Christian acts are ways of "co-creating, co-shaping, co-stewardship," and, in general, cooperating with God.[83]

This cooperation refers not just to grandiose deeds. We seek to cooperate with God even if that requires the most menial tasks of service. One is content with the Lord's food and clothing, to labor at day and to watch at night with the Lord. What is essential is this "with Christ." This laboring on our part need not be to our advantage, except the advantage of being with the Lord.[84] Stanley Hauerwas considers it un-Christian to suggest that God is involved in the mundane details of our life. For him, our work is just work. It is what we do, and it has nothing to do with cooperating with God, let alone with God's saving work.[85] John Paul II, by contrast, argues that God is very much involved with our ordinary work.[86] On this issue, I think the pope is clearly right. God also is very much involved in working for social justice and in forming friendships. But, lest these examples seem too easy, let me add that God is involved with going to movies and enjoying pizza—and everything else. The option being made here, then, should be clear. God is a God of history, and that means that there is nothing good that God's love does not embrace. Our mundane acts are not set apart from our religious life. Rather, these very acts are part and parcel of the covenantal relation between God and ourselves.

My thesis that the starting point of our moral life is to be with and to cooperate with God is open to misunderstandings, and I wish to address three. First, cooperating with God is not giving God a blank check. Divine command ethics can be criticized for reducing the plurality and richness of values to one value: do *whatever* God commands. The same problem would recur in the maxim "cooperate with whatever God is doing," were it not for important differences.[87] Love as participation requires taking account of the difference between God and ourselves. We have our own distinct part to play, and for that part we must exercise our own intelligence and freedom. We must discover to the best of our ability what God wants to do in *us*, not in other persons, and in our small slice of world history, not in that of others. To cooperate with God does not mean "do the same thing," but do our part, which is a creaturely part.[88] Jesus saw differences between himself and his Abba in function, in authority, and in being. Recall, for example, "sitting at my right hand or my left is not mine to give. That is for those to whom it has been reserved by my Father" (Mt 20:23). We must figure out what is our creaturely part. Therefore, presupposed for cooperating with God is a developed sense of discernment.[89] We may have to expend considerable intellectual and emotional effort in order to discern what is our part in cooperation. No straightforward deductions can be made from what we know of God in general to what we should do here and now. We strive for a concordance, a unity of God's heart with our own unique heart. Through our efforts at discernment, we discover "that certain intentions are *in accord with* or *in discord with*" the love that God and we share.[90]

Blind conformity is not required. God's love is not directed toward an arbitrary "whatever," and neither should ours be. Love is itself directed to the good. It attends to its objects as the particular good they are and as the particular good they can and ought to become. So our cooperation will be directed to the enhancement of particular goods in the world, and for that we cannot be blind. Of course, it is *possible* to blindly follow those decrees of God that we learn, for example, through Scripture. We can blindly obey as a way of showing that we love God. Timothy O'Connell calls this a loving legalism.[91] But if we are to be personally united with the mind and heart of God, it is important, within our limitations, to see and value the world's various goods as God does. Scripture and other sources can help us see, but we are fully engaged only when we in fact see for ourselves. Our cooperative actions, accordingly, will not be a blind willing of whatever God wills, but rather an intelligent and loving willing of what *we* see to be objectively good.

A second misunderstanding: loving cooperation is not an added motive. It is part of the meaning of what we are doing. Love for God answers not only "why" but also "what" questions about our actions. Our ethical acts are *not the same* as those of the atheist. Just as two people riding a train, one going to work and the other fleeing home, are not doing the same thing, even though within a limited time frame each seems to be doing nothing more than sitting, so we and the atheist are *not*, on the whole, doing the same thing.[92] In doing an ethical deed, we also want to cooperate with God. This "cooperation" is part of the intrinsic meaning of our act. A husband doesn't make love to his wife, and his wife make love to her husband, and the two just happen to be doing the same thing. Their coactivity is essential to the meaning of their acts. So too our conscious cooperation with God is a different sort of human act than the act we would do outside this communion. In cooperating with God's love for the world, we want not only to affirm and promote the fulfillment of creation, but also to increase "Christ's blessed hold on the universe."[93] To be sure, most of the time, our awareness that we are cooperating may be tacit or implicit. A wife will not and often should not have her family in the forefront of her mind as she debates an important legal case; still, if asked, she could readily answer that she is working for her family. The same woman as a Christian could, if asked, honestly say that she is cooperating with God's action in the judicial world. She is aware that she is cooperating with the God "who is over all, and works through all, and is in all" (Eph 4:5).

Third, cooperation with God is not simply a matter of imitating the example of God or of Christ. The problem with imitation is that, when we follow an example, we do so either blindly (the point discussed above) or we do so intelligently. If the latter, then once we have learned, we no longer need the one who taught the example. If so, God becomes a dispensable model. This will not do for Christians. Jesus says, "As I have done, so you must do" (Jn 13:15; also Eph 4:32, 5:1; 1 Jn 4:11). We Christians do as Jesus does, I suggest, not only because his actions are the right thing to do, but also because that is our way of being in relation to him. God's acts and Jesus' acts are indeed examples for us, but they are more than that. These acts are the ways that we can cooperate and thus live out our relation to God and Jesus. When Jesus says that loving our enemies proves that we are sons and daughters of God (Mt 5:45), this action "proves" the relationship in the way that apples prove that a particular branch belongs to an apple tree.

THE UNITY OF THE TWO COMMANDMENTS

We come to the question with which we began this chapter, how to connect the love of God and the love of humans. The problem, first highlighted by Augustine, is that we are given not one but two great commands from the Lord: "Love thy God with thy whole heart, and thy neighbor as thyself." Theologians have offered many solutions.[94] Some hold that these loves are simply two obligations set by God, with no other connection between them.[95] Some say that the love of God alone is religiously important; love and service of the neighbor have merely a worldly significance. In contrast, Martin Luther held that "the commandment of the love of God is brought down in its entirety into the love of neighbour."[96] Similarly, for Rahner, the "categorised explicit love of neighbour is the primary act of the love of God," while the categorized explicit love of God is secondary in comparison with this.[97] For some, love of neighbor is but one of many duties consequent to faith.[98] For others, love of God is one of the many duties consequent to an adequate love of self and its happiness. For some, love of neighbor is a path of purification in preparation for union with God, or meritorious of that union as reward, but not intrinsically related to the love of God. For others, love of God is a place of rest and refreshment, valuable only insofar as it readies us for the real work of love of neighbor. For yet others, love of neighbor is valuable as a test of love of God.[99] And some hold that love of neighbor is all that people need do, since God accepts love for neighbor as love for God.

Six Theses

The answer I propose is that, within our covenant with God, our love of neighbor and, indeed, of the world is our way of cooperating with God's love for them and thus is a way of being further united with God. This position might be put in two sets of three theses, the first set dealing with our love of God, the second set with our love of neighbor: (1) Our love of God is not identical with love of neighbor. (2) We can love God and not (yet) love our neighbor. (3) Our love of God leads to love of neighbor. (4) Our love of neighbor is not identical with love of God. (5) We can love our neighbor and not (yet) love God. (6) Our love of neighbor leads to the love of God.

First, the love of God is not the love of neighbor for the simple reason that God is God and not the neighbor. We can and do love God alone. That is our experience. Our emotional participation in God's life is possible and for Christians necessary. This love of God is our primary religio-ethical act. And it is a distinctive act: as Outka notes, "Love for God may involve discrete attitudes and actions whose very intelligibility . . . depends on their not being reducible to neighbor-love."[100] Love for God leads to worship and thanksgiving, and these actions are not simply preparations for neighbor love. They are directed "towards God precisely in so far as he is in himself, and without any mediation of the world, the goal of man in the supernatural order."[101] Going to church, for example, is not merely a community-building activity but primarily a way of loving God. Presumably many of us have experienced moments when we joyfully sang praise to God, moments when we felt awe and wonder at God's presence. These acts of prayer are not acts of neighbor love; rather, they are expressions of our love for God. This love appears when we say, "Thank you God for this Fall day," or when we feel ourselves affectively at peace with God without any particular reason. In the prayer of simplicity some of us experience God as an imageless presence we want to be with. Thus, we can and do love God, quite apart from loving our neighbor.

Second, to love God is not (yet) necessarily to love the neighbor. The love of God should lead to love of neighbor, but the relation is not a necessary one. We must distinguish between logical necessity and moral obligation. Our finitude and our freedom are misunderstood if it is said that love of God includes love of neighbor. We are incomplete and fragmented beings, and we have partialities and incompleteness in all our loves. Grisez fails to grasp the *difference* involved in our love when he writes: "God is perfect goodness. Every other good reflects and participates in his perfect goodness. Loving God is thus inseparable from loving created things to the full measure of their goodness."[102] Unfortunately, with our finitude it is impossible to love all created things or even all the things immediately around us. It is impossible for us to love to the full even the things we do love. But our limited love for creatures does not mean we do not love God, really love God. God is not these things, even though their goodness derives from God. One *ought* to connect these two loves, for they are metaphysically and covenantally connected, but one can love God and (not yet) love creatures, at least not this or that creature, and surely not all creatures to the full measure of their goodness. Aquinas correctly argues that we can love God alone, even as he holds that this is an imperfect love by comparison to a joint love of God and love of neighbor.[103]

It is perilous to insist that love of God necessarily includes love of neighbor. We can jump too quickly from loving God to loving neighbor, without adequately appreciating the absolute value of being in love with God. Love of God means at times being "alone" with God just for the sake of our covenantal relation. On the other hand, we can conclude too quickly that, because we do not love all neighbors or even our next-door neighbor, we do not love God at all. Since our neighbor is in principle everyone, if there were a necessary connection between the love of God and the love of all neighbors, then no human being this side of heaven could love God. Experience teaches that we can really love God, in however incomplete a fashion, and not love our neighbor, just as we can really love a woman, yet find her children only annoyances. We don't have to be perfect in an activity before it can be said to exist.

Third, union with God leads to union with God's loves, and so we will be inclined to love the neighbor whom God loves. There is a developmental, moral (not logical) necessity for lovers of God to become lovers of the world. The union of our minds and hearts with God's mind and heart helps us both to see our neighbors' precious value and to align ourselves with them in the direction of their own growth and fulfillment. Thus, union with God leads to, but is not identical with, love of the neighbor: "If God has loved us so, we must have the same love for one another" (1 Jn 4:11). We love God in part by freely consenting to what God wants to do through us, namely, serve God's people, above all in ways that will help them grow closer to God. "God will not forget your work and the love you have shown him by your service, past and present, to his holy people" (Heb 6:10). Thus we gradually make all our worldly acts flow from our fundamental love relation with God.[104]

I consider now the connection between the two loves in the reverse direction. The love of our neighbor—the fourth thesis—is not love for God. It is idolatry to make these two identical. If anything, love for neighbor is relativized by our love for God. We should not make the double affirmation of Augustine: "God is love" and "Love is God."[105] This is to confuse Creator and creature. Unity must not obliterate difference. Some authors raise the quite serious, though startling question, whether it can ever be right for a Christian to love the neighbor, for will not any love for the neighbor be diverted from God?[106] Paul himself recommended celibacy as a solution to such a problem (1 Cor 7:32–35). Outka notes that Paul's position leads to excessive detachment from others and implies that "God and man might somehow be rivals."[107]

The problem is, they can indeed be rivals.[108] We can make idols of an individual or institution, and this can detract from our love for God. Sometimes Harry loves Sally in such a way that she is the final horizon of his life, and all else is contextualized by how it relates to her. Love for neighbor can be disordered, and hence we usually speak of a "proper" or "right" or "ordered" love for neighbor. Love for neighbor must be subordi-

nated to God and coordinated with what God wants to do in us.[109] On
the other hand, our love for God can take us away from otherwise legitimate loves, e.g., a woman leaves family and friends or a potential suitor in
order to go into a monastery. Jesus delayed love's immediate impulse to
free Lazarus from sickness and death so that God might be glorified (Jn
11:5–6). His love for God restrained his love for Lazarus. Love of God
and love of neighbor ideally grow in like and not in inverse proportion,
but that is not guaranteed.

We can see the distinction between these two loves in another way. It
is obvious that atheists love their spouses and children; indeed they often
love the needy stranger better than Christians do.[110] There are psychological studies that show that believers are generally *less* loving than nonbelievers.[111] It is at the very least presumptuous to say that atheists know
not what they do, that they love God even though they do not know it.
Some may assert that atheists are in fact cooperating with God's love by
loving the neighbor, but this is hardly the same as love for God. In a
human analogy, I might support a cause that unbeknownst to me is the
pet project of my enemy. When I discover this information, I might
decide to contribute to another cause; at the very least I would tell myself
that I am supporting the good work, in spite of the fact that it is my enemy's pet project. So too an atheist can love the neighbor, being all the
while oblivious or resistant to the fact that this is what "God wants."

In reply, some say that "if we *really* love our neighbor, then we are loving God." Rahner, for example, typically qualifies love of neighbor by
terms such as "truly absolute" or "moral absoluteness and depth." His
position seems to be a fruitful tautology: a love of neighbor that attains its
absolute depth (God) is a love of God. Rahner expects much of "real" love
of neighbor: "The ultimate mystery of love of the neighbour only comes
fully into play, its absoluteness and the possibility of this absoluteness—
with regard to finite and sinful men—when it surpasses itself to be love of
God."[112] Three responses to these claims will help clarify my fifth thesis.
First, human consciousness is not so necessarily open to the infinite that
in every act of self-transcendence we always intend an infinite or absolute
horizon. We can, for example, memorize nonsense syllables or make up
relationships between random numbers, without believing that what we
are doing has any intelligibility beyond itself. More commonplace, our
daily activity is mainly a matter of "making our way around in the world."
Karl Barth rightly noted that many of our acts have simply a "relative and
limited transcendence, a movement of the creature in the creaturely
realm."[113] Donald Gelpi appeals to psychology and ordinary experience

to argue that we often live our lives within finite, not infinite horizons.[114] Therefore not every act of love by which we transcend ourselves attains God. Our worldly activity can be intelligent and loving, without any ultimate horizon. Second, some humans seem to experience the ultimate horizon as itself devoid of intelligibility.[115] Albert Camus has become the patron saint of all those who experience life as absurd, yet in spite of that experience defiantly devote their lives to loving and doing good for others. Third, even if it were true that in every act of loving the neighbor we also and in the same act necessarily affirm meaning and thus ultimately affirm God, still this sort of necessity is not the same thing as a conscious, free act of loving God.[116] Our glad affirmation of our neighbor might only begrudgingly include this necessary affirmation of God. Thus, the fifth thesis is that we can love our neighbor without loving God.

It should be recalled that I am trying to reflect on the experience of a lover, not that of an outside observer. One can argue that our love for our neighbor de facto affects God and, correlatively, our sin against our neighbor affects God. Jesus says, "He who welcomes you welcomes me, and he who welcomes me welcomes him who sent me" (Mt 10:40). Albert Nolan adds, "God is being crucified in South Africa today. 'Whatsoever you do to even the least of my brothers and sisters you do to me' (Mt 25:40, 45). There is no 'as if' about it."[117] While, from an outsider's viewpoint, all this is true, it is often not part of the experience of the agent, and therefore it has a different moral status. That is, a good act is not an act of love for God, if the one who performs it does not intend it to be such. God may reward (or punish) those who act well (or badly) toward the needy, and God may experience these acts as promoting what God wants to promote. But "loving deeds" that affect God and conform to God's purposes are not the same as acts of love for God. "Even *sinners* love their friends" (Lk 6:32). We must preserve the difference between God and neighbor.

Lastly, the love of neighbor leads to the love of God. Those who are deeply in love sense that they touch upon something divine.[118] Anyone who has known the deep satisfaction of reaching out to help another may have a similar experience: "He dispensed justice to the weak and the poor. . . . Is this not true knowledge of me?" (Jer 22:16). Anyone who has been caught up in wonder at the preciousness of a sleeping child may sense the sacredness of loving a neighbor. The love of a person leads, not inexorably but naturally, to an affirmation of God as the one who creates and sustains and embraces those we love. In loving our neighbor we may also become aware how actively alive God is in us, in our act of loving, and in those we love. Thus, love of neighbor reaches "its own radical depths and its final and definitive validity" when it "explicitly accepts its ground and its mysterious partner, namely, God."[119]

Coming to love God in loving the neighbor does not mean that we do good things for the neighbor in order to get a heavenly reward or that the neighbor is used as a steppingstone to God. This is not love of neighbors. Rather, in loving our neighbors we may experience how they participate in God's creative love. We experience them *as* children of God, since that is what they concretely are.[120] We love our neighbors themselves, but we experience their concrete selves as already belonging to God and opening out to the divine. Jules Toner notes, "This is very different from loving the man for himself because Christ loves him, but with no regard for him as having intrinsic value as a person, an image of God."[121] We love the intrinsic value of a person, but that intrinsic value includes being loved by God, and our affirmation of that intrinsic value is experienced as a love that cooperates with God who establishes and fosters that value.

In this section, I have charted two different experiential patterns of connecting love of God and love of neighbor.[122] In the first, we love God more or less directly, and then are moved to love all that God loves, which among worldly creatures preeminently are human beings. We love them *in Deo et per Deum.*[123] Moving from a sense of God, we experience their sacredness as their relation to God. In the second pattern, we move in a love experience from our neighbor to God. In experiencing the wonder and depth of the beloved, the act of love, or the love-relation, we also experience the gracious presence of God.[124] The connection between the love of God and love of neighbor is not, as I have said, logically or experientially necessary.[125] Still, a deep experience of either love should lead to the other.

Gradual Conversion to Coresponsibility

Presupposed in the preceding discussion is that being in love with God or anyone else is not an all or nothing activity. Love does not have to be a "total giving"; otherwise we probably never love. Love is also not a one-time event; it has a history.[126] There are stages in our love relations, e.g., "falling in love," "growing in love," and "abiding in love."[127] And within a given relationship, such stages repeat themselves. We experience a recurrent flow of joys shared and crises weathered, of conflicts overcome and new discoveries made. Steady harmony becomes its own reward, until it too needs to be transcended in favor of a yet fuller way of being together. And, though we might want to, we cannot simply decide the future of our loves once and for all. So we must recommit ourselves regularly in our growing relationships.[128] Gradually our most important relationships more or less consciously inform what we do. Our relations quietly shape, select, and exclude various alternatives even before we explicitly consider them. Gradually all "our actions are to some extent affected by our central love."[129] Our hope as Christians is that our love for God is our central love and that all our activities will be integrated into our covenant with God.

One obvious area for growth in cooperation with God's love is to love more people, including those we are inclined to hate. According to 1 John 4:20, those who say they love God but hate their neighbor are liars. Is this true, and if so, why? Theologians have for centuries puzzled out the connection implied in this statement. I think that John is best seen to be making an ethical claim, not a descriptive statement. That is, he is saying what those who love God will want to do, namely, love their neighbor. If he is making the descriptive statement that all who love God love all their neighbors, then the statement seems wrong. If he is saying that anyone who hates any neighbor cannot love God at all, then again the statement seems untrue to experience. Love of God may precede or follow love of others.[130] These loves, as I have argued above in the third and sixth theses, lead to each other; but they are not always found together.

To say that when I love God I am inclined to unite my love with God's love is not to assert that my cooperative actions will automatically follow. "The disciple is by definition one who has not yet arrived. . . . It is to be still on the way to full conversion and blessedness of life."[131] There are many known and unknown tendencies in the human heart, and even when we are attuned to God's movement, it does not follow that our whole self is attuned to God. Justification does not imply complete sanctification. Sainthood is a long process. Our past habits and determinisms may prevent us from being the good and holy person we otherwise want to be. There will be an ebb and flow in our loves. And there will be high-tide moments that may have no long-term effect on our character, but also low-tide moments that subtly effect permanent change. Even after a deep experience of God's love, "it is possible for the individual to reject this love soon after the experience. . . . The individual may revert to a former attitude or soon have new experiences that influence him toward some other outlook."[132] Or the allure of mystical union may be so captivating and so relativizing of the rest of one's life that it remains isolated from one's other loves. The mystic's integration of ecstasy with active life may be as difficult as the philosopher king's return to the cave. Mystics commonly say this return successfully occurs only in a late stage of the mystical life.[133] Thus, our love for God and the union of our spirit with God does not automatically entail that all we do will be in accord with that love (Rom 7:14–15). Graced union and our ethical life *ought* to be integrated, but they are not so inexorably connected that the sinner cannot be experiencing God in prayer and the saint cannot sin. Our multiple drives must gradually be informed by the spirit, just as our spirit needs gradually to enlist our drives into the realization of its own projects.

Thus there will be limits in our loving cooperation with God. God loves others whom we *cannot* love.[134] We may not be able to love these others (1) because of our own sinfulness, (2) because of our finitude (e.g., our developmental stage or ignorance or lack of time), or (3) because of the uniqueness of God's dynamism and destiny. Let me develop these three conditions.

The first case is common: it is our sinfulness that keeps us from loving what God loves. We are unable to fully entrust ourselves to God's love. God offers to be our "personal partner in love," but we refuse or are unable to accept.[135] Within a holistic religious view, Sin is "our refusal to commit ourselves to the history of salvation which God wants to enter on with us."[136] Presumably, we all have experiences where we choose to pursue some good or evil apart from our important relationships. We are aware that we cannot integrate that good or evil into these relationships. But we feel ourselves drawn or even "compelled" by some narrow desire. In order to satisfy that desire we push out of our consciousness those relationships which conflict with our desire. The same can happen in the most important relationship of our life, our covenant with God. We fail to cooperate with God's love because we are unwilling to allow certain aspects of our lives to be transformed by our love relation with Mystery. Even when we have somewhat accepted and affirmed and delighted in that relation, we still sin. We accept that love, but refuse its claim on our whole selves. We restrict or exclude God's action, limiting its scope or effectiveness. Overcoming sin often involves the experience that we are being called back into that primary relationship that promises to enlarge our life and enable us to be free.

The second limitation on our cooperation with God is our finitude, including our psychological development. Our finitude means we cannot even begin to dream of doing all that God wants to do. For example, God can personally love billions of people we will never even meet. Moreover, our finitude means that each of us can only do some of what human beings generally can do. And so our individual cooperation with God is less than what God does through the whole human race: "There are different works, but the same God who accomplishes all of them in everyone" (1 Cor 12:6). Furthermore, our psychological development is always incomplete. Presumably, in human relations, we have all encountered people who loved us more intensely than we could receive; our only recourse was to avoid their love for us. Our own defenses were too high to receive, and so we had to resist a response of love. So too it can be with our acceptance of God's love for us and our return love. Presumably, too, we have all loved someone whose range and depth of love so exceeded our own as to threaten our self-image. And so we found ourselves withdrawing out of fear of being stretched too far. So too it can be in our relation to our all-loving God.

Third, there are presumably features of God's love for creation that are uniquely possible to God alone. That is, human beings, both individually and corporately, cannot directly cooperate with these features. As I have tried to show, an experience of participation in the dynamism of others at one and the same time unites us with their dynamism and differentiates us from them. So too in our relation to God. We are capable of loving God, and in so loving we learn what we uniquely contribute to this shared life; but we also learn we are not God and therefore cannot do what God alone can contribute.

A Christian loves, within limits, what God loves. What then does *God* love? In brief, God loves God, the world, other persons, and me. Within our limits, what then should *we* love? The answer is the same: God, the world, other human beings, and myself. But whether we go to worship or to the soup kitchen, all should be done in response to and as part of our relation with God. This is not a matter of God first, after that others, and then perhaps one's self. God asks our whole heart all the time, and our love for creatures should increasingly be part of the way we cooperate with God.[137] The Christian moral life is a love relationship with God. The mystery of our lives is that we come to share in the life of the One who loves the universe.

CONCLUSION

In this chapter I have tried to explore a simple schema for our relationship with God. God loves us, we accept and return that love, and we form community with God. In that community, we gradually grow in our ability to love cooperatively with God. In the next chapters, I shall examine three kinds of this love.

NOTES

1.   Paul Wadell's *Friends of God* (New York: Peter Lang, 1991) gives an interesting Thomistic portrayal of our love for God, but he skips over how impossible it is, in Aquinas's thought, for God to have this kind of love for us. See also John Finnis, *Fundamentals of Ethics* (Washington: Georgetown Univ. Press, 1983), 148–49; Germain Grisez, *The Way of the Lord Jesus* (Chicago: Franciscan Herald Press, 1983), 599–603.

2.   James Gustafson, *Christ and the Moral Life* (Chicago: Univ. of Chicago Press, 1968), 260.

3.   Gene Outka, *Agape* (New Haven: Yale Univ. Press, 1976), 217–18. By contrast, Victor Paul Furnish, "Love of Neighbor in the New Testament," *Journal of Religious Ethics* 10 (Fall 1982): 330, notes that in Mark's rendition of the double command "the accent falls on the first injunction, not on the second." Stephen Post rightly critiques those who neglect the first commandment in his "The Purpose of Neighbor-Love," *Journal of Religious Ethics* 18 (Spring 1990): 181–93. Daniel Sheridan, "Maternal Affection for a Divine Son," *Horizons* 16 (Spring 1989): 66, observed that his students "presumed that loving God was loving your neighbor. . . . The specific love of God . . . was absent from the experience of most students." See also Karl Rahner, S.J., "Virtue," *Encyclopedia of Theology* (New York: Seabury, 1975), 1804.

4.   Daniel Maguire, *The Moral Core of Christianity* (Minneapolis: Fortress, 1993), 221.

5.   Grisez, *Way of the Lord Jesus*, 597.

6.   Richard Clifford, S.J., "The Hebrew Scriptures and the Theology of Creation," *Theological Studies* 46 (September 1985): 509, 514, 519.

7.   Stephen Mott, *Biblical Ethics and Social Change* (New York: Oxford, 1982), 10–15, 22–40; Gerry Heard, *Mystical and Ethical Experience* (Macon, GA: Mercer, 1985), 24.

8.   For an excellent, brief analysis of the nature of gifts, see Thomas Murray, "Gifts of the Body and the Needs of Strangers," *Hastings Center Report* 17 (April 1987): 30–38; for a study of the obligation to make a return for gifts, see Lawrence Becker, *Reciprocity* (New York: Routledge & Kegan Paul, 1986).

9.   Primitive experiences of God, as indicated by Rudolf Otto in *Idea of the Holy* (New York: Oxford Univ. Press, 1977), 12–33, are terrifying. The graciousness and savingness of God is brought out by other experiences; see Richard R. Niebuhr, *Experiential Religion* (New York: Harper & Row, 1972), 83–106.

10.   Gustafson, *Christ and the Moral Life*, 50–53.

11.   Karl Rahner, S.J., "Love as the Key Virtue," *Sacramentum Mundi* (New York: Herder and Herder, 1970), 6:344.

12.   William James, *Varieties of Religious Experience* (New Hyde Park, NY: University Books, 1963), 131–32; see also John Macquarrie, *Principles of a Christian Theology* (New York: Scribner, 1966), 150–55; Bernard Lonergan, S.J., *Method in Theology* (New York: Herder & Herder, 1972), 108. The problem of evil was faced in a courageous way by Carl Jung; for an analysis and a critique, see Robert Doran, S.J., "Jungian Psychology and Christian Spirituality," *Review for Religious* 38 (1979).

13.   Richard Gula, S.S., *Reason Informed By Faith* (New York: Paulist, 1989), 187.

14.   Cf. John Finnis, *Natural Law and Natural Rights* (Oxford: Clarendon, 1980), 406, and *Fundamentals of Ethics*, 147.

15. Karl Rahner, S.J., *Foundations of Christian Faith* (New York: Seabury, 1978), 120; see also Jules Toner, *The Experience of Love* (Washington: Corpus, 1968), 124–29.

16. Walter Brueggemann, "Covenant as a Subversive Paradigm," *Christian Century* (November 12, 1980): 1095.

17. Lucien Richard, O.M.I., "Toward a Renewed Theology of Creation," *Église et Théologie* 17 (1986): 157.

18. Heard, *Mystical and Ethical Experience*, 7; Daniel Day Williams, *The Spirit and the Forms of Love* (New York: Harper & Row, 1968), 33.

19. Enda McDonagh, "Love," *The New Dictionary of Theology*, ed. Joseph Komonchak et al. (Wilmington: Glazier, 1987), 609–10.

20. Michael Gilligan, *God and Evil* (New York: Paulist, 1976), 48–49.

21. D. Williams, *The Spirit and the Forms of Love*, 117.

22. Margaret Farley, R.S.M., "Fragments for an Ethic of Commitment in Thomas Aquinas," *Journal of Religion* 58 (Supplement 1978): S146; also Margaret Farley, *Personal Commitments* (New York: Harper and Row, 1986), 116–17.

23. Richard, "Renewed Theology of Creation," 156.

24. John Stacer, S.J., "Divine Reverence for Us," *Theological Studies* 44 (September 1983): 446, 448.

25. Hans Tiefel, "Severely Handicapped Newborns," *Questions about the Beginning of Life*, ed. Ed Schneider (Minneapolis: Augsburg, 1985), 162.

26. *ST* II–II.26.7.

27. William Lynch, S.J., *Images of Hope* (Notre Dame: Univ. of Notre Dame Press, 1965), 143.

28. Ronald Goetz, "The Suffering God: The Rise of a New Orthodoxy," *Christian Century* 103 (April 16, 1986): 387–88; David Smith, "Suffering, Medicine, and Christian Theology," *Moral Medicine*, eds. Stephen Lammers and Allen Verhey (Grand Rapids: Eerdmans, 1987), 255–61.

29. Rahner, "Love as the Key Virtue," 344.

30. Farley, *Personal Commitments*, 116, 120–21.

31. Irving Singer, *The Nature of Love* (Chicago: Univ. of Chicago Press, 1987), 1:253–55.

32. One of the ironies of history is that Augustine's text has been so quoted as to make it sound Pelagian. Augustine's full line is more nuanced. It begins, "It is for yourself that you have made us," indicating the prior movement of God; *The Confessions of St. Augustine*, trans. John Ryan (Garden City: Image, 1960), Bk. 1, Ch. 1, p. 43.

33. Paul Tillich, *The Shaking of the Foundations* (New York: Scribner's, 1948), 162.

34. For one who rejects this conclusion, see Finnis, *Natural Law and Natural Rights*, 409, and *Fundamentals of Ethics*, 148–49.

35. Evelyn Eaton Whitehead and James Whitehead, *Marrying Well* (Garden City: Doubleday, 1981), 227.

36. Farley, "Commitment in Thomas Aquinas," S139, 146–47.

37. Singer, *The Nature of Love*, 1:40.

38. Richard, "Renewed Theology of Creation," 155.

39. *ST* I.20.2. Still much in Catholic natural law theory made a friendship love between God and us all but unthinkable. See Thomas Higgins, S.J., *Man as Man* (Milwaukee: Bruce, 1949), 181–85. Making distinctions along confessional lines is, of

course, precarious. Thus, Calvinist theologian Lewis Smedes, *Mere Morality* (Grand Rapids: Eerdmans, 1983), 58, also rejects Nygren and affirms the intrinsic value of what God loves.

40. Dietrich von Hildebrand, *Ethics* (Chicago: Franciscan Herald, 1972), 235; Sandra Schneiders, I.H.M., *New Wineskins* (New York: Paulist, 1986), 222.

41. *ST* II–II.27.1.

42. Stacer, "Divine Reverence for Us," 443–44, 447.

43. Ann Belford Ulanov, "The God You Touch," *Parabola* 12 (August 1987): 32.

44. Paul Tillich, "To Whom Much Was Forgiven," *Parabola* 12 (August 1987): 42.

45. James Gustafson, *Ethics from a Theocentric Perspective* (Chicago: Univ. of Chicago Press, 1981), 1:307.

46. Schneiders, *New Wineskins*, 156–64.

47. Albert Nolan, *God in South Africa* (Grand Rapids: Eerdmans, 1988), 107.

48. Farley, *Personal Commitments*, 119.

49. Stacer, "Divine Reverence for Us," 444.

50. Outka, *Agape*, 49–50.

51. Outka, *Agape*, 8; see Anders Nygren, *Agape and Eros*, trans. Philip Watson (New York: Harper & Row, 1969), 95–102, 127–28.

52. Grisez, *Way of the Lord Jesus*, 603.

53. Higgins, *Man as Man*, 181–85. Grisez, *Way of the Lord Jesus*, 469, says vaguely that we can "somehow return good to the Lord for the good he has given us."

54. John Burnaby, "Love," *Dictionary of Christian Ethics*, ed. John Macquarrie (London: SCM Press, 1967), 198.

55. See Finnis, *Fundamentals of Ethics*, 148–49; M. C. D'Arcy, S.J., *The Mind and Heart of Love* (New York: Henry Holt, 1947), 225–26.

56. Cf. Roger Haight, S.J., "Foundational Issues in Jesuit Spirituality," *Studies in the Spirituality of Jesuits* 19 (September 1987): 39–40. Haight's statement that "prayer alone does not and cannot constitute a real union with God" is, I think, simply false. For him "practice *constitutes* the unity of the human with God."

57. For a different view, see D'Arcy, *Mind and Heart of Love*, 224–25.

58. *ST* I–II.28.2.

59. Otto, *Idea of the Holy*, 12–33.

60. Karl Barth, *Church Dogmatics* 3/4 (Edinburgh: T. & T. Clark, 1978), 339–40.

61. *Spiritual Exercises of St. Ignatius*, trans. Louis Puhl, S.J. (Westminster, MD: Newman, 1959), no. 193, p. 81; John Paul II, *Dives in Misericordia* (Boston: Daughters of St. Paul, 1980), no. 6, 8–9, 14.

62. *Sententiarum*, 3.27.1.1.

63. Josef Ratzinger, "Bishops, Theologians, and Morality," *Origins* 13 (March 15, 1984): 660.

64. Lonergan, *Method in Theology*, 106.

65. William F. May, "Code and Covenant or Philanthropy and Contract?" *On Moral Medicine*, eds. Stephen Lammers and Allen Verhey (Grand Rapids: Eerdmans, 1987), 83–96.

66. Robert Adams, "Pure Love," *Journal of Religious Ethics* 8 (1980): 96–97.

67. Grisez, *Way of the Lord Jesus*, 581. See also Letty Russell, *Future of Partnership* (Philadelphia: Westminster, 1979).

68. *ST* I–II.65.5; also *ST* II–II.23.1; *Sententiarum*, 3.27.2.1–2, 3.32.1.2.

69. McDonagh, "Love," 608.

70. Louis Dupré, "The Christian Experience of Mystical Union," *Journal of Religion* 69 (January 1989): 12.

71. John Paul II, *Original Unity of Man and Woman* (Boston: St. Paul Editions, 1981), 51. The inner tension between the terms "partner" and "absolute" is essential. Cf. Edward Vacek, S.J., "John Paul II and Cooperation with God," *The Annual of the Society of Christian Ethics* (1990), 81–107.

72. William Luijpen, *Existential Phenomenology* (Pittsburgh: Duquesne, 1969), 325.

73. William Earle, *The Autobiographical Consciousness* (Chicago: Quadrangle, 1972), 110–12; Jacques Leclercq, *La Philosophie morale de saint Thomas devant la pensée contemporaine* (Paris: Vrin, 1955), 345; Lois Gehr Livezey, "Rights, Goods, and Virtues," *Annual of the Society of Christian Ethics* (Washington: Georgetown Univ. Press, 1987), 57; Edward Collins Vacek, S.J., "Toward a Phenomenology of Love Lost," *Journal of Phenomenological Psychology* 20 (Spring 1989): 8–10. This position contrasts with that of some older natural law theologians who held that we should not love the nonpersonal world for its own sake; Etienne Gilson, *Moral Values and the Moral Life* (Hamden, CT: Shoe String Press, 1961), 218; Higgins, *Man as Man*, 181–82.

74. *ST* I.II.2.7; Jean Porter, "Desire for God," *Theological Studies* 47 (March 1986): 66–68; Karl Rahner, S.J., "Thomas Aquinas on the Incomprehensibility of God," *The Journal of Religion* 58 (Supplement 1978): S123–25.

75. For example, Higgins, *Man as Man*, 181–85, 344–48, devoted only 4 of 585 pages to "love of neighbor" and another 4 pages to "love of God." Anton Pegis, *Basic Writings of Saint Thomas Aquinas* (New York: Random House, 1945) translated vast sections of the *Summa*, but oddly stopped just prior to the section on charity.

76. Whitehead and Whitehead, *Marrying Well*, 234.

77. Pierre Teilhard de Chardin, *The Divine Milieu* (San Francisco: Harper & Row, 1968), 62. Teilhard adds (all in capital letters): "All endeavour cooperates to complete the world in *Christo Jesu*" (p. 56).

78. James Gustafson, *The Contribution of Theology to Medical Ethics* (Milwaukee: Marquette, 1975), 30–31, writes, "If God were sheer power without 'goodness,' if he were being without value, a theological point of view would be a-moral. . . . If the ultimate power willed the destruction of creation, there would be license not only for radical exploitation of life by humans in any given generation, but also for its ultimate demise. If God were indifferent to values, there would be no persistent moral thrust to human activity understood in a theological context. . . . Since God wills well-being, the theological moral point of view is one which directs human action toward the realization of potentialities for value that are present in nature and in history." Wendy Doniger O'Flaherty, "Separation of Heaven and Earth in Indian Mythology," *Cosmogony and Ethical Order*, eds. Robin Lovin and Frank Reynolds (Chicago: Univ. of Chicago Press, 1985), 178–79, shows that in some religious traditions there have been gods who fit these categories.

79. Mark Taylor, *God Is Love* (Atlanta: Scholars Press, 1986), 402–3.

80. Bernard of Clairvaux, *Treatise III: On Grace and Free Choice*, trans. Daniel O'Donovan (Kalamazoo: Cistercian Publications, 1977), 14, 47.106.

81. "Gaudium et spes," *Documents of Vatican II*, ed. Walter Abbott, S.J. (New York: America Press, 1966), no. 50, describes parents as "cooperators with the love of

God the Creator." The view presented here simply extends what the bishops said to all realms of life. See Stanley Harakas, *Toward Transfigured Life* (Minneapolis: Light & Life, 1983), 232; Gustafson, *Ethics from a Theocentric Perspective*, 1:242.

   82.   H. Richard Niebuhr, "The Social Gospel and the Mind of Jesus," *Journal of Religious Ethics* 16 (Spring 1988): 120.

   83.   Judith Plaskow, *Sex, Sin and Grace* (New York: University Press of America, 1980), 172.

   84.   *Spiritual Exercises of St. Ignatius*, no. 93, 95.

   85.   Stanley Hauerwas, "Work as Co-Creation," *Co-Creation and Capitalism*, eds. John Houck and Oliver Williams (Washington: University Press of America, 1983), 48–56.

   86.   See Vacek, "John Paul II and Cooperation with God," 81–107.

   87.   Thomas Ogletree, *Hospitality to the Stranger* (Philadelphia: Fortress, 1985), 115, raises this problem against Niebuhr's radical monotheism.

   88.   Gustafson, *The Contribution of Theology*, 52.

   89.   Avery Dulles, S.J., "Finding God's Will," *Jesuit Spirit in a Time of Change*, ed. Raymond Schroth (Westminster, MD: Newman, 1968), 9–22.

   90.   Gustafson, *Christ and the Moral Life*, 261–67; Patrick Byrne, "*Ressentiment* and the Preferential Option for the Poor," *Theological Studies* 54 (June 1993): 220, 233.

   91.   Timothy O'Connell, *Principles for a Catholic Morality* (New York: Seabury, 1978), 127.

   92.   Garth Hallett, *Christian Moral Reasoning* (Notre Dame: Univ. of Notre Dame Press, 1983), 10.

   93.   Teilhard de Chardin, *The Divine Milieu*, 63.

   94.   Outka, *Agape*, 15–16. For changes in Augustine's position, see Johannes van Bavel, O.S.A., "The Double Face of Love in Augustine," *Louvain Studies* 12 (1987): 116. See also Oliver O'Donovan, *The Problem of Self-Love in St. Augustine* (New Haven: Yale Univ. Press, 1980), 23; Oliver O'Donovan, *Resurrection and Moral Order* (Grand Rapids: Eerdmans, 1986), 230, 232; Paul Ramsey, *Basic Christian Ethics* (Chicago: Univ. of Chicago Press, 1978), 116–32; Karl Rahner, S.J., "Utopia and Reality," *Theology Digest* 32 (Summer 1985): 141; Heard, *Mystical and Ethical Experience*, 42–43, 56–71; Stephen Tyman, "Mysticism and Gnosticism in Heidegger," *Philosophy Today* 28 (Winter 1984): 364–65.

   95.   O'Donovan, *Resurrection and Moral Order*, 227.

   96.   Nygren cites this text from Luther with approval, *Agape and Eros*, 736.

   97.   Karl Rahner, S.J., "Reflections on the Unity of the Love of Neighbour and the Love of God," *Theological Investigations* (Baltimore: Helicon, 1969), 6:246–47.

   98.   Rahner, "Love as the Key Virtue," 346, notes this pattern in the tradition.

   99.   Outka, *Agape*, 44–45.

  100.   Outka, *Agape*, 52, also 216–17.

  101.   Karl Rahner, S.J. "Reflections on a Theology of Renunciation," *Theological Investigations* (New York: Crossroad, 1982), 3:51–52; *ST* II–II.182.2.

  102.   Grisez, *Way of the Lord Jesus*, 602.

  103.   *ST* II–II.27.8; *Sententiarum*, 3.30.1.4.

  104.   Karl Rahner, S.J., "Order," *Encyclopedia of Theology* (New York: Seabury, 1975), 1114–16.

  105.   Bavel, "Double Face of Love," 120–25; see also Nygren, *Agape and Eros*, 147.

106. Outka, *Agape*, 52–53.

107. Outka, *Agape*, 53; O'Donovan, *Resurrection and Moral Order*, 226–232.

108. Philip Quinn, "Tragic Dilemmas, Suffering Love, and Christian Life," *Journal of Religious Ethics* 17 (Spring 1989): 171, describes such a conflict in Endo's novel *Silence*. Earle, *The Autobiographical Consciousness*, 98–124, shows how the experience of being in love feels divine, complete, eternal, beyond good and evil.

109. C. S. Lewis, *The Four Loves* (New York: Harcourt Brace Jovanovich, 1960), 167–72; Charles Taylor, *Sources of the Self* (Cambridge: Harvard Univ. Press, 1989), 270.

110. James Gustafson, *Can Ethics Be Christian?* (Chicago: Univ. of Chicago Press, 1975), 1–24.

111. Paul Rigby and Paul O'Grady, "Agape and Altruism," *Journal of American Academy of Religion* 57 (1989): 731–32.

112. Rahner, "Love as the Key Virtue," 345–46; Rahner, "Unity of Love," 237. Rahner does, however, offer a developmental model for understanding love in "The 'Commandment' of Love in Relation to the Other Commandments," *Theological Investigations* (Baltimore: Helicon, 1977), 5:439–59. In his late work, *Foundations of Christian Faith*, 309, Rahner even says that this love of neighbor must develop into an explicit acceptance of its Ground. For a shoddily argued but valuable critique of Rahner's position, see Richard Roach, S.J., "An Excessive Claim: Rahner's Identification of Love of God with Love of Neighbour," *Studies in Religion* 5 (1975–76): 363; also Jean Porter, "Salvific Love and Charity," *Love Commandments*, eds. Edmund Santurri and William Werpehowski (Washington: Georgetown Univ. Press, 1992), 252–58.

113. Barth, *Church Dogmatics*, 473; cf. also Paul Tillich, *Systematic Theology* (New York: Harper & Row, 1967) 1:13.

114. Donald Gelpi, "Two Spiritual Paths: Thematic Grace vs. Transmuting Grace," *Spirituality Today* 35 (Fall & Winter 1983): 250–51, 348–49, 352.

115. Robert Solomon, *The Passions* (Garden City: Doubleday, 1976), 12–19.

116. Roach, "An Excessive Claim," 247–57, 360–72. Cf. C. S. Lewis, *The Four Loves*, 178.

117. Nolan, *God in South Africa*, 67. John Donahue, S.J., "The 'Parable' of the Sheep and the Goats," *Theological Studies* 47 (March 1986): 30, stresses that this famous Gospel passage is addressed to Christian disciples, not simply any human being, whether believer or not.

118. William Earle, *The Autobiographical Consciousness*, 98–121.

119. Rahner, *Foundations of Christian Faith*, 309; also Karl Rahner, S.J., "Virtue," *Encyclopedia of Theology* (New York: Seabury, 1975), 1805.

120. Oliver O'Donovan, *Problem of Self-Love in St. Augustine*, 32; O'Donovan, *Resurrection and Moral Order*, 228; cf. Nygren, *Agape and Eros*, 98, 214–15.

121. Toner, *The Experience of Love*, 107.

122. Gilbert Meilaender, *Friendship* (Notre Dame: Univ. of Notre Dame Press, 1981), 1–35.

123. Henri Bergson, *Two Sources of Morality* (New York: Holt, 1935), 45, 222.

124. Goetz, "The Suffering God," 387–88; D. Smith, "Suffering, Medicine, and Christian Theology," 255–61.

125. Outka, *Agape*, 186–89; cf. O'Donovan, *Resurrection and Moral Order*, 226–28.

126. Rahner, "Love as the Key Virtue," 339; see also Rahner, "The 'Commandment' of Love," 439–59; Toner, *The Experience of Love*, 95.

127. The phrases are revisions of the terms given by Singer, *The Nature of Love*, 3:383–88.

128. Farley, "Commitment in Thomas Aquinas," S141.

129. D'Arcy, *The Mind and Heart of Love*, 80; Outka, *Agape*, 133.

130. See Walter Conn, "Passionate Commitment: Dynamics of Affective Conversion," *Cross Currents* (Fall 1984): 329–36; Nancy Ring, "Sin and Transformation," *Chicago Studies* 23 (November 1984): 316–17.

131. Avery Dulles, S.J., "Imaging the Church for the 1980's," *Thought* 56 (June 1981): 130.

132. Heard, *Mystical and Ethical Experience*, 40.

133. Dupré, "Christian Experience of Mystical Union," 8–9.

134. Bruno Schüller, S.J., *Wholly Human*, (Washington: Georgetown Univ. Press, 1986), 28.

135. Karl Rahner, "Sin," *Encyclopedia of Theology* (New York: Crossroad, 1975), 1589.

136. Piet Schoonenberg, "Sin," *Sacramentum Mundi* (New York: Herder and Herder, 1970), 6:88.

137. Edward Vacek, S.J., "God's Action and Ours," *Emmanuel* 90 (September 1984): 370-76; Doran, "Jungian Psychology and Christian Spirituality," 503.

5

Agape

*You have heard the commandment, "You shall love your countryman
but hate your enemy." My command to you is: love your enemies, pray
for your persecutors. This will prove that you are sons of your heavenly
Father, for his sun rises on the bad and the good, he rains on the just
and the unjust. If you love those who love you, what merit is there in
that? Do not tax collectors do as much? . . . In a word, you must be
made perfect as your heavenly Father is perfect. (Mt 5:43–48)*

Numerous as the stars are the experiences of love. Some of these experiences are grouped into galaxies, most left unnamed and unexplored. Some
are deceptive like the morning star and the evening star, two names for the
same object that is not even a star. In this and the following chapters, I
group many of these experiences into three *kinds* of love: *agape, eros,* and
philia. The terms are classic. Their meaning, however, varies widely from
author to author.[1] While attending to past and present usage, I will offer
my own understanding of these three loves. I will show that each kind of
love fits the general idea of love, yet each is distinctive.

   In this chapter, after saying something about the feature that distinguishes the three loves, I look at Anders Nygren's deeply influential char-
acterization of the difference between agape and eros.[2] I then present my
own view of agape, concentrating on several controversial features. After
defending the emotional quality of agape, I consider four ways in which
agape is said to be related to the beloved's good. I also raise objections to a
rule of universal love and then present reasons for agape's preference for
the poor. After that I will speak of agape's generosity, its tendency to self-
sacrifice, and its fidelity. I conclude with a discussion of agape for God
and neighbor.

DISTINGUISHING FEATURE OF LOVES

Let me begin by setting down a crucial distinction I will use throughout
the rest of the book. We may love the beloved (1) for the sake of the
beloved, (2) for our own sake, or (3) for the sake of a relationship we have

with the beloved.[3] I call these love relations (1) agape, (2) eros, and (3) philia. Thus, I distinguish agape, eros, and philia by the phrase *"for the sake of."* The one for whose sake we love determines the kind of love we have. This distinction lies in our intention, in the meaning the act has for us, *not* in any *results* of the act. Thus, it may well be that in loving others we do the greatest good for ourselves. But if we love others *in order to* do the best for ourselves, we are not loving them for their sakes. If another act that was better for ourselves was available, we might abandon them and pursue that act. When we love others as a way of fulfilling ourselves, this love of others is eros, not agape. If, as some argue, God loves only in order to express God's nature,[4] then God does not love us *for our own sakes;* that is, God does not, in my terms, love us agapically.

In this chapter I take up agape, which has been emphasized more by Protestant authors, and in the following chapters I consider the traditional Catholic emphases of "eros" and "caritas" (philia). Though agape is usually called *the* distinctively Christian form of love, I shall argue that all three may be Christian. All three may be forms of cooperating with God. Each kind of love, however, creates or contributes to a different kind of relation with the beloved. For example, we may seem to do the "same act of giving" when we offer someone a hundred dollars, but the resulting relationships are different if we are giving the money in order to help someone in need, to grow in virtue, or to express our friendship. Needless to say, we can exercise more than one kind of love in any given activity. We are quite capable of mixed motives, and we usually have "mixed loves."[5]

NYGREN ON AGAPE

Agape has been (wrongly, I hope to show) called "the form of love which the New Testament commends to us"; it is said to name whatever is distinctive in Christian love.[6] What is agape? Let me begin with an example. During World War II, those Gentiles whom the Jews call "the Righteous" risked their lives to save Jews from the Nazis. The likely "return" on their generosity was death. To the extent that the concern they so heroically demonstrated was purely love of those Jews for their own sakes, this concern was agapic.

In the first part of this century, Nygren set the terms of the debate over the nature of agape and eros. In the judgment of one commentator, Nygren "so effectively posed issues about love that they have had a prominence in theology and ethics they never had before. . . . Thus, whatever the reader may think of it, one may justifiably regard his work as the beginning of the modern treatment of the subject."[7] Nygren claimed, with some justification, "Christian love, Agape, has never, strictly speaking, been the subject of dogmatic treatment."[8] Though one can easily challenge many of Nygren's scriptural and historical claims, his book has such clarity and initial persuasiveness that it is an excellent starting point for studying agape. His insights are splendid, his mistakes are instructive, and his views are still very much alive.[9]

Nygren and I share a major thesis: Christian ethics has been diminished by an eros-based ethics emphasizing personal happiness or fulfillment.[10] In this eudaimonistic ethics, human action is evaluated by whether it leads to our happiness, chiefly, the possession of God, who satisfies our human desires. When, however, our motive for action is the attainment of *our* happiness, the focus of our life is off-center. Christian life should be centered on union and cooperation with God. This relationship brings happiness of the deepest sort, but this happiness is not the reason for which we act. Nygren, therefore, rightly challenges one strand of Thomistic and Catholic thought. Nygren perceptively argues that the basic conversion we Christians must undergo is *not* one of shifting our desire from temporal things to heavenly things, from sensual or vital drives to more fulfilling spiritual pursuits. Rather, he says, our basic conversion should be from this sort of anthropocentric way of life to a theocentric one.[11]

It is impossible, Nygren says, to reconcile eros and agape. Between them there is "a universal, all-embracing opposition, touching every point."[12] I begin with Nygren's summary.

Eros is acquisitive desire.	Agape is sacrificial giving.
Eros is upward movement.	Agape comes down.
Eros is man's way to God.	Agape is God's way to man.
Eros is man's effort.	Agape is God's grace.
Eros is egocentric love.	Agape is unselfish love.
Eros seeks to gain its divine life.	Agape lives the life of God, therefore dares to "lose it."
Eros is the will to get, which depends on want and need.	Agape is freedom in giving, which depends on wealth and plenty.
Eros is primarily *man's* love; God is the *object* of eros.	Agape is primarly *God's* love; God *is* Agape.
Eros is determined by the quality of its object; it is not spontaneous, but "evoked," motivated.	Agape is sovereign and is directed to both "the evil and the good;" it is spontaneous, "overflowing," "unmotivated."
Eros *recognizes value* in its object and loves it.	Agape loves—and *creates value* in its object.[13]

It is perhaps obvious that within each column there is some overlap among the categories. What is more important is that the opposition between agape and eros is diametric. Nygren moves rationalistically, arguing that what one love has the other must not have. He is not alone in this approach. I will argue that this way of opposing the two loves is not biblical, theologically adequate, or experiential.[14] I begin by discussing the emotional character of agape because agape, since it is thought to be God-like, is often therefore described as a most dispassionate love. If one thinks of agape as unselfish and not ego-related, as sovereign and not dependent, as divine and not human, as spontaneous and not motivated, then it is only a short step to also think of it as unemotional.

AGAPE AS AN EMOTION

Agape is a kind of *love*. If the claims of the previous chapters are true, agape is therefore an *emotional* appreciation and concern for the good of the beloved. The reason for making this point is that writers often describe agape as beneficence or as an act of impartial justice; or they describe it as "uninterested willingness" or merely as "'objective' acknowledgment"; or they portray agape as paternalistic, benevolent action.[15] In brief, they describe agape as doing what is good for the other, without in any way being affected by the other. This position, I suspect, springs from the fatal failure to distinguish between *being affected* and *acting for our own sake*. The two are quite different. Agapists, I presume, commonly deny the place of the former in order to exclude the latter. They rightly hold that acting for our own sakes is characteristic not of agape but of eros. The problem is that in excluding "being affected" this position excludes love. Love, as we have seen, means that the beloved is a determining factor in the lover's own self-constitution. The prohibition of self-interest should not rule out recognizing the way the self is affected. Authors unfortunately often portray agape as if it were the sheer determination of the will, which runs roughshod over our aversions and is fed by something other than our attractions. Some authors praise self-sacrificial agape for others as "beyond the human" (and therefore as divine) because it bypasses or even represses the emotions that help make us human.

Such an unemotional love has a curious effect. Though the Good Samaritan story seems to require a transformation of the stranger into a neighbor, advocates of agape often require that the neighbor be turned into a stranger. That is, the neighbor is to be treated with a universal impartiality that is appropriate to all the human beings we do not personally know and care about.[16] Self-interest is expunged, but so also is interest. Thus, love is turned into a kind of justice. Respect for "humanity" is mistaken for "real, personal love."[17] While there is a sense in which we can love the human race, that love is not identical with a personal love for individuals. When we concretely love Maurice or Maureen, these persons are not for us just "human beings." As the young Aquinas wisely noted, to treat another person as "a human being" is to achieve a form of respectful justice, but it is not yet to love that person.[18] Considerably more of us is involved in saying "I love him" and even more in "I love you."

If we love someone, we are "enjoined to identify with the neighbor's point of view, to try to imagine what it is for him to live the life he does, to occupy the position he holds."[19] But this still is not sufficient for love, since a good detective or military planner will do the same for a criminal or an enemy.[20] Similarly, if we love someone, we will hardly deny them "respect," "regard," and "consideration," which are the favored terms of Gene Outka, one of the best-known commentators on agape. Still, this is not enough for love. If I respect the power of my enemies, show regard for my employees, and give equal consideration to everyone in a queue, I may be doing something appropriate toward these persons, but I still may not love them. We show respect for the rights and liberties of people we do not love. The words "respect," "regard," or "consideration" fall short of what we mean by love. Although it is not intended to do so, Outka's favored and oft-cited term for agape, namely, "equal regard," conveys the cold indifference of a government worker issuing welfare checks to all clients, doing so fairly and in accord with their common humanity.[21] By itself, the term "equal regard" lacks emotional affirmation. If I hate all equally, I have equal regard for all. If I have positive regard for all equally, I may only be practicing impartial justice or giving them acknowledgment.

Paul, who encourages us to "have the same attitude toward all," also tells us to "love one another with the affection of brothers" (Rom 12:10, 16). Something more than equal regard is called for. One thinks of St. Francis kissing the sick or Mother Teresa being moved by the plight of the dying. One recalls Jesus weeping over the Jerusalem that was set to kill him (Mt 23:37). One hears in Paul no dispassionate equal regard when he writes: "There is great grief and constant pain in my heart. Indeed, I could even wish to be separated from Christ for the sake of my brothers, my kinsmen" (Rom 9:2–3). These saints were moved by a real affection for those they loved. Their love was not a matter of unemotional respect for people. Their concern was not disinterested. The people they loved were not strangers whose distinctive differences were to them matters of relative indifference. Theirs was not only a sheer act of the will to "do the right thing." Thus, Paul touchingly writes: "While we were among you we were as gentle as any nursing mother fondling her little ones. So well disposed were we to you, in fact, that we wanted to share with you not only God's tidings but our very lives, so dear had you become to us" (1 Thes 2:7–8).

When our action originates in emotion, we are more fully engaged in our acts and not simply "going through the motions."[22] We love only when we have been *moved* and *attracted* to affirm the beloved's (real and ideal) goodness. Of course, it often happens that when we first meet a person who is unattractive to us, we have recourse to the thought of the basic value of every person; but this recollection should then evoke in us an actual experience of the preciousness of that person. In a word, we come to love the person.

We can, to be sure, do good for strangers out of sheer will, denying all feelings.[23] Rather than experiencing the emotions that arise in the presence of someone who is lovable, we may prescind from or deny these feelings and inclinations altogether. Without affection, we may be benevolent and beneficent to those in need, and these acts are valuable. Indeed, if we consider the frequent barbarism of human beings toward one another, then dispassionately treating each human being simply "with dignity and respect" seems already more than we can achieve. Set in contrast to our ongoing hostility and neglect of one another, unfeeling respect and equal regard would be a wonderful feat. But sensitive Christians, I think, find that respect and regard are too limited and controlled to be the human ideal.[24] The human spirit wants to do more than respect the basic value of persons. Some affectionate love is necessary. The human spirit wants to go beyond respect for the common humanity that makes us all the same. It wants to emotionally affirm both the dignity of our humanity and the uniqueness that makes us different.[25] The human spirit wants to love agapically.

GOOD OF THE BELOVED

The distinguishing feature of agape is that it is directed to the beloved for the beloved's sake. The "object" of agape is the beloved, its "aim" is the good of the beloved, and its "reason" is also the good of the beloved. Each of these three is essential. We might be oriented to Tom, but not to Tom's good; and this would not be agape. We can be directed to Tom's good, but our reason might be to benefit someone else, and this would not be agape. Only when we are directed to Tom's good for Tom's sake is there agape. Our agape for Tom might result in more good for ourselves or for someone other than Tom, but in agape these results are not our "reason" for loving Tom. Again, "reasons" here are not the same as results, even fore-seen results. Thus, if our "reason" to love Tom is to fulfill some need in ourselves, even our need to love, this is not agape for Tom. Of course, we can have two kinds of love at the same time, e.g., we can love another for the beloved's sake and also for our sake. There is nothing to prevent such a concurrence of loves, though tensions will likely arise between these loves.

Agape may be directed to *any "object"* that is good or capable of being good. The beloved, we saw in Chapter 2, might be a neighbor, a stranger, an idea, a cat, God, a group, or myself. Commonly, agape is described as "other-directed love" or "neighbor" love, where the neighbor is every human being except ourselves.[26] But there is no reason why we cannot have agapic love for ourselves, for God, or for subhuman creation, and we ought not have "equal regard" for God and our dog. I have insisted that there should be differences between the love that we have for a dog and a human being, or between God and human beings. But each of these can be agapic loves. If agape is essentially love for others, then it follows both that we cannot love ourselves agapically and that God does not love God agapically.

Agape is an affirmation of the *good* of the beloved. It is not simply knowledge of the beloved, nor is it sharing in a common activity with the beloved for the promotion of some other good. It is not cofeeling the experiences of another in a way that is indifferent to whether this sharing promotes the other's good. Agape also is directed to its *beloved for its own sake*. Agape for Tom is not, taken by itself, love for God, nor is it love of Tom for God's sake. I shall return to this issue at the end of the chapter.

Agape is directed to the good of the beloved, whether this good is *actual or only potential*. That is, agape is not oriented only to the neediness or incompleteness of others. Agape is not simply a helping love. We can agapically love our beloveds for the good that they already possess, delighting and affirming that good. In particular, we can love God with agape. And agape also opens us to ever greater riches already present in the beloved. But agape is usually directed to bringing about a new realization of good in the beloved. God's love for us brings us from purely potential persons into actuality. God's redeeming love gradually transforms us from actual sinners and potential saints into the justified and sanctified persons we can be.

Proportionate to Value

Describing agape as intent on the good of the beloved seems relatively straightforward. Enormous controversies, however, have developed over whether or in what way the beloved's goodness, actual or potential, should be a criterion for the exercise of agape. Nygren and many others argue some version of this thesis: agape is "indifferent to value."[27] Contrary to most commentators, I will defend the position that agape is directly related to the full value of the beloved. This issue is crucial, and I must give it extended treatment. I will examine four positions: with reference to the beloved, agape is directed to (1) no value, (2) sinfulness and disvalue, (3) basic human dignity, (4) full, individual good.

No value: Agapists often describe agape as having no reference to value. They do so, I think, in order to exclude three meanings of the terms "value" or "good." First, to talk of the beloved as good or as valuable can mean "good for me" or "valuable for my purposes." We have seen this distinction before. It has unfortunately been commonplace in Catholic thought to identify the good as whatever is "perfective of another," especially what is "good for me."[28] Using this notion of the good, Kierkegaard mistakenly held that any preferential love for a person must be a way of seeking a benefit for one's self and therefore is selfish.[29] The idea of agape excludes loving the goodness of another only insofar as this goodness benefits the lover. Outka tries to exclude this meaning of the good by describing agape for another as "identification with his interests in utter independence of the question of his attractiveness, of what he has to offer, of the reciprocity of the relationship, or repayment in the form of similar self-giving." Outka adds that agape is not present if we would stop loving when we no longer get any pleasure or reward from the relation.[30]

For similar reasons, Nygren finds no sense in speaking of a good self, "divine spark," "divine kernel," or "God in the neighbor." If any of these "good qualities" were present, they would be good reasons (i.e., good for us) for love; but if we had good reasons for love, it would be eros, not agape. Similarly, he argues, if God were motivated by human good, God's love would be eros, seeking to get something. But God does not need anything; God is sovereign. Nygren does not merely hold that love should be independent of relatively peripheral characteristics such as race, wealth, or social status. No, any supposed intrinsic worth of the person as person is out of court.[31] Nygren's position on human and divine agape makes the mistake, I think, of understanding the beloved's good as simply good for me rather than as the good in itself. He puts no stock in the typically Catholic theme that God the Creator pronounced creation good and that therefore it can be affirmed to be good.

Second, agapists want to exclude considerations of "good" or "value" where these terms suggest that the beloved might earn our love. In fact, the paradigm often given is love for our enemies or for infants because they do nothing to earn our love. As Paul Ramsey writes, "Love for enemy simply provides a crucial test for the presence or absence of regard for the neighbor for his own sake."[32] And Willard Gaylin colorfully writes, "The infant is universally adored by the typical parent, even though it is a totally narcissistic, self-involved, demanding, parasitic and uncharming (except in the eyes of those who love him) individual. . . . Love is showered on the infant, even though he does the kinds of things which normally only offend us. He urinates on us, passes gas and more in public, drools on us, disturbs our sleep, interrupts our meals, breaks our valued possessions, and upsets the tranquility of our lives—and we adore him for it."[33] Sinners, infants, enemies do not earn our love. But it is one thing to say that agape is not "earned" by the beloved,[34] and it is another to say that it is not based on the intrinsic value of the beloved. In fact, no one ever "earns" any kind of love.

Third, agapists sometimes exclude love for a supposed "intrinsic goodness" of the beloved because they think that this term means that human beings are good wholly apart from any relation to God. These authors rightly hold that our religious, moral, and ontological goodness essentially involves a relation to God, but they wrongly conclude that there is therefore no intrinsic goodness in creatures. Thus, out of a desire to affirm the sovereignty of God, theologians may deny any goodness at all in the creature. Nygren argues that "'all things are of God'—nothing is of man."[35] Thus, "Agape . . . *starts with the conviction of one's own lack of worth.*"[36] That is, since God alone is good, humans have no value. Nygren spurns the view that persons remain ontologically good as God's creatures even in their sinfulness. He also rejects the view that, under grace, sinners actually might again become good, indeed in a divinized manner. Catholic theology has not denied intrinsic goodness, but out of a concern for God's immutability more than God's sovereignty, it also has denied that our goodness makes any difference to God's love. It holds that God loves not our goodness, but only God's own goodness, and that we are but weak reflections of that goodness.[37] These positions imply a mistaken view of ontological participation. Though our goodness depends for its existence on God, still it is ours. We *are* in varying ways and to varying degrees good. If God does not love that goodness, God does not love us. As Timothy Jackson writes, "With the possible exception of the original act of creation, not even God's *agape* is unalloyed bestowal. God himself has granted creation a (partially) independent being which he calls 'good' in its own right; God himself is now a strong moral evaluator. The contingency of the world does not preclude its being valuable, any more than the contingency of my words precludes their being true appraisals of that value."[38]

Though Nygren holds that agape is indifferent to value, all talk of value is not out of court for him. He holds a position that sounds similar to my own: "*Agape is a value-creating principle.*" His position is quite different from my own, however, since he does not allow for any intrinsic value in the beloved. On the one hand, he can say that "the man who is loved by God has no value in himself." On the other hand, he says that the beloved of God "acquires worth." Value for Nygren, as for many in the Protestant tradition, seems to be merely imputed, for "what gives him value is precisely the fact that God loves him." Nygren rejects the view that human beings have an "infinite value of the soul." Agape is a value-creating act, but it does not really create value. Value is in the eye of the beholder, namely God. We are precious to God, but not really precious.[39] The question raised here is whether the moral and ontological goodness of the beloved is relevant to agape. Is agape indifferent to all value in the beloved? Is it enacted, to repeat Outka's phrase, "in utter independence of the question of his attractiveness"? I am arguing that agape essentially requires emotional affirmation of the beloved's own attractive goodness.[40]

Before pursuing that thesis further, let me readily admit that agape's supposed "indifference to value" plays an important function in Christian life. We love some people even though they are "not our type," indicating a willingness to go beyond the "good for me." At our best, we can love people who are rather repulsive to us; we can forgive and embrace people who are public sinners or who have offended us; sometimes we can love even those who continue as our enemies. We help a stranger, not knowing whether she is rich or poor, famous or even infamous, but only that she is human. Even if it does not mean indifference to all value, agape surely means a willingness to go beyond off-putting features.

Sinfulness and disvalue: The second basis given by theologians for agape is our sinfulness. Christ died for us while we were still sinners (Rom 5:8), a favorite passage of agapists. Nygren's conception of agape is ruled by one composite theological theme: the sovereign mercy of God. God is sovereign, dependent on nothing, and God offers us mercy rather than retributive justice. Nygren relies heavily on Matthew 5:43–48, "Love your enemies," along with its justification, "God makes the sun and the rain to fall on the good and bad alike." Although this text suggests that some humans are indeed good and others are bad, for Nygren the only relevant category for human beings is sinner. There is no good in human beings to motivate God since agape is offered to sinners.[41]

Since sinful humans are unworthy of God's love, Nygren concludes it is "futile to try to find a motive for God's love for the lost."[42] The possibility that the lost *are* nonetheless still *lovable* in some way is explicitly rejected by Nygren. That is, he will not allow that human beings, as images of God, are still bearers of intrinsic, albeit finite value. Nor are they lovable for what they may become. According to Nygren, God does not see the pearl of great price, perhaps buried under the mud of sin, because there is no such valuable pearl. There is mud all the way down. Nygren admits that if human beings were valuable, his theory of agape would be wrong. His defense of this position is revealing: if the sinner had some worth, God could offer no real forgiveness; forgiveness would merely be an acknowledgment of the goodness of the person, not the introduction of something new.[43] Sinfulness must, for Nygren, remain the basis for agape. He does not recognize love's creativity in affirming the actual good, overcoming the bad, and leading to as yet unrealized new goodness.

In a phrase that is very foreign to Catholic ears, Nygren concludes, *"Fellowship with God on the basis of sin, not of holiness."*[44] Nygren contrasts what he considers to be the false Catholic view with that of Martin Luther: "In Catholicism: fellowship with God on God's own level, on the basis of holiness; in Luther: fellowship with God on our level, on the basis of sin."[45] As is frequently the case in ecumenical disputes, the truth, I think, lies in the positive assertions of both sides, but not in their denials. The Lutheran view finds support in Paul's claim: "For our sakes God made him who did not know sin, to be sin." The Catholic view finds support in the way that Paul concludes this verse, "so that in him we might become the very holiness of God" (2 Cor 5:21). Holiness, in the Catholic view, is not forensic; we really "become" holy. But before considering that point, let me develop the point made by Nygren's assertion.

God does not avoid sinners: "God sent his Son in the likeness of sinful flesh" (Rom 8:3), and "in his own body he brought your sins to the cross" (1 Pt 2:24). On the other hand, "in him there was nothing sinful" (1 Jn 3:5). Put in my own language, God participates in our lives through love. And since we are sinners, God is *united* with us in our sinfulness. But since there is unity-in-*difference*, there is no sin in the Christ. Existential participation means a real sharing of life. To the extent that our lives are sinful, God can be affected by that alienation; hence, in that sense, there is alienation in God. There is a discordance between God and God's own people, whose lives God has freely accepted as God's own. That is, God has accepted this people, made them God's own responsibility, but is unable without their free consent to make them return love. In this sense of a love that is frustrated, alienation is found in God. Even though God does not sin, God can be related to us who are sinners, and that relation, which really characterizes the God of history, is an alienated relation.

Sin can be the basis of fellowship in another sense. As we have seen, love is directed to the not-yet-realized good. Love resists and moves to overcome evil. Insofar as we human beings are sinners, our sin can be said to be the basis of God's love in the sense that God responds to that deficiency and disorder in us as a condition that ought not be. Later in this chapter, I will discuss God's preference for the poor. Here I only call attention to the greatest "poverty," the absence or rejection of God from our lives. This poverty calls forth God's love.

Still, *pace* Nygren, love finds its primary basis in God's goodness and our created goodness. And since love is creative, we really can change from sinner to justified and from justified to sanctified. We can become the "holiness of God," again, by participating in God through love. Nygren puts little stock in the ancient theme that God the Redeemer even more wondrously renewed creation. He fails to appreciate the transforming power of love to intrinsically justify and sanctify. Love is for him not participation, but an activity that remains wholly with the lover, without real effect in the beloved. The beloved remains nothing but a sinner. By contrast, I have been arguing that, because of God's love, though we always remain to some degree sinners, we also can really share life with God and God really shares life with us. Accepting God's love moves us along our path from sin to sainthood. We who are always more or less ontologically good become morally and religiously good through God's creative and redeeming love for us and our response to that love.[46]

One final way to see that agape is directed to value is to reverse the perspective.[47] If we asked someone why they loved us, and they answered that they loved us because we were evil or loathsome or that their love had nothing to do with our value, we would rightly think that they did not love us.[48] We might feel pitied, but we would not feel loved. To be loved by such a promiscuous lover is even less affirming than to be wanted by a promiscuous sexual partner. The latter affirms at least some aspect of ourselves, while the former is unconcerned even about this much. Even when we feel unworthy, we want to be loved for what we are and can become. To learn that someone's love for us has nothing to do with any good in us is to learn that someone does not love us. To learn that someone's love for us is based on our sinfulness is to be encouraged to remain in our sin so that we can continue to be loved.

Basic human dignity: Outka holds that agape is equal regard for the *basic dignity* of all human persons: "(1) he is valued as . . . a person qua human existent and not because he is such-and-such a kind of person distinguishing him from others; and (2) a basic equality obtains whereby one neighbor's well-being is as valuable as another's."[49] Thus, Outka says, whatever is admirable or outrageous in persons is not valued one way or the other by agape. Agape shuns any comparisons between persons. It fosters equal consideration of all. No one shall be excluded on the basis of merit, talent, or any other similar criteria. No matter what the beloved does, "it still makes sense to talk of him as worthwhile."[50]

This position makes an essential point: love for other persons requires that, at a minimum, we affirm their basic human dignity. This minimum is in itself already enormously valuable. Indeed, this basic dignity is already a pearl of great price. Most other attributes are less important goods that pale in comparison with this great good. The affirmation of basic human dignity already prohibits two common forms of discrimination: first, no human being should be excluded on the basis of criteria such as nationality or sex, and second, no human being will be affirmed exclusively or exhaustively on the basis of such secondary criteria.[51] Agape forbids excluding human beings from the human race, not because agape is indifferent to value, but because this exclusion is a denial of their basic human value. In principle, then, agape extends to all human beings.

In this view, the good that agape affirms is the basic value of human life. The stranger, our enemies, or the handicapped each have this basic but quite precious kind of value, accordingly, they are more lovable than our favorite cat. We know next to nothing about the millions of starving persons in Africa, but we can be moved by the fact that they are human beings. This is not value-indifference, but apprehension of the great value of being human.

Agape is not only value-creating, but also disvalue-resisting, a point that frequently captures the attention of agapists. The major evil that agape resists is that of subordination of basic human dignity to lesser values.[52] We human beings, because of sin, are inclined to use or treat one another primarily in terms of some function or quality. We forget or even deny the basic and enormous value of being human, thereby missing the tree for its fruit. Agape resists the tendency to relate to others simply in terms of wealth or accomplishments or merit or beauty or talent or race or social standing. Agape insists that success is not essential to human dignity and that failures do not destroy it. Agape refuses to confuse instrumental value with basic well-being. Agape will not allow any person to be treated as cannon fodder or chattel for others. Preferences for one person over another must always take place only after basic human dignity has been effectively affirmed. The agapist worries that any preferences may "swamp universal human dignity" or cause concern for a common humanity to become mere "pious irrelevance."[53] These mistakes are all very real. Agapists rightly warn us not to treat people merely as a means and not to value people merely for some secondary qualities. We sinful human beings have a well-documented record of misjudging to our own advantage the value of the people about us, and so a bias in favor of the equality of all persons is often prudent. What this implies for social policy, Church teaching, and moral exhortation is that all people are proclaimed to be equal. This proclamation, I suggest, is a practical strategy, not a theoretical position. It is designed to resist our temptation to treat others as less than human. In all cases, agape must first intend the basic value of persons as human. But is this enough?

Before answering, I want to distinguish between a negative universal love and a positive universal love. The former demands only that no one be excluded on grounds that she or he is in some way unfit to be loved. The latter demands that we literally love all equally. But no human being can really love each of the six billion people of the earth. And no love would occur if we had to love every human to the same degree, no more and no less. Such love is in principle impossible for the finite and unique earthly beings we are. But even a negative universal love is not an adequate description of agape.

Outka well notes that "non-exclusiveness must somehow link with uniqueness. That is, attribution to everyone alike of an irreducible worth and dignity does not mean that people are indifferently interchangeable."[54] Even if we begin with basic human value, there is something distinctive about individual persons that is soon illumined if we love them. Generically equal human beings are interchangeable. Real human beings, however, have a unique identity which God and they (along with many outside influences) have brought and are bringing into being. In its reality and in its promise, this unique identity is something more than basic humanity. It is extremely precious, as any lover knows.[55]

When we love human beings, our union is limited to their generic humanity only to the extent of our ignorance. That is, if all we know about them is their basic humanity, then this is all that we can unite with. Even in such cases, however, we often try to imagine—without any confirming evidence—something of their unique identities, e.g., they are mothers with children or they are hungry. We know that even the "faceless" people we want to help have faces. As we meet them in person or in imagination, our love is directed not simply to generic human beings, but to individual persons.

Full, individual good: I want to argue that agape is and must be directed to the whole value of the beloved. Therefore, agape is a highly differentiated love, which is not directed to all equally. Can agape stop with "basic human dignity"? The problem is that persons are not simply generic human beings with basic human value. No true lover would ever tell the beloved that she or he was loved as an instance of basic humanity. No true lover thinks that an indefinite number of others could fill in for the beloved.[56] We sometimes say to another, "I love you just because you are you," where the apparent tautology in fact means to convey something unique beyond generic humanity and generic qualities.

Agape, to be true love, must look further: persons do not exist apart from their qualities. It is one thing to love persons *only for* their attributes, another to love them *apart from* their attributes, and still another to love them as beings that *exist in* their attributes.[57] Persons are not mere combinations of attributes, but beings who exist in and are modified by their attributes and actions. The fundamental act of personal being is deeper and more pervasive than all its partial self-enactments;[58] but this fundamental act does not exist apart from these enactments.

Even if we love the beloved only on the condition that the beloved has certain qualities, e.g., a generous and lively spirit, still there is no reason to deny that this is, in Jules Toner's language, a real, but "conditioned radical love" or conditional agape. It is not just a love of qualities, such that anyone with similar qualities would be loved as well. In fact, an experience of qualities without regard to the person who bears them is at most a rare experience, able to be approached only asymptotically and momentarily. We encounter persons, not qualities. In a "conditional agape," the lover "is not loving merely the qualities; he loves the person who has the qualities, but only on the condition that he has them. This is very different from loving him merely as the bearer of qualities."[59] Thus, "it is all right to be loved for our achievements and our kindnesses if not *only* for them. They are not alternatives to ourselves. They are part of that which defines ourselves."[60]

Problems arise when theorists demand that agape must be independent of all merit, qualities, functions, and the like. This demand would require agape to prescind from some of what the person really is. "In loving a woman as a person, a man does not love her for her admirable traits alone. He nevertheless loves them as *her* achievements and he loves her as the one who possesses them. Her attributes are more than just the cause of his love. They are part of the woman he loves, and in loving her he is also loving *them* . . . not as they might belong to someone else but as they belong to her."[61] Thus, we should be careful when we say, "God loves us regardless of what we do."[62] It is true that God loves us no matter what we do. But what people do may be good, and thus to say that God loves us regardless of what we do should not be understood to mean that God does not care about the good that we do. God's love not only "persists" through our sinful acts, it also relishes and fosters our good acts. Moreover, "what we do" cannot so easily be separated from "who we are." Who we are is partially characterized by our sin and by our virtue. And so God loves us who are sinners-and-saints.

What then of the concern of most theorists that agape not be dependent on such things as holiness, beauty, or intelligence? The answer is not that these sorts of things are irrelevant to agape, but rather that they are not the *primary* criterion of agape for human beings. The primary criterion is our basic humanity. As a consequence, agape will not permit us to dehumanize our enemies; rather it requires us to affirm their basic humanity. But agape includes more. Agape moves us to unite with and promote the good of beloveds—their whole good. The talented athlete shall be affirmed in (and not simply for) her ability. The skid-row bum shall be affirmed not only in his basic humanity, but also as the unique person he has made himself to be and as the better person he could further develop into. The criterion here is straightforward: agape accords to a being the full value that it really (and ideally) possesses.

This means that agape affirms differences. For Nygren, by contrast, God does *not* have a special love for Mary or Peter or Paul in contrast to Judas; he even holds that any talk of "God the Father's" special love for "God the Son" is a deviation from the true doctrine of agape.[63] Rather, I have argued, God's love affirms differences. The "Father's" love for the "Son" is a distinctive act of agape. God loves all creatures, and God loves them unequally, which is the foundation for why they are unequal in value. That is, all persons have more goodness than trees; some persons have more goodness than other persons; and these differences derive from God's love.[64] So too there can and should be differences in our agape.

The option being made here should by now be clear. For some, agape is not a response to anything in the beloved, since there is nothing worth responding to. However, if we say that agape is completely independent of value, including the basic value of being a human, then it is not clear how one might justify a greater love for God than for people or a greater love for people than for stones.[65] For others, agape is directed to sinners. This view makes it impossible that God could love God, that we could love infants or other moral innocents. And it fails to see how love is directed to the good, both real and ideal. For many ethicists, agape is characterized as a love that is directed to basic humanity, but to no further distinguishing features. I contend that such love can only be accomplished by a forced act of abstraction from the real persons we deal with. Encouraging such a love may even be counterproductive. Rather, agape, if it is really love, necessarily moves us to want to overcome this anonymity wherever possible. Furthermore, it makes little sense to say that we should love God quite apart from God's good qualities. Rather, agape may be directed to all "objects" in all their differences in value.

Practice of Agape

Theologians frequently do not literally mean what they say. They speak in the language of metaphor, hyperbole, paradox, allusion, analogy, and the like. One reason for using nonliteral language is that theology usually takes as one of its tasks the building up of the people of God, and so the language of exhortation is deliberately or inadvertently employed. One example of that hortatory style is the claim that agape requires us to love everyone equally. If that stipulation is taken literally, none of us could love agapically. One small reason why Christians don't strive harder to practice what they preach is that they are vaguely aware that what they preach is impossible.

Distinctions have to be made in the practice of agape, even for those who hold that agape is "equal regard." Outka puts the matter in a relatively noncontroversial, negative way: agape prohibits deciding "whether the other is to be cared for at all," but then he adds a controversial positive possibility: "it allows and perhaps requires that he be cared for appropriately."[66] This requirement undercuts the practical meaning of equal regard. Equality is an empty criterion when it comes to the positive practice of care. Something more akin to proportionality becomes relevant. Agape may be "identification with the beloved's interests," but these interests are different in different individuals. A love which treats people equally is inadequate.

Considered abstractly, all human beings share a common humanity. Considered abstractly, each has the same basic needs for life supports such as air, food, and shelter. Considered at a sufficiently high level of abstraction, each has the same psychological needs and social needs, each needs to know and love and will, each seeks for God. Concretely, however, these "common" traits are always already differentiated.[67] They are particularized by the individual person. We may strive to take all equally into account, but when we take who they really are into account, we find equality of practice is unethical. Equal regard cannot mean equal or identical treatment. It is an unwarranted prejudice to hold that all are born even with the same potential. The potential for living a full biological and psychological life is not equal, even from birth. The same may be said for intellectual potential and freedom. An equal amount of food for all will lead some to be fat, others to be thin. Most of us simply are *not able* to be an Einstein.[68] We even have differing capacities for relating to God due to differences in temperament.[69] Real human beings are neither actually nor potentially equal. Even if agape meant that we love all without exception, all without exception are different, and so we cannot and ought not offer equal treatment to all. "Equal" is only a negative criterion: do not *arbitrarily* treat one person less well than another. The equality of all people is a good and useful fiction that has been and continues to be very important for Christian social ethics. "It prevents us from overlooking certain urgent claims which lie outside our ordinary interests."[70]

The principle of equality derives more from the philosophical principle of universalizability than from Christian experience.[71] The biblical world is quite distant from such a principle—to its disadvantage but also to its advantage. The Bible knows mostly various interlockings of social position and familial or tribal relationships. The modern world consists of large numbers of relatively unknown people, and so it stresses equality and impartiality within "associational" interactions. In biblical times, the stranger tended to be an "outsider," that is, someone who does not "belong" to one's group. In modern times, the stranger is nearly everyone. Since, in public choices, we usually cannot know much about those who are involved and since what we can quickly learn, e.g., sex or race, is usually irrelevant, equality and impartiality are suitable for law. But this equality is not a good norm for the whole of our Christian lives.

The conditions of finitude require both that we select those we will love agapically and that we treat people differently. We often have to choose among the persons we will actively support, and sometimes we have to do harm, occasionally even mortal harm, against others.[72] While we may hope that somehow the harm will also help those whom we hurt, we realize that this hope may be unrealistic when we are required to resist those who harm others. Thus, distinctions have to be made in the *exercise* of agape.[73] Even if we could offer "indiscriminate acceptance" (whatever that might mean in the concrete), it must be followed by "discriminate response."[74] It hardly seems an agapic act to support the drug dealer in his "profession." Agape cannot, in Outka's fine metaphor, mean giving a blank check to the other. Perverse interests ought not be fostered.[75] Similarly, it is not a matter of indifference to the exercise of agape whether or not the beloved is growing in the direction of its own fullness. If a teacher is indifferent about whether his students are learning, his exercise of agape is seriously deficient. Love should not be so severed from concrete value.[76] *Unconditional* love surely means "I will love you even if that love does not do me any good." It also means "I will love you even if you are not doing yourself (or others) any good." But love by its nature does discriminate between good and bad. Unconditional love is in its exercise highly *conditioned* by the objective reality of the beloved: "I will love the real and potential good found uniquely in you; I will resist the real evil or immaturity in you." Thus, love is directed to and modified by the unique value of the beloved. Once the beloved is present, agape is without conditions for whether it will be exercised, but it is very conditioned by the identities of both lover and beloved in how it is exercised. Agapists often insist on the former, while they neglect the latter.

Contrary to the position of many agapists, God's love for human beings is not purely impartial or "nonpreferential."[77] In fact, one standard biblical meaning of the word "love" is "to prefer." God is one who sends the rain on the just and the unjust alike (Mt 5:45), but this God is also the one who separates the sheep from the goats, the one who chooses tiny Israel from all the nations, the one for whom Jesus is "my beloved," and the one whose Spirit blows where she wills. It should be noted, however, that I have *not* said that in practice agape always prefers those who are more valuable over those who are less. Even if, as I hold, people are not equal, this is not, as we shall next see, an argument that the smart or virtuous should get food first. Intelligence or virtue are not "relevant differences" for this distribution; simple hunger will do. Rather, I argue that agape is a love that takes account of reality, and reality includes the beloved's full value. Agape is directed to the whole (actual and possible, known and still to be discovered, present and to be created) value of the beloved. It is also, as we next see, directed to those who are most in need.

Preference for the Poor

Christianity is sometimes said to reverse the Greek tradition on love. In place of an eros love that flows from the needy to the rich that can fill their need, Christianity proclaims a love that flows from the full to the empty. "The Lord is exalted, yet the lowly he sees and the proud he knows from afar" (Ps 138:6). God chose Israel, the least of the nations: "Fear not, O worm Jacob, O maggot Israel; I will help you, says the Lord; your redeemer is the Holy One of Israel" (Is 41:14). God sided with Mary, the lowly handmaid, and cast aside the mighty (Lk 1:48). Christianity has known one who, though rich, became poor out of love for the poor (Phil 2:8). A Christian understanding of love, therefore, must keep in mind the love of superior to inferior, of God to creature, of rich to poor, of a community member to the outcast. Nygren put this point with his characteristic clarity: *"The stream of love must be directed downwards."*[78]

I suspect, nevertheless, that Christianity has never seriously held that love should be directed only to those who are poorer, more in need, or of "lesser value."[79] Otherwise love for God would be proscribed, not to mention many other loves such as love for the great saints. In fact, for Catholic theologians the dominant love has often been what Nygren describes as eros. For Aquinas, the stream of love best flows upward, toward that which will perfect the lover. What for Nygren is pagan love is for Aquinas both the way that God has created us and the way that God elevates us. If agape is essentially directed downward, as Nygren insists, then not only can we not love God but we may not even love our putatively equal neighbors with agape.

I hold that the movement of agape is not directed necessarily downward or upward. Agape is directed to the good of the beloved, whether those we love are "inferiors," "superiors," or "equals." We unite with the beloved in the direction of *its* greater good. Whether that good is more or less than our own is irrelevant to whether we can love agapically. We are not the reference point for the value-reality of the beloved. The beloved is. The beloved's actual and potential value is the good we care for.

Is there then any "privilege of the poor"? Two qualifications: first, it should be clear that being needy, disenfranchised, or powerless—in a word, "poor"—is not in and of itself valuable. One does not become better by being poor; otherwise it would be our loving duty to keep poor the poor. Similarly, if God always loves the poor more than others, then, from a religious viewpoint, the best thing we could do is to become poor and, again, keep the poor in their poverty. Our contribution to salvation, whether of a temporal or a spiritual nature, would be to deprive people. This is all counter to common sense and to the constant efforts of Christians. Accordingly, we should also be hesitant to say that agape necessarily "is composed of *compassion* and *mercy*" or that it is essentially forgiving.[80]

Agape is mercy and forgiveness only if the beloved is suffering or sinful. If God lifts the lowly, the lifting and the being lifted are what is good, not being lowly.

Second, since our love for God should be primary, love for the poor cannot be primary. Rather, our participation in God's love should lead us to love all without exception, to the extent that we are able. In the Scriptures, God surely loves the poor, but God also loves David, who was a king, and Jesus, whom the tradition describes as "perfect." And Jesus loved the rich young man (Mk 10:21). Further, though agapists commonly hold that Christian love favors those who are most in need or even least attractive to us, this encouragement should not be made a universal principle. For example, should our Christian criterion for a marriage partner be the person who is most offensive to us or who is most in need? If this kind of agape were the only Christian love, that would seem to follow. If it were the supreme Christian love, it would be the ideal to pursue and by which to judge ourselves. Marrying someone we liked would be acting like the pagans.[81]

Nevertheless, one of the most attractive features of Christian agape is that it inclines us to favor the most needy. But does that mean that we should choose, say, the least qualified engineer to design an airplane, simply on the grounds that she was the most needy? The agapist could well respond that out of love for those who will use the airplane, we should choose the best qualified. At the very least, this act involves preferring many rather well-off travelers over the needy one, a dangerous pattern if this were the only preference principle the agapist had. In decisions like this, a preference for the poor may only be valid when "all else is nearly equal," a condition that often does not occur.

Still, granting all this, it can be said that among human beings agape has a predilection for the poor because they are in greater need and therefore are more lovable *in the sense* that, generally speaking, more good can be done with and for them.[82] This reasoning parallels what utilitarian philosophers call marginal utility. Marginal utility builds on the commonsense notion that five dollars given to a poor woman more radically improves her life than five dollars given to a millionaire. A preference for the "poor" is usually a preference for those who are denied their basic human rights to housing, clothing, a share in the political process, and sufficient power to be able realistically to determine the course of their lives. The rich do not lack these basic goods. As we saw in the previous section, the good of basic humanity comes before any further qualities such as increase of status, beauty, pleasure, higher education, or athletic talents. These basic human rights are close to our basic humanity and thus one fosters enormously important values by helping others to obtain them.

To the extent that we are rich with agape, to that extent we can transcend ourselves and enter the lives of those who are in any way poor. It is agape's genius that we can unite with others in their need. Agape is sensitive to value. Thus, it is sensitive to a great disparity between what is and what could be. It is particularly sensitive to what is lacking when a fellow human being cannot live a normally decent life. Even if we are assured that we will always have cake, we can be sensitive to and ally ourselves with those who do not have bread. The experience of the beloved's needs—not any concern for ourselves that we too someday might be so needy[83]— moves agape into strong action with and for the poor. Thus, the richer we are in agape, the more we are inclined to devote ourselves to those who are in great need. From those who have been given much, much is expected (Lk 12:48). Those with ten talents of agape must be especially generous, but even those with one talent must extend themselves.

Thus, agape has a predilection for the "poor." This preference is not absolute (Mt 26:6–13). Enormously important and difficult questions arise about how to decide where to devote our energies, questions that I have neither the space nor the competence to solve. It seems clear, however, that normally there should be a lexical ordering in which the basic rights of all persons should first be taken care of.[84] On this ground, most of us stand condemned, since a great proportion of the world is presently deprived of its basic human rights while we pursue our own development. Still it is conceivable, following Rawls's maximin principle,[85] that the further advance of a few might be justified when, in the not-so-long run, it leads to the increased achievement of basic rights for all. One thinks of those rare cases when martial law—including the suspension of some, but not all human rights—might in fact temporarily be justified. One might for a while neglect housing in order to build a sawmill that would then be used to make lumber for housing. These are dangerous if commonplace exceptions, and I will say no more about such matters. Still, agape should be directed to the "poor" since they are the closest to being deprived of their humanity and since, other things being equal, they have the most to gain. Thus, Drew Christiansen writes,

> Some principles, such as the priority of basic needs or the inclusion of
> disadvantaged groups, will carry greater weight than others. Nonethe-
> less, the balancing of goods for the sake of the commonwealth raises

questions of sufficient complexity to preclude any final lexical ordering of norms. The common good functions above all as a coordinat-
ing principle, and the weight of relevant norms will alter depending
on circumstances. The goal of the coordination, however, remains
clear: *Everyone in the society ought to be able to share in an advancing
quality of life.* . . . The principle of solidarity charges privileged individuals, groups, and nations with making sacrifices, even from their
substance, to close the gap between themselves and the poor.[86]

The exact determination of these practical questions is, I think, at bottom
a matter of vocation and discernment. All must help the poor, but the
varieties of "poverty" are as extensive as the ways that human beings can
be "rich." People are "poor" in bread and "poor" in moral character. When
forced to choose between people who are economically poor through their
own fault and people equally poor through no fault of their own, an
agapically motivated person could go either way. The "undeserving poor"
are poor both in bread and in character. The "deserving poor," however,
are more likely to benefit from our assistance. Though agape does not of
itself solve practical questions, it does establish a life-pattern. Those who
are filled with agape will always be "bleeding hearts," just as God on the
cross had a bleeding heart.

SELFLESS LOVE

We have thus far seen that agape is directed to the beloved's full value for
the beloved's own sake. And it has a special eye for those most in need.
Now I want to look at some other characteristics of this love: it is spontaneous and generous; it is self-giving to the point of being self-sacrificial;
and it is faithful.

Spontaneous, Overflowing Generosity

Nygren asks, Why does God love us? The answer for him is simple: there
is no reason. God's love is spontaneous. Nygren, like many others, interprets this spontaneity or freedom to mean that there is nothing in the
beloved that motivates and in that sense determines God. Love's only reason is God's nature. Unlike Aquinas, Nygren does not draw this conclusion in order to save God's immutability. No, agape's downward
movement puts the lie to that philosophical theory.[87] Rather, if God
loves, it must be an absolutely free decision. If there were something in the
beloved, even some need, that could affect God, God would not have
sovereign freedom.

I have argued that love, including God's love, requires that the beloved codetermine both the lover and the particular act of love. Thus, God's spontaneity should not be understood to say that God is not moved or affected by the beloved. However much love wells up from a full heart, it is only a global emotion of fullness until it is intentionally directed to a particular object. To give an analogy: a doctor might find herself full of desire to help the victims of an earthquake who have been brought to a hospital. But she does not actually heal until she meets the people lying there, each of whom will require a different kind of healing. Thus, a love that does not yet love someone is not yet love in act. Not only must love be directed to specific objects, it partly takes its character from them. If a person were to say that he loved bowling and his dog, therefore he can love people, we would rightly scoff. The kind of love varies with its object. Love for a bowling ball cannot be the same as love for a person, and love for John concretely is not the same as love for Mary. When we love, we unite to some degree with the beloved, and thus we and our love are dependent on just who or what the beloved is.

The reason for recalling these phenomenological reflections is that many authors neglect this "intentional" nature of agape. They strongly insist that it does not make any difference whom we love, because agape possesses its quality, value, and significance independently of its object. Nygren offers from Luther an image: love is like gold, it is good in itself whether given to godly or ungodly persons.[88] This image treats love as a thing in itself and not as an act that requires and is dependent on its beloved.[89] That is, to pursue Luther's metaphor, gold given to an ungodly drunk for more alcohol would not be a gift of love. It is a mistake to protect agape's spontaneity by sealing love off from its object.

Still, agape is rightly characterized as "spontaneous and unmotivated." Deep in human persons there is a spontaneous desire not only to get but also to give. This desire is the stronger, the more a person is good. As Erich Fromm notes, "Giving is the highest expression of potency."[90] A good teacher *wants* to share her knowledge. A miser symbolizes those whose shrunken personhood, not limited resources, prevents them from being spontaneously generous. Whence this spontaneous goodness to others? Aquinas observed that it is the nature of the good to expand and generate itself in others.[91] The good God desires to share goodness. Humans do of course seek their own good but, made in the image of God and graced by God, they also desire to communicate their goodness.[92] It is in this sense that agape is spontaneous. It flows naturally out of a good heart. The deepest origin of our good activities is not a duty-bound will, but a heart full of love and joy. Agape gives from abundance.[93]

Those who are good not only spontaneously give; they give generously. All of us, presumably, have known moments when we felt so full of goodness that we were inclined to give to others in new and imaginative ways. That part of the Catholic metaphysical tradition that has emphasized an orderly creation has often neglected this expansive feature of love. Love goes beyond set boundaries. Agape has Dionysian moments within it. It rebels against a too well-ordered and controlled world. It rebels against bourgeois contentment and smugness. It eventually gets bored by a devotion without depth or extravagance. The dynamism of love disturbs the moderation that Greek-oriented humanists set up as the cultured ideal. As Martin D'Arcy colorfully writes, "The animus after setting everything in order to his own satisfaction has to take second place. He has to stand by and watch while the anima dances out of doors to another's piping."[94] The calculating person would never leave the ninety-nine for the one lost sheep (Mt 18:12). Agape forgives seventy times seven (Mt 18:22). It serves even unto its own death (Mt 20:28). "The boundlessness of such love, its heedlessness of self, its prodigality in pouring itself out for the neighbor without counting the costs is undeniable as we read its character on the pages of the New Testament."[95]

The experience of agape at times is one of ecstasy. We live beyond ourselves in another's life. We wholeheartedly affirm the beloved's existence and growth. In the ecstasy of love the value of the beloved often is felt more clearly than our own. We live for the beloved without close attention to our costs.[96] Our hearts are made to be full of passion; we are primed for an object worth dying for. As Max Scheler said, "Nothing great without passion."[97] When we are attracted by a profound ideal or cause or person, we experience that object as "deep calling to deep." This break from a closed world may be a descent to the nether realms of mystery religions or a flight beyond the world to God. But it can also mean a passionate devotion to this world. To be sure, our love for God must purify any inordinate attachments to the world; but passion must not be confused with an inordinate love of the world. When we passionately attach ourselves to God, we join with that God who "so loved the world that he gave his only Son" (Jn 3:16). Those who love God risk losing the world, the world they have become comfortable with, the world that they have structured to suit their own needs. In losing *this* world, they can, however, gain the world God loves.

Paradoxically, acts of "supererogation" are necessary. Agape's acts of supererogation are the "natural" outflow of a full heart.[98] Like Jesus, the saints do not simply calculate goods and evils. Rather their love often has a reckless quality to it. Living beyond minimum standards, they experi-

ence that for them "all falling short of the perfection of the Christian life
is some moral imperfection, some failure."[99] Acts of supererogation flow
from their passionate devotion to the beloved. Similarly, we can so unite
with those we love that their life becomes greatly determinative of our
action. We are drawn to do what they need and would or should do for
themselves. It becomes easy or "natural" to do for our beloveds what we
would do for ourselves or even what we would not do for ourselves. To be
sure, prudence may have to be exercised so that we do not needlessly harm
our own interests. But self-interest and self-control ought on occasion
yield to extravagant gestures of a passionate love.

Agape, thus, is not merely a matter of fulfilling a commandment.
Commandments can be fulfilled in an acquisitive way, e.g., as a way of
getting a reward or avoiding a punishment, and commandments usually
are not fulfilled in an "overflowing" way.[100] Agapic lovers do not do what
they are "told to do," nor do they simply obey the commands of the
beloved. Those sorts of acts would block up their devotion and turn it
into something else. At least at times agape has an extravagant quality.
Agape's boundlessness seldom appears in many theologies of agape. The
term "equal regard" seems itself minimalistic and calculating, even if that
is not what is intended. It does not do justice to the more expansive
moments of agape. Rather agape follows no set rule in its willingness to go
the extra mile (Mt 5:41) or to contribute one's last two coins (Mk 12:41–
44). What one would not demand of others flows freely from one's self.
That is, agape goes far beyond the principle of universalizability and the
golden rule. Agape can and should go beyond "the rock bottom rules"
that are necessary for any society to exist.[101]

Thus, agape's spontaneous generosity flows from loyalty and devotion. The "strenuous teachings" of Matthew 5:38–42 should be seen, not
as laws, but as examples of this spontaneity: we loan without interest to all
who want to borrow and seek out people who might want to beg from us;
when anyone sues us for whatever reason, we not only give them whatever
they seek, but add something extra for their effort; we do not use violence
against the violent.[102] These practices nicely capture the generous quality
of agape. And every Christian life must at least occasionally include such
acts of generous agape.

Turned into laws, however, these exhortations would make social life
impossible. Love tries to enhance the being of the beloved, and it does so
not only in the short term and for this or that person but in the long run
and for many persons. Yielding to every legal suit and giving our goods
away to everyone who asks, whether they are poor or rich, would soon

make society a lawless place and leave most of us unable to function. Rather, the lover's experience is one of being now and again "led to such actions by grace and not by his own resolve."[103]

There is, therefore, a need to be a discerning lover. In all moral living there is a mutually informing relation between our emotions and our reasoning. Reason functions as a moderator of the generosity of agape's devotion. But reason should not domesticate love's generosity, making it timid.[104] In cooperation with God, we can be extravagant lovers. No rule or even preference principle can, I think, be set down in advance for generosity. Christian discernment in community is necessary. Thus, we properly praise the sacrifice of life made by Maximilian Kolbe so that others might live, but when it comes, for example, to giving up both of our kidneys so that two others might live, we should hesitate. Ultimately we must discern what the love of God is calling us to do.[105]

Self-sacrifice and Self-giving

This passionate, generous devotion is the basis for another feature of agape: the lover at times willingly sacrifices for the sake of the beloved. "This is my body to be given for you" (Lk 22:19). Indeed, "when radical love is intense enough the lover's affirmation can be so completely given over to the beloved as to affirm the latter's being at the cost of the lover's own."[106] The testimony of the secular and sacred saints is that at our best we have a profound desire to give ourselves over to something larger than ourselves; we are even willing to sacrifice our life for that object of our devotion.

Any understanding of agape must include some place for the foolishness of the cross, the heroics of the battlefield, or the reckless daring required to rescue damsels in distress. Love's willingness to sacrifice is accounted for by love's ability to participate in and affirm the life of its beloved. The watchword is, "I want *you* to live fully." The lover's life, on occasion, becomes so absorbed in devotion to the beloved that there is no counting the costs. In its religious form, agape's devotion leads us to ignore our own loss if expended for God. Self-concern is suspended in this Dionysian ecstasy.[107] Agape's ecstasy may be the unexpected sacrifice by Sidney Carton at the end of Dickens's *Tale of Two Cities* or it may be the culmination of a lifetime such as Jesus' cross.

Not all would agree. D'Arcy hedges self-sacrifice: "A person as an end in himself, independent and unique and self-owning, cannot surrender himself so entirely as to deny or maim his own personal perfection."[108] This hedge is too high. It follows the Thomistic tradition that has always had a difficulty in understanding self-sacrifice. The perfection of the self is not an absolute limit. Ruled out would be a mother's sacrifice of her own self-development for her family. There would be little place for Jesus' cross. To be sure, we ought not be mindlessly self-sacrificial. A discerning prudence is called for. Not simply the prudence of self-interest, nor a prudence that simply calculates costs/benefits, but a prudence that restrains self-sacrifice until it is our time to take up our cross and follow Christ. When that time is, only a lover's heart can say.

Even in the best of worlds, there might still be sacrifice as an outflow of self-giving generosity. In our imperfect world some sacrifice will always be necessary. Human finitude and sin make it impossible for every being to achieve some modicum of fullness without some loss to others. Not everyone can have all they need or want. Finitude means that the classroom chair occupied by one cannot be occupied by another. Sin further renders any ideal harmony of all with all impossible. Thus, what is good for the one I love often will be possible only at some cost to myself.[109] We frequently face questions about who will sacrifice and who will benefit.

It is not easy to answer such questions. Some philosophers and theologians argue that self-sacrifice is an essential characteristic or even the distinguishing characteristic of agape.[110] Though many Christians recommend a complete and unreserved sacrifice of self as the highest ideal, there are at least three sets of problems with such a recommendation. Some have to do with the theory and some with the practice of self-sacrifice. First, some theoretical points. As a universal principle, self-sacrifice is self-contradictory. That is, if two persons each acted always self-sacrificially toward one another, neither could act self-sacrificially.[111] Each would insist on holding the door open for the other, and thus neither would enter. A perfectly altruistic and self-sacrificing community would have *more conflicts* than one in which self-interest prevails. In the latter, the interests of people often coincide. But in a completely self-sacrificing community, we would want to give to and not receive from persons who would want to give to and not receive from us. Unless it is qualified, the doctrine of self-sacrifice tells us to sacrifice always. Its inner logic strains against saving ourselves so that in the long run we might do more for others. Moreover, taken just by itself, an absolute doctrine of self-sacrifice gives us no way of choosing for whom to sacrifice if two or more people need help, as seems always the case.

Second, some religious problems: it is not easy to make the case that God wishes that we make a rule of self-sacrifice. Few if any of us want our friends to constantly sacrifice themselves. In fact, we want them to enjoy and fulfill themselves, and we often make sacrifices so that they do just that. By analogy, if God loves us, God wants us to live, and this living is not a matter of constant self-sacrifice, but rather of many acts of self-realization. Hence, God does not want us constantly to sacrifice ourselves, though, of course, on occasion this may be just what is required. Jesus did not endlessly sacrifice himself. He often lived moderately, sometimes even festively, until "the hour had come for him to pass from this world" (Jn 13:1).

Third, there are objections to the effects of recommending self-sacrifice. Liberationists note that a doctrine of self-sacrifice often works against the poor or marginalized: "By making self-sacrifice the primary criterion of the virtuous life, Christianity has given powerful religious validation to the situation of oppression. For those who lack power and status in a society, there is no motivational lever by which equality can be gained. . . . Indeed, this ideal tends to foster the reverse dynamic: an inducement to remain subjugated in testimony to one's disregard for self."[112] The oppressed of the world have sacrificed themselves for the rich and powerful, with little to show for their sacrifice but misery. Such "agape" actually promotes injustice.[113] Outka expresses further reservations about the consequences of a policy of self-sacrifice. We should not submit to the beloved's interests when this leads to exploitation. We should not give our neighbor all our property just because the neighbor wants it. At the very least, a principle of self-sacrifice needs the qualification that our sacrifice is for the good of the beloved. But that is not enough. Our rich neighbors would happily and profitably add our small piece of property to their estates. Some criterion of relative need seems also relevant. Equally obvious, we ought not sacrifice to help one person if that means that other people will suffer as a result.[114]

Obvious points. But not quite so obvious. Surely the model of Jesus, who gave his life for sinners, is essential in developing the ideal of agape, as is Jesus' injunction that we go the extra mile, give to those who beg, love our enemies (Mt 5:38–48).[115] Jesus tells us to turn the other cheek when the neighbor wants to hit us again, and to give our neighbor not only our coat but our shirt too (Lk 6:29). The "excessive" sacrifices we make may be expressive of intense devotion. The woman who anoints Jesus' feet is criticized for wasting precious oil that could be used for the poor, but Jesus defends her extravagant love even against the good that the apostles thought they could do for the poor with the oil (Mk 14:3–9). Christian agape encourages a way of life that, at least at times, is open to great self-sacrifice. In the Christian tradition of nonviolence, there "is an unwillingness to engage in the logic of self-defense (who gets whom first). It is also an unwillingness to engage in the logic of impartiality or equality; it is a refusal to demand even what one is minimally entitled to."[116] Thus, the logic of agape *may* lead to self-sacrifice, and not simply as an instrument to some good or as a by-product of service to others.[117] Self-sacrifice within a love relationship may express the depth of our devotion to the beloved. Self-sacrifice has an abiding place in Christian life.

On the whole, however, for describing agape "self-giving" is better than "self-sacrifice."[118] The latter puts the focus on one's loss, while the former highlights one's generosity, the other's gain, and the importance of union. Agapic lovers do not intend to negate their own interests, but to affirm those of the beloved.[119] Self-sacrifice is *not* essential to agape since what is good for the neighbor often also brings good for us. The fact that we gain through an action does not mean that agape is absent.[120] Imagine two alternatives. In the first we gain a little and the neighbor gains a lot. In the second, we lose a little and the neighbor gains a little. Self-sacrifice dictates the second choice, agape the first. Thus, "love need not be self-sacrificial. In responding affirmatively to another person, the lover creates something and need lose nothing in himself."[121] In sum, love's generosity and self-giving are

> a beautiful and natural overflow of one's forces. . . . *This* kind of love and sacrifice for the weaker, the sick, and the small springs from inner security and vital plentitude. In addition to this vital security, there is that other feeling of bliss and security, that awareness of safety in the fortress of ultimate being itself (Jesus calls it "kingdom of God"). The deeper and more central it is, the more man *can* and *may* be almost playfully "indifferent" to his "fate" in the peripheral zones of his existence.[122]

Faithful

We saw in Chapter 2 that love by its nature endures. Endurance is particularly strong in agape. Agape is "unalterable in that some attitudes toward the other are never set aside. . . . The loyalty enjoined is indefectible." Agape's "permanence involves persistence in the face of obstacles and continued concern for another's welfare despite lack of personal benefit."[123] The reason why agape is in principle the most enduring love is that its existence is not conditional on some return to us, on its success in fostering the beloved's good, or on some mutual relation with the beloved. We may sit long, seemingly pointless hours beside the bed of a sick stranger.

Our fidelity follows from the very nature of agape: it is love for the beloved's sake. Thus, unlike friendship, which is threatened or dissolved by conflict, this love remains firm even when the beloved rejects the lover.[124] The "Lord loves the people of Israel, though they turn to other gods" (Hos 3:1). Such fidelity is indeed powerful. Shakespeare said it well: "Love alters not when it alteration finds."

This agape says that "no matter what you do or become, I will love you." Agape's permanence is fidelity to the beloved which, though it changes in time, still is the same beloved. This fidelity, however, should not be understood to be an endless sameness. Agape also grows and changes. We want to love as much as we are able, and to love even more on the morrow. Agape's fidelity does not mean that it cannot adapt and evolve in accord with both our and the beloved's evolution. Much agapist literature so emphasizes that agape is independent of history or individual changes in the beloved that it appears to be in itself and in its exercise unchanging. For example, Reinhold Niebuhr held that disinterested love is "utterly independent of the claims and counterclaims of history."[125] Others add that agape should be "independent of changes in the particular states of the other. . . . Independence connotes that the love in question does not arise from and is not proportioned to anything a given neighbor individually possesses."[126]

I have seriously questioned whether this independence of all change is the Christian ideal. As finite subjects we change, and the finite objects of our love change, both thereby calling forth from us a proportionally altered love. The argument that love should be independent of all change in the beloved smacks of the Greek option of permanence over change. The guiding image seems to be a beneficent unmoved mover. There should be a rock-bottom stability to agape, but neither the lover nor, usually, the beloved is a rock. Agape alters in relation to both subject and object, without losing its permanence. It is a mistake to confuse the permanence of a rock with the fidelity that characterizes personal life at its best.

The virtue of fidelity is in itself bipolar: the lover is faithful both to the lover's own self and to the beloved. One common understanding of the virtues is that we act in a steadfast manner in order to be true to ourselves. Acting unvirtuously is then to deny ourselves (2 Tm 2:13). This position is not wholly wrong. Still if we are solely concerned with our own virtue, we are not loving the beloved for its own sake. Like other virtues, fidelity is in touch with reality and therefore love is faithful agape only when its exercise changes with changes in the beloved. Thus, God's love is endlessly responsive to us, leading us out of our sins and toward ever fuller holiness. And so too is our agapic love for another. Fidelity means that we will never stop loving, but it does not mean that we will always love in the same way.

Since God loves not only us but others and also all of creation, we cannot, as we saw in Chapter 4, conclude that what God is doing in the world will always be entirely for our good. Some loss to our own well-being will be necessary. The most that God's fidelity can assure us of is that God will be with us even in our losses. Our fidelity to God is manifest when we stay united with God, even when God asks of us great sacrifice. If we lose much or all, we still have the "one thing necessary" when we remain faithful to God. This God is the God of both our life and our death. This God is also the God of the resurrection, the God whose faithfulness does not allow our death wholly to wipe out the good we have become and done.[127]

OBJECTS OF AGAPE

Love of God

When they come to agape, theologians sometimes simply say, "*Agape* is understood first of all to refer to God's love for us."[128] This simple and basic Christian claim seems noncontroversial, but it evokes certain questions. First, what is the meaning of love? The meaning of "love" in such statements is rarely clarified. This is unfortunate since the meaning of love, as this book tries to point out, is hardly clear. Second, to say that agape is "*God's* love" tells us only who the "subject" of this love is. This point raises three questions: If agape is defined or distinguished as *God's* love, can it also be our love? And does saying that agape is "God's love" mean that other kinds of love are not "God's loves"? If they are not, are other kinds of love, e.g., philia or eros, neutral or even antithetical to salvation? I propose that agape, like *all* genuine loves, may be part of the life we share with God. Agape, then, is our love too. Subsequent chapters will show that eros and philia are also the loves we share with God. They too are "God's love."

Nygren argues that our agape should be "patterned on God's love."[129] But for him and his followers, this turns out to be theologically impossible. Consider the obvious problems that arise if one applies his descriptions of agape to love for God: for example, should Christians be indifferent to God's value? Is their love sovereign? Is their love for God directed downward, and to a sinner? Love must be spontaneous, generous, and free, but Nygren tells us that being moved by God's love means that God overwhelms and takes control of us. Thus agape is not really our act. For reasons such as these, many theologians are silent on whether we really can love God.[130] The first great commandment, though given by Jesus and central to Judaism and Christianity (Dt 6:5; Mt 27:37), turns out to be impossible.

By contrast, I have developed an understanding of existential participation that holds there can be two spontaneous acts, that is, two self-originated acts. God's love for us is spontaneous, and our human love for God can be a spontaneous response. Our response is free, uncoerced, even when it is itself a grace-enabled response. Love evokes love, but does not force it. Ours is a dependent and responding freedom. Nevertheless, our response is our own. While our agape is evoked by God, this does not mean that God's agape does all the work. We are real sources of our own acts. "Any who did accept him he empowered to become children of God" (Jn 1:12). Since we can meaningfully withhold ourselves from God, we can also meaningfully give ourselves to God.[131]

In response to God's grace, we can have an overflowing, generous love for God. "Of his fullness we have all had a share, love following upon love" (Jn 1:16). God loves us and we can affectively participate in God. Agape for God means that we affirm God for God's sake. Our delight in and relishing of God's goodness is not merely intellectual contemplation of God's goodness, but also an emotional union with that goodness, appreciated in and for itself, and not for what it can do for us. This love should, to the degree we are able, be proportionate to God's own goodness. It means that we unite with God's own dynamism, and do so in the direction of at least appreciating, if not also fostering, ever more value in the God who is related to creation. Our growth in union with God means that we are inclined to be caught up in wonder at the mystery of God. And that mystery—all the more so as it is involved in history—is inexhaustible.

God cannot force us to love God; otherwise it would not be our personal love for God. Our love for God can give God something that God doesn't have, namely, our own hearts and our own lives. We can offer ourselves to God (Rom 6:13). Those who say that any goodness we add to God already belongs to God fail to account for our difference from God. Rather, our loving heart, given to God, is not identical with God's heart and, therefore, is a genuine gift.[132] We are not mere tubes through which God's love flows from God back to God. We depend on God to initiate the love relation, but since the act of response must be ours, it also has its own originality. We can live ecstatically, forgetful of ourselves, willing to sacrifice, and faithful in response to God's fidelity to us.

Love of Neighbor

At the end of the last chapter I spoke about the relation between love for God and love for our neighbor. At the end of this chapter, I want to extend those reflections to agape. This chapter has said that to love our neighbors agapically means to love them for themselves. Should Christians, then, prescind from God in loving their neighbors? Günther Bornkamm observes concerning Matthew 25:31–46 that those at the last judgment protest that they would have loved those in need if they had known these persons were Christ himself. But their protest was not accepted. They are judged for not loving their neighbors for their own sake.[133] Is it then religiously sufficient to love our neighbors without a thought to God? Others, by contrast, have argued that we should love nothing for its own sake except God. All creatures are to be loved merely as means or stepping-stones to that one love.

Two responses suggest themselves. First, in loving our neighbors for who they really are, we can come to see that they really *are* related to God. They are continuously created, sustained, and embraced by God. For Christians, however much God is transcendent, God has not disappeared, leaving us able to interact only with creatures. God is actively loving our neighbors, and our neighbors are really involved in a variety of ways with God. We can experience this value of our neighbor as related to God when we love our neighbors *for themselves*. Their real relation to God is something we affirm in affirming them. We affirm their own dependent selves: made in God's image and redeemed by God.[134] We affirm them in their divine depths. Thus, when we love our neighbors for their own sakes, we encounter and are *also* able to love the God in whom they live and have their being. That is, we have two intertwined loves. We love our neighbors for their own sake, but in that love we also come to love God. The parable from Matthew 25:31–45 is, I think, misleading if it requires us to forget our relation to God in loving our neighbors for their own sakes. And it seems insufficient if it sanctions forgetting that relationship. What Christian would want to forget God! Rather, I propose, the parable invites us to be aware that God is present in those who are hungry, thirsty, without clothes, or in prison.

Second, let us look at the demand that we not love our neighbors for their own sake, but only God. When we love God we unite with God, and in so doing we are invited to love what God loves. God, who is not preoccupied like human beings with how the world may fit divine needs, is fully able to see and affirm the preciousness of the world. Furthermore—and this is the important point—God is able to love our neighbors for their own sakes. Otherwise God does not have, in my terms, an agapic love for them. God's love surely seems agapic: God so loved us that God sent the Son so that we might be saved and live (1 Jn 4:9–10). God seems genuinely to care about us for our own sakes. The classical position that God does not love us for our own sakes but only for God's own sake seems untrue both to experience and to the biblical story. Thus, our love for our neighbors can be genuinely for their own sake when we love our neighbors as part of our relation to God. Since God loves them agapically, that is, for their own sake, our love in cooperating with God's love also loves them for their own sake. To love others does not mean using love for them as a stepping-stone to loving God. Rather, loving them for their own sakes is part of our life with God.

CONCLUSION

In this chapter, I have discussed agape: love of our beloveds for their own sake. This love is centered on the beloved's value and is directed to the enhancement of that value. It is a faithful love that is spontaneous, generous, and willing to sacrifice. This love, however, is not the only love that should characterize Christian life. In the next two chapters, I extend these reflections to love for our own sakes.

NOTES

1. Oliver O'Donovan, *The Problem of Self-Love in St. Augustine* (New Haven: Yale, 1980), 10–11. Martin D'Arcy, S.J., *The Mind and Heart of Love* (New York: Henry Holt, 1947), 59, shows, for example, how two famous historians on love, deRougemont and Nygren, use eros and agape in almost opposite senses. Similarly, an ancient view of eros says that it seeks the infinite and scorns earthly communion (see D'Arcy, 60–62), while a contemporary view (James B. Nelson, *Embodiment* [Minneapolis: Augsburg, 1978], 110), sees eros as desire for a beloved sexual partner. For an excellent survey of various contrary and contradictory contemporary understandings of agape, see Gene Outka's classic text, *Agape: An Ethical Analysis* (New Haven: Yale Univ. Press, 1976). See also Wolfgang Nikolaus, "Eros und Agape," *Zeitschrift für Evangelische Ethik* 30 (1986): 399–420; Enda McDonagh, "Love," *New Dictionary of Theology*, ed. Joseph Komonchak et al. (Wilmington: Michael Glazier, 1987), 603.

2. Anders Nygren, *Agape and Eros* (New York: Harper & Row, 1969).

3. The beloved may be God, one's self, another human, a thing, etc. Two further classical varieties include love for the other in terms of a third party (e.g., John loves the

necklace for Mary) and love for the other in terms of its relation to someone we have a primary love for (e.g., John loves Sally because she is Mary's child).

4. Nygren, *Agape and Eros*, 75; James Hanigan, *As I Have Loved You* (New York: Paulist, 1986), 150–51.

5. D'Arcy, *Mind and Heart of Love*, 60.

6. Outka, *Agape*, 4, 7; Hanigan, *As I Have Loved You*, 149; C. S. Lewis, *The Four Loves* (New York: Harcourt Brace Jovanovich, 1960), 181, calls it the "highest form of love."

7. Outka, *Agape*, 1.

8. Nygren, *Agape and Eros*, 240 (all in italics in original).

9. Nygren in *Agape and Eros* extensively develops a history of agape. It is, he thinks, a history of a pristine and revolutionary idea that has been constantly polluted by eros. Even the Scriptures, he holds, are not free of this corruption (pp. 150ff). It was especially in the Synoptics and Paul and later in Luther that "the specifically Christian conception thrusts itself powerfully to the fore" (p. 29).

10. Nygren, *Agape and Eros*, 45.

11. Nygren, *Agape and Eros*, 223. *ST* I–II.1–5. For Aquinas, an impure heart is a heart withdrawn from God by being inclined to earthly things. Lacking an adequate theory of personal participation, Aquinas argues, "The nature of love is to transform the lover into the beloved; hence if we love base and perishable things, we are made base and unstable" (*Duo Praecepta*, 98a; *ST* II–II.25.3, II–II.44.1). In the life of the counsels, he writes, "A man will withdraw as much as possible from temporal things, even legitimate ones, because they occupy the mind and thereby hinder the actual movement of the heart towards God" (*ST* II–II.44.4; *Duo Praecepta*, 99b). "We make other things equal to God, when we love temporal and corruptible things at the same time with God" (*Duo Praecepta*, 100a).

12. Nygren, *Agape and Eros*, 205.

13. Nygren, *Agape and Eros*, 210. Nygren's summary is slightly shortened.

14. For example, Nygren neglects texts such as Luke 6:32 where *sinners* love (*agape*) those who love (*agape*) them. But in Nygren's theory, there cannot be good agape and bad agape, only God's agape; in fact, for him human love is not agape at all, but only self-love (*Agape and Eros*, 96–97). Though Nygren tries to build his argument on Scripture, his overall procedure of drawing sharp contrasts fits more a rationalistic frame of mind than fidelity to the diversity of Scripture. To Nygren, whatever agape has, eros cannot have; agape is Christian, eros is pagan; the first is theocentric, the second is egocentric (p. 205). A. H. Armstrong, "Platonic *Eros* and Christian *Agape*," *Downside Review* 79 (Spring 1961): 106–20, shows that Nygren's reading of nonbiblical history is also incorrect. See also the theological critique by Frederick Crowe, S.J., "Complacency and Concern in the Thought of St. Thomas," *Theological Studies* 20 (1959): 353–63.

15. See Karl Rahner, S.J., "Love as the Key Virtue," *Sacramentum Mundi* (New York: Herder and Herder, 1970), 6:340; Mark Taylor, *God Is Love* (Atlanta: Scholars Press, 1986), 308.

16. Paul Ramsey, *Basic Christian Ethics* (Chicago: Univ. of Chicago Press, 1978), 94–95, gets at this distinction by insisting that we find, not just some common humanity, but the "neighbor in every man." See also Oliver O'Donovan, *Resurrection and Moral Order* (Grand Rapids: Eerdmans, 1986), 240. On the other hand, it has been a Catholic tendency to turn the neighbor into one's own self; for example, Richard Gula, S.S, *Reason Informed by Faith* (New York: Paulist, 1989), 180.

17. D'Arcy, *Mind and Heart of Love*, 229; see also Charles Taylor, *Sources of the Self* (Cambridge: Harvard Univ. Press, 1989), 95.

18. *Sententiarum*, 3.29.1.2.

19. Outka, *Agape*, 262–63, also 311; John Gallagher, C.S.B., *The Basis For Christian Ethics* (New York: Paulist, 1985), 91.

20. Jules Toner, *The Experience of Love* (Washington: Corpus, 1968), 131.

21. Stanley Harakas, *Toward Transfigured Life* (Minneapolis: Light & Life, 1983), 163, provides the image. Though Harakas initially seems to disparage emotion in love, he then goes on to argue for more feeling in agape. Though we don't have to like those we love, he says, agape is fulfilled when "our whole inner world" (which presumably includes feeling and liking) is directed to them. Though he says we cannot have warm feelings for our enemies (p. 162), he also claims that agape becomes Christlike only when it is coupled with tender feeling, compassion, respect, warmth (p. 165).

22. Outka, *Agape*, 126.

23. The psychological danger here is that we force ourselves to live in terms of a "pseudo-ideal self," an "ideal" self that often kills our true self; Karen Horney, *Neurosis and Human Growth* (New York: Norton, 1950), 17–39.

24. D'Arcy, *Mind and Heart of Love*, 230.

25. Gene Outka makes agape highly differentiated in "Social Justice and Equal Access to Health Care," *On Moral Medicine*, eds. Stephen Lammers and Allen Verhey (Grand Rapids: Eerdmans, 1987), 638.

26. Cf. Hanigan, *As I Have Loved You*, 150.

27. Nygren, *Agape and Eros*, 77.

28. *Veritate*, 21.1–2, 22.1; *ST* I–II.27.1.

29. Paul Wadell, C.P., *Friendship and the Moral Life* (Notre Dame: Univ. of Notre Dame Press, 1989), 76. Wadell (pp. 97–98) indicates Augustine's ingenious solution to this problem of special friends: God is the one who does the selection by means of the "mechanism" of finitude. We should love those who, by God's design, happen to be near. This solution has the advantage of insisting that we should receive our friends as gifts from God. It has the disadvantage of denying that we do in fact and by right play a part in selecting our friends. Gilbert Meilaender, *Friendship* (Notre Dame: Univ. of Notre Dame Press, 1981), 20–21, 28, describes and rejects this position.

30. Outka, *Agape*, 208–9.

31. Nygren, *Agape and Eros*, 98–99, 215–16, 550.

32. Ramsey, *Basic Christian Ethics*, 99.

33. Willard Gaylin, *Feelings: Our Vital Signs* (New York: Harper & Row, 1979), 162.

34. Gallagher, *The Basis For Christian Ethics*, 93.

35. Nygren, *Agape and Eros*, 132; Lewis, *The Four Loves*, 180.

36. Nygren, *Agape and Eros*, 222 (italics in original).

37. Lewis, *The Four Loves*, 180.

38. Timothy Jackson, "The Disconsolation of Theology," *Journal of Religious Ethics* 20 (Spring 1992): 9.

39. Nygren, *Agape and Eros*, 78–80.

40. C. Taylor, *Sources of the Self*, 516; Robert Roberts, "Emotions Among the Virtues of the Christian Life," *Journal of Religious Ethics* 20 (Spring 1992): 43, denies that agape is a distinct emotion.

41. Nygren, *Agape and Eros*, 66, 68–70, 75, 104. Nygren omits all mention of texts such as Matthew 25:31–46, where the Son welcomes some persons and rejects others on the basis of differences in moral value.

42. Nygren, *Agape and Eros*, 89, also 70, 76.

43. Nygren, *Agape and Eros*, 79–80, 98–99, 215–16, 230, 550, 731. Cf. *Duo Praecepta*, 98a; *ST* I–II.110.1–2, 111.1, 111.5, II–II.8.4; *Sententiarum*, 3.27.2.1; *Veritate*, 27.1.

44. Nygren, *Agape and Eros*, 684, 687.

45. Nygren, *Agape and Eros*, 690; but compare, 734.

46. O'Donovan, *Problem of Self-Love*, 30.

47. M. C. Dillon, "Toward a Phenomenology of Love and Sexuality," *Soundings* 63 (Winter 1980): 357–60.

48. Lewis, *The Four Loves*, 181.

49. Outka, *Agape*, 12. It is hard to be certain what Outka himself holds, since he purports mainly to summarize other thinkers. Cf. also Ernest Wallwork, "Thou Shalt Love Thy Neighbor As Thyself: The Freudian Critique," *Journal of Religious Ethics* 10 (Fall 1982): 300–301.

50. Outka, *Agape*, 11.

51. Outka, *Agape*, 12–13, 261.

52. Outka, *Agape*, 261.

53. Outka, *Agape*, 261–62, 271–73.

54. Outka, *Agape*, 91–92, 260–61; Hanigan, *As I Have Loved You*, 151.

55. D'Arcy, *Mind and Heart of Love*, 229.

56. William Earle, *The Autobiographical Consciousness* (Chicago: Quadrangle, 1972), 117; Daniel Day Williams, *The Spirit and the Forms of Love* (New York: Harper & Row, 1968), 114. Soren Kierkegaard, "You Shall Love Your *Neighbour*," *Other Selves: Philosophers on Friendship*, ed. Michael Pakaluk (Indianapolis, IN: Hackett, 1991), 239, 244, makes the strongest case for understanding agape as being indifferently directed to everyone, quite apart from their bodies and psyches.

57. Robert Solomon, *Love: Emotion, Myth and Metaphor* (Garden City: Doubleday, 1981), 162–75; Singer, *The Nature of Love*, 3:401.

58. Toner, *The Experience of Love*, 101.

59. Toner, *The Experience of Love*, 105.

60. Gaylin, *Feelings: Our Vital Signs*, 163; Outka, *Agape*, 77–78, 90.

61. Singer, *The Nature of Love*, 3:399.

62. Wadell, *Friendship and the Moral Life*, 89; see also Outka, *Agape*, 260, 262.

63. Nygren, *Agape and Eros*, 152, 201.

64. *ST* I.20.3–4, II–II.26.7.

65. Outka, *Agape*, 167. A further complication, which I shall not treat here, is that some allowance must be made for the freedom involved in the act of bestowal: we and God choose some to become precious to us, some more than others.

66. Outka, *Agape*, 19–20.

67. Outka, 310; Timothy Jackson, "Christian Love and Political Violence, *Love Commandments*, eds. Edmund Santurri and William Werpehowski (Washington: Georgetown Univ. Press, 1992), 212.

68. See Outka, *Agape*, 264–67, 308. Contrary to Outka's claim, it is not historically true that all agree that "men are equally related to God and that this state of affairs

is equally valuable." For example, Aquinas and Scheler hold this position to be false; see Edward Vacek, S.J., "Personal Growth and the *'Ordo Amoris',*" *Listening* 21 (Fall 1986): 199–200.

69. See Chester Michael and Marie Norrisey, *Prayer and Temperament* (Charlottesville, VA: Open Door, 1984).

70. Mary Midgley, *Animals and Why They Matter* (New York: Penguin, 1983), 94.

71. Outka, *Agape,* 292. Ignoring, it would seem, Jesus' love of John (Jn 13:23), Victor Paul Furnish, "Love of Neighbor in the New Testament," *Journal of Religious Ethics* 10 (Fall 1982): 332, writes that in the New Testament, love means "refusing to show partiality."

72. William Luijpen, *Existential Phenomenology* (Pittsburgh: Duquesne, 1969), 317.

73. Hanigan, *As I Have Loved You,* 151.

74. Outka, *Agape,* 12–13, 20, 309. For the opposite view, see Ceslaus Spicq, O.P., *Agape in the New Testament* (St. Louis: Herder, 1963), 1:82.

75. Outka, *Agape,* 21.

76. Toner, *The Experience of Love,* 155–62; Stanley Hauerwas, "Love's Not All You Need," *Cross Currents* (Summer-Fall 1972): 229.

77. Meilaender, *Friendship,* 3.

78. Nygren, *Agape and Eros,* 735. There is, of course, an inconsistency here in Nygren. He cannot hold both that agape is indifferent to value and that it is directed downward to lower values or disvalues.

79. For an excellent analysis of some of the excessive claims that have been made on this topic, see Stephen Pope, "Proper and Improper Partiality and the Preferential Option for the Poor," *Theological Studies* 54 (June 1993): 242–71.

80. Spicq, *Agape in the New Testament,* 1:116.

81. For a Thomistic critique of this position, see Stephen Pope, "The Moral Centrality of Natural Priorities," *Annual of the Society of Christian Ethics* (1990), 109–30.

82. Pope, "Proper and Improper Partiality," 252.

83. Cf. *ST* II–II.30.2.

84. Outka, *Agape,* 92, concludes with the following hierarchy: "Needs typically will be emphasized before merit, other sorts of differences between persons beyond differential treatment based on different needs will be played down, and privilege will always have to be justified." Stephen Post, however, rightly notes that the first concern should be the neighbor's relation to God; "The Purpose of Neighbor-Love," *Journal of Religious Ethics* 18 (Spring 1990): 181–93.

85. John Rawls, *Theory of Justice* (Cambridge: Harvard Univ. Press, 1971), 152–56.

86. Drew Christiansen, S.J., "The Common Good and the Politics of Self-Interest," *Beyond Individualism,* ed. Don Gelpi, S.J. (Notre Dame: Univ. of Notre Dame Press, 1989), 81. Also see Outka, *Agape,* 310.

87. Nygren, *Agape and Eros,* 75–77, 152, 196–97, 201, 203–4. See also Hanigan, *As I Have Loved You,* 150–51.

88. Nygren, *Agape and Eros,* 730; Spicq, *Agape in the New Testament,* 1:139.

89. Outka, *Agape,* 280. See also Paul's usage in John McKenzie, S.J., *Dictionary of the Bible* (New York: Macmillan, 1975), 522; Nygren, *Agape and Eros,* 141.

90. Erich Fromm, *Art of Loving* (New York: Harper & Brothers, 1956), 23.

91. *ST* I–II.1.4, III.1.1; *Sententiarum*, 3.32.1.1. For a fine development of this theme, see W. Norris Clarke, S.J., "To Be Is To Be Self-Communicative," *Theology Digest* 33 (Winter 1986): 441ff.

92. *ST* I.19.2, 44.4.

93. Max Scheler, *Formalism in Ethics and a Non-Formal Ethics* (Evanston: Northwestern Univ. Press, 1973), 220–26; Nygren, *Agape and Eros*, 212, 736; Patrick Byrne, "*Ressentiment* and the Preferential Option for the Poor," *Theological Studies* 54 (June 1993): 226.

94. D'Arcy, *Mind and Heart of Love*, 242, also 234; C. Taylor, *Sources of the Self*, 116–18, 383, 412.

95. Kenneth Cauthen, *Process Ethics* (New York: Mellen, 1984), 129; also Nygren, *Agape and Eros*, 81–91, 115–23.

96. Lewis, *The Four Loves*, 168. To be sure, we would criticize someone who was not also making some sorts of comparisons—to risk one's life to rescue a beloved's ballpoint pen is foolishness. Even so, we can admire such devotion, shortsighted as it may be.

97. Max Scheler, *Selected Philosophical Essays* (Evanston: Northwestern Univ. Press, 1973), 131.

98. Outka, *Agape*, 296–97.

99. Vincent MacNamara, *Faith and Ethics* (Washington: Georgetown Univ. Press, 1985), 175; see also Garth Hallett, *Christian Neighbor-Love* (Washington: Georgetown Univ. Press, 1989), 35–37.

100. Nygren, *Agape and Eros*, 727–28.

101. Outka, *Agape*, 293–95, 309–10; cf. Ramsey, *Basic Christian Ethics*, 112–13.

102. Ramsey, *Basic Christian Ethics*, 66–67, 92.

103. Outka, *Agape*, 294–95.

104. Lewis, *The Four Loves*, 167–69.

105. Hallett, *Christian Neighbor-Love*, 7.

106. Toner, *The Experience of Love*, 142.

107. D'Arcy, *Mind and Heart of Love*, 73, 239.

108. D'Arcy, *Mind and Heart of Love*, 316.

109. Hauerwas, "Love's Not All You Need," 230.

110. Spicq, *Agape in the New Testament*, 1:87; Don Browning, *Religious Thought and Modern Psychologies* (Philadelphia: Fortress, 1983), 147–50; Toner, *The Experience of Love*, 143. The clearest and most extensive refutation of this view I have found is in Cauthen, *Process Ethics*, 137–46.

111. Outka, *Agape*, 276–77. This recommendation of self-sacrifice tends toward a further contradiction. If self-sacrifice is the best way for human beings to live, then I should adopt it as my policy. But my policy would then require me to give up the best way to live, namely, self-sacrificially. See Charles Harris, Jr., "Can Agape Be Universalized," *Journal of Religious Ethics* 6 (Spring 1978): 27–28.

112. Linell Cady, "Relational Love," *Embodied Love*, ed. Paula Cooey et al. (San Francisco: Harper & Row, 1987), 140.

113. Cauthen, *Process Ethics*, 146, 152.

114. Outka, *Agape*, 21–23, 275; Browning, *Religious Thought and Modern Psychologies*, 147–48.

115. Cauthen, *Process Ethics*, 154–55, presents another interpretation of these texts: "They can be seen as the most uncompromising statement possible of the fact that noth-

ing the other person can do can eliminate the free, spontaneous and unconditional affirmation of that person's inherent worth. Neither the compulsion of the Roman soldier's sword, the threat of the intruding attacker, the law-suit of the coat-seeking prosecutor, nor the hatred of the enemy can relieve us of the obligation to continue to affirm the humanity, the value, and the welfare of those who have not similar regard for our own personhood." Thus, he interprets these injunctions as forbidding restrictions on whether we will love. He does not turn them into laws for how to practice agape.

116. MacNamara, *Faith and Ethics*, 126.

117. Outka, *Agape*, 278–79; also Cauthen, *Process Ethics*, 144.

118. Fromm, *The Art of Loving*, 22–24; Toner, *The Experience of Love*, 143–44.

119. Cauthen, *Process Ethics*, 155; Outka, *Agape*, 208–9; also, George Newlands, *Theology of the Love of God* (Atlanta: John Knox, 1980), 19–20.

120. Outka, *Agape*, 279.

121. Singer, *The Nature of Love*, 1:7.

122. Max Scheler, *Ressentiment* (New York: Schocken, 1972), 89–91.

123. Outka, *Agape*, 11.

124. The biblical claim is not unambiguous. Consider, "if we deny [Christ] he will deny us. If we are unfaithful he will still remain faithful, for he cannot deny himself" (2 Tm 2:12–13). Some exegetes understand the second sentence to refer to Christ's fidelity to God. The first sentence announces a conditional love. See also Outka, *Agape*, 11.

125. Reinhold Niebuhr, *The Nature and Destiny of Man* (New York: Charles Scribner's Sons, 1943), 2:72.

126. Outka, *Agape*, 11, also 17.

127. D'Arcy, *Mind and Heart of Love*, 245–47.

128. Hannigan, *As I Have Loved You*, 149.

129. Nygren, *Agape and Eros*, 93.

130. Nygren, *Agape and Eros*, 93–94, 125–27, 213–14, 216–18, 260, 733–35; see also Gallagher, *The Basis For Christian Ethics*, 94.

131. Lewis, *The Four Loves*, 177–78; Outka, *Agape*, 51.

132. Germain Grisez, *The Way of the Lord Jesus* (Chicago: Franciscan Herald, 1983), 469.

133. Günther Bornkamm, *Jesus of Nazareth* (New York: Harper & Brothers, 1960), 110–11.

134. Hanigan, *As I Have Loved You*, 151; O'Donovan, *Resurrection*, 226–44.

6

Self-relating Actions

Whoever would save his life will lose it, whoever loses his life for my sake will save it. (Lk 9:24)

Christianity has been very ambivalent about self-love.[1] The New Testament itself has few if any injunctions to love ourselves and many texts that discourage it. As Anders Nygren says, "The commandment of self-love is alien to the New Testament commandment of love, and has grown up out of a wholly different soil from that of the New Testament. If there were not a desire on other grounds to include self-love among the ethical demands of Christianity, no one would be able to find in the commandment of love any reason for doing so. Self-love is man's natural condition, and also the reason for the perversity of his will."[2] Nygren is largely correct. Still, even if a *commandment* of self-love is not found in the New Testament, we can ask whether self-love itself is alien to the Scriptures. After all, the Scriptures are almost equally silent about love for God. Might not there be other grounds for considering self-love an ethical demand of Christianity? And, granting that self-love is our "natural condition" and one root of our sin, can self-love also be Christian and one element in our sanctification?

Usually, when Christians describe love, they describe it solely in terms of loving *others*, and they frequently insist that Christian love requires the loss of self. For example, David Scott writes,

> Love . . . demands a kind of total dispossession of the self. . . . love implies a losing of the self for the sake of the other. . . . There is a forgetfulness of the self in love, a putting oneself at the *disposal* of the other that is the direct antithesis of the self-containment of the man who seeks the increased appreciation of the glory of his own possibilities and accomplishments. . . . The fact that love, as understood in the Christian life, requires the radical loss of the self is strikingly portrayed in the New Testament.[3]

Here there is no place for self-love. Selflessness is required. It is even against love to want to appreciate the goodness of one's own possibilities and actualities. In a similar vein, Kierkegaard claimed, "Wherever Christianity is, there is also self-renunciation, which is Christianity's essential form"; for him, "self-love is condemnable."[4] Christians, according to Hans Tiefel, "are not pointed to their own fulfillment but to fulfilling the needs of others."[5] The evils of selfishness are a staple of Christian literature. Sin, Richard Gula writes, means turning inward and away from loving others.[6] In spite of all this, the *arguments* against self-love have usually been very sketchy, unnuanced, and one-sided. Why is self-love un-Christian? Why should we deny our goodness? In rooting out selfishness from our lives, must we also root out self-love?

Other theologians allow self-love, but accord it a decidedly inferior place. Paul Ramsey says love attributes "worth to the neighbor's needs infinitely superior to the claims of the self." He adds that "no more disastrous mistake can be made than to admit self-love onto the ground-floor of Christian obligation, however much concern for self-improvement, for example, may later come to be a secondary, though entirely essential, aspect of Christian vocation." Ramsey will not permit us to treat ourselves on an equal footing with others, since that would allow us to subtract from our obligations to others "as much as the just claims of self require."[7] Others first; the self only later.

Running parallel to the long tradition against self-love has been another tradition which favors self-love. Catholic ethics has often understood self-love as "the paradigmatic love."[8] Major sections of Aquinas's ethics and Catholic ethics after him are blithely self-centered. Virtue ethics almost inevitably relies on self-love since one of its central questions is, "What am I making of my life?" For many contemporary people, self-love tends to be the root of all good. Some psychologists hold that all-out efforts at self-actualization naturally lead to a world "so harmonious, so trusting, and so balanced, that all persons can pursue" their own self-love without detriment to the neighbor.[9] Indeed, as Teilhard de Chardin wrote of self-love, "the majority of people understand it easily enough" as the first duty of life.[10]

The tension between those who denounce self-love and those who affirm it is represented in the tension that lies between the scriptural claim that those who are now unfulfilled will be blessed (Lk 1:53) and the virtue tradition's claim that those who fulfill themselves now will gain greater future happiness. Both positions are over-simplifications, needing each other as correctives. In the Catholic tradition, this need for both positions took a curious form. Much Catholic *ethics* emphasized love of self, while much Catholic *spirituality* emphasized denial of the self.[11] The former showed how the self benefits in any love for others, while the latter argued that self-forgetfulness and self-denial were necessary for perfection. In the former, concern for self was justified as the way that God created us, while in the latter concern for self was considered a distraction from God-centeredness. In the former, the importance of developing the intellect and freedom was highlighted, while in the latter the quieting of mind and relinquishing of our own will was encouraged. For ethics, being in relation to the world and therefore having a well-attuned self has been the focus, while for spirituality, especially in the past, the focus has been on forgetting the world and concentrating on God beyond the world.

In the next chapter, I will develop a positive role for self-love. This chapter is mainly a critique of some common statements against self-love. After surveying the Christian tradition, Garth Hallett comments, "The number and quality of the advocates of Self-Denial impress me more than their arguments."[12] This chapter explains how and why the advocates of self-denial, self-forgetfulness, and self-subordination have overstated their case. I begin with a look at the tradition, including a famous historical debate over the appropriateness of a purely selfless love for God. I next set out six different views on the relation of self-love to love of God and love of neighbor. Then I will analyze several ways in which our actions are related to ourselves. After that I will discuss two kinds of egoism, and to them I will contrast personal responsibility. I will then argue that self-affirmation has a *necessary* place in several important religious acts. Finally, I will argue that God's love is not purely selfless, nor should ours be.

SOME SCRIPTURAL TEXTS

The New Testament exhorts us not to be concerned about our own lives (Lk 12:22). Jesus demands that we deny ourselves, take up our cross, and follow him (Mt 16:24; Mk 8:34). We are told that those who love their lives will lose them (Mt 10:39, 16:25) and that those who hate their lives will eternally preserve them (Jn 12:25). Jesus announces that "the greatest among you will be the one who serves the rest" (Mt 23:11). Paul tells us that "Christ did not please himself" (Rom 15:1), and he says that "no man should seek his own interest but rather that of his neighbor" (1 Cor 10:24; Phil 2:4). The author of 2 Timothy puts "lovers of self" among the trials endured in "terrible times" (2 Tm 3:2). Scripture scholar Günther Bornkamm concludes, "True love cannot justify or spare a corner for self-love."[13] Thus, a pervasive theme of the New Testament is the denial of self, not the love of self. The Scriptures seem to ignore any *positive* possibilities of self-love.[14] The phrase "as yourself" in the second great commandment is one of the rare texts that even mentions self-love, and its meaning is so opaque as to have yielded wildly different interpretations.[15]

On the other hand, the Scriptures are filled with the promise of life (Dt 7:12–8:20, 30:15–20) and more abundant life (Jn 10:10). These promises appeal to a good we want for ourselves. Whether it is a promise of new life now (1 Jn 3:14) or, more commonly, in the hereafter (e.g., 1 Cor 15:19–22; Mk 9:42), the promise appeals to our self-love. If we truly hated ourselves, we would not want to live forever. Thus, far from denying all self-love, Scripture seems to take it for granted. The Gospel injunctions of self-denial and self-hate may be understood as a form of Hebraic speech used to highlight priorities.[16] That is, the Bible tells us to *hate* ourselves (and fathers, mothers, etc.) when it means that we should not love ourselves (and other human beings) *more* than we love Christ and his God (Lk 14:26; Mt 10:37).

When Paul writes, "Observe that no one ever hates his own flesh; no he nourishes it and takes care of it" (Eph 5:29), Paul assumes self-love. In our psychological era, however, we are aware that Paul's observation is profoundly untrue of many people. A dramatic counterexample is that of an anorexic girl. Any counselor could give many cases of people who not only hate their own body, but deeply hate themselves.[17] "Man's inhumanity to man is equaled only by man's inhumanity to himself."[18] Hence it can be seriously asked in our times whether there is not an obligation to love oneself. Christians have taught that God loves us, that others should love us, but that the one person who should not love us is our own self. Is this teaching still valid and useful?

Those who denounce self-love or make it secondary to love of others need to consider some theological anomalies that follow. Do they really think that God does not have self-love or that God loves God less than others? Do they think that the one who boldly announced, "I am the way, the truth and the life" (Jn 14:6) did not really love himself? This is the Jesus who allowed himself to be anointed with perfume that could have been sold to help the poor (Mk 14:3–9).[19] If Jesus and his Abba can love themselves and accept being loved, the question arises: cannot Christians do the same?

CONDEMNATION OF PURE AGAPE FOR GOD

One intriguing way to get at the issue of self-love is to ask a central religious question: should we not at least love God wholly and entirely for

God's sake, with no thought for ourselves? In the seventeenth century, a fascinating dispute broke out between two Roman Catholic bishops, Jacques B. Bossuet and François Fénelon. According to Bossuet,

> We wish to be happy, and we cannot do otherwise. We cannot banish this motive from any one of our rational actions. . . . Love cannot be disinterested as far as beatitude is concerned. . . . It is an illusion to subtract the motive of personal happiness from our love towards God. . . . To love God is simply to love our own beatitude more distinctly. . . . The desire of reward (where God is the reward), far from detracting from love, is a quest for love's perfection; it is indeed love's adequate and perfect motive.[20]

Thus, for Bossuet, our own happiness should be our final motive for loving God. Bossuet's position followed a dominant line of Aquinas's metaphysical thought: every being necessarily acts for its own good, and the goal of our actions is to gain our own happiness, which is, ultimately, to possess God.[21]

Fénelon, who was a widely known and sought after spiritual director, opposed Bossuet and argued that any action performed out of regard for the agent's own interests—even if it is an interest in eternal bliss—is not Christian; rather, it is merely a sublime form of egoism. This objection has appeared obvious to many, and it is the same charge that Nygren made centuries later. In 1699 Innocent XII addressed a set of propositions derived from Fénelon. Among these propositions were the following:

> 1. There is an habitual state of the love of God, which is pure charity and without any admixture of the motive of one's personal interest. . . . God is no longer loved for the sake of merit, nor because of one's own perfection, nor because of the happiness to be found in loving him. . . .

> 5. In the same state of holy indifference we wish nothing for ourselves, all for God. We do not wish that we be perfect and happy for self-interest, but we wish all perfection and happiness only in so far as it pleases God to bring it about that we wish for these states by the impression of His grace.[22]

From a theocentric perspective, these propositions can hardly fail to impress persons of piety. Fénelon advocated the "pure love" of God and making God's good pleasure the basis of our own.

It is remarkable, then, that the Roman Catholic Church officially condemned and still condemns these positions. Grouping the above propositions under the title, "Concerning the Most Pure Love of God," Innocent XII rendered the following verdict: "Condemned and rejected as, either in the obvious sense of these words, or in the extended meaning of the thoughts, rash, scandalous, ill-sounding, offensive to pious ears, pernicious, and likewise erroneous in practice."[23] In the pattern of the Council of Trent, which condemned those who say that we ought not look for a reward for our good deeds, the pope condemned a selfless love of God. Commenting on Innocent XII's verdict, Kenneth Kirk says: "The 'Explanation of the Maxims' was condemned at Rome, after a history of intrigue which it would be difficult to outrival. But at the bar of Christian thought Fénelon's main position has been decisively vindicated."[24] Would that it were so simple. To try to make at least some sense of Innocent XII's broad and intemperate condemnation, I want to look more closely at what is at stake in this debate over the "pure love of God." At least six distinct positions on the relation between self-love and love of God are possible. Looking at these six positions will also help clarify what is at stake in the relation between self-love and love of neighbor.

The first position, which seems to be represented by Bossuet, says that the very meaning of love is to desire or seek what is "good for me." In the case of God, we love God insofar as God brings us happiness. Love of God for God's sake is, this position holds, conceptually incoherent. We always and only love what is good for us. Reversing Fénelon's emphasis, this position argues that love would never choose to bring great happiness to God if it brought pain or misery to us. In denying Fénelon's position, however, the pope did not commit himself to this alternative.

A second position says that love for God requires that "we must renounce all desires, even the noblest." This position has Stoic and Buddhist parallels. It sees in our desires the source of either frustration or selfishness. It takes literally the biblical axiom that, if we are to be alive to Christ, we must be dead to ourselves.[25] Grace alone is good. This position seems to deny the goodness of our created nature. If so, that would have been grounds for the pope's condemnation.

A third position makes a positive but exclusivistic proposal. The love of God is the only worthy religious motive, and all other interests or motives are religiously irrelevant or unworthy. This position does not claim that we should deny our inclinations, but only that actions based on them are not Christian. Self-love may be an unavoidable fact, but its religious significance is nil.[26] For a philosophical parallel, we might recall that Kant's enormously influential ethics builds a high wall between acting out of interest and acting out of duty; only the latter is of moral significance. Thus, for this third position, other motives often will be present, but only the pure love of God is worthy of a Christian; other desires or interests are merely "natural." The Catholic tradition resists this third approach if it means to deny that "grace builds on nature."

A fourth position affirms a pure love of God and it affirms other motives, but only *insofar* as God wills them. The Fénelon text condemned above held this position. François De Sales, among others in the tradition, proposed an imaginative test of the purity of one's love for God: one "would rather have hell with the will of God than Paradise without the will of God—yes indeed, he would prefer hell to Paradise if he knew that there were a little more of the divine good pleasure in the former than in the latter."[27] This *resignatio ad damnatum* does not reflect an attitude of "How bad I am!" Rather it is an act of greatness, of largess, of love. It is the spontaneous generosity characteristic of agape. It is not readily apparent why this position was condemned. However, if we recall what was said above in the chapter on participation, perhaps an error can be detected. This fourth position in effect denies the distinctive reality of the human person. It makes all depend on God *and* nothing on human beings who have their own proper will and desires. Jesus tells us to ask for what *we* want, indicating that our own desires are important and that God wants to hear what we want (Mt 7:7–11; Jn 15:16).

A fifth position asserts that the desire to win our life or gain happiness should never be part of our motive for loving God. We should not lose our lives *in order* to win eternal life. Rather, if we do the first, then God ensures the second. This position rightly warns that fostering our desires for happiness may cause us to forget God or to suppose that we can earn heaven. This position then recommends self-forgetfulness. The problem, we shall see, is that a strict policy of self-forgetfulness is neither possible nor desirable. The Gospel, which so often offers us the prospect of a more abundant life, is not very supportive of such a policy.

A sixth and more adequate position affirms a pure love of God, but also permits an eros love of God for the sake of our own happiness, as long as the latter love remains subordinate. For example, one traditional act of contrition says, "I am sorry for my sins because I dread the loss of heaven and the pains of hell, but most of all because they offend you, my God." It is sometimes added by advocates of this position that God uses and then purifies our naturally strong desire to love God for our own happiness, so that gradually we love God more and more for God's own sake. Our self-love is used by God to draw us to a fuller agapic love. But even as this pure love for God grows, an eros love of God for our own sakes need not diminish. In fact, the two loves can grow in like and not in inverse proportion. This view has been regularly held within the Catholic Church.

If, but only if, one must choose between love of God for God's sake and love of God for our own happiness, then Kirk seems right: "At the bar of Christian thought Fénelon's position has been decisively vindicated." The pure love of God is the superior love. It is difficult to imagine that Christianity encourages pursuit *solely* of our own interest, including our interest in beatitude. As Martin D'Arcy puts it, "The doctrine of enlightened selfishness has always attracted certain minds, but it will not do as an answer for a Christian."[28] Jesus on the cross does not offer us the supreme example of self-seeking, self-fulfillment, or self-interest. There is no hint in his character that he calculated his immediate sufferings as worth long-term rewards. The story of Gethsemane and the cross indicates that Jesus' complete devotion to God remained steadfast even when he felt forsaken by God: "My God, my God. . ." (Mt 27:46). If Jesus had been seeking simply his own happiness, as Bossuet claims humans must do, he was not the holy one to be imitated. Eros is not Christianity's first love.[29]

What sense, then, can we make of Innocent XII's condemnation cited above? The condemnation can be understood to affirm that there is *some* sense in which we can and must include ourselves and our interests *within* Christian life. Exactly how that is to be done has to be explained. The overall proposal of this book is that philia or covenantal love provides the best context for Christian life. Within that context, both other-directed agape and eros have their place. The wisdom of the Church, I think, resisted Fénelon's purist position. Many different kinds of love are appropriate to a full Christian life. Before I develop a positive place for self-love, however, I want to look at some typical misunderstandings of it, since self-love is often thought to be inappropriate for Christians.

EVALUATIONS OF SELF-LOVE

Christians have developed many understandings of self-love. Focusing on the relation between self-love and love of neighbor, I will look at six. For the first, "self-love" is a conceptual mistake. It is literally impossible because love always means loving an *other.* But we are not other than ourselves. Or it is impossible because love means reunion of what is separated or alienated, and we are not separated from ourselves.[30] These authors seem to presuppose that we are fully integrated beings. In the next chapter, I will argue that integration is a goal, not a given.

In the second understanding, self-love is "wholly nefarious."[31] In much theological literature it is synonymous with selfishness.[32] Two mortal consequences of self-love are considered inevitable: first, if we love ourselves, we will fail to love others, including God, or second, we will subordinate all others to ourselves. Thus, Nygren held that *homo incurvatus in se* could never love himself or herself in a well-ordered way. Similarly, philosopher Robert Solomon argues that "'self-love' is not love at all, but rather a misnamed species of . . . idolatry."[33]

For the third understanding, while loving others is to be encouraged and demanded, self-love is a neutral matter, neither blameworthy nor praiseworthy. This position follows the pattern of Scripture, where self-love is rarely commended, but also not usually named as sinful.[34] It is just part of the natural order and has nothing specially *religious* or Christian to commend it. For others, self-love is also *morally* neutral. Morality, they say, has to do only with our relations to our neighbor, not ourselves.[35] Others say that, since we spontaneously and gladly love ourselves, there is no duty and therefore no moral value attached to self-love. To use Karl Barth's metaphor, God doesn't need to blow on this flame—nor need we; it burns brightly enough by itself.[36]

The fourth alternative holds that self-love can be appropriate, but only as a means to serving our neighbor. In his Gifford Lectures, John Macmurray approaches this view: "It is the other who is important, not himself. . . . For himself he has no value in himself, but only for the other; consequently he cares for himself only for the sake of the other."[37] We love ourselves only so as not to be a burden to others, or to be better able to help others, or to be strong enough to prevent them from sinning. Such a position, obviously, is not ringing praise for self-love. It does, however, warrant some attention to ourselves: for example, we can learn our neighbor's needs by paying attention to our own wants and desires. As Ramsey remarked, we can learn how to be generous and forgiving by observing how indulgent we are toward ourselves.[38]

The fifth view permits self-love as long as it is, so to speak, only tacit and not part of our direct intention. This position observes that when we love others, we do in fact achieve our own highest fulfillment. That is, we should not love others for our sakes; but in loving others for their own sakes we de facto realize our best self: "It is one thing to say that the agent is unable to love others without loving himself, another that loving them is simply a way of loving himself."[39] When we experience deep fulfillment in loving others, we can say that such fulfillment is not our intention or goal. Rather, it is the way God made us. This view, then, does not explicitly deny self-love; rather, it encourages us to turn our focus away from ourselves and in so doing, we are assured, we will de facto do the best for ourselves. Again, this position makes no place for a direct love for self, and it generally assumes that complete self-forgetfulness is possible and wise.

The sixth understanding says that we can and should wholeheartedly and in the first place love ourselves for our own sakes. This sixth view, found in much pre-Vatican II moral Catholic theology, holds that self-love is primary and the origin of all other loves. One Thomist puts this thesis clearly:

> The first function of the moral good will be to direct the individual toward his real happiness. . . . That is why the first and fundamental moral will is a *concupiscent* will; the other moral wills of justice or of benevolence may specify it but can never change its interested nature. We have here uncovered the principle of the metaphysical subordination of benevolent love to concupiscent love, which principle has such a depth of meaning in the whole doctrine of St. Thomas.[40]

This description aptly describes *one* strand in Aquinas's thought, the strand that has been extremely influential in Catholic ethics. Aquinas, for example, held that we should never love another human being as much as ourselves.[41] In another place, Aquinas asks himself whether one ought to commit a sin if this would free others from sin and thereby help save their souls. He answers no, and the reason he gives is not that a sin would somehow offend God, but that persons ought to love themselves more than others.[42] Many Catholic ethicists have had few qualms about asserting the primacy of love for self. As one standard textbook put it, a person "is to love himself more than his fellow man."[43] Self-love was considered the "basic form of love, which all others are founded on," as well as the standard and paradigm for all other loves.[44] Charity or love for God has been commended for leading us to a higher form of personal fulfillment.[45] Catholic natural law moralists, who say that the ethical task is self-fulfillment, argue that this is not egoistic because this goal includes "its full individual, interpersonal, and societal self-transcending meaning and openness."[46] Still, the focus on self is evident: we must go to others because otherwise we would not fulfill ourselves. Germain Grisez puts the matter with characteristic boldness: *"Love is always in the first place a disposition to the fulfillment of the one loving."*[47] Grisez quickly adds: "This ought not be rejected moralistically as an expression of selfishness: rather it is a basic fact about created persons." Grisez then straightforwardly draws a remarkable conclusion: there is no essential difference between love of a steak and love of a friend. The fact that we devour the first but not the second makes no difference in regard to the nature of love. Both are for our own perfection. The "best love," for Grisez, is not described as devotion or availability to the other or even as communion, but as a "disposition to one's own perfect fulfillment."[48]

Thus, the sixth view holds that self-love is quite proper for a Christian. The position I will defend is different from all six of the above views. My argument is that self-love is indeed a legitimate love, but I do not argue that it always is or must be either the origin of other loves or prior to them or in conflict with them. Agape and philia need not be subordinate to concupiscent self-love, nor vice versa. Each has its proper place.

SELF-RELATED ACTIONS

Theological discussions of agape as other-centered have one unfortunate result: they obscure the self. Particularly in the twentieth century, no ethics can be adequate if it has a poorly developed place for the self. Insufficient attention to the self contributes to the view that love is not an emotion. An inadequate understanding of the self has also led to many mistaken arguments against self-love. More importantly, it has caused personal harm and hindered mutual relationships. I want to offer some distinctions that may help straighten out certain common confusions about self-love. I will look at certain ways that the self is involved in its own actions.

I will stipulate some terminology. The terms I discuss are: "self-enacting," "selfless," "selfish," "self-subordinating," "self-sacrificing," "self-giving," "self-forgetful," "self-aware," "self-attentive," "self-denying," "self-interested" "self-connecting," "self-disconnecting," "self-expressive," "self-satisfying," and "self-indifferent." These terms have only a loose meaning in common usage, and that looseness generates misconceptions. In explaining these terms, my positive goal is to draw attention to different ways that we consciously relate to our selves.[49] Many of the following distinctions will be useful throughout the rest of the book.

Self-enacting, Selfless, and Selfish

Every genuinely human action is *self-enacting*; that is, there is always a self who is the agent of its own activities. In this sense, persons never do literally "selfless" actions. Thus, "to rule out the self entirely is to make an abstraction of love which has no life."[50] The self, a concrete and unique self, is always involved. Common discourse, however, usually uses the word "selfless" to mean actions done by the self, that is, which are self-enacting, but which do not have as their motive the good that accrues to the self. Self-enacting actions may benefit one's self, or others, or usually both. *Selfless* acts intend only to benefit others (1 Cor 10:24). It is inevitable that in acting the self will fulfill or frustrate some tendency of its own; but not all actions intend the fulfillment or denial of these tendencies. In this sense, the act of dying for another may be selfless, even if it in fact leads to great fulfillment—it fulfills the profound human tendency to live for others, though it does not have that as its motive. By contrast, the act of killing one's self in suicide, normally, would not be a selfless act.

When our attitudes and acts promote our own self *and,* in order to do so, either deny or ignore what is due other persons or things, we call these attitudes and acts *selfish.* The qualifier "due" is necessary, since often in life we properly prescind from or even diminish some good of others; for example, the society that taxes its rich to help the poor is not acting selfishly. Selfish acts are, by definition, objectively sinful, since they prefer the self's good when it should yield to the good of others. Selfish persons, practically speaking, make themselves the value-center of the universe, and every other "thing," including God, has value or disvalue insofar as it is good or bad for themselves. Presumably, selfish persons do not make the intellectual mistake of thinking they are really the center of the world, but they practically interact with it on this basis. Others are treated as no more than an accessory to their own self.

It is frequently said that selfishness is the essence of sin, but this claim will not stand scrutiny. When persons worship false idols, they are inordinately devoted to other creatures, e.g, a nation. They can do so in a way that is destructive to themselves, and so their actions may be selfless. Thus, selfless or self-subordinating devotion to another is no guarantee of morally good action. Self-transcendence is not synonymous with virtue.

Self-subordinating, Self-sacrificing, and Self-giving

I call *self-subordinating* those acts which are directed predominantly to the advantage of another. Unlike selfless acts, these acts may also be motivated by our own good, but the emphasis is on the good of the other. If the agent also suffers some loss in doing these acts, then these acts may be called *self-sacrificial.* In order to be self-sacrificing, the agent must be aware of at least the possibility of some loss to self. One who accidentally loses some good is not acting self-sacrificially. And there is no sacrifice when agents choose harm for its own sake or when they do not value what they lose. Thus, persons who forgo sex or possessions because they think these are sinful or sources of sin do not act self-sacrificially. God can act self-sacrificially only if God can in some sense lose something good. Some traditional theologies seem to imply that while the greatest love may be to lay down one's life for one's friend (Jn 15:13), God is not able to exercise this "greatest love." The cross is clearly a sacrifice for Jesus, and it is a sacrifice for his God only if Jesus' sufferings also mean some loss for God.

In order to love adequately, our actions must often be self-subordinating. Self-subordination is not the same as self-sacrifice. When God, out of love for us, unites God's dynamism with ours, God consents to be devoted to our good. In itself, this does not, however, mean that God must lose something. Similarly, when we subordinate ourselves to another human being, we need not experience any loss. We do not lose our dignity, but rather grow in being. This is a fortiori true of our self-subordination before God. All acts of love are not self-sacrificing. Furthermore, self-subordination may take place not only in relationships with other persons, but also in our love for ourselves. Our thoughts, desires, tendencies, and other acts should be subordinated to the fundamental direction of our whole self. Unfortunately, these subordinate acts can usurp the primacy that should belong to our whole personhood. In such cases, our otherwise important tendencies towards self-preservation, self-assertion, and self-fulfillment bring about the loss of our moral personhood. When, for example, our desire for inner quiet blots out the commitments and responsibilities we have to others, then even internal tranquility can be at odds with our relational self.[51]

Finally, as we have seen, self-sacrifice is not the same as *self-giving*. When we give ourselves to another, we may experience no loss, but only gain. Contrary to what some write, self-transcendence does not always follow the pattern of death before new life. When we give ourselves in love to God, we are elevated, even as we gladly accept our subordinate position. Any gift of self leads to a unity in which we are partially determined by the dynamism of the beloved. But this determination can enrich us. Long ago, Plato described how love ennobles us when we unite with that which is greater than ourselves. I would add that a properly qualified devotion to creatures who are inferior to us may also be enriching.

Self-forgetful, Self-aware, and Self-attentive

Among those acts which are directed to others, some acts occur in a way that is virtually *self-forgetful*. Persons become absorbed in the object of their actions, as when someone finds a great book in the library, crouches down to read a paragraph, and twenty minutes later discovers that her left leg has fallen asleep. These self-forgetful acts are common enough, but obviously they usually pass unnoticed. In most cases, our actions include some level of explicit self-awareness. This *self-awareness* includes a concomitant sense either that we are performing a particular act or that it is occurring in us, as when thoughts run through our minds or when pain possesses our bodies. In self-forgetful acts, however, awareness of the self and its interests is outside explicit consciousness, e.g., the emergency room doctor forgets her fatigue since she is wholly intent on the bleeding man before her. *Self-attention* is that form of self-awareness that is consciously directed to one's self. Psychologists stress the importance of "paying attention" to one's self, and they work with the ills that happen when their clients fulfill others' desires while repressing their own. Self-attentiveness at its best flows from having "an affectional and empathic self-object," and at its worst it flows from self-distrust and can manifest itself in scrupulosity.[52]

Usually, our actions are accompanied by some self-awareness and self-attention. Our self-awareness appears, for example, when we correct ourselves while speaking. The presence of others can distract us from ourselves, but it can also increase our self-awareness and self-attention; in popular language, we become "self-conscious." Prayer may increase self-awareness and self-attention even as it makes us less "self-conscious." To the extent that we are acting self-confidently, our self-attention may be at a minimum; then we "live in" our actions without greatly monitoring them. When this happens, we may be said to be self-forgetful.[53] There is surely much to commend in absorbed spontaneity, not least as an antidote to unauthentic action. In fact, paying too close attention, e.g., to how we talk, walk, or feel, can lead to impaired function or even mental illness.[54]

Still, there is no special merit in forgetting oneself. The recommendation that we strive always to be self-forgetful is usually made in vain, not because we are so selfish, but because the nature of human consciousness is such that we are almost inevitably aware of ourselves as agents of our actions. Generous, self-subordinating persons who reckon the cost to themselves, but nonetheless act to benefit others, are virtuous even if they are acutely self-aware and self-attentive. They may, in fact, be more responsible than those who are heedlessly self-forgetful. There are dangers and advantages in these three ways of relating to the self. Self-forgetfulness may make us oblivious to our own value and responsibilities, self-awareness has the potential for self-righteousness, and self-attentiveness can distract us from concern for others. On the other hand, self-forgetfulness overcomes our tendency to prize first our own self-interest, while self-awareness and self-attentiveness can alert us to obstacles to freedom and enrich the fullness of our involvement. While acting self-forgetfully is a truly human way of acting, acting with deliberate self-awareness and self-attentiveness is often more fully human.[55]

Self-denying and Self-interested

Self-interested acts are at the opposite end of the spectrum from *self-denying* acts. The latter include renunciation or frustration of one or more inclinations, tendencies, or desires of a self, while the former aim immediately or mediately at their fulfillment. Acts of self-denial may be willed in service of some other good, or they may be a perverse rejection of self. Yielding to another, fasting from food, and martyrdom are examples of acts of self-denial that may be morally good; hurting ourselves, restricting our desire to know, and suicide may be examples of morally bad acts of self-denial. Thus, the biblical injunction to deny ourselves should not be blindly obeyed. We admire those who are self-sacrificing if we understand their actions to flow, not from a denial of the self's value, but from generosity. If those who deny themselves think that they are really "no damn good," their self-denial is itself wrong.

Self-interest, the interest we have in our own good, should be distinguished from our interests in the good of another person, thing, or cause.[56] It is a common mistake to say that since we always act for some interest or another, all acts are "self-interested." Self-interested acts are self-promoting. When we strive for the realization of our interest in another's good, we do realize an interest of ours, but we are not aiming at promoting ourselves. Describing all actions as "self-interested" obscures the altruistic and communal interests we also have.[57]

Self-interested action need not be "selfish." One of the central tasks for every being is to be and become itself. Our incompleteness is experienced as an invitation or demand for fulfillment, and we are the persons most responsible for achieving that fulfillment. Most human activity is at least partially self-interested. We would die if it were not so. Those who do not recognize their own self-interestedness are usually involved in broad and profound self-deception. Self-interest "is only a vice if it means an undue regard for self; unselfishness is only a virtue if it is countered by self-respect."[58]

Self-connecting and Self-disconnecting

Many acts can be performed either in self-forgetfulness or self-awareness. Certain acts, however, essentially include a desire for the self's explicit involvement. For example, Uncle Ed wants to be the one who buys ice cream for his nephew Ben; not just any benefactor will do. I call such actions *self-connecting*. In them, we desire not only that the recipient of our act may receive something, but also that we are the ones who bring it about. Such acts are essential in philia. When we engage in self-connecting acts directed towards others, we desire to strengthen or weaken our relation to them. For example, I want to get revenge, and my thirst for revenge would not be satisfied if some accident caused the evil I wanted to inflict. Similarly, with philia or family love, a father cares for his daughter in a way that he might not do for another youth. He acts not for his own enhancement, but he wants his act to connect himself to his daughter. His self-connecting actions may be genuinely altruistic. The biblical God often acts in a self-connecting way.

Self-connecting actions are particularly important in acts of self-love. When I am "good to myself," a different kind of act takes place from when another does a similar good for me: the difference is that I love myself. If it is important that I love myself, I must engage in some self-connecting acts. It is not enough that everyone else loves and takes care of me. Feeding myself is a quite different experience from having another feed me, even though the nutritional benefits may be the same. It is not enough that I indifferently happen to be the beneficiary of my own acts. For self-love, I must want to be the one who does good for myself. Our responsibility for ourselves is a self-connecting activity.

Self-disconnecting acts also occur. Victims of violence or incest often learn how to disconnect themselves from actions they are engaged in. When any of us are forced by circumstances or even by moral duty to do actions that we find disagreeable or "dirtying," one alternative is to disconnect ourselves from those actions even as we do them. The principle of double effect often required something like this sort of disassociation. Physicians who administered narcotics to terminally ill patients were required to say to themselves that they wanted to bring about pain relief, but that it was nature, not themselves, that was shortening life. Emotionally "dead" people often engage in actions that are at least partially *self-disconnected*. And Christians who want to be selfless often mistakenly think they must do the same. It is also sometimes suggested that an agapic love wills the good of another, but should be quite indifferent about who accomplishes that good. Its essential desire is that the beloved be benefited, and it would be a sign of pettiness to insist that we be the one to do the good deed.

Self-expressive, Self-satisfying, and Self-indifferent

An act may be performed in order to express the self, i.e., to objectify, externalize, or realize some attitude, thought, or emotion. The point of *self-expressive* acts is not directly what good or evil can be done, but rather the embodiment of some aspect of one's self. A destructive rage expresses one's anger; it is not a desire to break a particular vase. People act in certain ways in order to make a statement about who they are. Their "statement" expresses that they are trendy, or wealthy, or sophisticated. Self-expressive acts also spring from a desire to know and possess oneself. Thus, artists may paint to express themselves and in the process come to "know" their feelings. Two simple examples may clarify the difference between self-expression and love for another: a priest may preach as a chance to exhibit or unfold her gifts, or she may preach because she wants others to be transformed by the word of God; a nurse may minister because he has nurturing instincts he wants to realize, or he may provide care because he wants to alleviate suffering.[59] The purely self-expressive nurse would be sad if no one suffered; the purely self-expressive preacher would feel deprived if everyone was a perfect saint. They would lack occasions for their self-expression. Theology often portrays God's action as purely self-expressive: "God created us to express God's goodness." One interpretation of this proposition is that God creates us not for any good that might accrue either to God or to us, but simply as an "overflow of goodness." Just as the psalmist's lion goes about seeking indiscriminately whom it may devour, so God goes about seeking to express the divine self in a variety of ways.

Self-satisfying actions are those that are done for the pleasure we obtain in acting. We like playing solitaire; no other good is accomplished; and once done, we reshuffle the cards. We are not really "making a statement" about who we are by playing cards; we are not trying to bring about some new good; rather we are doing something simply for the satisfaction of doing it. All good actions can be satisfying, though most actions are not done solely for the sake of the satisfaction. Sometimes Christians have discouraged enjoyable actions because they fear that enjoyment or satisfaction makes the acts selfish. This is hardly the case.

We perform some actions impartially, that is, for the good of *any* human being. I will name these acts *self-indifferent*. (Less aptly, they are usually called "disinterested" actions; every human act, however, springs from some interest, though not every interest is "self-interested.") Those who exercise public office are often obligated to act as if they are self-indifferent; any good that comes to them is just a consequence of a good done for all; and they should disqualify themselves if their own interests would be specially promoted. Many ethicists claim that we ought always to treat ourselves no better (and no worse) than we treat any other of the billions of human beings. We, like everyone else, should count for one and no more than one. While we need not deny or forget ourselves, they say, our attitude toward ourselves and toward others should be exactly the same. In other words, while we bear responsibility for our own actions, we bear no special responsibility for and to ourself. This self-indifference is the gold standard in many utilitarian theories, and it is also central to many justice-oriented deontological theories. Ethicists employ various strategies to achieve this impartiality. John Rawls's veil of ignorance and the utilitarian's ideal observer are philosophical devices for approaching it. Agapists, at least when they do not reject self-love altogether, may forbid any special love for the self.

We human beings *can* achieve, at least sporadically, this indifference to ourselves. Despite its centrality in much modern philosophy, however, an unflinching self-indifference is hardly a desirable ideal for all actions. The Enlightenment's emphasis on universal equality achieved great gains by challenging morally irrelevant distinctions among persons, but it did so at cost of the rich diversity between persons and of many important kinds of relationships between persons. The principle of universalizability—so prized by analytic philosophers—is a useful corrective to unjust discrimination, but it bleaches out most of the color that makes life worth living. It also blinds us to human uniqueness and to the unique responsibility we have for ourselves.

Before ending this section, let me repeat that my two chief concerns have been, negatively, to indicate that not all self-related acts are selfish and, positively, to demonstrate that there are a variety of ways in which the self is involved in most of our acts. Christian life would be enormously impoverished if we ignored or tried to exclude consideration of our self.

EGOISM

The greatest enemy of Christian life is often thought to be not the devil, nor corrupting social structures, nor disordered loves of creatures, but simply selfishness. Christianity has not thought well about self-love in good part because it has often collapsed it into selfishness or egoism. I will consider two forms of selfishness: psychological egoism and ethical egoism. Then I will talk about a proper ethical responsibility for ourselves.

Psychological Egoism

A curious position that is widely espoused both in popular discourse and even in classical theology is psychological egoism. This view holds that all persons *necessarily* are motivated by their own advantage, even when they are doing good for others. For psychological egoism, selflessness is literally impossible. To some, this position is common sense. To others, it is a conclusion proved by science: among psychologists, there has been "a virtual consensus in favour of psychological egoism based on a research program of reliable and valid experimentation."[60] Ruthless self-criticism, psychological egoism holds, will always uncover a self-interested motive. A heroic act will be exposed as an attempt to overcome uncomfortable feelings, win praise, gain social acceptance, avoid blame, retain self-esteem, etc. Irving Singer observes, "According to Freud, all love is reducible to a desire *to be* loved: every interest in another object is just a circuitous device for satisfying self-love."[61] Even the great sacrifices we make for others will be found to be merely ways to win acceptance and love.

Christianity has long held its own versions of psychological egoism. It has been held that, after original sin, every human act is necessarily tainted or corrupted with selfishness.[62] The pagan mother who seems to be lovingly caring for her child is said in reality to be acting selfishly. God's grace alone makes a true or nonselfish love possible.[63] The presupposition is that by nature we are psychological egoists.

Psychological egoism is plausible both on experiential grounds and because of a conceptual ambiguity. Psychological egoism is not strictly refutable by experience since we never fully know our own motivation.[64] There seems always to be another or deeper or even more superficial motive that we are unaware of when we act. We join a monastery for what we think are the noblest of reasons; later, perhaps in therapy or during an annual retreat, we discover that our driving motive may really have been something quite irreligious: we wanted to please Mom or were afraid of sex or needed social status. Still later, we discover that we may in fact have had an admixture of noble and selfish motives, and we can't be completely sure which was or is primary. As we become more mature, most of us learn that we sometimes use good intentions to hide our selfish heart from ourselves. There seems to be no theoretical way to know whether we have reached our true or deepest motivation. The Council of Trent held that no one can be sure she or he is in the state of grace.[65] That means that no one can be sure that she or he is fundamentally motivated by the love of God. The thesis of the psychological egoist can experientially neither be proved nor disproved. But if it is true, much of Christianity and most of the evidence we have for our freedom are mistaken.

The psychological egoist denies that we ever can love others for their own sakes. "The question is not whether egoism is strong in human nature but whether we ever have any concern or desire for the welfare of others except as a means to our own, any concern for or interest in their welfare for its own sake, which is not derived from our concern for our own welfare."[66] Most of us answer that question by replying that we can because we do. We are fairly sure that we do generous acts for others that are not motivated by what we get for ourselves. For the reasons given in the previous paragraph, those who hold psychological egoism are themselves unable to show that we are always mistaken. If we cannot trust our experience about acting for others, then there is not much in the realm of human motivation we can be sure of, including the theory of psychological egoism. If we are by nature psychological egoists, then it is an enigma why we all try to deceive ourselves and not merely others into thinking that we do other-centered acts and that these acts are good and praiseworthy. Is it not rather that we disguise our selfish acts as altruistic because we think that selfishness is not necessary and that generosity to others is both possible and good?

The thesis of psychological egoism is also plausible because of an ambiguity in the way we commonly describe human action. Everyone acts for some reason or interest. Without reasons or interests, our activity would be merely arbitrary bits of behavior. These reasons or interests are ours and no one else's. Therefore, because we always act out of some interest of ours, it follows—so the argument goes—that we all are self-interested in everything we do. As Robert Ringer tersely put it, there are three kinds of people: while all people act in their own self-interest, some openly admit it, some admit it to themselves yet conceal it from others, and some deny it altogether.[67] Similarly, some Christians suggest that original sin corrupts all actions with selfish self-interest. They then exhort us honestly to confess our ever-present and inevitable sin.

In the previous section, I laid out the basis for rejecting this defense of psychological egoism. One moves from having interests to saying that such interests can only be "self-interested," i.e., for the advantage or well-being of the agent. But the fact that, to be rational, agents must have motives does not imply that all their motives are aimed at their own good. Their actions are *from* the self, i.e., they are "self-enacting," but they need not be *for* the self. Acting from some interest is not the same as acting in one's self-interest. Objective and subjective genitives are confused. Nygren makes this basic mistake: for him to be motivated is to be selfish. Rather we can be motivated by an interest in others for their own sakes.

Christians also encourage the theory of psychological egoism when they pray as if their desires could be only selfish. They ask God to eliminate their desires so that they can follow God's will. They universalize a disjunction: "Not my will but thy will be done." They fail to acknowledge that there can be a loving coherence between our desires and God's. The grace life we share with God need not defeat our nature, but may embrace it: Jesus says, "Ask, and you shall receive. Seek, and you will find" (Mt 7:7). Jesus is not encouraging selfishness. Our wants or desires are not always self-interested, let alone selfish. Rather, we may often selflessly and self-forgetfully desire to help someone. Indeed, the stronger our desire to help, the less attentive we may be to our own self-interests. Again the oft-made mistake is to say that, since we are doing "what we want," we are acting selfishly. Hence, we must give up our "wants." This view overlooks one distinguishing capacity of spiritual beings, namely, our ability to transcend our own needs. We can want good for the other for the other's sake. And our strongest desire can be to act in accord with God's desires.

In yet a fourth way, Christians foster the theory of psychological egoism when they denounce natural pleasure and enjoyment. Self-satisfying acts are lumped with selfish acts. A basic fact of human psychology is that good persons enjoy doing good deeds. There is a deep satisfaction even in making personal sacrifices for others.[68] From this fact, however, it does not follow that persons always do good in order to increase their own enjoyment. Such satisfactions *accompany* good action. While we often act for our own pleasure, acting for this motive will be effective chiefly with lesser pleasures. Sensitivity to human experience suggests the wisdom of the "hedonist paradox": those who seek only the enjoyment that accompanies the deeper human acts will distort these acts and thereby eventually miss the enjoyment that accompanies them. We can eat for pleasure, but if, when we spend time with a friend, we concentrate mainly on what pleasure we are getting, we will soon lose our friend. If, however, we concentrate on being with the friend, we will derive much pleasure from that relationship. The deeper enjoyments of life come *along with* movement toward the good and they come in relishing the good in itself that we experience.[69]

The language of psychological egoism pervades American culture. As the book *Habits of the Heart* makes clear, we have lost a publicly acceptable way of saying that we act for the sake of others.[70] We commonly talk as if we pursue only our own private interests, desires, or pleasures: for example, "I work with the homeless *because* it gives me such a good feeling," or "I teach inner city kids *because* I get so much out of it." Obviously missing from the teacher's "explanation" is the good of the students' learning. Self-benefit has become the only publicly acceptable motive. The teacher is not allowed to say, "I teach because the students are ignorant and need help." If the teacher were to discover that her students actually deteriorated under her tutelage, but replied that she would continue to teach "because" she enjoyed it, then it would be clear that she literally meant what she said. She teaches for her own enjoyment. But this is not what people normally mean. When people say they do things "because" they enjoy them, they usually mean that in giving they also experience deep satisfaction and joy. Their acts are not self-denying, but they are not for that reason selfish. In fact, we should take great pleasure in doing good, and this pleasure, the more intense it is, may increase the moral value of the act. Unfortunately, many agapists become suspicious the more we enjoy what we are doing, since, they fear, we might be acting for ourselves and not for the other. They miss the generating and supportive role of positive emotions. Such agapists undercut the good they try to promote.

Ethical Egoism

In contrast to psychological egoism, ethical egoism does not claim that we cannot but be self-interested. Rather, it claims that the deed which we *should* chose is the one which promotes our own interests.[71] "Charity begins at home" . . . and should remain there. We can promote the interests of others over our own, says the ethical egoist, but this would be moral folly. Advocates of ethical egoism can point out that it does not necessarily lead to a brutish, nasty world. Out of self-interest, people can and do cooperate to achieve some wonderfully human goals. Proponents of democratic capitalism sometimes point to the economic success of countries that vigorously promote self-interest. Ethical egoism can include principles of mutual aid, nonmaleficence, and concern for the feelings of others.[72] Hobbes's political theory shows how ethical egoism can be the basis of civil order. Rawls's system of social justice seems to presuppose ethical egoism,[73] and his conclusions have attracted many Christians.

Theologians, particularly Catholic ethicists, court ethical egoism when they justify other-love in terms of self-love. This approach is exemplified in Richard Gula's analysis of the parable of the Good Samaritan (Lk 10:30–37): "Whatever the priest and Levite saw when they looked in the ditch was clearly not themselves. So they continued on. The Samaritan, however, stops to help because he sees himself beaten and lying there wounded. He treats the victim as though he were caring for himself."[74] Christians also resemble ethical egoists when they argue, "We can be responsible only for ourselves, not for others." The ambiguity of their claim is perhaps evident. It is true if it means we cannot literally make others' decisions. We each must make an individual decision for Christ (Lk 12:49–53, 14:26; Jn 1:11–12). But it is false if it denies we can and must make decisions with and on behalf of others. Love for others, as we have seen, brings responsibility for them. Parents are responsible for their children, and Jesus was responsible for those whom God gave him (Jn 6:39). A Christian sense of solidarity, nicely imaged in Paul's metaphor of the body, indicates that we are responsible with and for the good of others. We are indeed morally responsible for what we do, but what we should do quite commonly is to promote the lives of others.

Christians also contribute to ethical egoism in another way. They suggest that even when we do good for others, what we most fundamentally should strive for is to be a good person, or, at least, to avoid becoming a bad person. That is, our final goal, even in altruistic acts, is our own moral goodness. This position holds that we should not be self-serving in any narrow sense of self-interest, but we can and must always serve one special interest, namely, our interest in being moral persons. Our primary question, they say, should always be: "How will this choice help me to become a better, richer, fuller person?" Virtue-oriented ethics frequently seems to advocate this position.[75] This focus on ourselves is made possible by a crucial feature of our moral lives. We become good in "doing good." Because it is always in some sense good for me to do what is right and bad for me to do what is wrong, ethical egoists argue that it is only reasonable to "do good and avoid evil." That is, we should choose to do the "right thing" *because* it will be for our good. The "right" is founded on our own good.

The Protestant tradition has rightly criticized the potential for self-absorption in virtue ethics. It fears that talk of virtues will usurp the place of grace, making it irrelevant. It fears that individuals will focus on their own resources rather than on God.[76] The result will be self-righteousness. If this happens, then virtue-oriented ethics leads to a kind of "ethical self-centeredness."[77] If a benevolent person's *only* concern is that she is becoming good by performing a good deed, she is directly intent not on achieving good for another but on making herself a do-gooder. If someone else does the good deed first, she feels cheated of her glorious opportunity to become more morally good. The world is a gymnasium for her to develop her moral character. She does not have a direct desire to bring about good. Otherwise she would rejoice that, even without her, the needy are provided for. The ideal situation for ethical self-centeredness is one in which, like a god, she is very rich and others are very poor, so that she can endlessly grow in virtue.

Another variation of this ethical self-centeredness sometimes occurs in persons who uphold certain moral positions, no matter what the consequences. Analogous to the "hedonist paradox," there is something like a "moralist paradox." Those who focus on being moral may miss the moral thing to do. The Kantian person who is so concerned to avoid becoming bad by lying to save a friend in fact betrays a friend and thereby arguably does an objectively immoral act. Or, to use a contemporary example, if a pacifist refuses to take up arms to defend friends lest he become a violent person, he thereby may share responsibility when the forces of evil are victorious. Deontologically oriented opponents of nuclear deterrence often mistakenly say they are responsible only for themselves and not for the fact that their absolute nuclear pacifism might induce an enemy to sin by starting a war; on the opposite extreme, those who wage a futile war lest they seem cowards equally err.[78] To be sure, it is dangerous to bend or break moral norms in order that some good be done or evil be avoided. But a refusal seriously to consider consequences may betray an ethical self-centeredness. The concern to keep one's hands clean may mean that the earth's soil is not tilled, and one is then responsible for the ensuing starvation.

A supreme form of ethical egoism occurs when our relation to God is reduced to a means to advance our own perfection. According to Kirk, after the Protestant reformation initially affirmed God's priority, it underwent a drastic shift and emphasized this-worldly activity. Prayer became focused less on worship and more on petition concerning life's needs and the tasks of service. Prayerful union with God turned into asking God for help in solving life's problems. Thus, "in Catholicism as in Protestantism, contemplation, or the ideal of communion with God as the culmination of approach to Him through worship, suffered a very serious eclipse."[79] Prayer became merely "a means and help we make use of to advance ourselves in perfection." Prayer became useful for bewailing one's faults, mortifying passion, and rooting out evil. Prayer, it was said, should be profitable, not simply a loving look at God. Eventually, as psychotherapy or self-help programs offered better aid in achieving goals, God became irrelevant. Prayer became a luxury that Christians could comfortably dispense with. That is, prayerful union with God, which had become merely ancillary to self-growth and social service, disappeared when better methods were found.[80]

In sum, I have shown how tendencies to psychological egoism and ethical egoism have not been absent from Christian theology and Christian life. Still, the preponderance of Christian thought is deeply committed to a life that includes generous and selfless service. I propose that theology, in spite of its good intentions, has contributed to these two egoisms because it has been aware, however inadequately, that it must give some recognition to self-love in Christian life.

Ethical Self-responsibility

Having warned against "ethical self-centeredness," I should quickly add that we do have a special responsibility for our own moral character. The moral life requires that we try to maintain or increase the good and to diminish the bad. Our own virtue is included in that good, even if it is not the only consideration. Our integrity is one part of our general responsibility, a responsibility that is directed to a larger realm of good than merely our own virtue. Because of our concern for the larger good, it is possible to tell an untruth to save the life of another, even when we know that deliberately, though justifiably, telling an untruth may weaken our own habitual pattern of being honest with others and therefore slightly incline us to tell further untruths. Our virtue is not the "end all and be all" of our lives. Ethical *self-responsibility* is not the same as ethical egoism. Normally, the explicit goal of our actions is to do some good and avoid or overcome some evil in the world; our goal is not simply to become good or evil persons. Jesus was friendly with prostitutes, even at potential risk to his own virtue; he did so for their good. Had he avoided this temptation, he would have abandoned those who needed him. Aquinas at times mistakenly reverses this perspective when he explains, for example, that we may sacrifice our very lives for our friends, not for their sakes, but because we love our own virtue more than our bodies.[81] Rather, I would say, we make this sacrifice because we love our friends and want them to survive.

Concern for our own integrity is important, since we are especially responsible for that part of reality which is ourselves. In all evil acts that we perform, there is harm done to the self. This harm is an important concern, but not the only concern. If Hitler, after killing millions of people, were to be chiefly concerned that he had not lived his life as kindly as possible, we would rightly be appalled that he still failed to appreciate the evil he had done. We would judge that he was consumed by ethical egoism. On the other hand, there are other acts, e.g., telling a white lie or failing to vote in a minor election, whose chief harm usually is what these acts do to our character. Acts of lust, cowardice or pettiness are often most harmful to our self.[82] These acts compromise some virtue in ourselves that we should preserve and foster. Though acting for the sake of one's virtue courts the dangers of self-righteousness, still we have a legitimate moral concern for our own virtue. We are responsible for ourselves, even if not only for ourselves. Because of our complexity, our various tendencies can complement or conflict with another. We should shape these tendencies into a more coherent self. To be sure, the self is coformed by other influences such as culture or God; but it is also cogiven as an "object" of our freedom. We are each finally responsible for forming this identity as personal.

Thus, self-responsibility, which is a form of self-love, includes crucial moral tasks that are not present in our love for our neighbor. *We* are finally responsible for accepting God's love for us; we are not finally responsible for the neighbor's acceptance of God's love. We can and must do what we can to foster the neighbor's union with God. But only we can make ourselves love partners of God. Among all the "objects" of God's love, there is only one that we are directly able to form in its free personhood. Essential to person-building is free self-determination, and this freedom we finally exercise only over ourselves. We can and must assist the freedom of others, but we cannot replace it. Even God cannot make us saints without our cooperation (Lk 7:30). In brief, we *can* love ourselves more *fully* than we *can* love our neighbor. We ought not strive to be wholly selfless or self-forgetful. To see this last point more clearly, I next want to show that several Christian acts are not possible without some attention to the self.

ESSENTIAL INVOLVEMENT OF THE SELF

Piety has encouraged Christians to "mortify themselves in all things possible," to live selflessly, to count not the cost to themselves but only the neighbor's benefit, to take no thought for themselves, to deny themselves, to treat themselves without favoritism, and even to hate themselves. Would we be better off if we practiced these maxims at every moment? I think not. I shall try to demonstrate this point by considering how some basic Christians acts—love, repentance, forgiveness, gratitude, sacrifice, and petitionary prayer—would be affected.[83]

Love

The advocates of self-forgetfulness rob love of its personal quality. Our love, say, for God is not only self-enacting in the sense that we freely perform this act. It is also self-connecting in the sense that we want to be the very ones who perform this particular act of love of God. As Robert Adams puts it, "Not to care, literally not to care at all, whether I will be the one who loves or hates God, so long as God's will be done, would not be an attitude of love toward God on my part, but of something much more impersonal."[84] A self-indifferent person might say that it does not matter who loves God so long as God is loved. Such a person approves the good, but has at best a very thin love of God. "That God be loved" is indeed a good to be approved; and such agapic love is, I think, possible; but it is a shrunken version of the Christian life. My full love occurs when *I* love *my* God. Similarly, discipleship requires love's self-connection. We would be poor disciples if, self-indifferently, we wanted Jesus to have disciples, but did not care whether we were among those disciples. A Christian cannot be satisfied with this detached attitude. Part of our identity as disciples is to desire to be one of the disciples.

Analogous things can be said about neighbor love and the propriety of self-denial versus self-satisfaction. A popular maxim is that we have to love others, but not like them, which means that we should affirm their good, but it is a matter of indifference whether we find anything attractive in them. To be sure, we do love people who do not satisfy many of our own needs and may even thwart quite a few. We may even experience considerable distaste in helping some people; our only satisfaction may be some fulfillment of our deep "drive" to love. That is, our actions may be largely self-disconnected. Still, a "saint" will find much to like in another person, and most of us would not feel cheered to learn that God loved us but did not like us. Each of us wants to be affirmed for ourselves, but we also want to be good for those who love us. We would rather not be the occasion of their self-denial and self-disconnection, but would prefer to be a source of their joy. We want them to like us, and similarly we should want to like others, i.e., experience satisfaction in loving them.

Self-denial and self-hate are not appropriate in the face of God's love. We have seen that, when God loves us, we should accept that love. We acknowledge that we are loved by God, and we should relish our status as beloved. This acceptance is not simply a matter of intellectually agreeing that God loves us; rather, it requires us to accept this love as part of who we are. Without a sense of our own worth and without at least an incipient affirmation of our self, we would not be accepting this love. An intellectual assent leaves our lives untouched; an emotional response of self-love transforms us. If, further, we cooperate with God's love for us, we must love ourselves. That is, our self-love must be self-connecting; we do not cooperate with God's particular love for *us* if we make no special difference to ourselves. God does not want us to be self-destructive sinners so that God can lovingly forgive us. That would be like a doctor wanting us to make ourselves sick so that the doctor would have something to do. By itself, a constant practice of self-indifference, self-denial, or self-hatred can frustrate God's love.

Repentance and Forgiveness

The advocates of self-forgetfulness, self-indifference, and selflessness cut the heart out of Christian conversion. Full repentance essentially requires inclusion and reference to our own self. Jesus says, "People who are in good health do not need a doctor; sick people do. . . . I have come to call, not the self-righteous, but sinners" (Mt 9:12–13). All of us must realize *our* sickness, before Christ will be able to change *our* hearts. To be sure, in some "thin" sense, we may be "sorry for" (and not simply "sorry about") the sins of humanity or of some other person. Still, whenever we have sinned, it is essential that we be sorry for our sins. It is not simply "humanity in one's person" that has sinned, to use a Kantian sounding phrase; rather, we have sinned. *We* must regret *our* involvement, *our* betrayal. Similarly, for the experience of being forgiven, it is not enough to acknowledge that Jesus died for humanity. Nor is a simple trust in God's general or universal mercy sufficient. God forgives, not simply humanity, but each of us, and a self-connecting response is requisite.

Repentance, forgiveness, and reconciliation are commonly misunderstood to be forms of self-disconnection. When we have done wrong, we are encouraged simply to forget the past and to "let bygones be bygones." Rather, it is essential to repentance that we regret *our* sin.[85] And for full reconciliation, when we have harmed others, we must both admit that we have harmed them and want to be forgiven by them, and they must both admit that they have been harmed and offer forgiveness. It is not enough for them to say that the offence was "nothing." That response is self-disconnecting. Full repentance and forgiving are acts that essentially require self-connection, not self-indifference or self-forgetfulness. The same, I think, can be said of our sins against God. God does not simply forget the past. Further, God cannot forgive unless God has experienced some offense. And we cannot genuinely beg forgiveness if we do not acknowledge that we have in some way harmed God and our relation with God. In short, repentance and forgiveness require self-connection on God's and our part.

Petitions and Gratitude

The advocates of self-denial, self-indifference, and selflessness undercut both petitionary prayer and thanksgiving. Jesus encourages us to pray for our needs (Mt 18:19; Jn 15:7). This encouragement would make no sense if we should be self-forgetful and not be concerned about our own needs. Many psalms would be unprayable if it were not permissible to be self-interested: "Oh Lord, hear my prayer, and let my cry come to you. . . . Incline your ear to me; in the day when I call, answer me speedily" (Ps 102:1–2). The Church has a long tradition of prayer as petition. In it we acknowledge our dependence and God's graciousness: like a parent, God will "give good things to anyone who asks him" (Mt 7:11). While it is laudable to pray for other persons, the Gospel also encourages us to pray for our own needs. But in order to pray for our own needs, we must have some awareness of ourselves and we must desire to have our needs fulfilled. In other words, if, as some say, self-interest is sinful, Jesus would be encouraging us to sin. It was not a sin for Jesus to ask that the cup pass from him (Mt 26:39).

The fullness of gratitude essentially requires self-interest. "I will give thanks to you, for you have answered me and have been my savior" (Ps 118:21). As we have seen, it is essential to a full love and a full repentance that we be self-connected in these acts. In neither of these two acts, however, is it essential that we be self-interested. In fact, an admixture of self-interest can at times block the full performance of these two acts. Love of God in order to get the "rewards" of heaven is a self-interested love that might abandon God for a "higher bidder." And true repentance is not simply motivated by a fear of punishments or by a childish fear that God will stop loving us if we don't repent. Indeed, such fear may indicate the same lack of God-centeredness that is the root of sin (1 Jn 4:18; Rm 1:28). Gratitude, however, requires self-interest.

We normally do not say that we are grateful to someone who has rescued some stranded travelers in a distant land. Unless we have some connection or involvement with those wayfarers, we more properly would praise the heroism of the rescuers than feel gratitude to them. At most, we have the sort of gratitude appropriate to one who believes that no one is an island apart from the main, or who holds Jesus' attitude that whatever you do for the least of my brothers and sisters you do for me. In these cases, there is some connection between ourselves and them. Gratitude is possible only insofar as those who receive a benefit somehow belong to us.[86] If a woman were merely grateful that some good had been done to the body of Christ and considered it merely incidental that the one who benefited happened to be herself, I think we would describe her as a person who was incapable of appreciating God's goodness to her. Self-indifference is not sufficient. Gratitude to God for God's graciousness to "humanity in her own person" is tantamount to a denial of her own personal dependence on and relation to God. Put strongly, an "inability to accept a gift *for oneself*, when one's own good was the chief goal of the giver, is *ungrateful.*"[87] Thus, without self-interest, the Christian virtue of gratitude is impossible.

One ploy, sometimes used by opponents of self-interest, suggests that, since it is good for rich benefactors to give, all we are doing by receiving is giving them an opportunity to exercise generosity. This affirms the giver, but it overlooks that the gift is given *to us.* We properly say thank you not simply in order to acknowledge that the benefactor is good, but to acknowledge and welcome the benefit and the bond that has been created or fostered. Without self-interest this could not happen. Purely other-centered agapists would be the last to know and relish God's love for them and the last to give thanks to God for God's gifts to them. The "for me" of Christ's death would remain opaque to such an agapist. In the liturgy, they might praise God, but they would not say thank you. In a word, an "agape feast" without self-love is impossible. Those who do not love themselves cannot give thanks to God.

Self-sacrifice and Self-gift

Finally, those who denounce or ignore self-love make personal sacrifices meaningless. Self-sacrifice is not really a sacrifice if we reckon that our self is evil, worthless, or otherwise of no account. Generous giving of ourselves is no gift if we hold that we are nothing but sinners. Indeed, if we are as corrupt as Nygren and others make us out to be, then it is an insult to offer this depraved self to God. Sacrifice and self-gift require handing over something that is precious to oneself; they require love of self.[88]

Proponents of self-indifference and the ethical norm of impartiality or "equal regard" are many. Christian praise of self-sacrifice, however, makes it clear that we should not always treat ourselves as one and only one, just like all others. Consider a standard example. Some soldier has to fall on a grenade, or else many will be killed. It is one thing for me to fall on the grenade; it is quite another to push the person next to me onto it. In each case, one person will die. The first act is noble and heroic; the second could rarely be justified. If every person impartially counted as one and only one, it would make no difference.

Christians often focus on Jesus' agape in dying for others, but his cross loses much of its personal meaning if he was impartially devoid of a special interest in his own life. If Jesus were self-indifferent, a purely rational analysis of his sacrifice might go something like this: Jesus looked at his life, saw that his death would bring about the good of humanity, and so made the rational calculation that benefit to many lives was better than one life lost. Hence, like any "minimally decent" person, Jesus offered his life: one loss is outweighed by many gains. His sacrifice on the cross, from this perspective, is rather nugatory.[89] The cross would be nothing noble, merely the obvious conclusion of cost-benefit analysis. Something is wrong with such thinking. Without some powerful tendency to save his own life, Jesus' sacrifice was small. Without Jesus' strong self-love, his anguish in the Garden of Gethsemane was just a moment of irrationality. It is, oddly, the agapic tradition which can make Jesus' sacrifice seem slight.

Again, an ideal of self-indifference or equal regard undercuts more commonplace acts of Christian sacrifice. If it is wrong, other things being equal, to place more of a burden on one human being than on another, then we should be hesitant to take up the burdens of our peers. Our own burdens are usually enough. They are our fair share. If, as Gene Outka writes, "Moral judgments . . . must disregard any references to particular individuals,"[90] then by carrying not only our own burdens but also those of others we would be violating justice and morality. If justice prizes self-indifference, then "justice may not only rule out the familiar move to the side of one's own interests. It may also rule out the less familiar move too far to the side of another's interests."[91] Love overrides this kind of justice when we sacrifice ourselves for others. We are able to do so precisely because we have a *special relationship to ourselves*. We ought not treat ourselves as one and only one, the same as all other human beings. This special relationship gives us a "right" and sometimes an obligation to ask of ourselves more than we appropriately demand of others.[92]

In sum, without a variety of self-affirming attitudes, we can repay debts, but not show our gratitude; we can forget, but not forgive; we can provide for others, but not fully love them.[93] Self-forgetting and self-denying and self-indifferent attitudes are indeed possible for Christians, and they have their time and place. But the fullness of Christian life requires a healthy concern for the self in its acts. A selfless life of pure self-sacrificial devotion is an impoverished Christian life.

GOD'S UNSELFLESS LOVE

In the previous section, I argued that several Christian acts require various self-connecting involvements. Christians cannot be always selfless or self-forgetting. In this section, I want to make a parallel argument about God's love for us. Since our love should be like God's (Mt 5:48), I want to show that even God's love is not simply selfless, self-denying, or self-indifferent.

God's love is commonly understood to be agapic in the sense of pure benevolence: out of God's goodness, God creates the finite beings of this world, redeems them from their alienation, and guides them to their fulfillment. In this traditional conception, God does not act for any benefit to God's self because God does not need anything. Rather God acts purely for our sakes. Such a purely benevolent God should be happy to remain anonymous, since a desire for recognition and response seems inappropriate for selfless benevolence. Some saints have said that, if it were possible, they would like to be able to do something for God without God knowing it; their own pure love of God would thereby be manifest—a gift given to God with no prospect of return. A fortiori, this attitude would be appropriate to a purely benevolent God. It should be a matter of indifference to a selfless God whether or not we are grateful.

This picture, of course, is not very biblical. Our tradition says that we have a jealous God (Na 1:2). God forbids the worship of idols who are false gods (Is 2:6–18). The people of Israel are "my house . . . my heritage . . . the beloved of my soul" (Jer 12:7–9). This God responds to the people's action: "I give you a king in my anger, and I take him away in my wrath" (Hos 13:11). The biblical God makes claims on us, "Give glory to the Lord, your God" (Jer 13:16); and this God is full of affection for Israel, "I have loved you, says the Lord" (Mal 1:2). When the people stray, God says, "My heart is overwhelmed, my pity is stirred" (Hos 11:8); then God enjoins them, "Return, O Israel, to the Lord, your God" (Hos 14:2).

If it were true that God's love was simply selfless, then God would have only *our* good at heart. God would affirm us solely for our sakes. It should make little difference to God whether we glorify or give thanks to God. A purely agapic God should have little complaint against atheistic humanists, as long as such persons are striving to live good human lives. This God should have even less complaint against pagans who with piety and reverence attribute their good fortune to humanity, idols, the stars, or Nature, since these persons would be fulfilling their human nature in ways roughly equivalent to those who worship the true God. And yet the Lord says, "Cursed is the man who trusts in human beings . . . whose heart turns away from the Lord" (Jer 17:5) and "This is your lot . . . because you have forgotten me and trusted in the lying idol" (Jer 13:25). Would a purely benevolent God cry out, "You have disowned me . . . turned your back upon me; and so I stretched out my hand to destroy you" (Jer 15:6)? Usually theologians have answered these questions by saying that the Bible speaks anthropomorphically or uses images for the sake of our weak understanding. Is it not, rather, the idea of a purely benevolent God that is itself a reductively anthropomorphic, rationalist view?

The *only* concerns a selfless God might have would be to overcome the ignorance of atheists and idolaters or the internal disorder that besets sinners. That is, such a God would not "care" that they do not love the true God, except insofar as the absence of this love might make them less fully human. Since most human goods do not have to be seen in relation to God in order for them to be reasonably well understood and appreciated—this has been the insistence of the natural law theory—the deficit of being an atheistic humanist might be minimal. A purely benevolent God might even encourage a colorful polytheism which for many people is more enlivening than a purified monotheism. In brief, if all that is at stake is that human beings need to be pious, grateful, devout, repentant, and so forth in order to flourish, then these attitudes and acts can rather adequately be fulfilled in idolatry, polytheism, or a suitably awe-filled atheistic humanism. And a purely benevolent God should be inclined to approve. Similarly, God's revelation would not be motivated by a desire to be known and loved. The deep desire we humans have to disclose ourselves and thereby begin to live in another's life would have no counterpart in God. In short, a selflessly loving God would reveal God's self only to the degree that it might be helpful for us, but not for the sake of any mutual relation that might be realized through this self-disclosure.

In cooperating with this selfless God's will, our love would likewise be anthropocentric. We would worship God only insofar as it is good for *us* to do so. We would be repentant only if it does us good to acknowledge our sins, not because it was important to God. When God says, "Come back to me with all your hearts," what God would really mean is: "Even though it is otherwise a matter of indifference to me whether you repent, *be good to yourselves* and acknowledge your inner disorientation." In cooperating with a purely selfless God, the first commandment for us would not be to love God with our whole heart and our whole mind and our whole body and our whole strength, but rather to love ourselves. Christianity would become nearly indistinguishable from humanism.

Such speculation rings false, I propose, because another kind of love, different from this selfless benevolence, more adequately characterizes God's relation to us. God has formed a covenant with us. As I shall argue in Chapter 8, the relation between God and ourselves is closer to philia than to selfless agape. God not only wills our good, but God does so in a self-connecting way *as* our covenant "partner." God is not satisfied if we thank some demi-god as our benefactor.[94] God wants to be *our* God. God not only wants us to acknowledge that we have been given much; God also wants us to acknowledge that God is the giver of those gifts and to be thankful. God's gift-giving is not simply an expression of God's goodness, nor is it enough for God that we have and enjoy these gifts. God is not like an absent parent who anonymously sends birthday gifts. Developing a relationship is also part of God's desire. God yearns for sinners, wanting them not only to stop their evil ways, but also to turn to God: "Come back to me with all your heart . . . return to the Lord, your God" (Jl 2:12).

INSUFFICIENCY OF PURELY SELFLESS AGAPE

In this final section I want to examine some further complications that follow from an ideal of a purely self-sacrificial, other-centered love. Such love has its place, but Christian life would be impoverished if this love were its exclusive ideal. First, as we have seen, from a purely theoretical viewpoint, it is *impossible* for everyone solely to give to others. It is impossible, not because sinful human beings will never do it nor because finite beings must receive in order to survive, both of which are true, but because logically it cannot happen. A giver requires a receiver, but a universal other-centered agape usually disallows genuine receiving.

Second, in practice, a purely other-centered life would lead (and, in my observation, sometimes does lead) to a duplicitous life. That is, it leads some to receive from others only for other-centered agapic reasons, namely, because it is good for others to give. Imagine going to the theater solely to encourage and support the actors, who themselves are acting solely in order to please the audience. No one would be there to enjoy himself or herself, and each group would succeed best if it kept the other ignorant of its real intentions. Is this not crazy? If we are trying to help someone and then discover that their only interest in being helped is that it is good for us to be a helper, we feel patronized. Our generosity has been emasculated.

Third, we make it harder for others to love us agapically if we do not live with eros. It is difficult to help people who sacrifice or deny themselves at every turn. Their own personhood "shrinks" to the extent that they have no desires for themselves. If they have no list of things that would make their lives better, others will be hard put to help them. The classical God who has no needs has been a difficult God to love. For God or human beings to live without eros is to make the agapic desires of others nearly impossible to fulfill. The cross of Christ is not the sole norm for Christian life. Christ sacrificed his life for others, but this is not all he did with his life. He also lived long and, we may presume, took pleasure from his Abba, his family, his disciples, and his world.

Fourth, to strive to live entirely selflessly or self-forgetfully is to become blind to and neglectful of one part of reality, namely, ourselves. In every act of love we perform, we are de facto enhanced. But, as William Luijpen notes, "It is impossible for man to disregard the fact that love, as active turning to the other, is equiprimordially the fulfillment of his own being."[95] We need not and should not try to remain permanently blind to this fact. We also need not deny the self-satisfying quality of loving and living fully. As Barth notes, "In every real man the will for life is also the will for joy. . . . Even at the highest level, he does not merely want 'to love God and man'. . . . No, in and with all these things, or side by side with them, at certain intervals or interludes, he also wants to have a little, and perhaps more than a little, enjoyment. It is hypocrisy to hide this from oneself. And the hypocrisy would be at the expense of the ethical truth that he should will to enjoy himself."[96]

Fifth, it is existentially contradictory to praise God for filling our needs, but then to insist that we should not have any concern for our own needs. The satisfaction of our needs is part of what makes life worth living, and the fulfillment of these needs is one reason for gratitude to God. If fulfilling these needs in others is good, then refusing to fulfill these same needs in ourselves is arbitrary.

Sixth, when we understand Christian moral life only in terms of affirming others, we exclude certain important questions about how we are going to live our lives. The virtue ethicists make an important point: periodically we should ask, "What kind of life is worth living, or what kind of life would fulfill the promise implicit in my particular talents, or the demands incumbent on someone with my endowment, or of what constitutes a rich, meaningful life."[97] That is, selflessness eliminates the self-responsibility that is central to morality.

Finally, an emphasis on self-sacrificial, other-centered love does little to solve another human failing, namely, our own self-hatred.[98] Aquinas's claim that human beings necessarily love themselves is not self-evident.[99] One discovery psychologists repeatedly make is that people do not love themselves.[100] Human beings often and profoundly hate themselves. Denizens of the twentieth century commonly recite to themselves a new commandment that may have been unthinkable in previous, prepsychological eras: "Thou shalt love thyself." Commandments typically arise when some important good is threatened.[101] The commandment of self-love is just such a response. Good Christians go to workshops to learn how to assert themselves, to know their desires, to better care for themselves. They do not think of these workshops as training in how better to sin, but rather in how to overcome a prevailing sin against themselves.[102] This "new commandment" arises from a growing awareness of the evil of self-hate. Many contemporary persons have discovered that they are incapable of a just anger, incapable of caring for their own needs, incapable of claiming their own dignity before others who would abuse them.[103] Yielding to others in all things leads them to a diffuse, unfocused, even self-destructive way of life, not Christian virtue.[104] Thus, some place must be found for a self-interested, self-attentive love of self.

CONCLUSION

The purpose of this chapter has been to establish the necessity of some regard for the self in any full Christian life. Though agapists commonly suggest that a selfless, self-indifferent, self-denying, self-sacrificing attitude is characteristic of all of Christian life, I have maintained that these attitudes are by no means the norm. Having carved out at least a small place for concern for the self, I now turn to a more careful analysis of the nature of self-love.

NOTES

1. Oliver O'Donovan, *The Problem of Self-Love in St. Augustine* (New Haven: Yale Univ. Press, 1980), 1–2; Morton Kelsey, *Caring* (New York: Paulist, 1981), 46–47; Jules Toner, *The Experience of Love* (Washington: Corpus Books, 1968), 89–90; Gilbert Meilaender, *Faith and Faithfulness* (Notre Dame: Univ. of Notre Dame Press, 1991), 55–56, 86–87.

2. Anders Nygren, *Agape and Eros* (New York: Harper & Row, 1969), 100–101.

3. David Scott, *Egocentrism and the Christian Life* (Dissertation: Princeton University, 1968), 4–5.

4. Søren Kierkegaard, "You Shall Love Your *Neighbour,*" *Other Selves: Philosophers on Friendship,* ed. Michael Pakaluk (Indianapolis, IN: Hackett, 1991), 243–44.

5. Hans Tiefel, "Severely Handicapped Newborns," *Questions about the Beginning of Life,* ed. Ed Schneider (Minneapolis: Augsburg, 1985), 162.

6. Richard Gula, S.S., *Reason Informed by Faith* (New York: Paulist, 1989), 101–102.

7. Paul Ramsey, *Basic Christian Ethics* (Chicago: Univ. of Chicago Press, 1978), 94, 101; William Werpehowski, "Covenant Love and Christian Faithfulness," *Journal of Religious Ethics,* 19 (Fall 1991): 106–10. Similarly, Dietrich von Hildebrand, *Ethics* (Chicago: Franciscan Herald, 1972), 186–87, 218–24, 273, is keen on seeing the importance of values outside of the self, but he has little positive to say about the value of the self as it naturally unfolds. Immanuel Kant, "Lecture on Friendship," *Other Selves,* 210–12, accords self-love "no moral merit."

8. Toner, *The Experience of Love*, 171.

9. Don Browning, *Religious Thought and Modern Psychologies* (Philadelphia: Fortress, 1983), 139; Konrad Hilpert, "Mehr Selbst Werden," *Stimmen der Zeit* 205 (April 1987): 272–73.

10. Pierre Teilhard de Chardin, *The Divine Milieu* (San Francisco: Harper & Row, 1968), 96.

11. Garth Hallett, *Christian Neighbor-Love* (Washington: Georgetown Univ. Press, 1989), 63, 133. Paradoxically, ethics often concentrated on how we sin, while spirituality focused on how we grow in holiness.

12. Hallett, *Christian Neighbor-Love*, 80.

13. Günther Bornkamm, *Jesus of Nazareth* (New York: Harper & Brothers, 1960), 114.

14. Victor Furnish, *Love Command in the New Testament* (New York: Abingdon, 1972), 207.

15. Hallett, *Christian Neighbor-Love*, 47–82.

16. John McKenzie, S.J., *Dictionary of the Bible* (New York: Macmillan, 1965), 341.

17. Ernest Wallwork, "Thou Shalt Love Thy Neighbor As Thyself: The Freudian Critique," *Journal of Religious Ethics* 10 (Fall 1982): 312.

18. Edmund Bergler, *Superego* (New York, 1952), x, cited in John Glaser, S.J., "Conscience and Superego," *Theological Studies* 32 (1971): 34.

19. Alistair Campbell, "Caring and Being Cared For," *Moral Medicine*, eds. Stephen Lammers and Allen Verhey (Grand Rapids: Eerdmans, 1987), 270.

20. *Instruction sur les états d'oraison*, *Oeuvres* 3 (Paris: Lefévre, 1836), 10, cited in Kenneth Kirk, *Vision of God* (New York: Harper & Row, 1966), 458.

21. *ST* I.5.1, 48.1, I–II.1.8, 2.1, 2.8, 3.8, 5.8, 6.Prol., 29.1, 29.4.

22. Henry Denzinger, ed., *Enchiridion Symbolorum* (St. Louis: B. Herder Book, 1957), nos. 1327, 1329, 1331.

23. Denzinger, *Enchiridion Symbolorum*, no.1349 (italics omitted).

24. Kirk, *Vision of God*, 463. Versus Kirk's verdict, it should be noted that many texts of the New Testament encourage acting for the sake of getting heavenly rewards or avoiding punishment in Gehenna.

25. Kirk, *Vision of God*, 461–63.

26. Gene Outka, *Agape* (New Haven: Yale Univ. Press, 1976), 287.

27. François de Sales, *Traité de l'amour de Dieu* (Paris: Gallimard, 1969), 770; also Ramsey, *Basic Christian Ethics*, 151.

28. Martin D'Arcy, S.J., *The Mind and Heart of Love* (New York: Henry Holt, 1947), 203.

29. Charles Kammer, *Ethics and Liberation* (Maryknoll: Orbis, 1988), 145–46.

30. Paul Tillich, *Love, Power, and Justice* (New York: Oxford Univ. Press, 1954), 33–34; also John Macmurray, *Persons in Relation* (Atlantic Highlands: Humanities Press, 1983), 94–95; Outka, *Agape*, 221.

31. Outka, *Agape*, 56.

32. The problems are at times rather semantic. Victor Paul Furnish, "Love of Neighbor in the New Testament," *Journal of Religious Ethics* 10 (Fall 1982): 332, says, "What is involved here is not 'self-love', but the acceptance of one's life as a gift and the affirmation that it is good." Why the acceptance and affirmation of one's life is not self-love is not made clear.

33. Robert Solomon, *Passions* (Garden City: Doubleday Anchor, 1977), 361–62.

34. Browning, *Religious Thought and Modern Psychologies*, 143, 154; Scott, *Egocentrism and the Christian Life*, 201.

35. Timothy O'Connell, *Principles for a Catholic Morality* (New York: Seabury, 1978), 111.

36. Cited in Outka, *Agape*, 289.

37. Macmurray, *Persons in Relation*, 158. Kenneth Cauthen, *Process Ethics* (New York: Mellen, 1984), 146–56, provides an excellent critique of this view.

38. Ramsey, *Basic Christian Ethics*, 99–100.

39. Outka, *Agape*, 287.

40. J. Rohmer, *La Finalité morale chez les théologiens de saint Augustin à Duns Scot* (Paris: 1939), 111–12, cited in Gérard Gilleman, S.J., *The Primacy of Charity in Moral Theology* (Westminster, MD: Newman, 1959), 104.

41. *ST* I–II.28.3, II–II.26.9, 11; *Caritate*, 9.

42. *ST* II–II.26.3–5; *Sententiarum*, 3.29.1.3, 1.5.

43. Thomas Higgins, S.J., *Man as Man* (Milwaukee: Bruce, 1949), 191. Henry Davis, S.J., *Moral and Pastoral Theology* (London: Sheed and Ward, 1945), 1:214, writes, "In respect of man's person, those sins are more grievous which are against oneself, than the same sins against parents, relatives, superiors, and others." Josef Pieper, *About Love* (Chicago: Franciscan Herald, 1974), 84, adds that the primacy of self-love must be accepted soberly as simply the way God created us.

44. Pieper, *About Love*, 82.

45. Germain Grisez, *Way of the Lord Jesus* (Chicago: Franciscan Herald Press, 1983), 600. William O'Connor, "The Nature of the Good," *Thought* 24 (December 1949): 641, gives the metaphysical understanding of the good that underlies this position: "In order that the perfection may be called good, it must be capable of *perfecting the subject that seeks* it. This perfecting relation is *essential* to *the good* wherever it is found... and means as a consequence that the search for the good *necessarily* implies a *lack* in a *subject* that the good can fill" (all italics mine). See also Pieper, *About Love*, 83.

46. Josef Fuchs, S.J., *Christian Ethics in a Secular Arena* (Washington: Georgetown Univ. Press, 1984), 119.

47. Grisez, *Way of the Lord Jesus*, 575 (all in bold print in original). Grisez and Joseph Boyle, Jr., *Life and Death with Liberty and Justice* (Notre Dame: Univ. of Notre Dame Press, 1979), 362–68, make acting for transcendent principles acceptable only if it accords with self-fulfillment.

48. Grisez, *Way of the Lord Jesus*, 575–77. Eugene Borowitz, *Contemporary Christologies* (New York: Paulist, 1980), 134, provides a poignant Jewish comment on this understanding of Christianity: "To Jews, Christians and their churches have not, do not and are not likely to care as much for others as they care for themselves, their institutions or their fellow Christians, much less to deny themselves for others or, as the Christ did, to sacrifice themselves for them. They surely have not sacrificed themselves for us."

49. Our actions also may, *mutatis mutandis*, be said to be "other-enacting," "other-forgetful," etc., or "relation-enacting," "relation-forgetful," etc.

50. D'Arcy, *Mind and Heart*, 70.

51. Josef Pieper, *The Four Cardinal Virtues* (Notre Dame: Notre Dame Press, 1966), 149.

52. Alice Miller, *The Drama of the Gifted Child* (New York: Basic Books, 1981), *xiv*, 21.

53. Kirk, *Vision of God*, 556.

54. Max Scheler, "The Psychology of So-Called Compensation Hysteria and the Real Battle against Illness," *Journal of Phenomenological Psychology* 15 (Fall 1984): 125–43.

55. Cf. Von Hildebrand, *Ethics*, 323–37.

56. John Brentlinger, "The Nature of Love," *Eros, Agape, and Philia*, ed. Alan Soble (New York: Paragon, 1989), 140–41.

57. Daniel Rush Finn, "Self-Interest, Markets, and the Four Problems of Economic Life," *Annual of Society of Christian Ethics* (1989), 36.

58. D'Arcy, *Mind and Heart*, 308. The fact that D'Arcy begins the quoted sentence with "selfishness" where I have written "self-interest" indicates the need for a richer vocabulary such as this section proposes.

59. Von Hildebrand, *Ethics*, 220. Obviously, in real life, most people have mixed motives.

60. Paul Rigby and Paul O'Grady, "Agape and Altruism," *Journal of American Academy of Religion* 57 (1989): 721. Because this research, for methodological reasons, eschews motivation and concentrates on behavior, it is not, to my mind, very convincing. The authors, however, adduce other research that *might* show that *sometimes* people act altruistically.

61. Irving Singer, *The Nature of Love* (Chicago: Univ. of Chicago, 1987), 1:29; Toner, *The Experience of Love*, 90. For a refutation of this claim, see Wallwork, "Love Thy Neighbor: Freudian Critique," 268–90.

62. C. S. Lewis, *The Four Loves* (New York: Harcourt Brace Jovanovich, 1960), 177.

63. Rarely is any argument given for this position. It is clear from experience that we sometimes act selfishly and sometimes nonselfishly. The latter is as "natural" as the former; cf. D'Arcy, *Mind and Heart*, 216–17.

64. Rigby and O'Grady, "Agape and Altruism," 723–25.

65. Denzinger, *Enchiridion Symbolorum*, no. 802.

66. William Frankena, *Ethics* (Englewood Cliffs: Prentice-Hall, 1973), 21.

67. Robert Ringer, *Winning through Intimidation* (New York: Funk & Washalls, 1973), 39.

68. Outka, *Agape*, 286; Toner, *The Experience of Love*, 84–86.

69. Lawrence Blum, "Vocation, Friendship, and Community," *Identity, Character, and Morality*, eds. Owen Flanagan and Amélie Oksenberg Rorty (Cambridge: MIT Press, 1990), 193–95.

70. Robert Bellah et al., *Habits of the Heart* (Berkeley: Univ. of California, 1985), well document this tendency.

71. Browning, *Religious Thought and Modern Psychologies*, 71–73, correctly puts many well-known humanistic psychologists in this camp. See also William Wilcox, "Egoists, Consequentialists, and Their Friends," *Philosophy & Public Affairs* 16 (Winter 1987): 77.

72. Vincent MacNamara, *Faith and Ethics* (Washington: Georgetown Univ. Press, 1985), 162.

73. John Rawls, *Theory of Justice* (Cambridge: Harvard Univ. Press, 1971), 11.

74. Gula, *Reason Informed By Faith*, 180.

75. Outka, *Agape*, 128. Outka provides a splendid chapter on agape as a virtue. We might expect him to embrace a theory of virtue, but, for him, morality refers primarily to action (p. 196).

76. Outka, *Agape*, 147–49.

77. Kirk, *Vision of God*, 554–55.

78. This form of ethical self-centeredness is not the same as self-sacrificial devotion to some cause or principle. Such devotion is most difficult to explain, but it stands near the pinnacle of moral living. Acts done to realize the good are themselves good even if they do not succeed. A self-sacrificial witness to ideals is a powerful and ennobling way of affirming and participating in those ideals.

79. Kirk, *Vision of God*, 431, see also 414–31.

80. Kirk, *Vision of God*, 438–41.

81. *Sententiarum*, 3.29.1.5. Elsewhere, Aquinas says our central delight is in our own virtue, so we don't need friends for delight (*ST* I–II.4.8, II–II.44.3). On the other hand, he says something different in *ST* II–II.24.9. Cf. Hallett, *Christian Neighbor-Love*, 83–110.

82. Hans Reiner, *Duty and Inclination* (Boston: Nijhoff, 1983), 169–73, 212.

83. The following owes much to Robert Adams, "Pure Love," *Journal of Religious Ethics* 8 (1980): 90–98.

84. Adams, "Pure Love," 90.

85. Max Scheler, "Repentance and Rebirth," *On the Eternal in Man* (Hamden, CT: Shoe String, 1972), 33–65.

86. Fred Berger, "Gratitude," *Ethics* 85 (July 1975): 299.

87. Adams, "Pure Love," 94; Meilaender, *Faith and Faithfulness*, 96–97.

88. Teilhard de Chardin, *The Divine Milieu*, 95. I mean "sacrifice" in the contemporary usage of the word, not in the etymological sense of making something holy, which requires no loss, but only an elevation.

89. I find this conclusion to be the (unintended) consequence of the position held by Hallett, *Christian Neighbor-Love*, 7.

90. Outka, *Agape*, 292.

91. Outka, *Agape*, 301.

92. Outka, *Agape*, 303–4. In discussing the "normal case," Outka says that one can assume that both parties are "pressing to have their own interests fully respected." As some feminists have argued, women and the poor often do not press their own self-interest or rights. Their special relation to themselves at this period in history may give them a right to ask *less* of themselves. See also Michael Slote, "Some Advantages of Virtue Ethics," *Identity, Character, and Morality*, eds. Owen Flanagan and Amélie Oksenberg Rorty (Cambridge: MIT Press, 1990), 429–47.

93. Kirk, *Vision of God*, 554.

94. Kant showed that much that is typically ascribed to God could just as well be performed by a demi-god; cf. William Luijpen, O.S.A., *Phenomenology and Atheism* (Pittsburgh: Duquesne, 1964), 37–38.

95. William Luijpen, *Existential Phenomenology* (Pittsburgh: Duquesne, 1969), 319; D'Arcy, *Mind and Heart*, 70; Max Scheler, *Ressentiment* (New York: Schocken, 1972), 93.

96. Karl Barth, *Church Dogmatics* 3/4 (Edinburgh: T. & T. Clark, 1978), 375.

97.   Charles Taylor, *Sources of the Self* (Cambridge: Harvard Univ. Press, 1989), 14.

98.   Carol Gilligan, *In a Different Voice* (Cambridge: Harvard Univ. Press, 1982), 82, shows how the acceptance of self-sacrifice as "the" meaning of love has had a strange consequence: "The morality of self-sacrifice had justified the abortion." D'Arcy, *Mind and Heart*, 216–17, tries to make the case that we, like all animals, have two basic desires, one to enhance ourselves and a second to sacrifice ourselves. I am not convinced, but if so, then self-love is needed not just as a corrective to self-hate, but also as a balance to our tendency to self-sacrifice.

99.   In a few passages which are too seldom noted by commentators, Aquinas sets aside metaphysics and notes that sinners in fact may hate their own connatural good (*ST* II–II.25.7, 34.5). According to our essential nature, he says, we love ourselves; but "when a thing acts contrary to its nature, that which is natural to it is corrupted little by little," and eventually hatred takes over; hence, "hatred of one's connatural good cannot be first, but is something last, because such hatred is a proof of an already corrupt nature." Daily experience and contemporary psychology teach that this hatred comes not only at the end of a long process of self-corruption, but begins much earlier (sadly, in childhood) and is for many a lifelong source of harm to themselves and others.

100.   Browning, *Religious Thought and Modern Psychologies*, 142–54.

101.   Edward Collins Vacek, S.J., "The Function of Norms In Social Existence," *Analecta Husserliana*, ed. Anna-Teresa Tymieniecka (Boston: Reidel, 1986), 20:380–89.

102.   Scott, *Egocentrism and the Christian Life*, 205, takes this assertion of one's own will as a distinctive feature of egocentricity.

103.   Giles Milhaven, *Good Anger* (Kansas City: Sheed & Ward, 1989), 137.

104.   Gene Outka, "Universal Love and Impartiality," *Love Commandments*, eds. Edmund Santurri and William Werpehowski (Washington: Georgetown Univ. Press, 1992), 53–57.

7

Self-love

You shall love your neighbor as yourself. (Lev 19:18; Mk 12:31)

A life solely of selfless, self-forgetting, self-sacrificial agape would be seriously deficient. It would not be Christian. Such was the negative conclusion of the last chapter. We can and should exercise other-directed agape, but Christian life includes more. The positive conclusion of this chapter is that direct and indirect loves for the self are good and Christian. Self-love should not be contrasted with other-love as pagan to Christian. Rather, self-love is vitally important in any full Christian life.[1]

Let me briefly restate the problem. One strand of Christianity has not been favorable to any form of self-love. Paul offered the watchword: "Love seeks not its own" (1 Cor 8:5). Anders Nygren speaks for many when he claims that the commandment "Thou shalt love thy neighbor as thyself" should not be read to include self-love but to exclude it.[2] Agape should extend to all human beings, except oneself. Indeed, there is *no* Christian *self-love:* "The resources of natural human life are exhausted in and with egocentric love. There is nothing in the life and activity of the natural man which does not bear the marks of . . . seeking its own. It is therefore wholly under the domination of sin, and on that basis there is no possibility of manifesting love in the Christian sense of the word."[3] Rather, "Agape and the theology of the cross are [for St. Paul] quite simply one and the same thing."[4] For Nygren, Christian love is self-giving and sacrificial, while self-love is acquisitive. Paul exhibited the self-sacrificial nature of agape when he was willing to be cut off from Christ for the sake of his people (Rom 9:3).

On the other hand, we have seen that another strand of Christianity makes self-love central. For Thomas Aquinas, as this chapter shall further detail, love for another human being was less important than love for one's self; indeed, love for other human beings was justified in terms of self-love.[5] Aquinas denied that Paul was really willing to sacrifice himself for his Jewish people.[6] Aquinas thus is at the opposite pole from Nygren. Aquinas appreciates the special relation that persons have to themselves.

Is self-love sinful or is it salutary? An answer depends in part on what we mean by "self-love," a term whose meaning is quite ambiguous.[7] I will discuss two forms of self-love: agape for self and eros. For my purposes, the distinction can bring out two importantly different aspects of our love for ourselves. The first is a direct love of self, the second is indirect. In the first, the immediate object of love is our own self; in the second, the immediate object is something other than ourselves, which we love as a way of loving ourselves. With the first, we love ourselves for our own sake: agapic self-love. With the second, we love another for our own sake: eros.

In this chapter, I first discuss an agapic love for the self. Then I consider the great Catholic apologist for eros, Thomas Aquinas. Next I lay out the general characteristics of eros and show how it is different from agape. Then I give a theological account of self-love. I conclude with a section on how agapic and erotic loves for self, neighbor, and God may be in harmony but also may be in conflict.

AGAPE FOR SELF

We are to love our beloveds for their own sakes, agape says. Can we deliberately and directly love ourselves for our own sakes? If stranded alone for a lifetime on a desert island, would we be morally and religiously required to care for ourselves? Some theologians say that such activity is permissible, but morally indifferent.[8] Others call it sin or idolatry.[9] I am arguing that it is morally and religiously good.

Let me recall to attention that I am examining our conscious intentions. Some transcendental Thomists note that in affirming another we are at the same time de facto and *necessarily* deciding about ourselves and determining ourselves for the good, even if we are neither aware of this fact nor intending to do this. What they say may be true, but it is not what Christians have questioned when thinking about self-love. Some Thomists even argue that in truly loving our neighbor we are also loving not only ourselves, but also all of reality.[10] I mention this point—with which I disagree—only to indicate that they and I are doing different things. When we love our neighbor, we don't ordinarily love all reality. When we love our neighbor, we may give almost no thought to ourselves. Still, can we consciously make ourselves our own beloved?

Self-affirmation and Integration

As I noted in Chapter 3, we human beings are a unity of different, often divergent, and only partially integrated tendencies. Self-love is a self-referential action in which we try to bring this multiplicity into greater unity.

It is naive to think that this integration will occur "naturally" or automatically. The development of a self that has a wide range of inclinations, a depth to those inclinations, and an order among those inclinations is a near miraculous achievement. Becoming a reasonably balanced, broadly interested, and deep human being is a stupendous feat.

Self-referential actions are notoriously difficult to explain. Consider, for example, self-deceit. How can we lie to ourselves? In order to do so, we have to simultaneously know something and keep it from ourselves. That seeming contradiction can and does happen. We can quite sincerely deny something that, we later admit, "in another part of ourselves" we knew to be true. Jesus regularly preached against the Pharisees, many of whom presumably were quite sincere. His preaching often seems designed not so much to teach them something they did not know, but to shock them into recognition of their own self-deception (Lk 11:37–12:3). We can deceive ourselves.[11]

We can also hate ourselves or love ourselves. Some scholars, as we have seen, reject self-love because, they say, love needs some separation to overcome. Indeed, it is not easy to see how we can act in a self-transcending way toward our own self. But we do perform this self-referential act. As Karl Rahner wrote, this emotional "self-affirmation is not simply surrender to the instinctive drives of the 'struggle for existence,' but is based on objective recognition of the value and dignity of the subject within reality as a whole and in relation to God. This God-given excellence is not loved simply because it is one's own, but because it *is* and is of value."[12] Agapic self-love is neither an unselfconscious feeling of wholeness nor simply our biological and psychological tendency to grow. This self-love engages our consciousness in a reflexive way.

In agapic self-love we direct our emotional affirmation toward ourselves in particular acts and in a more habitual way. We may be filled with love or hate for ourselves, or our self-love and self-hate may be only minor, passing features of our lives. We can also love or hate some *aspect* or the *whole* of ourselves. Self-love means that we affirm our good tendencies, both actual and ideal, and that we affirm whatever leads to the rectification of our evil tendencies or disordered affections. Love is, we have seen, an emotional affirmation of the dynamism of the beloved in the direction of the beloved's own good. It is the task of direct self-love to overcome an unwholesome self-hate and to integrate good tendencies into an overall, positive direction for our lives.[13] Our love for ourselves means both that we affirm those dynamisms in ourselves that foster our identity as whole and that we decline to affirm those dynamisms that lead either to disintegration or degradation. We affirm the saint in us and we dissent from the sinner in us. We promote "healthy self-integration, personal identity and centeredness."[14] If we can and should value these qualities in others, we can and should especially value them in ourselves since we are each responsible for our own lives. It seems odd to hold, as many do, that it is good for others to fill our various needs, but not good for us to actively do so (Rom 15:1–2).

Agapic self-love is at the root of many of life's widely valued tasks. For example, the choice to pursue a liberal education should be a choice to begin a new phase in our self-development (Prov 19:8).[15] This self-development is intrinsically valuable, whether or not it helps us to find employment or serve others.[16] Out of self-love we also affirm our natural tendencies toward self-preservation and self-actualization: eating and drinking, playing and praying, mating and musing, and so forth.[17] An habitual self-love lies behind many of our spontaneous, emotional responses. For example, anger, as a form of self-assertion, can be quite good.[18] Self-love also lies behind our concern for our own personal integrity and identity. We rightly do not pursue some possibilities that may be good for others because these possibilities are "not us." At stake in any of our activities is our own identity, and our self-love preserves and fosters that identity. We love who we are and who we are becoming. Thus, since we form our own identity with every personal act we perform, we can be rightly concerned about the effects of an act on our own virtue. We consent to those tendencies in us that mold us as members of God's Kingdom. In exercising this agapic love, we are faithful to our best selves and to God.

If agapic love for others is one "solution" to the problem of human selfishness, agapic love for self is a solution to another human problem. Our contemporary world is filled with many forms of self-alienation. In response to this problem, contemporary philosophers and theologians have raised eloquent pleas for authenticity, spontaneity, integrity, and the uniqueness of the self.[19] Given psychologists' testimony that so many of us live alienated lives, there is a "duty" of self-love.[20] Freud's "discovery" that the human psyche is characterized not only by eros but also by *thanatos* should not have come as news to Christians who have long affirmed the self-corrosive power of sin. Still, Christians surprisingly seem to have assumed that a healthy self-love would take care of itself and that, therefore, we need exhort ourselves only to other-love.[21] The opposite is frequently the case. Some people agapically love others, even while hating themselves. Many people readily sacrifice themselves for others, but feel guilty when they do something good for themselves.[22] Therefore, some emotional affirmation of the goodness of our own self may be quite necessary.

If a perfect stranger needed a heart transplant, should we offer our own heart? This would truly be the self-sacrificing gift that agapists recommend. Most people, however, would say that we have no such obligation. At the very least, they would want to make sure that such apparent generosity did not mask a lack of proper self-love.[23] Jesus, who submitted to the cross "for us and for our salvation," was not "unChristian" when he first asked to be spared the cup (Mt 26:39). He lived many years before that supreme sacrifice. If, without some special reason, a woman refuses to eat or take care of her health or if she neglects her talents, something is amiss. Less self-evident, perhaps, but equally true, if she did not delight in her own good and be dismayed at her own bad tendencies, she would hardly be living a full human life. The second great commandment indicates that self-love is important. To be sure, the phrase "as yourselves" is notoriously vague.[24] Still, a rather plain reading of the text indicates that if we are to love our neighbors as ourselves, then we are to love ourselves. The phrase would have little meaning if we were not to love ourselves.

Characteristics of Agapic Self-love

I have already discussed agape in Chapter 5. Here I will briefly apply some of the characteristics of agape to a direct love of the self. This love is a real love. It is an *emotional* apprehension and consent to our own ever-becoming selves. It is an emotional participation in our own lives. We encourage and assure ourselves; we allow ourselves to enjoy and relish what we are doing and who we are. By contrast, thinkers trained in the analytic tradition tend to describe self-love as a nearly emotionless self-respect: "to being one's own master, to exercising self-control and resisting temptations, to tenaciously following one's own lights when the occasion arises or in defense of one's liberty."[25] All of these are, of course, essential. They are virtues of the will; but they are a pale shadow of self-love.

Agapic self-love is a *creative* love directed to our own growth. Filled with a sense of our own (finite and dependent) goodness, we affirm and appreciate that goodness and want it to develop. The *overflowingness* of agapic love includes a promotion of our own best interests. We "overflow," so to speak, into those areas of our own being that are as yet unfilled. Though there is a grave danger of phariseeism and self-righteousness in being alive to and concerned with our own growth, still this form of love can be appropriate. In fact, this self-affirmation, far from increasing egoism, can actually diminish it, since when we are full of a sense of our own goodness we have less need to denigrate, use, or parasitically identify with the goodness of others as ways of bolstering a sense of our own worth.[26] Instead, when we affirm and confirm the direction of our lives toward the good, we also become freer to love others.

We can and should *bestow* value upon our own unique existence; that is, we grant it a special significance for ourselves. In other words, we have and want a special responsibility for ourselves. This agapic love can mean a real *generosity* to ourselves. The dangers here, of course, are many. But when we have done our part to take care of the needs of our neighbor, it can be proper, at least on occasion, to be specially good to ourselves, whether that be in the form of extra prayer, a martini, or a long vacation. At the same time, we can and do make agapic *sacrifices* for ourselves. Out of a devotion to our long-term developing identity, we can deny the full play of many of our needs for the sake of some future goal, for example, the sacrifices necessary to pursue a scholarly career. We can ask more of ourselves than we can of others. A genuine love of self is not easy; indeed it is the task of a lifetime.

AQUINAS ON EROS

If Nygren can be considered the apostle of agape, Aquinas can be the apostle of eros. In Chapter 5, I devoted considerable attention to Nygren's view of agape; here I concentrate on Aquinas's view of eros. Before beginning, let me freely acknowledge that I am tracing only one strand in Aquinas's thought. It is, I think, the dominant strand. It is a strand that has massively influenced Catholic natural law ethics. But Thomas has other strands. He has some place for agape. And, as we shall see in the next chapter, he also had a theory of friendship.[27]

Aquinas and Nygren generally agree on the nature of eros. The major difference between them is that Aquinas thinks it is central and good, while Nygren thinks it is self-centered and pagan.[28] Nygren traces the eros theme back to the Greeks, where he finds its purest form in Plato, who praises the human tendency to strive upward in the direction of the ideal world in order to obtain union with the divine.[29] Eros, then, is not sensual love as contrasted to heavenly love. In fact, eros motivates some of the best human activities: the pursuit of the truth, goodness and beauty, indeed the desire to possess God.[30] Accordingly, Plato's eros seemed to Aquinas and others to be a natural ally for Christian love; but for Nygren this is emphatically not the case. Rather, eros is the "born rival" and "principal adversary" of agape.[31]

Before we can decide whether this is so, we need to look at Aquinas's theory of eros. Drawing upon the Greek heritage, Aquinas understands love and hate as aspects of that basic drive by which all beings *seek* whatever is *good for themselves* and resist whatever is not: "Just as each thing is naturally attuned and adapted to that which is suitable to it, wherein consists natural love, so it has a natural dissonance from that which opposes and destroys it, and this is natural hatred."[32] The fundamental axiom for Aquinas is: "Every nature *desires* its own being and *its own perfection*."[33]

Thus, human beings seek their own perfection, and so for them the *good* is whatever helps them attain that perfection. "The term good is applicable first and foremost to a being that is perfective of another after the manner of an end."[34] In other words, the good, as Aquinas generally views it, is *"principaliter"* the good for me (or another), not the good in itself which is to be affirmed for itself. "The proper object of love is the good, because love involves a certain connaturality or attraction of the lover for the loved. To everyone, that is good which is connatural and proportionate to itself."[35] By this proportion, Aquinas here means that we love something insofar as it is for our own good, and we flee it insofar as it does not serve our good. Only what is truly suitable to us will count as good. The love described here is what Aquinas usually calls the love of concupiscence.[36] In a love of concupiscence, "the lover, properly speaking, loves himself."[37] Thus, this strand of Aquinas's thought comes close to *psychological egoism*. Aquinas asserts, on metaphysical grounds, that "a man necessarily must love himself; and it is impossible for man to hate himself."[38] In fact, all beings necessarily seek their own good. Indeed, all human beings love themselves more than all other human beings.[39]

At times Aquinas's thought borders on *ethical egoism*. A typical problem in understanding agape toward others—not to mention practicing it—is the self-transcendence of love. In going beyond our self, will we not lose our self? If we live in another, do we not betray ourselves? Here, however, the problem is the reverse. If we are striving to achieve our own perfection, will we ever really go beyond ourselves? Aquinas usually makes our love for others depend on self-love. "The root of love is the similarity of the beloved to the lover because thus the beloved is good and suitable to himself."[40] We must, he says, love ourselves above others, since we are most similar to ourselves; then we are to love others to the degree that they are like us, e.g., our children, spouse, parents, fellow citizens, and so forth.[41] Aquinas explains these natural loves not in terms of the other but in terms of the self: "Therefore the love which one has for his wife and son is more included in the love by which a person loves himself than is the love which he has for his parents. But this is not to love the son for son's sake, but rather for one's own sake."[42] In answer to the question whether we need friends or other people either on earth or in heaven, Aquinas answers, No, not essentially. Aquinas recognizes two kinds of perfection, one in which persons are internally perfected and another which occurs through human relationships; and he considers the nonrelational perfection to be higher.[43] Our central delight is in our own virtue. Here on earth, however, friends can be appropriate means through which we attain our end. In heaven, God suffices for us, though friends may be an added extra.[44]

Aquinas sometimes sounds like an eudaimonistic utilitarian: "Of necessity, every man desires happiness. . . . Happy is the man that has all he desires."[45] In somewhat Pelagian fashion, Aquinas asks how we can attain happiness.[46] Though Aquinas did not in fact do so,[47] much Catholic ethics under the inspiration of this question tended to make morality a science of human happiness and of the various means to achieve our final happiness. Religiously, Aquinas courts this *anthropocentrism* by proposing two correlative premises: "Happiness means the acquisition of the last end"[48] and God is that which completely satisfies the human appetite.[49] Nygren agrees that "Eros is man's way to God,"[50] but Nygren spurns this eros as human self-centeredness. Aquinas generally welcomes this eros: "Since everything desires its own perfection, a man desires for his ultimate end that which he desires as the perfect and fulfilling good of himself."[51] For Aquinas the end of our acts is *one's self*, not some end beyond the self: "Natural love is said to be of the end, not as of that end to which good is willed, but rather as of that good which one wills for oneself."[52] God is desired insofar as God is perfective of one's self. According to Aquinas, "We are induced to desire Him, by which we most love ourselves, willing for ourselves the highest good."[53]

These tendencies in Aquinas's thought toward egoism are troubling. We are capable of loving objects that are good in themselves or good for others, but not good for us. And whatever is other or outside this suitability to the self should not be ignored or hated. To the contrary, Christians have wanted to say that, like God, we can and should love the poor, needy, and sinful—those who seem least suitable for perfecting our self. To be sure, we do not love their poverty, neediness, or sin. And Aquinas acknowledges that their incomplete share in the fullness of life's goods itself may make a *special* claim on our beneficence.[54] Still, the point here is that we can and should love those who are different from ourselves, including those who will not benefit us.

In sum, this view of human love essentially includes a return to self. Humans have their own *exitus et reditus*, they go out in love in order to perfect themselves. And in seeking their own end, creatures seek God, for "God alone perfectly satisfies man's will,"[55] and "man's last end is the attainment or enjoyment" of God.[56] God is envisioned as an object of our desire for that which perfects us. The human person is viewed as needy, and God is envisioned as fulfilling that need. In fact, in a remarkable if not also embarrassing passage, Aquinas says that if God did not fulfill our need, "there would be no reason for loving Him."[57]

EROS

It was views such as the one we have seen in Aquinas that infuriated Nygren and pushed him into the opposite extreme. Still, there is much good sense in Aquinas's position. He well describes one healthy love. Psychological egoism, ethical egoism, and anthropocentrism are finally wrong. But each is wrong to the extent that it is partial. Stripped of the qualifiers that we can or should *only* promote our good, his understanding of eros captures an important truth of human life. Martin D'Arcy only somewhat overstated the case when he said, "Self-love is synonymous with life, or the desire to live."[58] We human beings need others to attain our own fulfillment, and this fulfillment is a worthy goal.

Characteristics of Eros

Eros is defined differently by different authors. Here I understand it as love for other persons or things not for their sakes, but *for the lover's sake*.[59] We can have eros for a beautiful painting, for nuclear physics, for a poodle, for our son, or for God. Eros springs from and is directed to fulfilling the interests or development of the self. Eros affirms the other in view of the benefits the lover receives. These benefits might include goods received in return from the beloved, a certain enrichment from being united to the beloved, or merely the fulfillment that comes from acting. Eros ceases once those benefits are no longer in prospect. For example, we may buy a cat as a pet, and then we come to love our Garfield. We lavish care on him, even make sacrifices for him; but our basic motive is our own enrichment. And we may get rid of Garfield if he becomes too much of a burden, or we may decide to keep him if only because we could not bear his absence.

Eros is a form of self-love, but it is distinguished from agapic self-love because it proceeds *by way of love for the other*. Eros is a real *love* for others. "If the object were *merely* instrumental, we could not be said to love it."[60]

The beloved, in at least some aspect of its goodness, is genuinely affirmed. Still, the object is affirmed or promoted under the condition that this love in the short or long run redound to the good of the self. The father who lovingly encourages his children's education genuinely wants their advancement; but his love is eros if he would cut off support when "parenting" no longer brings him satisfaction.

Our normal loves are highly marked by eros: we love others in part because of what they do for us. The structure of human consciousness ensures the possibility of self-love in all we do. When we love others, we freely allow their unique goodness to modify our identity; then, to the degree that this process is itself conscious and free, we are likely to affirm the enriched person we become through our love. Furthermore, whenever we extend ourselves toward others, we are exercising our talents, thereby developing ourselves, and this is satisfying. Since we can hardly stay long unaware of how we too grow even in our most other-centered acts, an element of self-love likely will accompany all of our acts. Only persons who genuinely hate themselves will resist this accompanying self-love. Those who strive to be consistently self-indifferent or self-forgetful will try to bracket any inclinations to self-love. For the rest of us, some self-love will usually be present and welcomed.

The process of self-love is often only *tacit*. For instance, we commonly experience fulfillment in devotion to some cause, even when that fulfillment is not our *primary* reason for involvement. We enjoy and affirm this accompanying fulfillment, even when such enjoyment is not our primary goal. That is, some eros often goes along with agape. Conversely, we typically experience emptiness when we are not devoted to someone or something beyond ourselves. It seems not only possible, but legitimate, to want to be involved with a cause *in part* for the fulfillment (or overcoming of emptiness) that accompanies such devotion. If the sole motive for involvement is our own fulfillment, then we are not really devoted to the person or cause. But we human beings are complex enough to have true commitments that are accompanied by self-love. Again, we sometimes take on certain projects because of their own intrinsic worth, but after a while we discover that the satisfaction of the involvement diminishes. Needless to say, we can continue our involvement because of the worth of the project. But it often happens that, if someone else can take our place, we move on to yet other involvements. The project retains its value, but it no longer challenges us, no longer sufficiently expands us; and so we move on to other projects because our self-fulfillment is also worthwhile.[61]

Objective love: Eros is genuinely love of the *other*. It is not solely love of self. "What separates authentic erotic love from narcissism is the otherness of the other."[62] Eros is not, as is commonly asserted, identical with love of self. We can hate things out of love for ourselves, and the hate is not eros. Rather eros "is also an affective affirmation of its object—even though not for itself but for another and not in its totality but only under that aspect" which is good for ourselves.[63]

Not every desire is love. We have many kinds of desires, e.g., the desire to win, the desire to humiliate. Eros is not even identical with our desires for whatever will contribute to our perfection. As an act of agapic self-love, we might want to eat carrots because they are healthy for us, but we might honestly say we do not love carrots. As I use the term, eros is truly *love* for the other. Eros emotionally unites the lover with the beloved and therein affirms the beloved's value, but does so for the sake of the perfection that thereby accrues to the lover.

The relations we have with this world are of many kinds. Most are not distinguishably love relationships. We may but usually do not love the earth we walk on and from which we derive our food. We may but usually do not love the hundreds of people on the subway train going downtown with us; we have a basic human respect for them; and frankly we might even wish that a good number of them would have stayed home. Still we can and at times do love the "objects" of our world. Sometimes we love them for themselves; perhaps more commonly we love them for what they contribute to our life.

Eros is an *objective* love, not a subjectivism that distorts reality for our own purposes. It affirms the other in (at least some of) its real and ideal value. We might love our teacher and be glad when she advances in knowledge, but we are glad because we will thereby have a better teacher. We affirm what is really her own growth in value, but do so for our advantage. Genuine eros does not distort the good to fit our own needs; rather, we want to conform to the good as it is; otherwise we will not really be fulfilled by the beloved's good.

Eros takes many forms. In eros's sensual *epithymic* form, we are, for example, attracted to the sexual sense-pleasure we receive from our lover, and his value is then relative to our desire for that pleasure.[64] In eros's psychological form, we may seek someone who will make us feel comfortable or cheerful. In eros's spiritual form, we move toward ever more beautiful or intelligible objects, hoping to have some share in their sublimity. In its religious form, eros wants God to be perfect because otherwise our quest for the perfectly fulfilling good would seem thwarted. The Scriptures

frequently appeal to these forms of eros: you should love God and neighbor, and then "you will be repaid at the resurrection of the just" (Lk
14:14). We shall reap a hundredfold for any sacrifices we make (Mk
10:29). The psalmist can sing, "I love the Lord because he has heard my
voice in supplication," an eros love (Ps 116:1). In each of these forms of
eros, the beloved is genuinely affirmed and loved, but only insofar as,
under one or more aspects, the beloved is good for the lover.[65]

Not necessarily acquisitive: It is important to note that, contrary
to Nygren, eros is *not* mere *acquisitiveness*, trying to turn everything into
our own possession. We can love a painting or a sunset, and not intend to
possess them. We give ourselves to a teacher in order to gain her knowledge. We ecstatically "melt"[66] into God. In fact, the eros lover often wants
to *be* "possessed" by the beloved.[67] This is as true of religious eros as it is
of two teenagers in love. Hence, eros is not necessarily a possessive love.
Rather, eros often desires to *belong* to a superior being. Eros is "a passionate attraction to the valuable and a desire to be united with it."[68] One
exotic religious example of this eros occurs when a Dionysian frenzy takes
possession of believers and they are transported into the dark world of the
mystery religions or into mystical ecstasy.[69] More garden-variety examples
occur: we desire to be with important or famous or powerful people. We
are moved to love them, that is, to unite with them, but not to possess
them. Were we truly to possess them, they would lose their luster, and
eros would not achieve its aim of self-enhancement. Persons who have
been possessed by us have been reduced to a thing and thus would no
longer be attractive to us. But these distortions are not necessary to eros.

Eros is often wrongly criticized as only "taking" from others. Eros can
also want to share. For example, some persons want and need to talk.
They love a good listener, sometimes any minimally decent listener. They
are clearly not agapic people, trying to help others. They love themselves
through another. They seek someone, e.g., a therapist, to whom they can
unburden their problems. Or they may need simply to share their experiences with someone. They may come to love their listener. In these cases,
persons erotically love someone who will allow them to "give" or share
themselves, sometimes in most private or intimate ways. And not seldom
does it take great *agape* to *receive* from such persons.

Furthermore, eros should not be seen simply as "taking" since without eros we can needlessly deprive others. One need only imagine sexual
relations or a good meal with a spouse who didn't really love these activities. Our spouse's lack of enjoyment would deprive us. Eros seeks its own

fulfillment, but it often essentially depends on the beloved also achieving erotic fulfillment. Mutual eros can be more desirable than eros in one person and agape in another. Eros moves us out beyond ourselves to foster and then share in the pleasures of others. In so doing it wants the other to live a rich life.

For Plato eros springs from both need and energy. Nygren and others emphasize the "emptiness and want" aspect.[70] Aquinas emphasized the energy or *dynamic* aspect of eros, that is, the ability of a being to maintain, restore, and increase its own self through relating to others. Aquinas provides a lengthy defense of a thesis that might be described as "alikes like alikes," in other words, we like to be with our own kind.[71] Strong or talented people like to be with other strong or talented people. Eros is not merely emptiness; it may also be a fullness that wants to be with others. It feels enriched in their company and seeks that company for enrichment.

Affirms value: Because it is love, eros is an *affirmation* of the *other's* (at least relative to us) *value.* If we discover that apples do not, as we had thought, keep the doctor away, then we can no longer love them for their healthful property. Our reason for loving them had been that *they* really had some nutritional or medicinal value. Similarly we want our paramour to be good-looking or our students to be intelligent. These are their values, even when they are valued for what they do to enhance our life. Eros can be directed to either unique or generic values in the beloved: only you can bring me happiness or any decent student will do.

Like agape, an eros love for the neighbor intends the *good of the beloved.* This is an important point if eros is to be a genuine love. We can love our wife for the prestige she brings us, and we may lavish as much care on her as we would if we loved her simply for herself. In fact, we often better care for others when we love them for our own sakes than when we love them solely for their sakes. Eros may even lead to goods for each party that are otherwise unlikely without the eros. Driving our sister's kids to school is a service done out of love for her, but we probably would not extend this favor for long if she did not return the favor. Everyone may benefit through eros.

Because our eros is a kind of love, we are directed to the *greater value* of the beloved; in fact, it is to our interest that the beloved's values we prize be seen in and grow to their fullness. The more they are enhanced, the more we are enhanced. Eros-filled persons can see richness in the smallest or simplest of things. For such persons, small is also beautiful. They have the capacity to seek an enormous range and variety of goods, and they have a desire to taste the delights and wonders of life. Those who are in a relationship with God aspire to enjoy with God in an ever fuller way all of God's world.

Love in all forms, as we have seen, is not content to affirm what is and to remedy what is defective. It is *creative*, moving toward the new and not yet appreciated or realized. Eros can be very creative, whether in dreaming up new cuisine or in discovering ever more ways to give itself over to God. Eros develops new and, at times, uncharted relationships in order to discover new possibilities of the self. The guardians of order are suspicious of this eros. We saw earlier that agape may have a lawless form. This agape goes beyond a sober reasonableness to expend itself in devotion and even sacrifice. There is also a "lawless" form of eros that breaks from the sober restraint of reason and from the tidiness of order. This lawless form moves the self to be unwilling to be content with the universal, the ordinary, the expected. In its positive form, this eros reflects the search for one's self, a protest in favor of one's individuality, the plea for one's uniqueness. It is an affirmation of the self in a freedom which goes beyond "merely the unfolding and actualization" of already given potentialities.[72] In its degraded form, it is subjectivism or an uncontrolled itch for novelty.[73]

As was true of agape, so it is also true of eros that this love is *valuable in itself*, whatever the results that may flow from it. This is not to say that all exercise of eros is appropriate, any more than all exercise of agape is appropriate. Just as self-sacrificing devotion to one's pet poodle can be immoral, so also eros for a painting is wrong if it leads one to steal the painting. In itself eros is not wrong, but it becomes wrong when it is not modified by reason and other loves. Our eros is God-given and therefore is to be affirmed along with all God's gifts.

Eros, as a form of love, emotionally *unites* us with various goods. With persons, we may just relish their presence and feel good when we are with them. Someone who is "in love" is permeated with this sort of eros. Eros, then, is no external, "using" relation, but rather a union of our self with the beloved. James Hanigan rightly describes eros as a passionate "desire to become one with the beloved"; toward persons this love seeks a union that is "personal, exclusive, and forever."[74] Christians, especially the mystics, often have talked about their relation to God in these terms. Eros is an *emotional* union with the beloved. It is not merely a rational calculation of the advantages that another might bring to us. We are enlivened by the presence of our beloveds. We delight in them. We feel ennobled in the presence of beings of high value. We feel nourished even by lower values, at least if these values do not take us from higher fulfillments. The Bible often describes the relationship of God toward human beings in terms of emotional attachment: God is a jealous, demanding God, who expects our all (Ex 20:5, 34:14; Dt 4:23–24).

Eros is capable of great *devotion* to the beloved. Two romantically involved lovers will make great *sacrifices* for one another. And when Juliet dies, Romeo is ready to end his life because his life now has no purpose. His life lacks the one person who can fulfill his eros. If his love were simply agape, then he would have no reason to end his life. He might be sad for her, or even happy that she is in heaven. But neither of these reasons would be cause for him to despair. He wants to end his life because he now lacks the life-giving fulfillment that he derived through eros. Without her, he feels his emptiness will never be filled.

Potentially stable: At least some acts of eros move toward *permanence.* Peter says, "Lord, to whom shall we go? You have the words of *everlasting life*" (Jn 6:67). Hanigan and others, however, find eros "too unstable."[75] They dismiss too quickly the durability of a deep eros. They seem more guided by a Greek aversion to change than by the ever shifting intricacies of an abiding personal relationship. The God of the Bible offers the rewards of an exclusive, personal, and lasting covenant, but this covenant goes through all the ups and downs common to human life. Jesus encourages his disciples to seek "a never-failing treasure with the Lord. . . . Wherever your treasure lies, there your heart will be" (Lk 12:33). These acts of eros may abide forever.

To be sure, eros will leave the beloved behind when the beloved no longer promises fulfillment. But there is no reason to say that all beloveds will be discarded, for some beloveds—above all, God—can permanently provide fulfillment. Even transient loves such as a love for baseball have about them the quality of "I wish this could last forever." We may grow weary or tired of the things that we love, but this is a feature of our finitude, not specifically of eros. It happens with agape too. Even contemplation of great ideas and marvelous beauty becomes, for us terrestrial beings, rather boring after a while. One can examine a painting over and over, but the very makeup of our bodies requires that we leave the painting after a while. In the midst of these variations, however, a habitual eros love can endure. We want to go back again and again to see the painting or be with our hero. Eros may be quiescent for a long while, but given the occasion it returns in full vigor. Consider the love that married couples have for one another. It surely has an eros component, even though this will wax and wane rhythmically over time. But it lasts, or can last. And with the death of a spouse, a husband will experience an enormous loss to himself. The "Song of Songs," which extols if anything an eros love, ends with the claim that "love is stronger than death" (Sg 8:6). Eros can even survive death.

Unwillable: Finally, like other loves, eros may be free, *without* being simply *willable*. Love's essential correlation with and therefore dependence on the object puts any love beyond our total control. Hanigan says that eros is unsuitable as a foundational Christian love because it is not "capable of being willed as a matter of free choice."[76] It must be replied once again that *no* love that is more than just external behavior can be simply willed as a matter of free choice. Much behavior can be willed, but matters of the heart cannot. Indeed, every aspect of the Christian life must in some sense be a gift of grace and thus cannot simply be "willed as a matter of free choice." The will can elicit into act basic graced attitudes that are already present and allow them to flourish. It can freely consent to the love that arises at the invitation of the goodness of the other. But it cannot simply decide to make *any* kind of love happen.

Differences from Agape

Eros is distinguished from agape by being *self-interested*. We love the beloved for our own sake. This is a matter of our conscious intentions, not of greater or lesser good achieved. In fact, the good obtained by the beloved may be greater than our own. To give a political parallel: if the only way we can gain power is to ally ourselves with a senator who will thereby have even more power, we might decide to assist this senator because without her we will have nothing. Our contribution to her career is conditional upon whether it brings advantage to us. When she goes out of office, our support stops.

Agape, by contrast, would support another even when it brings no advantage to us. Agape acts independently of self-interest. It could so happen that we reap the greater advantage through our agapic love. Again, using a political parallel, a senator might kindly help us develop our skills as a fledgling politician, but it may turn out that we become a brilliant asset to her career. The fact that she reaps the greater benefits does not of itself turn her agape into eros. Agape is tested by the lack of personal advantage, but it is not proved by that lack. Eros is proved by drying up when we are no longer nourished. Jesus puts this test to his disciples when he tells them that it is not his to give a seat in heaven, and then he asks them if they can drink with him a bitter cup. "The Son of Man has not come to be served but to serve—to give his life in ransom for the many" (Mk 10:38–45).

There is no metaphysical necessity that what is good for others cannot also be good for ourselves. Our agapic love for our neighbor will always in some sense be good for us. If the most profound act of human beings is to love, then agape will be self-fulfilling. It fulfills us to be a lover. But, apart from this fulfillment, there is no necessary metaphysical harmony such that what is good for our neighbor will also be good for us. Apart from the intrinsic value of love itself, agape may be bad for us. We may have to make significant sacrifices. As Kenneth Cauthen writes,

> It would be tempting at this point to appeal to the paradox of self-realization through self-sacrifice. . . . Yet there is a tragic dimension to life found in the inescapable fact that serving some ends eliminates others. . . . It is not always true that the highest good of the self is coincident with service of others. . . . The soldier who dies for his country in a just war cannot live to become the poet his soul longs to be. . . . Sacrifice of self is not always the road to self-realization in every sense of the word.[77]

Love is itself good; its exercise is its own reward; and when Christians love in concert with God, they elevate themselves by uniting with their origin and goal. Still, the exercise of agape may leave many of our richest potentials unfulfilled. Indeed, it may lead to the sacrifice of our life.

Restricted scope: Because eros is exercised for our own sake, its scope will be *more restricted* than agape's. Not all good things are "good for me" (1 Cor 6:12). Agape can love all beings for themselves, and hence it has no limitation of scope. Poisonous snakes are not good for us, and we will not easily love them erotically. (Since we human beings are richly complex, there may well be ways for eros to be evoked: we are pleased by the graceful way that snakes move, or we develop an attachment for our pet snake.) But we should not conclude from the more restricted scope of eros that it is not Christian. A more universal love is not necessarily better than a particular love. Would, for example, a love for Jesus be less valuable than a love for several of his executioners?

Scripture describes God's love as both universal and particular. On the one hand, there is "the man Christ Jesus who gave himself as a ransom for *all*" (1 Tm 2:5) and Jesus' remark that the rain falls on the just and unjust alike (Mt 5:45). On the other hand, God's love is often highly particularistic and value-dependent. The goats and sheep are selected according to what they have done (Mt 25:31–46); and God chooses *some* for salvation (2 Tm 2:10). Jesus not only favored the disciples over many others, but he favored some disciples more than others (Jn 15:16, 19:26).[78]

Hanigan complains against eros that it "would be a human impossibility" to "enter into erotic love relationships with everyone."[79] To be sure. But we can ask whether there is any love that we might extend to everyone, short of some vague well-wishing. Every love tends to become particular in practice. Only a love for "being" would be truly universal; and in its Dionysian and mystic forms, eros seeks this kind of union with "being." Moreover, eros can move us to pursue truth, beauty, goodness, justice, and peace; and those goals surely have a *universal* scope. Rather, eros is more limited in scope than agape because aspects of the object that are not good for us cannot be loved erotically, whereas they can be loved agapically.

Need-dependent: Agape proceeds out of a fullness or from a overflow of goodness. As we have seen, eros is a movement born both of "want" and "energy." It is an energetic movement toward the value that will fill its longing.[80] For Nygren eros tends to be only neediness or desire, and desire ceases when it possesses that which it seeks.[81] Aquinas rightly holds, however, that eros will not cease when it once possesses what it seeks, for eros will then delight in what it possesses.[82] Thus, eros is not necessarily restless. Still, the difference between agape and eros is that the latter essentially springs from some sort of "need."

This "need," however, must not be narrowly conceived. We are in need of others because we are relational beings. Human beings exist in an open and largely unfulfilled relation to other human beings, to the world, and ultimately to God. The movement of eros *begins* with this largely unfulfilled *relatedness* to all beings and Being. Paradoxically, the more this emptiness is fulfilled, the more we are capacitated for wider and deeper relationships. That is, fulfilling a "need" creates further "needs." Our potential for relations increases by fulfilling our potential. "Those who have, will get more" (Mt 25:29). When we are feeling nourished by those we love, we grow in our desire to be in touch with a richer and deeper reality.

Agape can be self-indifferent. It wants others to love us only if it is good for them to do so. By contrast, an important kind of eros is the need to be needed. We often become attached to others when their need of us heightens our sense of our own value. While it is true that all of us want to be loved for our own sakes, we also want to be loved "erotically." We want to be sought for the good we can contribute to others.[83] When another loves us for the good we bring them, our own goodness is confirmed and enhanced. For example, we want to be chosen for a basketball team; being chosen means that in the eyes of someone we will be good for the team. If we learn we have been chosen only agapically—perhaps because we were the least athletic—we might welcome the opportunity to play, but we would not feel valued in the way we want to be. Similarly, to be chosen for a marriage partner means that the woman we love sees us as good for her. Would we have it any other way? And if we freely welcome love from others—and not only because it is good for them to love, but also because it is good for us—then we are exercising a form of self-love.

Of course, the fact that we are valued does not make us valuable. Another may only be projecting onto us some unmet need. But when others really love us erotically, their love confirms our value and fosters it. In fact, their love usually opens up for us unsuspected aspects of our value. Another's accurate eros for us is creative of our identity. They bring out the best in us or at least some aspect we may not have been so aware of. On the other hand, we may be valued only for some of what we are, or for aspects of ourselves that are not very central, or even for what we do not esteem in ourselves. We may be affirmed for our brawn, or for our curves, or for our vicious streak. These affirmations may genuinely reveal something about us, but we will feel in the long run demeaned if these aspects are the only ones that another loves in us or if they are traits we do not approve. Further, when others love us only for the way we satisfy them, they may be inclined to discourage certain positive changes in us lest they lose what they find fulfilling.

Most theologies do not speak of God's eros. God, it is said, does not need anything from us. I do not agree. To be sure, God is secure no matter what we do. But God loves us. That means that God has united God's own heart with our heart. *In* that relation, God wants our fulfillment for ourselves; but, as one involved with us, God also wants our fulfillment for God's relational self. God will not be able to be *our* Redeemer unless we love God in return. Speaking anthropomorphically, but nonetheless appropriately, once God has decided to redeem, God the Redeemer needs to be needed. The biblical God is portrayed as frustrated, angry, and disappointed when God's identity as our Savior is effectively thwarted by us (Is 30:1; Jer 12:7–9). God is concerned about the covenant, for our sake, to be sure, but also for God's now committed sake. "I, the Lord, am your

God who, as God, brought you out of Egypt that I, the Lord, may be your God" (Nm 15:41). As Günther Bornkamm notes, "It would be impossible to deny the aspect of a passionate longing in the love with which God loves man."[84]

THEOLOGY OF SELF-LOVE

Though some may urge that it is imprudent to argue for self-love in an era commonly described as self-centered, an articulation of the theological grounds for self-love may help locate the proper place and limits of this love. Denigration of all self-love itself causes great harm because good self-loves are thrown out with the bad and because, in reaction to this aberrance, not only good but also bad self-loves are undifferentiatedly affirmed. The fact that God loves God's self should have provided a clue to theologians that self-love is not selfishness.[85]

Theological approach: The religious defense of self-love I offer may seem peculiar to those outside of theology. Theologians sometimes get in the strange position of arguing from the obscure to the obvious. For example, one hears that, because the nature of the Trinity is one of inter-personal relations, a husband ought to love his wife. Those outside of theology, I presume, must shake their heads and say that, if it is not clear that a husband should love his wife, any recourse to intra-Trinitarian life hardly clarifies matters. Similarly, the goodness of self-love is to many people obvious, and grounding it in God seems to explain the obvious by the mysterious. The point is well taken. My goal here is different. I want to show how self-love fits within the theological framework developed earlier in this book. A theological justification of self-love is particularly called for, since Christianity has looked so unkindly on self-love. My hope is that a religious vision might have a role, however modest, in redeeming or enriching the meaning of self-love (Prv 29:18).

To that end, allow me briefly to summarize the theology of this book. God loves us. That has been the starting point. The God we know and proclaim is a God who loves us through the activity of creation, redemption, and sanctification. This is a God who can say with great passion, "I will make with them an eternal covenant, never to cease doing good to them. . . . I will take delight in doing good to them. I will replant them firmly in this land, with all my heart and soul" (Jer 32:37–41). This God passionately wants our own good. God is emotionally involved with us, with the development and growth of who we are. God creates us as good, and moves us toward our own fullest goodness.[86] Our response to God's love is to accept God's love for us and to unite ourselves with God. That acceptance includes acceptance of ourselves as created by God, as redeemed from our sinfulness and limits, and as invited into ever closer union with God.

What follows from this basic theme is that we can and should love ourselves. The relation between ourselves and God is one of participation. God is not ourselves, and we are not God, but we share with God a union of love. This unity-in-difference means that God cannot love us as fully as God wants if we do not cooperate. The very nature of personhood is such that our free cooperation is necessary for our development as persons. Therefore, our cooperation with God's love in building our own personal identity is essential and irreplaceable. One way we cooperate is to love ourselves. When we love ourselves, we strive to become who we are. "Who we are," however, is very complex. We are beings who enact ourselves by relating to ourselves, to others, to our world, and to God. Our relation to ourselves should at bottom be one of love. Through an agapic self-love, we affirm and delight in our power to enact and develop our many natural and learned inclinations and capacities. Through eros, we affirm and delight in all others insofar as they bring us growth.

Creation—personal flourishing: The God who creates us wants us to flourish. God's love affirms us in our selves and wants us to attain our own perfection. That perfection includes above all living in a love relation with God. Paul claims that "God makes all things work together for the good of those who have been called" (Rom 8:26). This is strictly true only in the sense that both our diminishments and our fulfillments can contribute to our relationship with God. Our chief good is to be in relation to God. Our good also necessarily includes love for ourselves, others, and our world, to the extent that these loves are compatible with our relation to God. Therefore, in response to God's love for *us*, we can and should affirm our own good. God loves us through us. Without our cooperation, God would be hard put to make that divine love practically effective.

Our flourishing is human flourishing, and that means that we live in rhythms of "receiving" and "giving," receiving from others what we need in order to flourish and giving to others since we also need to give in order to flourish. We can give and receive without consideration of what that giving and receiving does for us—that is the point of agape. But we can and inevitably must at times also give and receive with some consideration to what the giving and receiving does for us. To be sure, the development of others must always be taken into account by us, and that may require self-sacrifice. And we cannot develop all our potential, since human possibilities are innumerable and not all are possible: we may have the capacity to be a cloistered nun or a politician, but we cannot be both. Still, some fulfillments we can and should provide for ourselves. In so doing, as Aquinas argues, God's providence for creation continues.[87]

Redemption and sanctification: It is legitimate to want to overcome the emptiness and self-frustration that arises from sin. It is legitimate to want to be *good*, that is, to be and grow in right relation to creation. It is legitimate to want to be *holy*, that is, to be and to grow in relation to God. Each of these desires is dangerous, since, as we saw in the last chapter, each can be sought self-righteously, that is, as if it referred to some isolated quality about ourselves and not to a relation to God and others. We cannot autonomously forgive our own sins; virtue cannot be directly willed but must gradually develop as a set of habitual responses to creation and God; and holiness has to be received. Still, since moral goodness and holiness are fulfillments of our life, we can aspire to some measure of them. We cannot be saved without our cooperation, and this salvation includes freely consenting to our own growth in goodness and holiness.

Our desire to overcome sin and to come into union with God is not some Pelagian or pagan trait. This union is what *God's* redeeming and sanctifying activity inspires us to seek. These desires of ours are responses to God's inviting love. We accept God's love for us, and we are transformed in that acceptance. As transformed, we want to be good and holy. We are right to desire fulfillment of the relationship offered us by God. In so doing, we love ourselves.

Eros in the eschaton: The doctrines of creation, redemption, and sanctification encourage self-love. So does the doctrine of eschatology. Jesus insists that we ask for what we need, a demand that would be inappropriate if Jesus disapproved of self-love (Mk 1:40). What we need above all is a relationship with God. We can and must love God for God's own sake, but we can also love God for our own sake. Out of our own need, we can love God in "hope for our heavenly reward" or because we "dread the loss of heaven." If there is a "crown of life, which the Lord has promised to those that love him" (Jas 1:12, 2:5), we can hope for that crown. That is, we hope that *we* will be in relation with God and we dread the loss to *ourselves* if we could not love God. This is not to deny that what we most

want is for God to be glorified, but it is also legitimate to want the fulfillment that arises from our own relation to God.

Pictures of heaven as a sort of lazy living in God's green pastures,
where all the roads are paved with gold and all our friends gather in endless banquets, have a delightful naivete about them. The images mistake
the lesser goods of heavenly life for its central joy: we will see and love
God "face to face" (1 Cor 13:12). But this naivete should not be mis-
judged as merely a peasant's fantasy. These images spring from the realization that we need the world in order to be fulfilled. Our bodies—which
are ourselves—exist only in relation to a world. Without our bodies, we
are not human beings. Without other persons, we also are not persons. As
personal beings, we need others for our own fulfillment. Even after the
resurrection, Jesus was not above some freshly caught and roasted fish,
eaten with friends (Lk 24:42–43).

Jesus frequently presented images of heaven that appeal to self-love.
Thus, the Kingdom that Christians may hope for is more like a wedding
banquet with others than solitary worship (Lk 14:15–24). In the
eschaton, it will be good for us to be with those who share in God's life.
An argument can be marshaled that we would not be truly happy in
heaven without the presence of our fellow human beings. Aquinas, as we
saw, describes God as all-sufficing and therefore deems the fellowship of
others as, so to speak, an added extra. But God's goodness is not the
neighbor's goodness, since God is not the neighbor. The theory of participation I developed argues that creatures are more than deficient reflections of God's goodness. For the fullness of eschatological joy, we will
continue to need other persons. The theory of *apocatastasis*, suitably modified to be a hope and not a dogma, acknowledges not only God's ability
to save all, but also that our fulfillment demands the presence of friends
and creation.[88]

Sinful self-denial: The importance of self-love can be seen through
a reverse consideration. Not to love ourselves is prima facie not to cooperate with the love that God has for us. It is sinful. Christianity is not
engaged in recruiting an elite corp of dead men and women. We must die
to ourselves, where this means die to our selfishness, and we may have to
deny ourselves, when this is what is required to stay faithful to our sisters
and brothers and especially to God. But God does not desire our death
(Ez 18:32). We have all been with lifeless, emotionally "dead" people.
Such people have no strong delights or desires for themselves. Surely this

is not the ideal of Christian life. A human life without eros is a life devoid of some of the major features of our identity.[89] To choose such a life is to choose to be a deficient human being. If we cannot enjoy life's pleasures and goods, we are less perfect than those who can.

Jesus of course preached and practiced self-denial. It should not be forgotten, however, that he did so as one who had an abundance of life in himself. Out of strength comes the ability to be weak. Jesus, who washed the feet of his disciples, reminded them, "You call me Teacher and Lord, and fittingly enough for that is what I am" (Jn 13:13). It is for the strong to humble themselves. It was a vigorous and self-confident Paul who learned unsuspected strengths in weakness (2 Cor 12:9–10). It is the strong who need to be open to the lessons found in weakness. The weak can be hurt by such exhortations. Weakness should not be prized for itself. Only those who have or who can get what they want are truly able to deny themselves; otherwise there is no sacrifice. The strong can risk being weak, the secure can dare to be vulnerable, those who love life can freely give it up for others. Those without eros, however, have little to lose. They may find it easy to practice the self-denial involved in "equal regard," but only because no one has any special significance or makes any particular difference to them.

To deprive one's self of a good is prima facie an evil. It can be justified. It can be noble when justified. All worldly goods must at some time be given up. But this does not make denial a good in itself. We can for a worthy reason, e.g., our health, cut off our arm, but this loss is not good in itself. So too we can refuse to erotically love God and the world, but this is a real loss. Whether we eat or drink, we should do all in the Lord (1 Cor 10:31; Rom 14:3–6). This Pauline view might be taken to mean that these sensuous activities are not forbidden as long as they are done in the Lord. Eating and drinking might be considered simply as biological acts of nourishment, to be performed in obedience to God's command. But surely a richer meaning is possible. Eating and drinking in the Lord can be a love feast, a time of sharing with the Lord. The point here is that for us to choose not to live erotically is prima facie to frustrate God's desire that we live fully. Other things being equal, we are right to love our place at the banquet of this world.

Special relation to ourselves: Since God loves each of us individually, we have under God a special responsibility for our individual selves. Since we are that created good which is most constantly present to ourselves, whose needs we are usually most able to fill, and whose moral self we alone are able to form, we are therefore our own nearest "neighbor." We should not treat ourselves as one and only one among many. The so-called impartial or self-indifferent attitude, while possible and at times appropriate, is normally inappropriate. Normally a special responsibility arises wherever there is only one person who can realize a particular important good. Here, no one else can love us as we can love ourselves. To be sure, others may in fact love us "more" than we love ourselves. But, our love for ourselves is irreplaceable and indispensable. We have talents and a personal identity that we alone can develop. We have a relational self that we alone can enact. Others may "father" our daughter, but they cannot be her father. Thus, each of us should "value his own history as one for which there is no identical replacement."[90]

Our lives are primarily our own responsibility. As Outka notes, "I cannot always seek to do for others what I can and ought to do for myself. I ought to further my neighbor's happiness, but I ought not to choose his way of life for him. Yet I do regard my way of life as meaningfully *mine*, something for which I am directly accountable."[91] Since freedom is crucially *self*-determination, we cannot exercise it for others. That is, there are things we can do for ourselves that we cannot do for others. Indeed, we must do them for ourselves, and must not do them for others. If we did not do them for ourselves, we would not be human. If we did them for others, we would not allow them to be human.

We have a special responsibility in the ordinary course of our lives to do those things that are part of our flourishing, including enjoying life. Such a position has not been obvious. The Western tradition has held a different view, especially when it comes to enjoyment or pleasure. Paul says that, like Christ, we should please others but not ourselves (Rom 15:1–2). And philosopher W. D. Ross claimed, "The desire to produce an indifferent pleasure for another is good, and the desire to produce it for oneself is indifferent. . . . since one's relation to oneself is entirely different from one's relation to any other person."[92] Though Ross thinks his position is "perfectly clear," I suggest that we have not less but more responsibility for our lives than we do for others. And that includes providing pleasure for ourselves. Moreover, apart perhaps from some rudimentary sense-pleasures, we cannot "produce" pleasure in others. Their free cooperation is necessary for them to enjoy most pleasures. This free consent is not something we can produce in them; but we can "produce" it in ourselves. Providing for ourselves pleasure and other enjoyments (which is not the same as living solely for pleasure [2 Tm 3:4; Jas 5:5]) is itself a good thing and not merely an indifferent thing.[93] Doing this good thing for ourselves, and in general doing any act of self-love, is good.

To be sure, doing good things for ourselves and enjoying ourselves usually are not experienced as part of our "duty" but only as something we want to do. But fulfilling our healthy desires is one way we teleologically further our perfection. That is, it is moral, even if it does not feel like a duty, but only something we spontaneously want. Aquinas's view that we all seek our own happiness may be an incomplete basis for ethics, but it points to one important aspect of our life. God would be cruel if God made us beings who like to enjoy themselves, but then forbade us to seek that enjoyment. "For every man, moreover, to eat and drink and enjoy the fruit of all his labor is a gift of God" (Eccl 3:13). Jesus himself admits that "the Son of Man appeared eating and drinking" (Mt 11:19), an activity that got him accused of being a glutton and a drunkard; and he encouraged the disciples to eat and drink whatever is provided (Lk 10:7). Indeed, for many contemporary people, self-love has, as I have noted, become a real duty—a third great commandment—through which they counteract their spontaneous, if neurotic, inclination to deny and hate themselves. In addition to warning people of the dangers of eros, the Church should also proclaim that there is too little eros in life.[94]

"FOR THE SAKE OF"—SELF, NEIGHBOR, GOD

Love of Neighbor

I have used the phrase "for the sake of" to distinguish agape and eros. This distinction introduces complications and potential dangers I want to address. To begin, we can love our neighbor for the neighbor's sake, for our own sake, or for God's sake. Philosophers and theologians have evaluated these loves in several ways. First, some say that it is impossible or unethical to love our neighbors for their own sake, while others say it is a natural love, and still others say that this kind of love can happen only through grace. Second, if we love our neighbor for our own sake, some say it is not really love, while others say that this is the nature of all love. Third, if we love our neighbor for God's sake, some say that this is true Christian love, while others say that this is not love at all since we do not actually love our neighbor.[95] In reflecting on such alternatives, I will indicate options made throughout this book.

First, what of loving the neighbor for our own sake? There seems no strong reason to say that loving another for our sake is necessarily wrong.

Such a love, as this chapter has been at pains to demonstrate, can be a genuine love, an emotional affirmation of the neighbor's good. The possibility of selfishness should not blind us to the possibility of a Christian eros. Still, at the end of this chapter on self-love, I do not want to pass over some *dangers* in loving others for our own sake. One typical problem with eros is not that we treat our neighbors as if they had no value, but rather that we affirm only part of their value, namely, that part which promotes our self-interest. We potentially miss their basic human dignity because we are interested only in that aspect of them that benefits ourselves. Another problem occurs when eros becomes our chief or exclusive love. Outka makes this point well:

> In relation to everyone else the agent's predominant aim is individual and private satisfaction. . . . The ultimate goal of the agent's aspirations is in any case some prospective state of his own. This goal dominantly pervades every relation to others. In social relations, cooperative action is only an obvious device for securing from others what is instrumental to the agent's private ends. In personal relations, enrichment to the self determines the degree to which the other is found interesting and desirable. Whoever thus enriches is if possible possessed, in one way or another, without overriding regard for the other's independent needs and desires. . . . the sublimity of the objects to which the agent aspires may have little effect on the character of his relation to any of them.[96]

The problem here is not the presence of eros in our lives; the problem occurs when every other thing is seen predominantly or *only* in relation to ourselves. This is a selfish existence.

Second, it is morally good to love others for their own sake. That is the role of agape. When the Son of Man judges the nations (Mt 25:31–46), he does not ask whether those who welcomed strangers and clothed the naked had done so for his sake. Indeed, those who failed to do so give the impression that they would have helped if they had known they would have thereby served him. It is the king who makes the connection between himself and the poor. It is not necessary for those who help to see the king in the poor. A religious motive was not necessary. The *danger* in such a view is that it seems to make explicit and personal love of God irrelevant. Anonymous Christianity becomes as good as explicit Christianity. Surely, something is wrong with such a view.

Third, we can love the neighbor for another's sake, and the special problem here is love for God's sake. If we love a child for the sake of his mother, do we not turn the child into a mere token or sign of our love for his mother? While this sort of thing does happen, it does not really fit my description of either eros or agape. In either, we genuinely love the child or the neighbor. Eros is not any use of an object to attain our own ends. So here the love of the child could be a genuine love for the child, even though its further "reason" is love of the mother. A father often loves his own children both for themselves and for the sake of his wife, not to mention for his own sake. Mixed loves are common.

What if we love our neighbor for God's sake? Do we turn the neighbor into a mere means for loving God? Does the neighbor become merely a rung on the ladder of our assent to God, to be discarded when we have ascended to higher things?[97] Is love of neighbor simply a test to prove our love for God?[98] These are real *dangers*. Eros has often been understood to be a love that moved to higher and higher goods; once it attained a higher good, there was no need to love lesser things since they were only so many deficient forms of the higher good. Why love the "imitation" when one has the real thing? Love for the neighbor in this sense may make the neighbor a mere steppingstone to loving God. Some understand phrases such as "loving Christ in the neighbor" or "loving the neighbor in Christ" to mean that we don't really love the neighbor, but look beyond the neighbor to God. The neighbor becomes a mere cipher, and the only one really loved is God.

I began a response to these problems in Chapter 5. Love of the neighbor for God's sake can and should really be love for the neighbor. The neighbor is not God, and so love for the neighbor is not love for God. Our neighbors deserve a love that is directed directly to them. They have their own value that is not merely a deficient form of what is in God. And it must also be *our* love for them, not just God's love somehow passing through us.[99] Still, when we love the neighbor for God's sake, the neighbor need not be the *final* reason for our love—but then the neighbor should never be. Our goal as Christians is not to love our neighbors solely for their own sake. This does not mean that we cannot love them for their own sake, but only that, as we grow more in love with God, our goal is to love them *in Deo*, that is, as part of our cooperating with God's love. We can love them without a thought to God, but that is not what we want to do. We want to love them for themselves, but also as part of our relation with God. Human consciousness encompasses such complexity. Thus, to love the neighbor in God does not turn them into a mere means for us to "express" or "show" or "prove" our love for God. Love of neighbor is not simply a "test" of our love of God. Love of neighbor is also not, in

Platonic fashion, a steppingstone to love of God, which would involve a sort of "trading up" that is foreign to personal love.[100] Rather, to love them in God is to love them as part of our relation to God. When we love God, we unite with God who loves our neighbor. So our love for them is one way in which, united with God, we enter more deeply into God's own activity of loving them for themselves.

In Chapter 5 we saw a second way in which the love of God and love of neighbor may be related. Loving the neighbor for God's sake may also mean that we love them as participants in God's life. As creatures, they share in God's goodness. As specially graced by God, they are marked as (potential) friends of God.[101] We find God's love *alive in them*, and to the extent that we deeply love them, we come closer to the mystery of God active in them. They are different from God, but they share in God's own life. Hence we can also love them for the sake of participating in God who is alive in them. God, as the redeeming Ground of their being, can be loved in loving them.

There is perhaps a third meaning of "loving our neighbors for God's sake." Throughout this book, the term "for the sake of" has pointed to the one whose fulfillment is our goal and criterion. If it is the case, as I have suggested, that God's relational self is fulfilled by the ongoing perfection of creation, then in loving our neighbor we are also fostering God's fulfillment. The neighbor is not used; rather, in fostering the neighbor's fulfillment, God also is fulfilled. So, in this third sense, the neighbor's fulfillment is the only way that some aspect of God's relational self can be fulfilled. We love them "for God's sake."

Love of Self

We can love ourselves for our own sake, for another's sake, and for God's sake. This chapter has discussed loving ourselves for our own sake. What I have just said about loving the neighbor for God's sake is, *mutatis mutandis,* applicable to loving ourselves for God's sake. So I will only briefly look at loving ourselves for the neighbor's sake. Many who are worried about self-love are willing to accept self-love only when it is done to enable us to love our neighbor. If there were no neighbors, this love apparently would not be justified. Obviously, I do not agree. Still, there are legitimate ways in which we can love ourselves for the sake of our neighbor.

First, love for self also ordinarily promotes the necessary condition for loving another. We will not long be able to love others unless we get enough food, sleep, and recreation. The sequence of things we do for ourselves for the sake of others can be quite long and indirect: we brush our teeth so that we will not get cavities and have to go to the dentist, which would mean a loss of money and time that could better be devoted to those who are more needy.[102] Further, knowing that a "happy person" is more likely to be agapically generous than one who feels only inner emptiness or self-disgust, we might seek those things that make us happy. We might love ourselves for others' sakes.

Second, love of self gives clues as to what others may need. I do not hold the position that we can only affirm in others what is similar in ourselves.[103] The opposite is often the case: we see good in others that we then want to realize in ourselves. But surely we do get some idea of the needs of others when we pay attention to our own needs. Without such self-care, it is likely that we will not notice similar needs in others. Self-love, curiously, serves as a paradigm for other-love.[104]

Love for God

We can love God for God's sake, for our own sake, or for our neighbor's sake. The last is quite common. Petitionary prayer often has the form of loving God for what God can do for our children or friends or nation. Spouses like to worship together because it brings them closer together; if they got nothing out of it, they might stop. Loving God for the neighbor's sake is similar to loving God for our own sake.

In comparing agapic love for God with erotic love for God, it is worth noting that in practice our tradition, perhaps wisely, does not insist on the distinction.[105] The interweaving of eros and agape toward God is abundantly testified to in the Scriptures. For example, "We will worship at your holy temple [an agapic activity] and give thanks to your name [eros], because of your kindness [eros] and your truth [possibly agape]; for you have made great above all things your name [agape] and your promise [eros]. When I called, you answered me [eros]" (Ps 138:2). Much of the Hebrew Bible is concerned with God's promise to Israel. This promise is surely a promise of good things for Israel, and Israel is motivated to remain faithful to the covenant for the sake of obtaining the good promised. The New Testament likewise is filled with promises of a better life for those who are faithful disciples of Jesus. The New Testament draws many connections between our actions and our reward, but usually leaves the nature of the connection ambiguous. For example, the claim "whoever loses his life will save it" (Lk 9:24, 17:33; Jn 12:25) does not say that we should lose our lives in order to save them, an appeal to eros, nor does it say that we should lose our lives no matter the consequence to ourselves, an appeal to agape. The ambiguity has a certain theological appropriateness. Otherwise, on the one hand, our sacrifice could be said to have a claim on God, and salvation would no longer be God's free gift. We would be encouraged to Pelagianism, doing our part and then demanding that God reward us. On the other hand, our salvation is not given to us wholly without our desire for it. Rather there is a "reward" *in* our very devotion to God, and by God's graciousness there is also a "reward" *for* the devotion, namely, a closer relation to God.

We saw at the beginning of the previous chapter that the Roman Catholic Church condemns those who hold that we should have a purely agapic love of God. Surely, we can have an agapic love of God. Jesus' death on the cross is testimony to this possibility. Christian martyrs, who did not abandon God for the sake of earthly self-interest, nevertheless hoped that God would not abandon them. And many of our prayers, both liturgical and private, spring from eros. We pray for our community or for ourselves, asking to be freed from illness or floods or ignorance or fear. We do so out of a proper self-love. But we also do so out of a love of God. God is to be affirmed as good in God's own being; but God is also loved as good for us. Ignatius of Loyola states that we are made to praise, reverence, and serve God; but then he adds that "by this means" we save our souls.[106] Agape and eros are joined. When we participate through love in another, this blurring is nearly inevitable. We say, for instance, "You are *my* joy" and "You are *my* life." In every emotion, we intend the value of the "object" and we are affected. Ordinary emotional language refuses to neatly separate love's unity and difference; and that is fine for living, however difficult it makes precise technical discourse. In loving God, we affirm God, and we are positively enhanced. We need not deny or blind ourselves to the fact that the God we love is both wholly other and a gracious giver. There is a compatibility, through God's graciousness, between agape and eros, both of which will be present in Christian life.

Priorities

We are to be lovers, but we often have to make choices among our loves. This book hopes only to set the framework within which such decisions might be located, not to determine concrete decisions. Can we, nonetheless, make some general observations about the various loves we have thus far discussed? That is the question for this final section.

Discernment: In practice, should we always love ourselves or others first? Relatively little will be said, because I think that this is the matter of daily individual discernment. Still, I can make a few comments. It is clear that there will be conflicts in our lives. We may have to choose not only between two or more neighbors, but also between these others and ourselves.[107] The latter is the concern for this chapter. What promotes our good may not be good for our neighbor, and vice versa. What is good for us may not be in accord with God's more universal love. The sacrifices we make for others should not be simply our own autonomous acts of generosity, but must be warranted as ways of participating in God's love. The special love we have for ourselves must likewise be warranted as a way of participating in this love.[108] That is, we have to make choices between our own fulfillment and another's fulfillment, but these choices should be part of handing ourselves over to God in love.

No one rule: In his remarkable book, *Christian Neighbor-Love*, Garth Hallett shows that there are texts in the Bible or in tradition that support a variety of preference rules. He claims to show, however, that self-subordination is in fact the priority rule the New Testament commends.[109] My position throughout this book is that there is no general answer to the question of whether in particular decisions we should give primacy to ourselves or others. Each possibility may be called for. We saw above when talking of self-sacrifice that we may well be called to sacrifice ourselves for the sake of the neighbor, if that is what God's love requires. God loves us individually, but God loves more than just us. And we may have to subordinate ourselves to others whom God wants to promote. Still, there is also a place for glad self-affirmation. If God loves us, it is hard to see how cooperating with that love could mean a consistent policy of always yielding to others first. To be sure, God's love may "concentrate" on others, e.g., a preference for the poor, and, thus, cooperating with God may mean that we focus on others, even to the point of at times forgetting or denying ourselves. But that is quite different from a preference rule that demands that we always deny or forget or subordinate ourselves.

The ongoing result of "original sin" is not self-love, but an array of disordered loves.[110] While we can love ourselves too much, we can also love others too much or in an inordinate way. Submission to others and even self-giving devotion to other human beings can be excessive. Cooperation with God's love for ourselves will mean that we will not always yield to the desires and needs of others. Those who recommend self-forgetfulness or self-subordination as a policy often do not consider the consequences of their proposal. If we should adopt a policy that leads to forgetting our own hunger, desire for sleep, or need for pleasure, then life would be short and nasty or filled with a sense of failure. A strict criterion of self-subordination holds that only when others' needs are met may we fulfill our own needs. But it is almost always the case that there is someone who is in need, indeed, in much greater need than we are.

Paul Ramsey, like many others, sets down a hard and fast rule: Christian love "means 'treating similar cases *dissimilarly*,' 'regarding the good of any other individual as *more* than your own'."[111] But though he repeatedly makes the claim, he gives no satisfying explanation for the strict priority of other-preference. By contrast, I have suggested that there is in ordinary life a certain primacy to self-love. But this too is not a hard and fast rule. It seems obvious that people take care of themselves, and ordinarily this is preferable to having others care for them. It is not merely a matter of convenience that we feed ourselves and not one another. We are the persons who are most responsible for ourselves. Besides, an absolute welfare state where everyone cared for others but did not care for themselves would hardly be ideal.

Thus, no single rule can be given, other than that we should love and cooperate with God. Even if we were to try to follow a policy of favoring others over ourselves, there should ordinarily be some limits. Our health might give way to another's interest in health, but our health should not give way to another's mild pleasure. Our honesty and sense of self-respect should usually take priority over another's comfort, even if on another occasion we might be willing to tell a lie or submit to a murderous rapist to save the life of our child.

In arguing that our own self often comes first, I do not mean to side with the Thomistic line that we should always prefer ourselves to other individuals.[112] Other-centered and self-sacrificial agape is essential in the Christian's heart. There are roughly equivalent dangers of excessive self-assertion and self-giving. The danger of self-love is selfishness. The danger of other-love is that we treat ourselves merely as a *means* for the fulfillment of the interests of others.[113] At a minimum, we should ordinarily take into account the needs and interests of others, but this rule does not forbid devoting much of our lives to our own development. We are men and women for others, but we are also worthy of our own love.[114]

Supererogation: Christians spontaneously approve persons who generously give or sacrifice themselves for the sake of others. The sacrifices we make for our own lives, however authentic, do not win such strong approval. We admire the young Lincoln who sacrificed so much to become educated, but we admire much more the Lincoln who sacrificed his life to serve his country. The reason lies in the largeness of heart that self-sacrifice for others indicates. "There is no greater love than this: to lay down one's life for one's friends" (Jn 15:13). Jesus' sacrifice was not a matter of laying his life down for the sake of developing his own virtue. Rather, enormous virtue, the virtue of a deep love, is presupposed and expressed in making a sacrifice for others. In sacrificing for others, Jesus exhibited God's own generosity. And so can we. "Such as my love has been for you, so must your love be for each other" (Jn 13:34). That is our greatness.

Nonetheless and hesitantly, I add a qualification. If the life of service to God and others is not to become "fanatical, unrelenting, and oppressive," some place must be given to caring for ourselves.[115] Surely we admire and approve saints like Dorothy Day and Mother Teresa. Still, the Christian's moral duty to the "poor," whom we always have with us (Jn 12:8), needs to be complemented with some affirmation of our own person. The problem is that "some neighbor somewhere is always worse off than myself,"[116] especially since the whole world now is our neighborhood. If we must always yield to those who are worse off—not to mention those who are better off (Mt 5:39–41)—then effectively all care of our own needs will be proscribed. Ordinarily, I think, God does not make such a demand of us. Christian life is not relentlessly self-subordinating. Cooperating with God generally permits and even encourages a robust and energetic living, which is only possible through some considerable love for ourselves.

The ordinary care we have for ourselves can be contrasted with those acts of great generosity which the tradition called supererogatory. Ordinarily, most of us spend significant amounts of money to provide housing or food for ourselves. We consider that "ordinary morality." Most of us, however, would consider it extraordinary to spend equal or greater amounts for others, particularly when we do not have great resources. We think that it is part of ordinary morality to spend, say, ten thousand dollars on ourselves and to give a thousand dollars to others. We would consider it supererogatory to reverse that proportion. That is, we are ordinarily required to love ourselves more immediately and constantly than others. We ordinarily have a special responsibility for ourselves.

Nevertheless, we are also able to ask more from ourselves than from others.[117] And we should. Every life needs at least some "supererogatory" acts if it is to be human. We need to live more than ordinary lives. We need to stretch beyond the comfortable. "Ordinary morality" is not enough even for "ordinary people." The story of Dives and Lazarus should haunt the conscience of all of us who are in any way affluent (Lk 16:19–26). Christians spontaneously disapprove of Dives sitting content at his own table. The image of Jesus who came to serve is an image of a man who made the supreme sacrifice of his life. Still, he did so only once. He allowed time for prayer, for feasting, for speaking his heart to those he called friends. Surely there were in Israel at the time (not to mention in the whole world) many people who could have used his cloak; there were many who could have used his company for an extra mile. There were many people he could have healed, but he did not. He had other things to do, including taking time to be alone (Mk 1:35, 45). Jesus sent his disciples out without a purse, yet he also told them that those who have a purse must keep it, and his own group of disciples carried a purse (Lk 22:35–36; Jn 13:29). As we have seen, Jesus, who announced good news to the poor, also defended the woman who poured costly ointment over him when the money from it could have been given to the poor (Jn 12:3–8).

Concern for the poor, when it becomes an absolute priority, can become for most of us an impossible, defeating "infinite moral duty." God's love for us can and indeed must free us to do *more* than our fair share in easing the burdens of the world; but for most of us this priority cannot become the whole of our lives. As I have often noted before, Christian living is a multifaceted life and, except for special vocations, no one aspect of it should exclude the others. Perhaps no more can be said than that we must live in a dialectical tension of self-affirmation and other-affirmation, each under the grace or vocation that we receive from God.[118]

CONCLUSION

I have tried to make a positive, theological case for the place of self-love. Love of self is, at least in our age, a third "commandment" alongside love of God and love of others. But agape and eros are not enough for a complete Christian life. In the next chapter I turn to friendships as the centerpiece of the triptych.

NOTES

1. A. H. Armstrong, "Platonic *Eros* and Christian *Agape,*" *Downside Review* 79 (Spring 1961): 105; Bernard Häring, *Free and Faithful in Christ* (New York: Seabury, 1979), 2:429.

2. Anders Nygren, *Agape and Eros* (New York: Harper & Row, 1969), 100–101, 130–32, 217; Gilbert Meilaender, *Faith and Faithfulness* (Notre Dame: Univ. of Notre Dame Press, 1991), 55–56, 86–88.

3. Nygren, *Agape and Eros*, 723.

4. Nygren, *Agape and Eros*, 117.

5. *ST* II–II.26.3–5, 26.9–11, 27.6; *Sententiarum*, 3.29.1.3, 1.5; *Caritate*, 9, 11. The same position can be found in Augustine: Oliver O'Donovan, *The Problem of Self-Love in St. Augustine* (New Haven: Yale Univ. Press, 1980), 119–20.

6. *ST* II–II.27.8; *Caritate*, 11.

7. Gene Outka, *Agape* (New Haven: Yale Univ. Press, 1976), 55.

8. Kenneth Cauthen, *Process Ethics* (New York: Mellen, 1984), 147; Timothy O'Connell, *Principles for a Catholic Morality* (New York: Seabury, 1978), 111.

9. Paul Ramsey, *Basic Christian Ethics* (Chicago: Univ. of Chicago Press, 1978), 301.

10. O'Connell, *Principles for a Catholic Morality*, 62.

11. Sidney Callahan, *In Good Conscience* (San Francisco: Harper, 1991), 153–70.

12. Karl Rahner, S.J., "Love as the Key Virtue," *Sacramentum Mundi* (New York: Herder and Herder, 1970), 6:341.

13. Morton Kelsey, *Caring* (New York: Paulist, 1981), 46–48; S. Callahan, *In Good Conscience*, 134–42, 148–60.

14. Outka, *Agape*, 290.

15. Konrad Hilpert, "Mehr Selbst Werden," *Stimmen der Zeit* 205 (April 1987): 274–76.

16. Jonathan Jacobs, *Virtue and Self-Knowledge* (Englewood Cliffs: Prentice-Hall, 1989), 18–19. John Paul II insists that work too is important, but that is because for him, as also for Vatican II, work itself can develop the self. See Edward Vacek, S.J., "Work," *The New Dictionary of Theology*, ed. Joseph Komonchak et al. (Wilmington: Michael Glazier, 1987), 1098–1105.

17. Cauthen, *Process Ethics*, 180.

18. Giles Milhaven, *Good Anger* (Kansas City: Sheed & Ward, 1989), 137.

19. Hilpert, "Mehr Selbst Werden," 268–69.

20. Cauthen, *Process Ethics*, 149.

21. Ramsey, *Basic Christian Ethics*, 115.

22. Carol Gilligan, *In a Different Voice* (Cambridge: Harvard Univ. Press, 1982), 100, also 74.

23. Charles Harris, Jr., "Can Agape Be Universalized," *Journal of Religious Ethics* 6 (Spring 1978): 25.

24. Garth Hallett, S.J., *Christian Neighbor-Love* (Washington: Georgetown Univ. Press, 1989), 1–14.

25. Outka, *Agape*, 71, also 35, 55, 221, 287.

26. Irving Singer, *The Nature of Love* (Chicago: Univ. of Chicago Press, 1987), 3:433.

27. Martin D'Arcy, S.J., *The Mind and Heart of Love* (New York: Henry Holt, 1947), 96–117; Frederick Crowe, "Complacency and Concern in the Thought of St. Thomas," *Theological Studies* 20 (March, June, August 1959): 8; Robert Johann, *The Metaphysics of Love* (Glen Rock, NJ: Paulist, 1966), 16–17, 128; James Keenan, S.J. *Goodness and Rightness in Thomas Aquinas's Summa Theologiae* (Washington: Georgetown Univ. Press, 1992), 119–43. One name that Aquinas gives for "agape" is "love of friendship" (*ST* I–II.26.4, also I.5.6; *Sententiarum*, 3.29.1.3), which is different from charity or friendship-love. It is, I would argue, a mark of his underdeveloped thinking on this

topic that he uses two similar terms for different loves. Also, Aquinas ordinarily will not allow an agapic love for subhuman creation. This, I think, is a mistake. For Aquinas, subhuman creation is often seen as either useful or pleasant, but not as good in itself (*ST* II–II.25.3; *Sententiarum*, 3.32.1.1–2; *Caritate*, 7). Love for creation is suspect (*Duo Praecepta*, 98a, 98b, 100a; *ST* II–II.44.1, 44.4).

28. Jean Porter, *The Recovery of Virtue* (Louisville: Westminster/John Knox Press, 1990), 47; Nygren, *Agape and Eros*, 216.

29. Nygren, *Agape and Eros*, 161–63, 173–75, 182. Nygren examines mainly religious eros, and hence for him its movement is thought to be essentially upward. But the needs of human beings are many, and our loves can also be directed to fellow human beings and other creatures. Nygren spurns such a downward love by saying it is blindness (p. 212). See also Plato, "Socrates Speaks at a Banquet," *Eros, Agape, and Philia*, ed. Alan Soble (New York: Paragon, 1989), 46–56.

30. Armstrong, "Platonic *Eros* and Christian *Agape*," 105–21.

31. Nygren, *Agape and Eros*, 50–53.

32. *ST* I–II.29.1; Crowe, "Complacency and Concern," 24.

33. *ST* I.48.1 (my italics), also 5.1.

34. *Veritate*, 21.1–2, 22.1.

35. *ST* I–II.27.1, 36.2, also I.5.3, 16.3, 19.9, 48.1; *Veritate*, 21.1, 22.1.

36. For Aquinas, "man has a love-of-concupiscence towards the good that he wishes to some other thing and a love-of-friendship towards him to whom he wishes good." (Though Aquinas uses the word "friend" here, this is not his usual meaning for friendship [*ST* I–II.26.4, also I.5.6; *Sententiarum*, 3.29.1.3]). This love of concupiscence is not exactly the same as what I am calling eros. A love of concupiscence does not require that we love something for ourselves, only that what is loved is loved for something other than itself. In this sense, we might love a child for the sake of her mother (*ST* II–II.26.3, 27.3).

37. *ST* I–II.27.3, 28.3, 75.4, II–II.44.7.

38. *ST* I–II.29.4; but see II–II.34.5.

39. *ST* I–II.27.3, 28.3; God and the common good are exceptions (I.60.5).

40. *Sententiarum*, 3.27.1.1; *ST* II–II.25.4; for one critique of this position, see Plato, "Lysis," *Other Selves: Philosophers on Friendship*, ed. Michael Pakaluk (Indianapolis, IN: Hackett, 1991), nos. 214–15, pp. 15–17.

41. *Sententiarum*, 3.29.1.6.

42. *Caritate*, 9; *ST* II–II.26.9, 30.1. Similarly, Aquinas says that St. Paul in Ephesians 5:33 did *not* mean "a man ought to love his wife equally with himself, but that a man's love for himself is the reason for his love of his wife, since she is one with him" (*ST* II–II.26.11; *Caritate*, 9).

43. *Sententiarum*, 3.27.1.4.

44. *ST* I–II.4.8, II–II.44.3.

45. *ST* I–II.5.8.

46. *ST* I–II.2.Prol, 3.1, 6.Prol, also 1.4, 2.7–8, 3.1–2, 3.8, II–II.23.7.

47. Cf. John Langan, "Beatitude and Moral Law in St. Thomas," *Journal of Religious Ethics* 5 (1977): 186; Jean Porter, "Desire for God," *Theological Studies* 47 (March 1986): 65.

48. *ST* I–II.1.8.

49. *ST* I–II.2.7–8, 3.8.

50. Nygren, *Agape and Eros*, 210, also 160–63, 170–72.

51. *ST* I–II.1.5.

52. *ST* I.60.4.

53. *Caritate*, 7; Johann, *The Metaphysics of Love*, 67. Aquinas addresses a long series of questions to show that no creaturely good, but only God, will satisfy us (*ST* I–II.1–8). In this sense, God is a "means" to human perfection and satisfaction; and the anthropocentric view holds sway. (If Aquinas had wanted to show that God is the ultimate end to whom we should *devote* ourselves, then an entirely different approach would have been appropriate.) To use Aquinas's usual definition of good, God is good in the sense that God perfects human beings. (Aquinas explicitly resists this conclusion when speaking of angels [*ST* I.60.5]. But it seems inevitable, or at least it has seemed so to many Thomistic ethicists.) "Since everything desires its own perfection, a man desires for his ultimate end that which he desires as the perfect and completing good for his own self" (*ST* I–II.1.5, also I–II.1.4, 1.6, 1.8).

54. Patrick Byrne, *"Ressentiment* and the Preferential Option for the Poor," and Stephen Pope, "Proper and Improper Partiality and the Preferential Option for the Poor," *Theological Studies* 54 (June 1993), 226–28, 262–63.

55. *ST* I.44.4, I–II.3.1.

56. *ST* I–II.3.1.

57. *ST* II–II.26.13; the opposite in I.60.5, II–II.17.8, 23.5. The one set of exceptions that Aquinas, somewhat ad hoc, makes to his general rule that we seek our own happiness is another (doubtful, I think) general rule that we naturally subordinate ourselves to the common or universal good, indeed to God since parts naturally affirm the whole (*ST* I–II.109.3, I.60.4–5, II–II.58.5, 65.1–2; *Caritate*, 4, 10, 12). Aquinas faces Paul's claim that charity does not seek its own through the same device. Paul, he says, really means that we love, not other individuals, but the common good more than ourselves (*ST* II–II.26.3–5; *Sententiarum*, 3.29.1.3, 1.5). Cf. Keenan, *Goodness and Rightness*, 125–27.

58. D'Arcy, *Mind and Heart*, 216.

59. I have somewhat arbitrarily defined eros as love of someone or something *other* than myself simply for purposes of clarity. Strictly speaking, eros for one's own self is nearly identical with agapic self-love, since agape for self is love of self for its, i.e., my own sake and eros is love of (my) self for my own sake.

60. Singer, *The Nature of Love*, 1:39. Cf. Vincent Genovesi, S.J., *In Pursuit of Love: Catholic Morality and Human Sexuality* (Wilmington: Glazier, 1987), 33, who says that eros is not love at all.

61. This is not to deny that certain commitments, e.g., marriage, deserve our fidelity even when they no longer seem fulfilling, nor that such commitments often are fulfilling only through selfless fidelity.

62. M. C. Dillon, "Romantic Love, Enduring Love, and Authentic Love," *Soundings* 66 (Summer 1983): 146.

63. Jules Toner, *The Experience of Love* (Washington: Corpus, 1968), 177.

64. The most difficult case is our love (*epithymia*) for *things* that are pleasurable or agreeable. We devour the banana that we "love." Still even here I think it can be said that we want bananas to exist and to be good as bananas, and in particular we want this banana to be an excellent banana. The fact that we subordinate the banana to ourselves does not mean that we do not affirm its value; rather, its value is relative to our taste and hunger and affirmed as such.

65. Genovesi, *In Pursuit of Love*, 29–30, mistakenly suggests that if I am concerned for the effects others have on me, then I will be responsive to "what these others *have*, not *who* they *are*." There is no solid basis for this claim.

66. *ST* I–II.28.6.

67. James Hanigan, *As I Have Loved You* (New York: Paulist, 1986), 148.

68. Sallie McFague, *Models of God* (Philadelphia: Fortress, 1987), 131.

69. Max Scheler, *The Nature of Sympathy* (Hamden: CT: Shoe String, 1970), 25, 34, 77–95.

70. Armstrong, "Platonic *Eros* and Christian *Agape*," 107, shows how this view is not faithful even to Plato, whom Nygren cites. Tillich wrongly makes this poverty "the root of love in all its forms," *Systematic Theology* (Chicago: Univ. of Chicago Press, 1967) 2:52.

71. *ST* I–II.27.3; *Sententiarum*, 3.27.2.1. I do not think Aquinas's arguments are successful. It is also necessary for Christians to like those who are dissimilar; see Hallett, *Christian Neighbor-Love*, 66.

72. Karl Rahner, S.J., "Order," *Encyclopedia of Theology* (New York: Seabury, 1975), 1118.

73. Charles Taylor, *Sources of the Self* (Cambridge: Harvard Univ. Press, 1989), 375–76; Edward Vacek, S.J., "Popular Ethical Subjectivism: Four Preludes to Objectivity," *Horizons* 11 (Spring 1984): 42-60.

74. Hanigan, *As I Have Loved You*, 148–49. Hanigan nonetheless says that this eros is "not a form of love that can be commended to people as a moral stance toward the neighbor."

75. Hanigan, *As I Have Loved You*, 148.

76. Hanigan, *As I Have Loved You*, 149.

77. Cauthen, *Process Ethics*, 167–68.

78. In the New Testament, God also withholds the truth and keeps people from repenting (Mk 4:12; 2 Tm 2:26).

79. Hanigan, *As I Have Loved You*, 149.

80. Nygren, *Agape and Eros*, 175–77.

81. Nygren, *Agape and Eros*, 177–81, 211–12. Nygren says that for Aristotle the gods can and do love creatures; had Nygren pursued this ability of the gods to "delight" in human beings, his view of love might have been more adequate (pp. 201–2).

82. *ST* I.19.2.

83. Josef Pieper, *About Love* (Chicago: Franciscan Herald, 1974), 93.

84. Günther Bornkamm, *Jesus of Nazareth* (New York: Harper & Brothers, 1960), 116.

85. Rahner, "Love as the Key Virtue," 341.

86. Nygren, *Agape and Eros*, 222, notes that *"Eros starts with the assumption of the Divine origin and worth of the soul."* Nygren differs from my presentation in that he rejected this assumption, while I accept it.

87. *ST* I–II.91.2.

88. John R. Sachs, S.J., *The Christian Vision of Humanity* (Collegeville, MN: Glazier, 1991), 96–101; Edward Collins Vacek, S.J., "Towards a Phenomenology of Love Lost," *Journal of Phenomenological Psychology* 20 (Spring 1989): 9–19.

89. Outka, *Agape*, 267.

90. Outka, *Agape*, 291.

91. Outka, *Agape*, 305.

92. W. D. Ross, *The Right and the Good* (Indianapolis: Hackett, 1988), 168.

93. Karl Barth, *Church Dogmatics* 3/4 (Edinburgh: T. & T. Clark, 1978), 375.

94. For St. Ignatius one very important, evocative question is: what is it that *I* desire? See Edward Kinerk, S.J., "Eliciting Great Desires," *Studies in the Spirituality of Jesuits* 16 (November 1984): 1–29. Also relevant here is the observation of E. M. Forster (cited in Outka, *Agape*, 291): "Unselfish people, as a rule, are deathly dull. They have no colour."

95. Gordon Graham, *Idea of Christian Charity* (Notre Dame: Univ. of Notre Dame Press, 1990), 125–26.

96. Outka, *Agape*, 56–57.

97. Nygren, *Agape and Eros*, 214–17, also 179–81.

98. Bornkamm, *Jesus of Nazareth*, 110–11.

99. In eliminating a religious eros, Nygren eliminates the human lover. "The Christian has nothing of his own to give"; his love for neighbor is God's love infused into him and "passed on" to others (*Agape and Eros*, 129–30, 216, 733–34). See D'Arcy, *Mind and Heart*, 71, also 77–78.

100. Robert Nozick, "Love's Bond," *The Philosophy of (Erotic) Love*, ed. Robert Solomon (Lawrence, KS: University Press of Kansas, 1991), 423; Oliver O'Donovan, *Resurrection and Moral Order* (Grand Rapids: Eerdmans, 1986), 226–44.

101. James Keenan, *Goodness and Rightness*, 135.

102. Ramsey, *Basic Christian Ethics*, 163.

103. *ST* II–II.25.4; *Caritate*, 9.

104. Ramsey, *Basic Christian Ethics*, 100.

105. O'Donovan, *Resurrection*, 249–52.

106. *Spiritual Exercises of St. Ignatius*, trans. Louis Puhl, S.J. (Westminster, MD: Newman, 1959), no. 23, p. 12.

107. O'Donovan, *Problem of Self-Love*, 103, 134, points out that Augustine denies any possible clash: "The idea that one person's individual interests could clash with another's was simply a mistake: the only true interests had to be communal because the only true goodness was God." Augustine at times gave way to totalitarian or collectivist leanings and at other times could be quite individualist.

108. Karl Barth, *Church Dogmatics*, 385, 387; Bernard Häring, *The Law of Christ* (Westminster, MD: Newman, 1963), 1:49.

109. Hallett, *Christian Neighbor-Love*, 5, 60–61. His definition of self-subordination is stricter than the one I proposed above in Chapter 6.

110. Don Browning, *Religious Thought and Modern Psychologies* (Philadelphia: Fortress, 1983), 143.

111. Ramsey, *Basic Christian Ethics*, 243. Hans Reiner, *Duty and Inclination* (Boston: Nijhoff, 1983), 140–42, recognizes what he calls an absolute value of one's own existence, but unfortunately he holds that relative values such as pleasures or comforts are nonabsolute when sought for the self, but absolute when sought for another. Then he holds that self-values always should yield to values obtained for others.

112. *Sententiarum*, 3.29.1.5. One wonders how this fits Jesus. Cf. Hallett, *Christian Neighbor-Love*, 66. Aquinas corrects for this bias, however, by arguing elsewhere in terms of a questionable whole-part reasoning (*ST* I–II.109.3, I.60.4–5, II–II.58.5, 65.1–

2; *Caritate*, 4, 10, 12). Singulars are inferior in comparison with that which is more universal (*ST* II–II.8.3). The individual may be sacrificed for the sake of the community.

113. D'Arcy, *Mind and Heart*, 291.

114. Cauthen, *Process Ethics*, 169.

115. Cauthen, *Process Ethics*, 174–78, well poses this question. His solutions are as good as any I have read, though they do not quite satisfy.

116. Cauthen, *Process Ethics*, 175.

117. Michael Slote, "Morality and Self-Other Asymmetry," *Journal of Philosophy* 81 (April 1984): 179ff.

118. Cauthen, *Process Ethics*, 176. Cauthen lists several tensions that must be preserved: (1) "the nearest with less deprivation and the neediest who may be far away"; (2) "the essential needs of survival, security and health and those enriching values which add quality and breadth to welfare"; (3) "short-term and long-term investments"; (4) the principles of "merit, achievement, and effort" (pp. 178–79).

8

Philia

I call you friends. . . . The command I give you is this, that you love one another. (Jn 15:15, 17)

In the previous chapters, I have argued that both agape and eros have a place in Christian life. I now extend this claim to mutual love, which I will name "philia." I advocate a pluralist approach, rejecting the view that there is only one form of Christian love. Eros and agape, which can stand by themselves, function best within a philia relationship, though philia is not merely a combination of these other two.

Most Christian authors praise a self-sacrificing love or a love that works *for* the other; some praise a love by which we live *from* others; unfortunately, only a few argue at length on behalf of a love that means being *with* others. When the Church thinks of saints, it thinks mostly of those who sacrifice themselves and not of those who nourish friendships such as marriages. Theologians who reflect on love commonly emphasize those New Testament texts that highlight agape. They skip over the many texts that emphasize interpersonal relationships. They may say that covenant and community are central. But when they describe love, they focus on the kind of love one selflessly offers to enemies, or strangers, or universal humanity.[1] In a word, communal life is neglected. Daniel Day Williams challenged this one-sidedness: "It simply is not true that the *agape* of the New Testament is nothing but the grace of God poured out without motive upon the unworthy. It is also the spirit of rejoicing, of friendship, and of the new life with its foretaste of the blessedness of life with God and with the brethren."[2]

In Chapter 2, I deliberately did not develop the mutually bonding power of love. I favored words like "align" and "affirm" because we can love things and persons without mutuality taking place. We can love those who do not love us. Our "union" with the beloved need not be "communion."[3] The central thesis of this book, however, is that communion or philia is the foundation and goal of Christian life. This love is a "power that creates unity and forms the human community ever more extensively

and intensively."[4] Indeed, all human love finds its culmination and ultimate goal in a community of solidarity with and in God.[5]

Philia is the love that enables people to live in communion.[6] It draws
people together into "special relationships." Philosophers sometimes use
this phrase as a technical term to designate those groups we form with one
another on the basis of special characteristics beyond our common
humanity.[7] "Special relationships" include friendships, but also such
groups as family, the Body of Christ, or a nation, the sort of groups that
were the topic of Chapter 3. Philia also is the love that constitutes our
"friendship with God," which was the topic of Chapter 4.[8] Each of these
special relationships are formed by philia, though each will have its own
distinctive embodiment of that love. For example, a special kind of friendship is necessary before sexual intercourse is appropriate; not just any love,
not even any philia love, will do.[9] In each of these quite distinct relationships there is something more involved than simply love for individuals.
Philia is the love that informs these groups that are or should be so central
in every life.

Philia is distinguished from agape and eros by the *mutuality* of the
relation it creates.[10] In philia, as in all love, we love our beloveds. But in
philia we love them not for their own sake, as separate individuals, nor for
our sake (nor for the sake of yet another party), but for the sake of the
mutual relationship we share with them. While retaining their identity,
persons through philia "share a commitment to the continued well-being
of the relational life uniting them."[11]

I open this discussion by locating philia in the Christian tradition. I
then examine the distinctiveness of philia as mutuality. Next I show that
philia has the characteristics found in any love. After that, I take up the
main objection some theologians and philosophers make against such
"special relationships." Finally, I discuss the role of philia in ordinary life.

PHILIA IN CHRISTIAN TRADITION

The agapic tradition in Christianity commonly focuses on those sections
of Jesus' great sermon in which he tells us to love our enemies, turn the
other cheek, go the extra mile, lend freely. Jesus asks rhetorically, "If you
love those who love you, what merit is there in that? . . . Do not pagans do
as much?" He chides, "Even the sinners love those who love them." The
agapist underscores Jesus' claim that to love the just and the unjust alike is
to be "perfect as your heavenly Father is perfect" (Mt 5:39–48; Lk 6:27–
35). Understandably, then, the Christian tradition has praised this agapic
love. This love imitates God's love, the love most clearly shown when Jesus

died for us while we were yet sinners (Rom 5:8). Agapic love is, if not exclusive to Christianity, surely characteristic of it.

Furthermore, Jesus undercut the special relations formed by familial or ethnic ties. We are to hate father and mother; our true brothers and sisters are those who do the will of God (Mt 12:49–50). Jesus was not received by his own people (Lk 4:24); rather, the Gentiles become God's people, not by virtue of membership in a group, but by an individual conversion of the heart. Thus, a certain independence from ordinary communal ties and a certain willingness to "go it alone" for the sake of God or others is essential to being a Christian.

To say all this, however, does not warrant the conclusion that agape is the ideal or even the only Christian love. Jesus' rhetorical maxims existentially undercut themselves when taken as a rule for life. Should we hope that enemies will hate us so that we can love them? If our enemies were to become friends, would we then no longer be able to love them in a Christian way? When everyone is in heaven, will there then be no Christian love? Jesus surely did not expect his disciples to love only enemies or to love all alike. When Jesus asks Simon Peter, "Do you love me more than these?" (Jn 21:15), the fitting answer for Peter was *not*, as some agapists might have it, to profess that he had "equal regard" for Jesus, "independently of any personal characteristics or qualities" in Jesus. It would have been even less appropriate for Peter to respond that, since, according to Jesus, there is no merit in loving those who love us, he, Peter, loved Jesus' enemies more than Jesus. Rather, love in the Kingdom involves more than love for enemies and strangers. As Morton Kelsey chided, Jesus underestimated how hard it can be to love those who love us.[12]

Agapists usually ignore a whole range of scriptural passages that appeal to *special relationships*, particularly in familial terms. "If anyone does not provide for his own relatives and especially for members of his immediate family, he has denied the faith; he is worse than an unbeliever" (1 Tm 5:8). Agapists cite the text, "Love your enemies, pray for your persecutors." But Jesus immediately adds, "This will prove that you are *sons* of your heavenly *Father*" (Mt 5:44–45). That is, the origin of our love for our enemies is a special "familial" relation with God. And we learn about God by observing how a human father acts (Mt 7:11).[13]

We are to one another not simply sinners or strangers lying along the wayside; we are also disciples of Christ, members of his body. Discipleship requires a more communal love than either agape or eros. The members of the early Christian community "were of one heart and one mind" (Acts 4:32). They were, as we are, children of God, heirs, and sharers in the divine nature (Gal 3:26, 4:5–7; Rom 8:14–17; Col 1:18; 1 Jn 3:9; 2 Pt 1:4). Jesus says that there is no greater love than to lay down one's life for another, but these others are described not as strangers but as "friends" (Jn 15:13). Friendship is the context out of which this great sacrifice arises.

God, who "used to speak to Moses *face to face,*" says to Moses, "This request, too, which you have made, I will carry out, because . . . you are my intimate *friend*" (Ex 33:11–12). God is the "husband" of Israel (Hos 2:18). In the Incarnation, "The Word became flesh and made his dwelling *among us*"; by him, we are "empowered to become *children* of God" (Jn 1:14, 12). Jesus loves "his *own* in the world" (Jn 13:1). At the end of his public life, he renames his relation to the disciples, "I no longer speak of you as slaves. . . . Instead, I call you *friends*" (Jn 15:14–15). After the resurrection Jesus instructs the women to report the good news to "my *brothers*" (Mt 28:10); and he says that he is "ascending to *my Father* and *your Father*" (Jn 20:18). In the New Testament, God's ancient promise is recalled: "I will dwell with them. . . . I will be *their God* and they shall be *my people*. . . . I will welcome you and be a *father* to you, and you will be my *sons* and *daughters*" (2 Cor 6:16–18).[14] In each case a "special relation" is affirmed. God loves sinners, but the eschatological ideal is a communion of saints, friends in the Lord. God loves all persons, but forms special relationships with certain persons and groups.[15]

Christians similarly live in familial relationships: we are to one another sisters and "brothers, beloved of the Lord" (2 Thes 2:13). Through the Spirit, we too can cry out *Abba* (Rom 8:15). We are "predestined to share the image of his *Son*, that the Son might be the *first-born* of many *brothers*" and *sisters* (Rom 8:29). John can exclaim: "See what love the *Father* has bestowed on us in letting us be called *children* of God! Yet *that is what we are*" (1 Jn 3:1). And because we are children of God, we are "brothers" and sisters to one another (1 Jn 3:9–10, 14). Paul and John talk almost exclusively of a Christian's love for members of the community, not for enemies or strangers.[16] To one another we owe mutual love (Rom 13:8). While once we were no people, now we are "a chosen *race*, a royal priesthood, a holy *nation*, a *people*" that God claims for "his own" (1 Pt 2:9–10). Scripture abundantly mixes these types of relationships: nationhood, people, family, and friend. Each is a "special relationship," the sort of thing that agapists neglect or reject.

Gilbert Meilaender offers five reasons why philia has often been displaced by agape in recent Christian theology.[17] First, philia is a preferential love in which certain attractive features of the friend influence whom we love, whereas agape is said to be indifferent to the beloved's attractiveness and therefore more universal. Second, philia is marked by a bond that essentially includes reciprocity, whereas agape is more broadly directed, extending even to sinners, enemies, and strangers who likely will not return love. Third, philia is said to be unstable because it changes when the beloved changes, whereas agape is said to be marked by an everlasting fidelity. Fourth, philia stresses a this-worldly communion, whereas agape finds its justification in an other-worldly sphere. Finally, philia encourages simply being with one another, whereas agape fosters service and work for others. I have already criticized some of these contrasts, and I shall address others in what follows. The point here is to note that philia has been rejected or displaced in favor of an individualistic, nonmutual and task-oriented love.[18]

Karl Rahner, by contrast, seems to have held that all love is essentially mutual.[19] He sides with the traditional view that neither God nor we can love the damned. He argues that we can love sinners or enemies only if we can hope that someday they will return our love. It seems to me, however, that we can and often do love those who will not love us in return. We may hope for their return love, but this is not a condition for our love. A dying father could love his infant daughter. And all of us can love enemies whom we are morally certain will never, at least in this life, love us in return. Rather than say all love must be mutual, it seems better to hold that there are agapic and eros loves that are not and may never be philia.

Still, philia is an essential love in Christian life. Love for strangers and sinners and enemies is part of, but not the whole of, Christian life.[20] As the above scriptural texts indicate, a forgiving, suffering, self-sacrificial love is not the only kind of love that God shows. A love for strangers is not the ideal of Christian life. Christianity has a richer ideal than the Enlightenment requirement of a universalistic love for human beings just as human beings. Even the Stoic ideal, which greatly influenced Christianity and which held that "all men are brothers and therefore in familial relation to one another, is much richer."[21] Paul asks for much more when he enjoins, "Love one another with the affection of brothers" (Rom 12:10). In addition to agape, philia with its special relationships deserves a place in Christian life.

DISTINGUISHED BY MUTUALITY

Friendship. Few of us live without friends, and still fewer want to live without them. Most of us give at least occasional thought to what makes friendships work and what causes them to fall apart. It is remarkable, then, that so few philosophers and theologians have given sustained thought to friendship. Aristotle is one exception, devoting two of ten chapters of his *Ethics* to the subject; Cicero and Aquinas also took up the topic. In the main, however, it has been and is a neglected area.[22] This is odd since special relationships such as friendships are such an important part of almost every human life.[23] Friendship is not just a means to good living, but partly constitutive of it. Aristotle began his study of friendship with what seemed to him to be a commonplace observation: "Without friends no one would choose to live, though he had all other goods." Aristotle asked rhetorically what good it would be to have possessions if one could not give them away, particularly to one's friends.[24] It has not been sufficiently obvious to Christian thinkers, who have had similar views about possessions and "all other goods," that life without friends is not a life worth living. Doubtless, ethics should reflect on interactions between strangers. But Christianity has to make clearer that it also knows a "richer sense of special moral relationships, embodied" in such groups as families, friendships, congregations, or professions.[25]

A Distinctive Love

Philia is love of the beloved for the sake of a mutual relation with the beloved. Five examples may help to distinguish philia from both agape and eros. First, consider a decision we might make to leave an affluent life in order to spend time with the poor. We might want to live with poor people to satisfy our curiosity or to exercise our talents. To love poor people for these reasons is eros, loving them for our own sakes. We could, however, go to live with them out of agape, making great sacrifices solely to help them. Beyond both eros and agape, we could make the change out of solidarity with them. This philia love would be concerned not primarily with gaining some good either for ourselves or for the poor, but with accepting their lot as a way of sharing their lives. Our philia might not, in any obvious way, improve their lot, and it might worsen ours. But it is a noble love.[26] "He emptied himself . . . being born in the likeness of men. He was known to be of human estate" (Phil 2:7–8).

A second example: a friend has moved out of town. I call to find out how he is doing and to let him know how much I miss him. He says he's never been happier, that he thought he would miss me but he doesn't. With agape, I would be glad that his happiness is greater than ever and that he is not suffering any pain of loss. With eros, I would feel my loss more intensely. With philia, I would be disappointed for a quite different reason. Philia wants the other to be happy, to be sure; but it wants to be part of the reason for that happiness; it wants to share in that happiness, to coexperience it; and it wants its own happiness or unhappiness to be shared. It wants to share life.

A third example: a woman may correctly judge that her regular presence in a man's life will hinder his relation with his wife, and she may judge that his wife can do more good for him than she could ever do. So out of love for his good, that is, love for him for his own sake, she withdraws. Since he will no longer be actively loved in the unique way she can love him, she may sincerely regret *his* loss, out of love for him for his sake. She may also regret *her* loss. Here a selfless agapic love is in conflict with the self-connecting philia and Eros she would otherwise have for him.

A fourth example: if a woman comes upon two boys, both of whom were equally injured in a car accident, but one of whom is her child, can she help her son first? According to some agapists, there would either be no reason to do so or she should be advised to sacrifice a relation that is close to her in favor of the stranger. Under eros, she would help her child because that act would in the long run be best for her. Under philia, she should help her son because she is bound by a special relation to him.

A fifth example: consider the sacrament of marriage, which—not incidental to the purposes of this chapter—embodies a love analogous to Christ's love for the Church (Eph 5:25). Would anyone seriously hold that in looking for a prospective spouse we should look for the person who was most a sinner, most our enemy, most wretched, and generally the least compatible with ourselves? The agapic injunctions of Matthew 5:43–48 are not very helpful here. On the other hand, common experience indicates that if the spouses have only eros, the marriage will not survive. Rather, spouses require that special form of philia, called "conjugal love," which, according to Vatican II, forms them into a "community of love."[27]

There are two aspects of philia. We love others *for the sake of the mutual relationship* we share with them, and we love them *as* partners in that relationship. This love "involves a cherishing of the joint experience which is one's life with another as well as a cherishing of the particular person who has lived through it with us."[28] Thus, our "reason" for loving them is the special relationship we share with them; they are loved not just for themselves nor as someone "good for us," but rather as those with whom we want to share a mutual relation.[29] In philia, unlike pure agape and eros, there is a communal life which, so to speak, circulates between the members. The members love and are loved in terms of their special relationship. Their love flows from the relationship and is directed back to it.[30] Each person of the relationship is loved, but with a view to enhancing their membership in the relationship. Of course, others outside the relationship may also be loved. And they may even be loved because of the relationship. Thus, Christians love nonbelievers as an outflow of their membership in the Christian community. But nonbelievers are not loved *as members* of the relationship.

Through a philia love two or more persons form a community.[31] Each member in an essentially self-connecting way affirms herself or himself and the other(s) as members of the community. As Gene Outka puts it, this "love refers, in part or altogether, to a quality of relation *between* persons and/or groups. Those actions are loving which *establish* or *enhance* some sort of exchange between the parties, developing a sense of community."[32]

Meaning of Mutuality

I will not attempt here a complete phenomenology of philia.[33] In Chapter 4, I developed at considerable length the basic structure of a mutual relationship. That structure deserves repeating: someone loves me; I accept that love; I love that person; the person accepts my love; we form a community; and then we cooperate as members of that community. This basic pattern of mutuality is *analogously* present in all philia relations.[34] Since philia is distinguished from agape and eros by mutuality, I will develop some of the characteristics of mutuality. In broad outline, mutuality is (1) a form of sharing life (2) through interaction of free persons (3) who communicate themselves to one another (4) in a way that is progressively involving.

Shared life: Mutuality is more than merely having some common interest, hobby, or goal.[35] If Jack is interested in Jill, and Mike is interested in Jill, the two may well be enemies, not friends. Rather, there must be some desire to share life with the other. Partners in a philia relationship do not simply look at some common object; they must also "face each other."[36] Otherwise, like two divorced parents who both love their child, they have a similar focus, but not a mutual love.

Mutuality is more than two parallel loves: Jack loves Jill and Jill loves Jack, yet each does so independently of the love of the other. Each might not even know of the other's love. Or if they are aware of that love, they may not much care about being loved by the other. Or if they care, they may not want to be loved in response to their own loving but rather to be loved quite apart from their loving. That is, they may both be fiercely independent agapic or eros lovers, each wanting to enrich or be enriched by the other, but not willing to build a shared life. Favors may be traded, so to speak, but no community is built.[37] Mutuality, by contrast, means that each of us acts as a member of a relationship. Each of us belongs to the other(s) by belonging to the relationship. "We, who are many, are one body in Christ, and individually we are members one of another" (Rom 12:5). Our relationship grows or declines through the acts that we perform for and/or with one another *as* members and through the acts we perform for the sake of the group itself.

In a mutual love, I must not only know of my love for you and your love for me, but I must also *affectively welcome* your love for me and mine for you as part of the relationship that we want to form. I must care that you love me and I must relish my place as one member of our relationship. And you must do the same. Otherwise there is no mutual relation. In other words, our acts of loving and accepting love must be consented to as part of a relationship we form together. Not only do we give and receive love, but our acts of giving and receiving are themselves an *enactment of the relationship* we share.

Mutual relationships are like dancing. In dance, two persons engage in a shared activity; each is caught up in a rhythm to which each contributes.[38] The dancers' unity-in-difference is revealed in those moments where each partner seems to know where the other will next move. Each, in varying ways, leads and is led; and both act together. By contrast, novice dancers think about the rules of the particular dance step or they worry about their feet. Accomplished dancers give themselves over to the movement. They come alive, achieving heights of performance they could never achieve alone. In surrendering to the ensemble, they distinguish and fulfill themselves. Similarly in philia, persons give themselves over to the relationship, learn therein its distinctive discipline, and thereby create a good that they could not separately achieve. Many important human activities—ranging from conversation to sexual intercourse to communal worship—require mutuality; and most of our activities are enriched by being shared. Philia relationships not only are in themselves intrinsic goods, but they also make possible many other essential human goods.

In a mutual love, we want to *make a difference* in how our partners live. And when we are touched (physically or emotionally) by our beloved, we welcome that touch and respond to it as part of our relationship. Thus, we transform one another's way of being in the world.[39] We consult our partners not just because they may have better insights, but also because we want *their* views to influence and form our own. Our receptivity acknowledges not only the goodness of their perspective but also the desired mutuality of our relationship. Thus, Catholics willingly allow their own Church to have a greater influence on their lives than the views of Buddhism or Islam. Philosophical prudence suggests that we gather insights wherever they bloom. But we listen more to the insights of our own community since following those insights further bonds us to our community. Sometimes we do what our partners want simply as an expression of our special relationship with them. Thus, Naomi beautifully says to Ruth, "Wherever you go I will go, wherever you lodge I will lodge, your people shall be my people, and your God my God. Wherever you die I will die, and there be buried" (Ru 1:16).

The activities we do as part of our relationship fulfill the "need" we have to share life. As Aquinas says, friends want "to live together, speak together, and be united together in other like things."[40] Nevertheless we can act *as a member* even when we are apart.[41] For example, Francis Xavier worked alone in China, but the Society of Jesus was present there through him. And we can *share in* the activity of our community even when as individuals we are not active. Thus, Christians can sleep, confident that their Church is still praying, forgiving, and working for justice throughout the world.

Each of our communities develops its own *"way of proceeding"* in the world. Each community has its priority principles: some communities look for ways to help the poor, while others look only for ways to become rich. Each community has its own special virtues such as humility or a get-ahead aggressiveness. Each community has its own favored objects; for example, most Protestants have a different attitude toward Mary, the mother of Jesus, than Catholics. Each community has its *shared world* whose history extends backward in time and forward into the future. The places we have visited, the traditions we carry on, the liturgies we pray together are part of our shared world. Those who are outside our shared world may visit these same places or pray these same prayers, but their experiences are different because they are not part of our communal life.

Interaction of free persons: Philia's special relationships are not restricted to I-thou encounters. In many "special relationships," the members are a "he" or a "she," not an "it," but also not a "thou." Such relationships still have a personal nature. That is, mutual love takes various personal forms depending on the kind of community it forms. Relations within a church community should be different from the intimacy of a family and the impartiality of a state. Still, in each relationship, a dialogue of lives occurs that involves members in ways that are unpredictable. With each different "special relationship," a different facet of one's personal self is realized that no other philia love can bring about.[42]

In meeting another person, we engage someone who is, in varying degrees, *free*. The interaction will be frustrated or ended whenever one party tries to control the response of the others. As an extreme example: if a man rapes a woman, in the very moment that he possesses her, he loses *her*.[43] He will have only a self-disconnected body. Similarly, when we try to make God be our servant, the one who does our bidding, the one who must answer all our prayers, the one who must be concerned only for us, we lose *God*. A true encounter is always with someone whom we cannot control. We can influence and be influenced, but not control and be controlled. We evoke, but cannot force, personal change in one another. In our encounters, what we "take" from persons can never be their personal self, unless it is freely given. What we "give" of ourselves must be freely accepted or else it is not fully given. And what we do together must be a concordance of free persons.

Self-communication: Mutuality among persons is possible only with freely offered self-revelation. We can learn much about persons through detached observation. But mutuality occurs only when they want to communicate themselves to us. And we must want to receive that self-disclosure. Some people litter the world with information about themselves that no one wants to hear. Other people are unwilling to let themselves be known. And still others are unable or unwilling to receive the self-disclosure of people they should be concerned about. A church or a nation that will not permit its members to speak is not a philia-based group. A God who will not listen cannot be a "friend." Philia requires all members, to the degree they are able, to try to disclose themselves to the others and to receive the others' self-disclosure.

Mutual self-disclosure is different from the unilateral self-disclosure that occurs, for example, with a confessor or a counsellor. To be sure, the kind and depth of self-disclosure in these protected therapeutic situations is frequently greater than what is revealed in most mutual relations. Confessors often hear things that are revealed to no one else because of the confidentiality promised. That is, they will not act on or communicate to others what has been communicated to them.[44] But, valuable as this therapeutic situation is, it is not enough for the human heart. Our personal lives would not be better off if everyone could act only as therapists or clients. In such an arrangement, there would be someone to whom we could deeply disclose our life and someone else who would deeply confide to us, but there would be no mutuality.

We human beings want and need mutual self-disclosure. We want what we say to make a difference in the life of someone who makes a difference to us. We want the other at times to act on what we say. As students, we want our teachers to take account of our objections or our difficulties in understanding. As church members, we want our leaders to take account of our own perspectives in the way they guide the Church. By contrast, the therapist, at least in principle, does not live differently because of what we say or do. The counsellor listens in order to help us. Counsellors do not reveal their own lives except insofar as such revelation may help us. Counsellors should be agapic lovers, and the symbol of their success is the healed client who no longer needs them. Clients are legitimately self-interested, continuing the relationship only as long as they receive benefit. With friends or partners, by contrast, we communicate our lives in order to contribute to one another and to the special relationship we share. The therapeutic session should not be the model for full living.

In our mutual self-communication, we speak ourselves to *another*, which means that we have to be intelligible to the other's self. To communicate, we must be able to see the world at least somewhat through the other's eyes, without losing our own perspective. We thereby learn to overcome the immature tendency to see the world only through our own eyes.[45] To communicate we need, secondly, to make *ourselves* intelligible to the other. We must to some degree know ourselves. We do not, however, have to know ourselves before we speak, since often the limits and contours of our own distinctive self become delineated only in the self-disclosure.[46] Thirdly, we not only speak ourselves to another, but we do so as part of our *relationship* and as a way of further forming its *shared world.*

When we communicate ourselves, we become *vulnerable*. Philia essentially includes a vulnerability that can be absent from agape.[47] James Nelson well observes: "Agape comes from one who is self-sufficient and strong. . . . not only is it more blessed to give than to receive, it is also easier. A man can stay in control of things when he is not indebted to another, when he is self-sufficient and not needy, when others depend on his largesse, not he on theirs."[48] What we risk in mutuality is the identity we have thus far formed. We open ourselves to what is beyond our control.[49] As Williams writes, "It is not the essence of man to try to make himself invulnerable. That is sin. It is the essence of man to find the meaning of his life in a community of mutual responsiveness and sharing." So it is for us, and so it is for God. Williams continues: "God makes himself vulnerable to receive into his being what the world does in its freedom, and to respond to the world's action."[50] Unlike Aristotle's god, the

Christian God became vulnerable in becoming "our" God. Self-sufficiency is not what God has chosen. Process theologians quickly add that God's vulnerability—this being able to be affected by the beloved—is a fuller or more perfect way of being. A god who cannot be vulnerable is less perfect because that god cannot enter into a mutual love.

Progressively involving: Mutuality may be *fulfilled or unfulfilled*, and in varying degrees. Many of us, for example, have experienced a desire to be married or in a friendship even before the right person came along. That is, the relationship we sought was as yet unrealized. It was unfulfilled. When the right person appeared, we loved that person in part for the sake of realizing the desired mutual relation. Needless to say, when this desire was filled by a real partner, the community that resulted was at least somewhat different from what we had imagined. Real partners always modify our dreams.

Philia's inception and development are open-endedly convoluted. Consider an opening scenario: I smile at the woman across the room, and she acknowledges my smile and accepts it. Her return smile is a response to me that she could withhold, and I recognize her smile as freely returned. My warm gaze toward her is now a response to her response and, if continued, may lead her to further respond. An evolving, involving mutual relation begins.[51] I desire to be desired by the one I desire. I come to love her, and she comes to love me. I know that she loves me, and I love her *as* loving me; and she knows that I love her, and she loves me *as* loving her. I also know that she knows both that I love her and that I love her as thus affectively turned toward me; and so on.[52] This verbal convolution suggests the complicated and evolving nature of mutuality.

In philia relations, I do not love the beloved as a separate person. I love the beloved as related to me. I really love her, but the "her" that I love is, in part, a person who loves me. I too do not simply have a separate identity, but rather an identity that is, in part, that of one who loves her and is loved by her. Needless to say, the identity of each of us is not limited to the relationship we have to one another. And I can love aspects of her that are not turned toward me. That is, I can also have an agapic relation to her. Philia is that love that we have for one another as mutually involved, and this involvement increases the more we share our lives. In loving her, my own ability to love is expanded, and this means that my own lovableness is increased. And since my lovableness is increased, she is more able to love me. And since in loving me her lovableness is increased,

I am more able to love her.[53] Our philia relation itself thereby increases. Each response offers the promise of a deeper relation.

When an "outsider" affirms my friend (or a member of my community), I can be grateful to the outsider for what he has done for my friend. In affirming my friend he has affirmed someone with whom I share life. In *this* sense, the outsider has done something for *me*, for that part of me that is involved with my friend. Thus, "as often as you did it for one of my least brothers, you did it for me" (Mt 25:40). When *I* do something for my friend, however, my act is part of our shared life. Even if the deed I and the outsider do for my friend seems the "same," it is not the same because my act has the added meaning of being part of our shared life. Conversely, a harm done to a friend is greater than the "same" harm done to a stranger because, in addition to the violation of both persons, the friendship bond is also violated.

As partners we organize at least some of our activities in terms of our philia relationship. The deeper the relation, the more completely will our activities be "normed" by what they do for our relationship. The activities we choose to engage in will be selected and evaluated in terms of how they will modify our communal life.[54] In fact, special relationships provide the *basis* for much of our *moral life*. That is, we make many of our choices *as* a friend, *as* a father, *as* a citizen, and so forth.

Our philia relationships have a history: they contain moments that are valuable in themselves as well as moments that are meaningful only because of our long-term relationships. Each phase of our relationship prepares for the next phase.[55] It may be that for periods of time, mutuality will not be possible. But the goal of a mutually shared life over time is essential to philia.[56] Philia relations sometimes grow gradually and at other times in dramatic ways but grow they must or else they wither. In brief, partners are present to and in one another; they value and affirm one another as partners; and they move one another along in an "endless" dialogue that is left off today and taken up tomorrow. The result is a historically evolving shared life.

Conflicts: Still, all is not automatic growth. It can and does happen that the good of one or another member requires the dissolution of a friendship. Two "lovers" break up so that one person can pursue a new career or vocation. This dissolution springs not from the philia itself; it may come from another kind of love. Thus, my agape for my friend may lead me to encourage his career move, and his eros likewise leads him to pack his bags. Our mutual philia wants him to stay. We usually experience both agape and eros toward those with whom we share special relationships, but these loves can conflict with philia.[57]

There can also be practical conflicts between and within different philia relationships. Our love for one friend may have to be foregone in favor of love for another. Love for our parents may regularly be in tension with love for our spouse. A philia relationship with God might conflict with other loves, even with loves that, in the abstract, might ordinarily flow from our covenant with God. Jesus' death, which expressed his fidelity to his Abba, severed him from his earthly community. Jesus said that if the disciples truly loved him, they would rejoice that he leave them "to go to his Father" (Jn 14:28). Further, their philia for him will cause them to be hated by those who otherwise would be their friends (Lk 21:16–17).

Mutuality is not the same as "social cooperativeness," something that can be done without affection and is present in voluntary associations. Nor is mutuality the same as harmony, at least if harmony is envisioned as a state without conflicts.[58] Because two or more distinct persons are involved, the potential for conflict is always present. This conflict need not destroy a special relation. As a unity-in-distinction, a mutual relation should allow for and even foster differences, at least where these differences do not weaken the unity and especially where these differences lead to a richer unity. Thus, for example, our unity with God does not prevent us from voicing our disagreements to God. Otherwise our self-disclosure would be unnecessarily limited and our relationship with God needlessly truncated.

Moments of conflict and tension are almost inevitable. Since the identities and destinies of the two (or more) persons are not identical, communion is never completely secure. We need to learn when we are genuinely contributing to another and to the relationship, and when we are simply imposing our own perspective or needs. We need an objective knowledge of self, other, and the relationship to discern when overall unity requires separate action and when it requires acting together. Our respective selves and our relationship grow through an ever changing mix of communicating, yielding, resisting, independent acting, and cooperating.

The possibility of violating communion is always present, and this possibility may be greatest in our relationship with God. The temptation both to make God in our own image and to consider God our "faithful servant" is immense, since God is not "a being" like creatures. God does not resist in the way that a fellow human being might do, and the effect of our actions on our relation to God is less evident. God's reactions to our

attempts at going it alone or our refusals to cooperate are often not immediately or directly felt. The Bible, to be sure, has many references to God's
resistance to human sin, indicated in punishments such as the Babylonian
exile. But since these "punishments" are often delayed (Is 48:9), we cannot
argue that our prosperity indicates God's blessing. And since not every evil
is a punishment for sin (Jn 9:3), we cannot be sure that our adversity is due
to God's judgment. Sadly, the wicked often seem to prosper (Mal 3:14–
15), and some of the good die young. Even a loss of a sense of God's presence may not be the result of our infidelity to God, but only an invitation
to a deeper relationship. Thus, considerable reflection is needed to know
when we are cooperating with God and when, for example, we are taking
advantage of a false or too small image of God. "Real meeting" and real
growth in our relation to God in this life always have an unremovable element of ambiguity. All the deepest and most important aspects of life do.

PHILIA POSSESSES LOVE'S CHARACTERISTICS

In the previous sections I have argued that the tradition clearly recognizes
philia relationships, that it is not the same as agape or eros, and that it is
essentially a mutual relation. Since agape and eros are commonly taken to
be the two main forms of love, I want now to show that philia also possesses the general characteristics of love. And since a variety of "charges"
have been made against philia, I want to defend it against these criticisms.

Spiritual self-transcendence: Through philia we transcend our
individual, private needs and interests.[59] We join ourselves to something
beyond ourselves when we make friends, form a family, or join a church.
Contrary to what agapists often claim, partners in our special relationships are not prized simply for what they contribute to us. That is, philia
is not simply eros. To the contrary, the "infinite value" of persons is often
first learned in special relationships.

We cannot even fully appreciate and realize our own "infinite value" if
we do not devote ourselves to others. When we seek only our own fulfillment, we eventually become shallow. We can never reach human fulfillment when all the world is valued only as so many objects for our own
self-development.[60] The existence of a friend calls us forth from this
unbalanced life. The friend and the friendship exist and deserve love even
when we seem to derive nothing from them. They draw us out of ourselves and invite us to self-transcendence. As Aquinas notes, "He who
loves goes out from himself, insofar as he wills the good of his friend."
That is, "he wants his friend to be, and to have good things."[61]

Indeed, our special relationships almost invariably contain considerable suffering and disutility that we endure or even gladly accept for the sake of the relationship itself. Aquinas wisely remarked: due to a union of affections, when one's friend suffers, "he counts his friend's hurt as his own, so that he grieves for his friend's hurt as though he were hurt himself." The reason for this, Aquinas says, is that, "the lover dwells in the beloved . . . so that it seems as though in his friend he felt the good or suffered the evil. Hence it is proper to friends to want the same things, and to grieve and rejoice at the same."[62] We take pleasure when our friends succeed, but we also want to share in their trials and sufferings. We feel our friendship has been denied if our friends withhold bad news on the grounds, say, that they wanted to spare us and that we could do nothing to help anyway. Friendship means we want to share in good times and in bad. We willingly go to the bedside of a dying or perhaps even comatose friend, knowing in advance that it will be painful to be there. We would consider ourselves faithless if we abandoned our friend for the sake of being with others who might be more enjoyable or helpful.

In cases like these, neither agape nor eros provides a sufficiently rich explanation of our actions. The suggestion has been made that we visit the dying friend because we imagine our own dying process and then—since we will want others to be with us when we are dying—we do for others what we hope will be done for ourselves.[63] Not only does this Thomistic analysis seem crude, as if every action we perform must have an eros dimension, but it also fails to reflect our ordinary experience. It is hard to imagine Mary at the foot of the cross engaging in this sort of reasoning. We criticize the apostles for their lack of fidelity, not for failing to pursue their long-term self-interest. The suggestion may also be made that we go to the hospital out of agape, and this surely is a more likely explanation. Still, this will not explain why we want to be not with just any dying person, but with our friend. We go because we want to honor and continue the friendship we have.

Thus, friendship is more than agape. Aquinas draws upon a long tradition when he writes that a true friend is "a *second self*. . . 'a friend is half of one's own soul'. . . . love consists precisely in such a union. . . . This is a union of hearts."[64] The phrase "another self" can, however, obscure the self-transcending quality of philia.[65] Eros-based theories of love tend to understand the beloved as somehow myself so that loving another can still be understood as good for myself. To the contrary, as the above examples suggest, we can love another quite apart from whether this love brings any good to ourselves.[66] Philia is a form of participation, i.e., a unity-indifference, a form of sharing in the life of persons or groups who remain *other* than myself. My friend is *not* "another me," but is in fact quite different from me.[67] I know that my friend's joy or suffering is not the same as my own, even as it is still significant to me. If my friend has suffered a loss, then for me to remain indifferent because it is not my loss would indicate that I am not really a friend. Philia requires self-transcendence.

Valuable and value-oriented: Philia is directed both to the good of the relationship and to the good of its individual members. These are distinguishable. Each may be affirmed, and happily these goods usually grow together. Like all loves, philia affirms its beloveds in the direction of their greater value. We want our partners to flourish, but we want them to flourish in those aspects of their lives that constitute and contribute to their membership in our communion.[68] We also want the relationship itself to flourish. When partners give gifts to one another, the friendship is itself affirmed and strengthened, and this very increase is intended by philia. Adams notes: "The Christian interest in harmonious relations, as a goal of love, seems to go beyond any merely instrumental value they may have. And I believe that moral intuition, as well as Scriptural authority, favors regarding the desire for friendly relations, for their own sake, as a good motive."[69] The Church's resistance to divorce stems from its awareness that a marital relationship has a value over and above what the two individuals get from the relationship. This is clearest when a "family" is involved, but it is also true of the friendship of the "couple." It may, of course, happen that hostility so characterizes the relation that a separation would be advisable. But something, namely, the good of the relationship itself, is lost when this occurs, even if something is gained by the individual parties. Similarly, prayer is not simply a means to personal perfection. The principal "point" of worship or prayerful contemplation is maintaining and fostering the relationship we have with God.

As a kind of love, philia is *good in itself.* Indeed, philia is among the most valuable activities we perform, well worth its "costs." Though it ordinarily brings great benefits to each party, philia is not based on a calculation of good consequences for the individual members. As Outka notes, "Clearly my friend and I each derive individual happiness from the relation. But that is not all, nor is it controlling. For the friendship is also an end in itself."[70] Philia's goodness appears in moments of quiet satisfaction or in the sacrifices we self-forgetfully make for one another. Its value shines out in the way that acts done for "friends" are felt to be easy, while the "same" acts for strangers are more onerous. Its intrinsic goodness also becomes apparent when its absence fills the soul with a hunger that only it can satisfy.

Philia relationships are themselves great goods, and therefore they are worth the time and energy invested in them. Most of us spend countless hours in creating, maintaining, and fostering our relationships. We play with one another, go for walks with one another, talk on the phone just to keep up. We "waste time" together that could be "more profitably spent," were it not for the fact that the relationships we thereby maintain and build are among the highest goods of our lives. We want the special relationship itself to flourish. To take an example from a different domain: we love our nation, and we rightly promote it. We are interested in national affairs beyond those that directly affect our lives. We discuss and vote as a way of calling our nation to its own best identity. We recognize that we take our identity in part from belonging to our own nation, and we are responsible for its growth. Conversely, the nation is responsible for its citizens and it must help them to attain their own best selves.

Philia does not calculate reciprocal advantages, at least not very carefully.[71] It is the overall relationship that is important. Still, these reciprocal advantages are part of the relation. If they are persistently absent, the relation likely is not mutual. "A friendship will stagnate and die if either person does nothing but give or nothing but receive, nothing but challenge or nothing but appreciate."[72] If I go to the hospital to be with my friend, I am not seeking my own good. If later my friend does not visit me when I am in the hospital, I rightly feel something is missing. I did not go to the hospital in order that my friend would later do the same for me, but the return favor is nonetheless due as part of our mutual relationship.

Philia, of course, is not the only good, and sometimes its good should yield to other goods that may be more important or pressing. At times a given philia relation may have to be set aside, diminished, or denied for the sake of the individuals involved. For example, when a wife wants to pursue further education, this may come at some cost to her relationship with her children and husband. Their affirmation of her own pursuit may of course unite them all more closely, but her education may also lead her to be less involved in the family. To the degree that the philia relation is highly prized, individual pursuits will be somewhat restrained. To the degree that individual fulfillment is highly prized, special relationships may suffer. No simple formula can establish priority principles between individual fulfillment and group fulfillment. We commonly leave our college friends for the sake of a job in a new town. We do not do the same with our spouse. And we should never forsake our relation to God for any earthly good. We may have to give up all else, including our lives, for that relationship.

Philia is *inventive and creative.* Philia makes possible ever deeper penetration into the depths of beauty and goodness of a mutual relationship. Thus, spouses sometimes exclaim, "I never suspected marriage could be so good." In other words, philia brings about new and unexpected value both in the members and in their relation. Philia is also creative in the sense that this love fosters in both lover and beloved a set of enriching needs, expectations, and loyalties that would not be present without the love.[73]

Contrary to some traditional theories, philia is not restricted solely to those who are equals.[74] Rather, it creatively overcomes differences. Christ *made* friends of public sinners, and through that friendship they left their sin. In his youthful work, Aquinas made this very point: "Love *makes* it happen that the beloved be suitable and rather connatural to the lover."[75] This happens in at least three ways. First, philia brings about communion by uniting minds and hearts and creating a shared world. Second, philia "renders irrelevant whatever discrepancies in wealth, status, power, social position, education or talents exist between" partners.[76] In any community, there will be weaker and stronger members, and so contributions to communal life will be unequal. But the common life of the community looms larger than the difference between individuals. As a result, Paul notes, those who would otherwise likely be denigrated are treated with greater honor and respect (1 Cor 12:22–26). Third, an ongoing relationship reveals the deep value of people whom we would otherwise see only in a more superficial light.[77] When we befriend the poor, we discover their own preciousness as well as their unique perspective. Thus, philia creatively promotes a life that is fuller than we could achieve by ourselves. This is above all true of that most unequal of relationships, our relation to God. We can never be God's equal, but through God's creative love we can be God's friends and children.

Emotional: Philia is a self-connecting love. Robert Adams argues: "It is an abuse of the word 'love' to say that one *loves* a person, or any other object, if one does not care, except instrumentally, about one's relation to that object."[78] If I could use the word "philia" where Adams uses the broad word "love," then I am in full agreement. Agape, by contrast, can take the attitude of not caring that I am the benefactor, only that the beloved be benefited. Agape does not care about developing a relation with the beloved, which may be why it is attractive to those who don't want to "be involved" even when they "get involved." That is, they want agapically to help others, but do not want the vulnerability that philia brings.

Philia is an *emotional* relation.[79] As partners, we are affected by one another. The others are on our mind and in our heart, and the things that concern them concern us.[80] As Fred Berger observes, "It is not enough that our friend does the right things in our interrelationship; it is equally important that he does them (at least in part) because he *likes* and *cares* for us."[81] We do not simply have emotional feelings for the individual members of our groups. There are also shared feelings within and for the group itself. This is not to say that every individual member feels the same emotion at the same time. But there are communal emotions that the individual can share. For example, United States citizens felt a common horror when John F. Kennedy died. Most Christians feel a communal bittersweet sadness on Good Friday and a common exultation on Easter. As members of Christ's body, Christians can and should feel bad over the sin of a fellow Christian.

Enduring: A philia relationship calls for fidelity to its members and to the relationship itself. Like the other loves, philia tends to *permanence* or to lifelong fidelity. Peter's friendship, though not his courage, appears in his exclamation, "Lord, at your side I am prepared to face imprisonment and death itself" (Lk 22:33). Some theologians, however, disparage friendship. Outka praises agape because it "is unalterable; to abandon it would never be appropriate. Alternately, friendship may fluctuate; it depends at least in part on mutual liking, and usually on admiration and esteem as well."[82] Kenneth Cauthen argues that a love that requires mutuality will be inherently unstable. Following Reinhold Niebuhr, he describes this love as "infested with anxiety."[83]

Though there is some truth in these concerns about philia's permanence, qualifications are in order. First, we should compare real and ideal philia with real and ideal agape. It is obvious that real friendships often end, but it is equally obvious that the real exercise of agape also fails. The latter may be sinful or sad, but so may the former. Agape in principle ought not end. Neither should philia. Second, a perfect agape would be free of anxiety, but so would a perfect philia (1 Jn 4:18). Unfortunately, the human condition can infect any love with anxiety, including our love for God. Susceptibility to instability or anxiety is part of all human life. Those who complain about the fickleness of friendship usually are thinking of friendships based on pleasure or utility, not of friendships based on the intrinsic goodness of the friends.[84] Friendship among the "persons" of the Trinity or among the saints in heaven indicates that philia can in principle endure forever.

Third, agape, as I have described it, is itself based on the value of the other, both real and ideal; and this value grows or declines. Hence, agape itself changes in its execution. Something similar is true of philia. If, as the above objection holds, philia depends on mutual liking and on admiration and esteem, then philia is able to be sustained as long as we are able to like, admire, and esteem the beloved. Why must these be impermanent? God can permanently like, esteem, even admire whatever goodness there is in us. We too can do the same.

Philia, however, is not strictly dependent on fluctuating feelings of liking, admiring, or esteeming. Its endurance is manifest even in ordinary interpersonal relationships and in our relation to God. Most of us who try to pray go through periods when we are unable to experience God's presence and therefore unable to experience the ordinary delight that accompanies being with God.[85] Like Jesus on the cross, we have to trust that this special relation to God continues. We can do no more, and so we hand ourselves over into the darkness which is God's transcendence, trusting in the relationship we have known. We remain faithful to God in spite of this desolation. This faithful love is obviously not eros, for eros is what is being purified. It is also not agape, for in the dark nights the prayerful person generally is not able sincerely to affirm God's goodness for its own sake. God doesn't seem at all good; rather, God just seems absent. During these periods, the main love present is philia, here as faithfulness to a seemingly dead relation. The same also happens in our philia relationships with other human beings. Family members often remain amazingly faithful to one another through seemingly impossible difficulties. Philia is not dependent simply on the individual's particular attitudes at any given moment. Whether as institution, e.g., marriage, or as implicit commitment, e.g., ordinary friendship, philia can hold us even when we have lost sight of the value of the other or of the good of the relationship.

These hard cases suggest a further problem for philia's power to endure. The beloved may so change that I cannot fully share in her life.[86] To the extent that my friend becomes absorbed in a life of crime, to that extent I cannot be her friend. I ought to bear an agapic love for what is authentic in her, hoping that she will reform her ways, but our friendship must change. To say this, however, is not to deny that in philia, as in all personal loves, I love the *other*-in-her-qualities, not the qualities alone. Therefore, I can, presumably, preserve some sort of limited friendship with her, even though I cannot live in an open-ended sharing of life with her. And I can continue to invite her into the kind of relationship with me that itself will incline her to become good again. The classic image of the mother who is faithful to her wayward son exemplifies how a special philia relation can persevere. These special relationships can last as long as the partners last, though sometimes only in an unfilled way. Philia promises forever. One cannot intelligibly say, I want you to be my friend or my God for a week. Nevertheless, philia relations are more fragile than agape because they necessarily have a history. Agape may occur in episodic acts. Philia requires a history of mutual involvement.[87] Thus, philia is subject to the erosion of time's passage.

There are other related reasons why it is more difficult for philia than agape to endure. Because our agape for others in principle is not concerned for our own well-being, it should not cease when the consequences to ourselves are negative. With agape we can do what is best for others, without worrying about whether this is also good for ourselves and for our relationships. Philia is more fragile because it is more complex. It necessarily must also consider these other goods. Philia is also more fragile because it takes two (or more) to make this relation. In a mutual love, the you that I love is a you-related-in-love-to-me. As Jules Toner writes, "In communion what I do depends not only on your being lovable, but on your being in act as lover toward me."[88] If you withhold that love for me, then I can no longer engage in a mutual love, but must content myself with other kinds of love and live with an unfulfilled philia. Further, we finite human beings usually cannot sustain an unfulfilled or unbalanced special relation forever. As Linell Cady writes, "All relationships must, for limited periods, be able to withstand the refusal or failure of one spouse to act for the common good; but, if chronic, the union will inevitably fail. . . . Although a strong communal life can withstand such betrayals, if they become habitual and widespread, the life of the community inevitably withers and dies."[89]

When a friendship fails, the friendship is a failed or now unfulfilled friendship. Through the grace of God it may someday be restored. That is, friendship has a peculiar durability that outlasts its actual, fulfilled existence. We sometimes make overtures to a former friend, and part of the intelligibility of those overtures is that something once existed that ideally should have continued. Out of loyalty to the commitment once made and to the common life once shared, we desire to restore the friendship to what it once promised to become. The bond persists as a failed and presently unfulfilled promise. If it is restored, we need not start a new friendship, but only restore our relationship. Hence, contrary to what some agapists claim, philia has its own kind of permanence and stability.

Universality: Some philosophers and theologians favor agape over philia because, they hold, it has the advantage of being a universal love. James Hanigan, for example, argues that, since a personal friendship with everyone is a human impossibility and hence cannot be universal, it lies outside what is essential for Christian life.[90] Hanigan, like others, seems to have uncritically accepted a Kantian criterion of universality as normative for any Christian love. Neither the Bible nor tradition nor common experience warrant that criterion. Agape is itself universal in aspiration only, since understandably it too must be particular in practice. All finite human loves are directed to some objects and not others. On earth we cannot actually love all individual persons with agape, eros, or philia.

Nevertheless, while philia in practice is particular, it too is in principle universal. All of us, I presume, have had the experience of developing a friendship with persons whom we initially found unattractive. Generalized, such experiences indicate that philia *can* be universal. That is, people can in principle develop special relations with everyone by finding a variety of grounds for those relations. A look at history indicates that people have found quite different bases even for their romantic loves. In the medieval period it was held that likes attract likes, in the Romantic period it was claimed that opposites attract, and in our own period we speak of lovers complementing one another.[91] It seems both possible and desirable to have as many special relationships as possible, and on a variety of bases. Heaven, to take again the limit case, is a universal communion of friends.

Not able to be directly willed: Finally, like other loves, philia is not something we can just decide to have.[92] Philia, however, is even more beyond our command than the other two loves. Both agape and eros are dependent on the goodness of the beloved, but they do not depend on the free consent of the other. Philia requires that the other accept our love and also love us in return. And so even if we could will in ourself a "friendly love" (which we cannot), we cannot will a mutual love, since we cannot command others to accept and return love to us.

Philia relationships are beyond our direct will for another reason. Some of our special relations begin prior to any possible choice, e.g., we are born into our family or baptized into our church as infants. In order for these special relations to become fully human philia relations, we can and must subsequently accept and ratify them, but this consent is not a matter of willing them into existence. In these and other philia relations, mutual love may grow imperceptibly and may never be *explicitly* chosen for itself. The bond will be implicitly consented to through the choices we make to do things in accord with the relationship. There are some philia relations, however, that are so important that, once they have arisen, we want to ratify them through an explicit commitment, e.g., marriage. We want to bind our future and to safeguard the relationship against the contingencies of life as well as our own inconsistencies. We want to declare and not just consciously live in and from the relation.[93] Still, even in these cases, it is a matter not of willing the relation into existence. Rather we consent to it as and after it arises.

Once philia has arisen, it includes significant responsibilities within and for the relationship. As we have seen, it is false to say that we are responsible only for ourselves. We live in moral solidarity with others. We share history with them. We share in their lives and therefore in their freedom. We become coresponsible for them. We are responsible for the community whose history we share. This responsibility is a matter of a unity-in-difference in which each of us preserves our own proper responsibility (the distinction) but also shares in the responsibility of the others and of the group (unity). In making our choices, we consider how a course of action will affect not only ourselves, but also the other partners and the relationship itself.

Perhaps one reason for the general neglect of the topic of friendship in ethics is precisely because it is so far from our "control." Any moral theory that focuses solely on what we can autonomously decide or command will have no central place for friendship. Also, any moral theory that focuses solely on acts will have little place for friendship, because friendship evolves over time and is sustained as much by attitudes as by acts. An act-centered ethics walks in shallow waters, and an autonomous duty ethic is suitable mainly for navigating the narrow gorges along the river of life. An ethics that is more adequate to life will include relationships that are only indirectly able to be willed. The deepest exercise of our freedom is found in consenting to these relations.

SPECIAL RELATIONSHIPS?

I have yet to face one major objection often raised against philia. Philia essentially includes partiality, and that, it is said, leads to immorality.[94] Examples are commonplace: a mother worries more about her child's cold than about thousands freezing to death in a distant country; a father gives a job to his son rather than to someone better qualified; a congresswoman seeks pork-barrel benefits for her state even though they threaten to break the federal budget. Where egoism says, "I'm going to get mine, and more," philia seems to say, "We're going to get ours, and get it first." Thus, philia relations are often accused of being nothing more than *egoisme à deux*.

Agapists, Outka says, feel "a characteristic unease about the restrictedness of special relationships." To counteract the human tendency to neglect those outside our special relationships, they suggest an alternative: "The agapist prefers to begin at the other end, with the negative restraints and positive injunctions applicable in any human relation."[95] This alternative proposes that, first, we should not violate any person and, second, each and every human being should be treated as having basic dignity. In Chapter 5, I formulated another understanding of agape that includes these two points, but is more general. It also is less suspicious of special relationships. This principle says: "Do not treat persons or things as of less value than each actually and potentially has, *and* do treat persons or things as bearers of the value they actually or potentially have." Applied to persons, this formulation includes the minimum basic dignity of persons (otherwise love would not be directed to the value they really have) but it also includes those other values that are part of the uniqueness of a person. This formulation has priority rules: first, no person shall be treated as less than a person; second, everyone shall be treated with the respect that accords to being a person; third, everyone shall be treated in accord with his or her complete (actual and potential) value. This formulation permits us to say that in general every child of the world deserves not to be abused and deserves to be positively supported in its basic needs before we advance to "extras" for our own children. Hence, in the present order most of us in the Western world share a sinful blindness to a lack of adequate resources for many of the children (and adults) of the world. Basic human rights generally ought first to be secured for everyone.

As David Hollenbach has well said, rights "are not only immunities from interference by others. They are also empowerments that enable those who exercise them to be active participants in the life of the various communities to which they belong. . . . liberation is *from* bondage *into* community—into a community of persons who are both free and coresponsible for one another's fates."[96] In other words, the basic right to belong to the *human community* requires rights such as to food and shelter. In this context, then, we can see why the United States Catholic bishops defined human rights as "the minimum conditions for life in community."[97] For example, what is wrong in murder is not just that an individual's right to life is violated but also that a person is excluded from our human community. Every human being belongs to that "thin" but fundamental relationship we call the human community. This belonging in part accounts for why we treat human beings, even the most vulnerable or handicapped, as valuable in a way that no other animal is.

But membership in the human community is not enough for a full human life. Basic human rights are valuable in themselves, of course, but they take on their full significance in terms of our "special relationships." We also belong to many smaller, but "thicker" relationships such as our church, nation, and family. These thicker relations establish the loyalties, patterns of expectations, practices, and so forth that inform most of our actions. These special relationships more fully engage the rich uniqueness of each person. In fact, I suggest, we best begin our ethical reflections with these special relations since in them the depth of the value of persons is best discovered and affirmed.

Many agapists say that agape forbids *any criterion of selection* among persons and *any favored relationships.*[98] Fortunately, few agapists are as consistent as Kierkegaard, who refused to marry his beloved Regina on the grounds that such an act would violate agape. Rather, since special relationships are themselves good, it is fitting and proper that we select persons with whom we think we can make the best or at least a satisfactory special relationship. It would be, for example, a violation of the nature of marriage if we married the first person who happened to be nearby,[99] whether male or female, whether young or old, whether attractive to us or nearly disgusting, whether sinfully abusive or lovingly tender.

Should Christians, then, have a "characteristic unease about special relationships"? In fact, the unease Outka names is characteristic mainly of the Protestant authors he studies. By contrast, the Catholics Outka cites are generally quite enthusiastic about special relationships. A "Catholic" approach tends to *begin* with special relationships, lead *through* them to the dignity of all human beings, and set as a *goal* the richest possible variety of special relationships. Without special relations, most people, including the poorest, would be worse off. For example, it is better for children that they be cared for by their own parents, not simply by all members of the human race. Adults too can flourish only if they are members in a variety of special relationships.

It is true that we rarely sacrifice more for the stranger or enemy than for "our own," but this generally is not a moral failure. The new mother who is up night after night to feed her child makes enormous sacrifices. The fact that she is sacrificing for "her own" child does not take away her generosity. To give up sleep for two or three nights for a stranger is rightly considered quite virtuous. Parents give up scores of nights' sleep and hundreds of thousands of dollars to raise and educate their children. Even if they would not do so for the children of strangers, this does not mean that they make no sacrifices. The fact that such a yoke is easy, such a burden light, does not make philia any less human and Christian.

Thus, special relations are not immoral just because they are partial. Rather, they are part of the fullness of Christian life. Even God's love is partial. Speaking to Israel, God says, "You alone have I favored, more than all the families of the earth." This special relationship is accompanied by special retribution: "Therefore I will punish you for all your crimes" (Am 3:2) and special demands: "Seek me, that you may live" (Am 5:4). God chooses some from Israel to be the elect in the new covenant, and God chooses Gentiles to replace those who have been cut off. Such are God's "inscrutable ways" (Rom 11:7, 17, 33). Recent Catholic theology has emphasized the "scandal of particularity" in the Incarnation: though God has a relation to all, God has a special relation to a first-century Jew named Jesus. This "favoritism" does not mean that God may not select others for different favors. We too may and should have a number of "special friends," each special in different ways. Our various special loves may be just so many different ways of cooperating with God's multicolored love.

Catholic history, of course, also provides abundant evidence of the pitfalls in prizing particular relationships, e.g., the thesis of *extra ecclesiam nulla salus*, or the impression given that forgiveness and grace are not available outside the sacraments, or the strict division of the Church into teachers and learners. Therefore the disadvantages of beginning with special relationships should be acknowledged along with the advantages.[100] The Enlightenment exposed many of the abuses that an emphasis on special relations is prone to. But now our own age has the task of exposing the abuses and distortions that an emphasis on equalitarian individualism brings. Philosophers and theologians are finding that exclusive reliance on universal human dignity is insufficient. As Daniel Callahan writes, such Enlightenment views "deny the concreteness and irregularities of real communities . . . eschew vision and speculation about goals and meaning, and . . . enshrine the discourse of wary strangers (especially that of rights) as the preferred mode of daily relations."[101]

Philia aims at the complete development of the beloved. It does so, however, only insofar as this development is consonant with our relationships. This limitation is accepted because being in a mutual relation makes possible a deeper way of being human than either pure agape or eros can achieve. Thus, Christians can and should encourage philia. Agape is not, as it is for Outka, the "supreme ethical principle."[102] Philia is also not a supreme ethical principle in the sense that it can be trumped by no other principle or love. The other loves ideally lead to and serve it.[103] Still, no human life can be complete without all three forms of love. As Garth Hallett wisely observes, "The tactic of eliminating rival loves rather than ordering them leads to incoherence and impoverishment."[104] To this point I now turn in the final section of this chapter.

THE THREE LOVES IN HUMAN LIFE

Correcting deficiencies: Each of the three loves we have discussed counteracts basic human disorders. First, agape corrects for selfishness, which is ever ready to mask itself as healthy self-love. "When the problem of human life is egocentrism . . . the remedy is self-sacrifice."[105] Or when the problem is overweening pride, agape enables us to appreciate the value of others in and for themselves. Or when the problem is that our philia relations tend to become exclusive not simply in the sense that we form "friendships" only with some, but in the sense that we exclude some human beings altogether from our love, perhaps even harming them, then agape insists that we must value the welfare of all human beings, whether they are community members or not. Special relationships ought not contravene an openness to all persons.[106]

When, second, the problem is that we have little appreciation for ourselves, the remedy is self-love or eros.[107] When the problem is depression or self-hate, eros for the world may enliven us. When the problem is sloth, often self-affirmation will energize us. Self-love is not necessarily in opposition to love for others. It is false to assume "that the more one loves himself for his own sake the less he can love others for theirs."[108] Self-love increases our sense of our own goodness, and since goodness tends to overflow, those who love themselves may in fact love others more.

Third, beyond these sorts of disorders, it may be that "the basic problem of man's life . . . is to overcome aloneness and separation and the disharmonies of life that are consequent on separation and loneliness. . . . The only adequate solution for that problem is the union which is love,"[109] that is, philia. Self-love or an agapic love will not of themselves overcome this basic loneliness. We want to be in various mutual relationships with others. The basic human sin has been described in many ways, usually as pride or selfishness, as either trying to take the place of God or trying to make everything serve us, as a lack of agape or too much eros. From the viewpoint of philia, sin has a different face: "Sin is the turning-away . . . from interdependencies with all other beings, including the matrix of being from whom all life comes."[110] Philia corrects the temptation to think that life is nothing more than individuals walking next to, or behind, or in front of others, but not with others. All these disorders are present in human life, and a variety of loves is necessary to counteract them.

Independence and belonging: Life's rhythm includes attachment, detachment, and new attachment. As children, we are strongly guided by eros loves within a family-philia context. Our growth toward maturity is a growth toward agape, toward loving others for their own sakes. It is also a growth toward loving ourselves for our own sakes and not simply as parts of the communities that nourish us. Autonomy gradually replaces heteronomous living through another. We slowly establish internal control and personal boundaries so that there is a self to give and not simply someone who lives (in however internalized a fashion) out of others' expectations.[111] Maturity, however, requires more than independence. We must learn to give ourselves to others in mutual relationships. Finally, in death, we are detached from the earthly form of our special relationships, and we hope for new forms of attachment to those same earthly realities (Jn 14:18). Relationships are the "beginning" and "end" of this maturational process. We begin in dependence, achieve some independence, and move toward interdependence.

Though this growth can be depicted as sequential stages, the process of attachment, detachment, and free attachment, of dependence, independence, and personal belonging, is, of course, much more complex. For example, even as adults, we are still breaking away from our parents. And we can get "stuck" in this process, getting lost and absorbed in our relationships, or becoming isolated in autonomy's individualism. When the process goes well, however, we come to learn the preciousness of every person.[112] We learn that everybody has an inner life; everybody is some mother's child; everybody is potentially somebody's special friend. Can anyone who deeply loves agree with Anders Nygren when he says that human beings are simply worthless sinners? The "infinite value of the soul" in every person that Nygren could not find is discoverable through all forms of love.[113]

Agape, eros, and philia: Both eros and agape are necessary for human flourishing. "To give, therefore, as well as to take, is inherent in living organisms. . . . Two loves co-exist in every living thing."[114] But more is needed than these two loves. We also need that form of love by which we belong in a community. We not only give and take; we also share. That is, we exist in special relationships. "The fundamental human craving is to belong, to count in the community of being, to have one's freedom in and with the response of others, to enjoy God as one who makes us members of one society."[115] This belonging motivates many of our actions and it forms part of the reason for much of the give and take of life. We "give" to the beloved because we already belong to the beloved; and, *as* belonging, we feel free to "take." When belonging is primary, we may "take" without necessarily taking anything away from the whole. The student who takes most from a lively class is frequently the one who contributes most. When we "take communion," we enact and enrich the whole Church. Those who are unwilling to take and receive from others and the common good reveal an unwillingness to belong in a mutual relationship. In a philia relation, it is important not only that all partners give love, but also that they want to receive love.[116] "At the center is an ideal of a community of selves enjoying mutual self-realization"; sacrifices will be made only "when the larger good of the community or the greater needs of some call for the disproportionate contribution of self-giving from others. 'To each according to need, from each according to ability'" is then an appropriate norm.[117]

Human life typically includes all three loves in rhythmically occurring ways.[118] Philia can transform agape and eros, making them a part of the ongoing mutual relation it creates. When these transformed acts of agape and eros occur within our mutual relations, they are evaluated not just in themselves, but also by whether they flow from and contribute to the relationship. On the whole, friends enjoy and profit from their relationship. At times, however, they make great sacrifices in order to be faithful not just to the good of the members but also to the good of the relationship itself.[119]

Agape, eros, and philia each have their own goodness. In this book I have frequently sought a set of priority rules that could solve practical questions about whom or what we should love first and about which kind of love is most important in Christian life. I have found none other than that we should love God above all else. I cannot say we should always or never love our neighbor or ourselves or even other creatures first or last. And there is no lexical rule that says philia always or never trumps either agape or eros. There is time and place for each love. We would not want our friends constantly to deny, forget, or subordinate themselves for us, and we should not expect ourselves to do so for them. In a philia relation, each of us is not only permitted but on occasion required to put ourselves first. It is not even a good moral rule (*parenesis* is something else) that all should always give as much or more than they receive. Today we appropriately may "give" a little, and tomorrow we appropriately may need to "take" a lot. In communal life, we give and take in varying degrees and in different ways. Only over a longer period can we judge whether the various loves have each played an appropriate role.[120]

Usually, of course, our philia relationships are good for both the lover and the beloved. If not, questions eventually and properly arise. These questions arise not because the sole point of the relation is to enhance independent persons. Rather, they arise because, negatively, the relation itself may diminish if one or other partner significantly diminishes and because, positively, the relation's richness usually grows as one or other partner grows. If, however, a relationship would be forsaken simply because we no longer were "getting something out of it," this abandonment indicates that we did not really value the philia relation itself, but only the benefits we derived. If we love another solely in order to receive a return love or solely to achieve the fulfillment that comes from loving, then eros and not philia is present.[121] Philia creates, expresses, and enhances a mutual relationship. Philia fulfills us, but that fulfillment is not its primary consideration. If one partner has to make a sacrifice for the sake of the relationship, this should be regretted by all. The greatest love may be *shown* by laying down one's life for our friends (Jn 15:13), but making this sacrifice is not the point of any genuine love.

Though agape and eros in daily life are often extended to many people with whom we have no obvious special relations, we should not conclude that agape or eros is antithetical to special relations. When we love real persons for their own sakes or for our own sakes, we frequently find ourselves inclined then to develop some sort of special relationship with them. Agape and eros can lead to, hope for, or even require mutuality, because part of the very good of both the lover and the beloved may well be to be involved in a mutual relationship. When Jesus invited disciples, he might have done so agapically, simply for their sakes (or for the sake of still others), but he seems to have done so with a goal of fellowship: "I call you friends" (Jn 15:15). As these personal relationships develop, "inevitably the quintessence of agape is altered. The purest and more perfect manifestation is not in self-sacrifice, but in those instances of personal devotion where a response in kind is forthcoming."[122] The self-giving of agape may find a return self-giving, and this leads to a mutual relation.

The self-fulfillment in eros may discover someone who is fulfilled by a return love, and this too can lead to philia. As D'Arcy writes, "The *perfection* of love . . . is to be found in personal friendship, whether between a man and a woman, between man and man, or between man and God."[123] Christians envision the eschatological victory of God as a unity of all things, where God is all in all.

CONCLUSION

Philosophy and theology often reflect on our moral lives as if we were isolated individuals performing isolated acts aimed at other isolated individuals. A theological focus on agape or eros without philia tends to feed this individualism. Most of our daily moral acts, however, have to do with our communal relationships. We belong to special relationships, are loyal to special others, and enact special roles. Friendship, trust, and loyalty are essential in our daily lives.[124] Duties to strangers are important, of course, but they are not the paradigm of Christian living. In this book I have taken the position that beginning with special relationships is the theologically preferable option: God treats us less as aliens, as sinners, or as creatures who share nothing of divine life and more as daughters or sons, as friends, and as covenant partners. This book arises out of the convictions that God relates to us in special relationships, that human selfhood begins in such relations, particularly in the family, and that the fullness of human personhood is possible only through deep philia relationships. In this chapter I have begun to spell out the meaning of these special relationships. In the next chapter, I conclude this book by reflecting particularly on our special relationship with God.

NOTES

1. See Vincent Genovesi, S.J., *In Pursuit of Love* (Wilmington: Glazier, 1987), 28–30; Paul Ramsey, *Basic Christian Ethics* (Chicago: Univ. of Chicago Press, 1978), 159–60; John Macmurray, *Persons in Relation* (Atlantic Highlands: Humanities, 1983), 159; Oliver O'Donovan, *Resurrection and Moral Order* (Grand Rapids: Eerdmans, 1986), 228–29. Gilbert Meilaender, *Friendship* (Notre Dame: Univ. of Notre Dame Press, 1981), 32, 53, distinguishes Christian love from friendship, even though he wants to find a place for friendship in Christian life. Ceslaus Spicq, O.P., *Agape in the New Testament* (St. Louis: Herder, 1966), 3:33, 86–102, struggles to divide agape from philia. On the other hand, Paul Wadell, C.P., *Friendship and the Moral Life* (Notre Dame: Univ. of Notre Dame Press, 1989), 70–74, tries to show how agape and philia are really the same. Stephen Post, "The Inadequacy of Selflessness," *Journal of American Academy of*

Religion 56 (1988): 213, struggles to affirm the centrality of mutuality; he is more persuasive in "Love and the Order of Beneficence," *Soundings* 75 (Winter 1992): 499–516.

2. Daniel Day Williams, *The Spirit and the Forms of Love* (New York: Harper & Row, 1968), 46.

3. Aristotle, *Nichomachean Ethics* (1170b10–14) in *Basic Works of Aristotle*, ed. Richard McKeon (New York: Random House, 1941), colorfully noted that the deep union of friendship requires sharing in life, not just "feeding in the same place, as with cattle." See also *Sententiarum*, 3.27.1.1; *ST* II–II.25.12.

4. Max Scheler, "The Meaning of Suffering," *Centennial Essays*, ed. Manfred Frings (The Hague: Martinus Nijhoff, 1974), 132; Max Scheler, *Philosophical Perspectives* (Boston: Beacon, 1958), 116; Max Scheler, *Genius des Krieges und der deutsche Krieg* (Leipzig: Weisen, 1917), 8.

5. Max Scheler, *Formalism in Ethics and a Non-Formal Ethics of Value* (Evanston: Northwestern Univ. Press, 1973), 533–41; Max Scheler, *On the Eternal in Man* (Hamden, CT: Shoe String Press, 1972), 374–77, 390; Max Scheler, *The Nature of Sympathy* (Hamden, CT: Shoe String Press, 1973), 128–29, 164–65, 194–95; Oliver O'Donovan, *The Problem of Self-Love in St. Augustine* (New Haven: Yale Univ. Press, 1980), 129.

6. Aristotle, *Nicomachean Ethics*, 1155a (McKeon: 1058), says that friendship either is a virtue or implies virtue. I here distinguish philia as the virtue of mutual love from friendship as the special relationship that philia creates. See also John Cooper, "Aristotle on Friendship," *Essays on Aristotle's Ethics*, ed. Amélie Oksenberg Rorty (Berkeley: Univ. of California Press, 1980), 301–2.

7. Not all "special relationships" are formed by love. For example, the employer-employee relation is founded on reciprocal advantages or justice. The master-slave relationship is hardly one of mutual love. In this chapter, I focus on those special relationships that are created through mutual love.

8. John Stacer, S.J., "Divine Reverence for Us," *Theological Studies* 44 (September 1983): 441; Sallie McFague, *Models of God* (Philadelphia: Fortress, 1987), 153. The early Christians called themselves "friends of God" and "brethren" of one another; Meilaender, *Friendship*, 2.

9. For another example, see Daniel Callahan, "What Do Children Owe Elderly Parents?" *Hastings Center Report* 15 (April 1985): 34–36, on why the parent-child relation is not simply a friendship.

10. Jules Toner, *The Experience of Love* (Washington: Corpus, 1968), 42–43; Timothy Sedgwick, *Sacramental Ethics* (Philadelphia: Fortress, 1987), 79–80; Karen Lebacqz, "Love Your Enemy: Sex, Power, and Christian Ethics," *Annual of the Society of Christian Ethics* (1990), 12. Victor Furnish, *Love Command in the New Testament* (New York: Abingdon, 1972), 209–10, writes that Christian love does not require a response, but then adds that it requires community. Paul Ramsey, *Nine Modern Moralists* (Englewood Cliffs: Prentice-Hall, 1962), 146, rejects distinctions among loves.

11. Linell Cady, "Relational Love," *Embodied Love*, ed. Paula Cooey et al. (San Francisco: Harper & Row, 1987), 141.

12. Morton Kelsey, *Caring* (New York: Paulist, 1981), 88–89; Eric Fromm, *Art of Loving* (New York: Harper & Brothers, 1956), 48, similarly underestimates the difficulty.

13. Arthur Dyck, "Loving Impartiality in Moral Cognition," *Annual of Society of Christian Ethics* (1989), 63.

14. See Karl Rahner, S.J., "Love as the Key Virtue," *Sacramentum Mundi* (New York: Herder and Herder, 1970), 6:343–44.

15. Joseph Allen, "The Inclusive Covenant and Special Covenants," *Selected Papers* (American Society of Christian Ethics, 1979), 108–13, traces the need for special communities to finitude, and he suggests that God relates to us only in an "inclusive covenant." There seems to be no basis either in tradition or in reason for these claims.

16. Spicq, *Agape in the New Testament*, 2:332.

17. Meilaender, *Friendship*, 3.

18. Stephen Pope, "The Moral Centrality of Natural Priorities," *Annual of the Society of Christian Ethics* (1990), 120–22.

19. Rahner, "Virtue," *Encyclopedia of Theology*, ed. Karl Rahner, S.J. (New York: Seabury, 1975), 1801; Rahner, "Love as the Key Virtue," 343. Perhaps not surprisingly, the Catholic Rahner argues his point by saying that some eros must be part of every love.

20. McFague, *Models of God*, 102.

21. Irving Singer, *The Nature of Love* (Chicago: Univ. of Chicago Press, 1987), 1:201.

22. Meilaender, *Friendship*, 1; for a fine set of classical texts, see *Other Selves: Philosophers on Friendship*, ed. Michael Pakaluk (Indianapolis, IN: Hackett, 1991).

23. Cooper, "Aristotle on Friendship," 318–34, shows how difficult it is to prove this assertion.

24. Aristotle, *Nicomachean Ethics*, 1155a, 1159a, 1169b (McKeon: 1058, 1067, 1088); cf. also Cicero, "On Friendship," xiii–xv, in *Other Selves*, 97–100; Charles Pinches, "Friendship and Tragedy," *First Things* (May 1990): 40.

25. Courtney Campbell, "Religion and Moral Meaning in Bioethics," *Hastings Center Report* 20 (Supplement July/August 1990): S9–10.

26. This nobility is different from Aristotle's noble friendship, where the latter is based on the intellectual, moral, or religious goodness of the friends. Cooper, "Aristotle on Friendship," 303–15; Toner, *The Experience of Love*, 44–46.

27. "The Church Today," *Documents of Vatican II*, ed. Walter Abbott, S.J. (New York: America, 1966), nos. 47–50.

28. Singer, *The Nature of Love*, 3:386.

29. Walter Conn, "Passionate Commitment," *Cross Currents* (Fall 1984): 334; Lawrence Blum, "Vocation, Friendship, and Community," *Identity, Character, and Morality*, eds. Owen Flanagan and Amélie Oksenberg Rorty (Cambridge: MIT Press, 1990), 173–98.

30. James Keenan, S.J., *Goodness and Rightness in Thomas Aquinas's* Summa Theologiae (Washington: Georgetown Univ. Press, 1992), 126.

31. It is, I suppose, possible for a person to be a friend to himself or herself. If so, then agape, eros, and philia may be indistinguishable when the self is the beloved.

32. Outka, *Agape*, 36.

33. Elsewhere I have begun such a project; see Edward Vacek, S.J., "Toward a Phenomenology of Love Lost," *Journal of Phenomenological Psychology* 20 (Spring 1989): 1–19.

34. Groups are unlike most friendships in that they usually exist prior to new members entering them. Further, we may love the group before it accepts us.

35. James Hanigan, *As I Have Loved You* (New York: Paulist, 1986), 146–47, and others hold a contrary view. See also Wadell, *Friendship and the Moral Life*, 136.

36. Toner, *The Experience of Love*, 188.

37. Aristotle, *Nicomachean Ethics*, 1156a (McKeon: 1060–61); *ST* I–II.26.4; *Caritate*, 8; *Duo Praecepta*, 101a; Toner, *The Experience of Love*, 48; Kenneth Cauthen, *Process Ethics* (New York: Mellen, 1984), 143–45; Cooper, "Aristotle on Friendship," 304; Wadell, *Friendship and the Moral Life*, 56–69. Immanuel Kant, in his "Lecture on Friendship," in *Other Selves*, 210–17, comes close to describing friendship more as bilateral exchanges or gifts than as mutuality. The contrary position is developed by Elizabeth Telfer in "Friendship," in *Other Selves*, 250–51.

38. Tom Driver and Herbert Richardson, "The Meaning of Orgasm," *God, Sex, and the Social Project*, ed. James Grace (New York: Mellen, 1978), 184–200.

39. Roger Scruton, *Sexual Desire* (New York: Free Press, 1986), 228.

40. *ST* I–II.28.1.

41. This notion seems to be missing in Aristotle; cf. Cooper, "Aristotle on Friendship," 302, 327–28.

42. Toner, *The Experience of Love*, 197; Charles Taylor, *Sources of the Self* (Cambridge: Harvard Univ. Press, 1989), 375, 383; cf. Robert Johann, *The Meaning of Love* (Westminster, MD: Newman, 1955), 34.

43. Kathryn Pauly Morgan admirably explores the enormous existential difficulties of mutual love in her "Romantic Love, Altruism, and Self-Respect: An Analysis of Beauvoir," *The Philosophy of (Erotic) Love*, ed. Robert Solomon (Lawrence, KS: Univ. Press of Kansas, 1991), 391–414.

44. Edward Vacek, S.J., "Confidentiality," *The New Dictionary of Sacramental Worship*, ed. Peter Fink, S.J. (Collegeville, MN: Liturgical Press, 1990), 247–52.

45. Martin D'Arcy, S.J., *The Mind and Heart of Love* (New York: Henry Holt, 1947), 210.

46. C. Taylor, *Sources of the Self*, 375, 383.

47. Cooper, "Aristotle on Friendship," 331.

48. James Nelson, *The Intimate Connection* (Philadelphia: Westminster, 1988), 55.

49. Evelyn Eaton Whitehead and James Whitehead, *Marrying Well* (Garden City: Doubleday, 1981), 224; C. Taylor, *Sources of the Self*, 383–85.

50. Williams, *Spirit and Forms*, 136; see also Whitehead and Whitehead, *Marrying Well*, 224. By contrast, D'Arcy, *Mind and Heart*, 314, first argues extensively that "in true loving we receive and give," but then when it comes to God says only that "we receive life and receive it more abundantly."

51. Nancy Ring, "Sin and Transformation," *Chicago Studies* 23 (November 1984): 316; Diana Fritz Cates, "Towards an Ethic of Shared Selfhood," *Annual of the Society of Christian Ethics* (1991), 249–54.

52. Toner, *The Experience of Love*, 187, 192, 194.

53. Toner, *The Experience of Love*, 193.

54. Robert Nozick, "Love's Bond," *The Philosophy of (Erotic) Love*, 417–32.

55. Stacer, "Divine Reverence for Us," 440–42.

56. Christine Gudorf, "Parenting, Mutual Love, and Sacrifice," *Women's Consciousness, Women's Conscience*, ed. Barbara Hilkert Andolsen et al. (New York: Harper & Row, 1985), 105.

57. William Wilcox, "Egoists, Consequentialists, and Their Friends," *Philosophy & Public Affairs* 16 (Winter 1987): 78.

58. Outka, *Agape*, 43, 175.

59.   Margaret Farley, "The Church and the Family," *Horizons* 10 (Spring 1983): 60.

60.   D'Arcy, *Mind and Heart,* 228.

61.   *ST* I–II.28.3; *Sententiarum,* 3.28.1.1.

62.   *ST* I–II.28.2, II–II.30.2, also I.20.1.

63.   *ST* II–II.30.2.

64.   *ST* I.20.1, I–II.26.4, 28.1, II–II.25.2, 25.3.

65.   *ST* I–II.28.1. Since Aquinas says this love is like a substantial union, "whereby one loves oneself," it has often—not without textual warrant—been interpreted to mean that friendship love is really a form of self-love. Aquinas resists this interpretation, for he adds that in a concupiscential love the movement of love "remains finally within him," but "in a friendship-love, a man's affection goes out from itself simply because he wishes and does good to his friend, by caring and providing for him, for his sake" (*ST* I–II.28.3).

66.   Cicero, "On Friendship," *xvi,* in *Other Selves,* 100.

67.   Søren Kierkegaard, in "You Shall Love Your *Neighbour,*" in *Other Selves,* 241, 244.

68.   Aristotle, *Nicomachean Ethics,* 1157b (McKeon: 1063); also, *ST* I–II.28.1.

69.   Robert Adams, "Pure Love," *Journal of Religious Ethics* 8 (1980): 97.

70.   Outka, *Agape,* 37–38.

71.   Outka, *Agape,* 281–82; Ernest Wallwork, "Thou Shalt Love Thy Neighbor As Thyself: The Freudian Critique," *Journal of Religious Ethics* 10 (Fall 1982): 291–92.

72.   Stacer, "Divine Reverence for Us," 440–42.

73.   Meilaender, *Friendship,* 14.

74.   Cicero, "On Friendship," *xix–xx,* in *Other Selves,* 104–5; cf. Aristotle, *Nicomachean Ethics,* 1158b–59a (McKeon: 1061).

75.   *Sententiarum,* 3.27.1.3. Aquinas also reverses the order: similarity causes love; *Sententiarum,* 3.27.2.1; *ST* I–II.27.3; though see *ST* II–II.25.6. Unfortunately, Aquinas also set down as a *general* principle that "we ought to hate in others that which is dissimilar to us, and to destroy it whenever possible" (*Sententiarum,* 3.28.1.4, 30.1.1).

76.   Sandra Schneiders, I.H.M., *New Wineskins* (New York: Paulist, 1986), 223.

77.   Gilbert Meilaender, *Faith and Faithfulness,* 47.

78.   Adams, "Pure Love," 96.

79.   Cooper, "Aristotle on Friendship," 335; Lawrence Becker, *Reciprocity* (New York: Routledge & Kegan Paul, 1986), 93.

80.   *Sententiarum,* 3.27.1.1; *Duo Praecepta,* 101b.

81.   Fred Berger, "Gratitude," *Ethics* 85 (July 1975): 308.

82.   Outka, *Agape,* 282; also Meilaender, *Friendship,* 53–67. One should question the prejudice in favor of immutability that pervades this literature.

83.   Kenneth Cauthen, *Process Ethics* (New York: Mellen, 1984), 138.

84.   Aristotle, *Nicomachean Ethics,* 1156a–b (McKeon: 1060–61). See also Outka, *Agape,* 271.

85.   For a brief survey of criteria for the dark night, see Constance FitzGerald, O.C.D., "Impasse and Dark Night," *Living with Apocalypse,* ed. Tilden H. Edwards (San Francisco: Harper and Row, 1984), 93–115.

86.   Telfer, "Friendship," 255.

87.   Rosemary Haughton, *The Passionate God* (New York: Paulist, 1981), 27.

88.   Toner, *The Experience of Love*, 193.

89.   Cady, "Relational Love," 141.

90.   Hanigan, *As I Have Loved You*, 146–47; Don Browning, *Religious Thought and Modern Psychologies* (Philadelphia: Fortress, 1983), 150–54; O'Donovan, *Resurrection and Moral Order*, 240. Wadell, *Friendship and the Moral Life*, 74, reverses this pattern when he makes agape merely a universalized friendship, thereby missing the mutuality that is essential to philia but not to agape. See also Outka, *Agape*, 41.

91.   Singer, *The Nature of Love*, 3:18.

92.   Hanigan, *As I Have Loved You*, 146–47, holds that philia is not the Christian love, and his main reason seems to be that this love cannot be commanded, but, as we have seen and he himself admits, no love can be commanded.

93.   Margaret Farley, R.S.M., *Personal Commitments* (New York: Harper & Row, 1986), 34–37; also M. C. Dillon, "Romantic Love, Enduring Love, and Authentic Love," *Soundings* 66 (Summer 1983): 138–40; Stephen Rowntree, S.J., "Johnny Loves Mary Forever: What Therapy Doesn't Know about Love," *Beyond Individualism*, ed. Don Gelpi, S.J. (Notre Dame: Univ. of Notre Dame Press, 1989), 35–41; Telfer, "Friendship," 256–57.

94.   Wadell, *Friendship and the Moral Life*, 70–71.

95.   Outka, *Agape*, 272–73; Meilaender, *Friendship*, 4–5, 28, 34.

96.   David Hollenbach, S.J., "The Common Good Revisited," *Theological Studies* 50 (March 1989): 90, 93.

97.   National Conference of Catholic Bishops, *Economic Justice for All* (Washington: NCCB, 1986), no. 79.

98.   Wadell, *Friendship and the Moral Life*, 70–71.

99.   O'Donovan, *Problem of Self-Love*, 122–23.

100.   Marilyn Friedman, "Feminism and Modern Friendship," *Ethics* 99 (January 1989): 275–90; Thomas Murray, "Gifts of the Body and the Needs of Strangers," *Hastings Center Report* 17 (April 1987): 34–36.

101.   Daniel Callahan, "Religion and the Secularization of Bioethics," *Hastings Center Report* 20 (Supplement July/August 1990): S4.

102.   Outka, *Agape*, 278.

103.   *ST* II–II.25.4; Outka, *Agape*, 37–38.

104.   Garth Hallett, *Christian Neighbor-Love* (Washington: Georgetown Univ. Press, 1989), 79.

105.   Sedgwick, *Sacramental Ethics*, 79–82.

106.   Outka, *Agape*, 274; Meilaender, *Friendship*, 30–31. This openness is not the same as being willing to have these others share in the friendships we already have formed. That is, the dynamic of the relation we have with one or a few may be unique and would be distorted by the presence of other persons within that bond, e.g., marriage.

107.   Barbara Hilkert Andolsen, "Agape in Feminist Ethics," *Journal of Religious Ethics* 9 (Spring 1981): 73–77.

108.   Outka, *Agape*, 288.

109.   Toner, *The Experience of Love*, 55; Williams, *Spirit and Forms*, 146.

110.   McFague, *Models of God*, 139.

111.   Eileen O'Hea, C.S.J., "Surrendering to the Divine Other," *Review for Religious* 49 (May/June 1990): 431–33.

112.   Wadell, *Friendship and the Moral Life*, 81; also see Edward Vacek, S.J., "Popular Ethical Subjectivism," *Horizons* 11 (1984): 44–46.

113.   Nygren, *Agape and Eros* (New York: Harper & Row, 1969), 78. I take the term "infinite value" to be a metaphor. Like similar terms it mostly means "do not compare." Here I use it only to refer to the preciousness of the individual.

114.   D'Arcy, *Mind and Heart*, 217.

115.   Williams, *Spirit and Forms*, 146.

116.   Williams, *Spirit and Forms*, 120.

117.   Cauthen, *Process Ethics*, 171.

118.   Letty Russell, *Future of Partnership* (Philadelphia: Westminster, 1979), 41. Thomas Shannon, "Marriage—Mutuality and Equality," *New Theology Review* 3 (August 1990): 6–22, nicely illustrates how neither agape nor eros are sufficient for understanding marriage. It is not necessary that there be only one reason for which we act. Gudorf, "Parenting, Mutual Love, and Sacrifice," 101–10, ably shows a "mixed love" within family life, though she misses the point of "for the sake of," confusing results with reasons. The fact that parents grow through loving their children does not mean that they love their children in order that they might grow. Wallwork, "Love Thy Neighbor: Freudian Critique," 274–77, points out that for Freud relationships will not last long if there is not some narcissistic gratification in them.

119.   Aristotle, *Nicomachean Ethics*, 1157b (McKeon: 1063); Cady, "Relational Love," 141–43; Sedgwick, *Sacramental Ethics*, 86; Cauthen, *Process Ethics*, 160.

120.   Becker, *Reciprocity*, 186–95.

121.   Toner, *The Experience of Love*, 196–97.

122.   Outka, *Agape*, 36–37, 268–69, 280.

123.   D'Arcy, *Mind and Heart*, 24.

124.   Cady, "Relational Love," 140; Berger, "Gratitude," 309.

9

Friendship with God

Beloved, let us love one another because love is of God; everyone who loves is begotten of God and has knowledge of God. The man without love has known nothing of God, for God is love. (1 Jn 4:7–8)

The central theme of this book is that we can have a love relationship with God and that we can love ourselves and our neighbors as part of that love relationship. This friendship with God is the heart of Christian life.

TRADITION ON PHILIA WITH GOD

John, the "apostle of love," offered many descriptions of the philia relationship between God and humans. Jesus makes the bold claim, "I am in the Father and the Father is in me" (Jn 14:10). This love involves both their difference from one another and their unity: Jesus claims, "The Father is greater than I" (Jn 14:28), and he also proclaims, "The Father and I are one" (Jn 10:30). The relation between Jesus and his "Father" is mutual and it has a shared world: he prays to God, "Just as all that belongs to me is yours, so all that belongs to you is mine" (Jn 17:10). This mutual relation leads to Jesus' cooperation: "My Father is at work until now, and I am at work as well" (Jn 5:17); the work that Jesus does, he does "in my Father's name" (Jn 10:25).

Jesus' philia relationship with his God continues in his disciples: "That they may be one, as we are one—I living in them, you living in me—that their unity may be complete. . . . you loved them as you loved me. . . . your love for me may live in them, and I may live in them" (Jn 17:22–26). Jesus has loved them: "You are my friends" (Jn 15:14; Lk 12:4); and God has been affected by their return love: "My Father has been glorified in your bearing much fruit and becoming my disciples" (Jn 15:8). Indeed, God's own love is perfected in them (1 Jn 4:12). Jesus' friends will go on to bear even greater fruit than he has produced (Jn 14:12). John sums up the relationship between God and humanity in profoundly mutual terms: "God is love, and he who abides in love abides in God and God in him" (1 Jn 4:16).

In its public prayer, the Catholic Church continues this philia language, combining familial and friendship terms. In its eucharist, the Church prays: *"Father,* hear the prayers of the *family* you have gathered here before you. In mercy and love, unite all your *children* wherever they may be. Welcome into your kingdom all who have left this world in your *friendship."*[1] In its spirituality, the Church has emphasized communion with God. Aquinas reflected on our relationship to God not so much in terms of our alienation and sin, but in terms of philia: *"Charity* is a kind of friendship of man to God through which man loves God, *and God man."*[2] For Aquinas, this love includes "a returning of love for love along with a certain communing of one with another. . . . Now this fellowship of man with God, which consists in a kind of intimate living with Him, is begun here in our present life through grace."[3]   Similarly, Karol Wojtyla, now John Paul II, described God's saving grace in terms of community, friendship, and family: "The work of salvation signifies a particular union with God, or rather a *communion.* . . . God, in his superabundant love, adopts man as his *son* and *lives with him as a friend.* Thus revelation is not only the manifestation of the mystery of God, but is also an invitation, by accepting which man *participates in the work of salvation."*[4]

THE SUPERNATURAL REVISITED

Our philia relation with God gives us a way to freshly interpret classical theological language for grace. The tradition had recourse to a "supernature" to make our friendship or filial relationship with God possible. It was assumed that friendship can occur only between equals. Therefore God had to infuse in us something of a divine nature so that we could be "friends." This requirement is, as we have seen, not necessary. Love unites beings who are different, and philia is possible as long as some mutuality is possible. On God's part, grace is God's self-gift to us. On our part, as Karl Rahner argues,

> Grace is not a second nature superimposed on natural nature; it is the opening out of the natural spiritual essential ground of man towards the immediate possession of God, the teleological orientation of man's natural spiritual nature towards the life of God. The supernatural virtues . . . are the orientation of [the spiritual faculties] and their natural virtues towards the life of God. . . . 'Theological virtues' is the rather portentous name for the experience of the accepted grace of God, which is, ultimately, God himself.[5]

Since we can freely refuse or accept God's love, we live either in sinful nature or graced nature.

In the language of classical theology, human beings are rational animals. As animals, we are bound to the limits of this earth. As rational and as loved by God, however, we are able to respond to One who is beyond these limits. That is, we have a *potentia obedientalis* and a "supernatural existential": we are open to receive God's love and have the ability to respond to God's love.[6] God's love effects in us a new capacity for love analogously to the way another human person's love for us evokes in us a new ability to love. That is, when we accept being loved we are transformed by that very act of acceptance. We accept God's "sanctifying grace."[7] And in genuinely returning God's love, we do not merely add a new object for our love. Rather, our very *ordo amoris* is itself expanded. Thus, by accepting that we are loved and by loving anew, we come into a new way of being.

Uncreated grace, which is God's love, becomes in us "created grace" when we accept God's loving participation in our lives.[8] By uncreated grace, God "has made himself man's personal partner in love."[9] God enters into an interpersonal "dialogue" with us, a dialogue that invites us to live and love in an expanded way.[10] God communicates God's own self and thereby informs, reforms, and transforms our lives.[11] In receiving this self-gift, we do not lose our humanity. We are "supernaturally elevated" in the sense that we now love not only with our own mind and heart but also in union with God's. Our elevated humanity then becomes, in Rahner's bold words, "the other mode of existence of God himself."[12] Through philia God lives in us and we live in God.

Grace does not turn psychological egoists into selfless lovers. We are by nature able to agapically love our friends or even enemies, even if we do so only sporadically. Rather, what grace primarily brings about is that we become friends with God. We cannot do that by ourselves because, as we have seen, it takes "two" to make a friendship. Grace also enables us to cooperate with God in loving the world. When our good deeds flow from this relation, we experience in ourselves what the tradition called "cooperative grace."[13] Our activities flow from and are enacted for the sake of our friendship with God. Because we are in this new relation, we find that we are more able to do that which is good and holy. We face life's tasks and difficulties with more equanimity and strength because we sense that we are not alone. In classical terms, we experience a new strength called "actual grace." Our God is with us, concerned about us, sharing our life, and so we experience in ourselves new and more abundant life (Jn 10:10).

DOCTRINAL IMPLICATIONS

If "God is love" and "love is of God" (1 Jn 4:7–8), then we should expect our doctrine of God to be affected by our theory of love, and vice versa. And, indeed, such has been the case. Anders Nygren spoke for many when he described God as primarily a sovereign savior whose love means mercy to sinners.[14] Accordingly, many Christians claim that agape for strangers and enemies is the preeminent "Christian love."[15] In Nygren's approach, the Johannine view of love, while admirable in many respects, "weakened down" and lost the "purity" found in the synoptic and Pauline views of agape.[16] By contrast, I have taken a more Johannine position that begins with God as our "Father" and Jesus as our brother or friend. This position does not deny sin, but situates sin and salvation within these relationships. Accordingly, the preeminent Christian love is philia among friends and neighbors. As Aquinas writes, "Friendship is the *most perfect* in what pertains to love."[17]

This view of Christian love requires us to reconsider our image of God and our doctrine of salvation.[18] Many theologians have hesitated to say that grace is friendship with God because such a statement implies that *God* is really a friend to us. The doctrine of God, they say, implies that God cannot "become" anything, let alone a friend. Theologians have also hesitated to say that *we* really are friends to God.[19] The doctrine of salvation, they say, implies that we human beings are too wretched to really be friends with God. Let us look at these two concerns.

First, can God become a friend to us? A common understanding of agape rules out any mutuality and therefore friendship between God and ourselves. This point appears in Gene Outka's description of a typically Protestant view of agape:

> The criterion for agapeistic actions appears to be only what *exemplifies* or *expresses* something resident in a person, irrespective of all questions of response and reciprocity. Whether the enemy remains my enemy or whether the beloved is aware of my devotion are considerations for which the criterion itself appears to authorize no interest.[20]

Catholic theologians such as Germain Grisez have often argued something similar when they claim that God "creates all things *not to acquire anything*, but solely to *express* his goodness."[21]

If God's love for us is agapic in these ways, then a number of distortions follow. Should we say that God creates purely "to express his goodness"? I have argued that an act of pure self-expression is not really an act of love for another but only an act of *self*-love. One can grant God's acts of creating and redeeming do express God's goodness. But, surely, God's love means that God is also concerned that goodness of *creation* itself is expressed, realized, and fostered.[22] And is it true that God does not care whether we are aware of God's love? If that were true, why would God have revealed God's own self? Also is it really true that God does not care whether we respond or whether we remain an enemy? If that were true, what would it mean to say that God's son died to save us from our sins, to consecrate us, and to bring us to glory as brothers and sisters (Heb 2:9–11)? This view of agape distorts our idea of God's love. If God loves agnostics and sinners, God wants them to become believers and saints.

Again, should we, without qualification, say that God cannot and does not want, in Grisez's words, to "acquire anything" in a relationship with us? I have argued that God does not have what God wants to "acquire," namely, our hearts, until we give them to God. The Church prays, "May [Christ] make us an everlasting gift to you."[23] If Christ makes us a gift to God, can we not presume that God receives that gift and thereby "gains something?" Thus, when we join Christ's offering and offer ourselves in love to God, God gains a friend—a paltry, measly, almost insignificant, often traitorous friend, but a friend nonetheless. Furthermore, the Gospel paradox that by losing one's self, one gains one's self (Lk 17:33) is also a revelation about God. By "losing" God's self-sufficiency, God becomes our God. God gains a new relational identity.

Second, can we become friends to God? This is the question of salvation. The Reformers well understood that "the nature of man is his essentially relational mode of being."[24] Being out of relation to God is the meaning of depravity. However well our intellect, will, and heart otherwise function, they fail their primary purpose if they are not active in relation to God. In *this* sense, fulfilling "natural law" is sinful if by "nature" one means the self apart from its relation to God. Sin, as Rahner notes, is a refusal to live in union with the God who "has made himself man's personal partner in love." That is, it is a "rejection of God's personal love."[25]

How then are we saved? Agape-based theories of salvation such as Nygren's tend to make salvation quite independent from how we live our lives. Since Nygren holds that God's saving love is detached from any good or evil in us, the way to conduct our lives would seem to have little or no bearing on our salvation. God's saving love may even, to paraphrase

Outka's description, not care whether the sinner remains a sinner. If so, salvation becomes forensic. Eros-based theories of salvation, on the other hand, usually emphasize our human efforts to obtain our perfection. The way we live has everything to do with our salvation. We must constantly purify our loves and constantly grow in love for that which will finally satisfy us, namely, God. Our own salvation is our quest.

One Catholic attempt to avoid both these problems explains that God has freely decided to reward our good works with eternal salvation. This solution has the merit of preserving both God's primacy and the significance of human action. As John Langan writes, "Christians have generally supposed that they [gain eternal happiness] only indirectly, that is, in some way that is dependent on God's judgment and his just distribution of rewards to the good and punishments to the evil."[26] Is this adequate? I think not.

Salvation means that we are invited into a personal, intimate, mutual relation with God. Salvation is the gift of and growth in a philia relationship with God. Eros-based theories are wrong because no one can produce or earn or even merit such a relationship. Achieving salvation through our good works is impossible, not because of some divine decree or prerogative, but because of the philia nature of salvation. Trying to win God's love is misguided because we already are loved by God. Indeed, it is offensive to try to earn any personal relationship, especially when it is already freely offered. A personal relationship is also not an issue of justice.[27] We don't owe someone our friendship; above all, God does not owe us friendship. Our love relationship with God is God's free gift and our free response.

Paradoxically, when we begin to accept this relationship, we come to realize how far we are from full intimacy with God.[28] When we allow ourselves to feel loved by God, we are able to let go of our defenses and see both our evil and our good. We walk along the path of our salvation. Our good actions are then seen to be not simply our own initiatives. They are already our acts of cooperation with God. If so, then there is already blessedness in the very doing of them. The relationship itself is the primary blessing; its absence is the primary meaning of damnation. Morally good action is not an indirect condition for meriting beatitude, but rather a partial possession of beatitude.

If God abides in us and we in God (1 Jn 4:10), then this salvation, far from being forensic, means rather that we can emotionally and affirmatively participate in God's life. As Walter Kern writes, "The dogma of grace means real 'intersubjectivity' between God and man, a living fellowship of love, not two 'one-way streets', but a common current to and fro."[29] When we live in this philia relationship, we live in a new way.[30] We put off our old selves and begin to live with new selves (Eph 4:24; Col 3:10).

In this new life, we are a "new creation" capable of new acts (Gal 6:15; 2 Cor 5:17–20). What are these "new acts" we can do? The primary answer, of course, is that we can love God. After that, and within that, love for God enables us to share in God's ongoing work (Jn 9:4). Our friendship with God allows us to relive the past, for God has been there; it allows us to live in the present moment, for God is active there; and it allows us to live for the future, since God wants to bring about that future. The Church's prayer is, "Help us to *embrace the world* you have given us, that we may *transform* the darkness of its pain into the life and joy of Easter."[31] When we love God and cooperate with God's love in transforming the world, we already share the life and the joy of Easter.

A SIMPLE SUMMARY

Natural law theologians commonly say, "*Our* ways *are* God's ways"; that is, our naturally good human ways are the way God has created us. But other Christians insist, "*God's* ways *are not* our ways"; that is, as creatures and sinners, we are different from God. The theme of this book is that we must hold together both God's ways and our good human ways, affirming both, preserving their distinction, and uniting them in friendship. God's ways and our ways are united in a covenant that accentuates the distinction between God and ourselves. God can do so much that we cannot do, and together with God we can do much that God cannot do without us.

Out of love for us God accepts our human way as part of God's way, but God's love opens us out to a new way of being human. In response, we accept God's way as part of our way, and we thereby allow God a new way to be God. Our new way of being means reformation from sin and sharing in divine life. God's new way of Being is to become our Creator, Redeemer, and Sanctifier, that is, the Christian God. Our covenant with God involves multiple forms of activity both on our part and God's: it is now creative, now restraining, now sustaining, now forgiving, now enjoying, and always directed to richer life. Whether we promote our lives or sacrifice them, we live fully only when we live in *union* with God. The new heaven and new earth occurs when God shares in our lives and we share in God's life. In other words, ours can be an ongoing love affair with God. Like any love affair, this relation has its ups and downs, its moments of distance and renewal. Like any love affair, this relation can last a lifetime, and longer.

Anders Nygren and Thomas Aquinas offered two classic alternatives to this covenantal view. If God is truly sovereign, reflected Nygren, then God is everything and we are nothing. God's love passes through us as through so many empty tubes toward our neighbors. If God is truly the highest good, reflected Aquinas, then our love for God is our way of striving to get what is most fulfilling for ourselves. Our goal is to pass beyond the world and our friends until we at last gain possession of that good which completely satisfies. If God is truly merciful, reflected Nygren, then God's love is directed downward to sinners who have no value. If God is truly perfect, reflected Aquinas, then our love is directed upward but contributes nothing to God. Aquinas had an alternative position, and so did Nygren, but they did not extensively develop this alternative. Each said that through grace we could have a friendship or fellowship with God. This book has developed this alternative a little further.

Friendship does not require equality, though it does require mutuality. But how can there be anything in common between God and humanity? The answer I have proposed is rather simple. Love means sharing in the life of the beloved. Hence, humanity and God can have the life of one another in common. We human persons are not trapped in our own skins, and God is not trapped in divine self-sufficiency. We live not only in ourselves, but also in God. As lovers, we can be more than ourselves. In fact, we become ourselves only by becoming involved with more than ourselves. Similarly, our Christian God is not a solipsist, all wrapped up in the divine self. Our God too has gone out of the divine self to share in our lives. Thus, God has a history that is lived in this world and especially lived in our lives. God begins this history by lovingly creating the world. God begins a special phase of this history by lovingly creating each of us.

This book has developed these theological themes by reflecting on our experiences of human love. Those experiences are a rich but too often neglected resource for theology. A strange, but rather commonplace thing happens when others love us. They affirm us and, if we are sensitive, we feel invited to change. We can resist their affirmation, and we feel our hearts harden. But we can yield to it, allowing others to share our life. If we do so, we find that we grow both softer and stronger. We are more sensitive to the goodness of the world about us, and we can do things we would otherwise not have thought possible. We feel ennobled, as if we had greater possibilities of goodness than we ever dreamed of, and we are inclined to make those possibilities become real. Thus, when we feel loved, we are inclined to love ourselves. We feel "good enough" about being less than perfect. But we also want to be our best selves, living toward the ideal that our lover puts before us, an ideal that our lover continuously takes from us and regularly revises in the light of how we have grown or failed.

Another strange and commonplace thing happens when others love us. Feeling their presence in our life, and accepting their presence, we want to love them in response. We want to affirm those who are affirming us. We want to share in their lives. Of course, this can be too burdensome, demanding too many changes in our preferred way of proceeding. But we can do it. The union of their spirit with ours invites us to unite our spirit with theirs. And when we love them in return, we too no longer live just in ourselves, but we live in them. Our spirit is not so much divided as increased by loving them.

A further strange, commonplace, and miraculous thing happens when others love us and we, in response, love them. We become mutually concerned about our friendship. We want it to increase. We want to be together. We want to share one another's successes and failures, sufferings and joys. We want to do things together. Our projects are of interest to our friends, and their projects are of interest to us. We want to cooperate with one another. But because of our reverence for our friends, we do not want to take from them their unique contribution to whatever we do together, nor do they want to take ours from us. Our respective differences mutually contribute to rather than detract from what is so important to us, namely, our friendship. We encourage, cajole, chastise, or invite them, but we want them to be free in responding.

We want, whenever we can, to get to know and love the world that our friends love, especially the people they love. Whenever other involvements threaten our relationship, however, we ask questions of priority. We ask whether our own relationship is more important. If it is, we ask how to bring these other involvements into some subordinate position, or how to eliminate them altogether. Each of us makes decisions by looking to see how these decisions will fit within our friendship. We don't give orders to one another. We don't set up rules for our friends to follow. Rather, we gradually develop together "our way of proceeding." We are confident we have at least a lifetime together to work such things out.

Sometimes our love is almost wholly centered on one another. Happy about our friendship, we find that we want to do good for our friends. We are even willing to sacrifice and die for them. Sometimes our love is more concerned with our own selves, for we too are worthy of love. But we also want to do good for still others. We want to share with an expanding circle of other people the good that we have experienced. "A good man produces goodness from the good in his heart" (Lk 6:45), and we feel full of overflowing goodness. We even feel strong enough to love those who are strangers or enemies. And we are especially concerned for people who seem to have so little of the goods we possess. We want them all to flourish. We want them to know love.

All that I have said here about a human love relationship is true in its own fashion of our love relationship with God. God is love, so it is proper for God to love God and to love us. It is proper for us human beings to love ourselves, for in that way we cooperate with God. It is also proper for us to love our neighbors, for God is doing that too. It is above all proper for us to love God, and that is the best we can ever do.

CONCLUSION

This, then, is a simple summary of the simple vision that has guided this book. It also is a simple statement of the foundation of Christian ethics. God loves us; and for us to live is to respond in love to God and to all God loves. Once we have felt that love, then, with the lawyer in Luke's Gospel, we can reply that this is the heart of our Christian life:

> *You shall love the Lord your God,*
> *with all your heart,*
> *with all your soul,*
> *with all your strength,*
> *and with all your mind;*
> *and your neighbor as yourself.*

And, if this is our reply, then God's response is:

> *You have answered correctly.*
> *Do this and you shall live. (Lk 10:25–26)*

NOTES

1.   Third Eucharistic Prayer, *The Sacramentary* (Catholic Book Publishers, 1974), 554–55 (italics mine).

2.   *Sententiarum*, 3.27.2.1 (italics mine). Also, *ST* I.19.2. Aquinas offered some promising leads for understanding the relation between God and Christians as one of friendship. But the language of self-love and self-fulfillment predominated in Thomistic ethics. In the *Summa Theologiae*, friendship with God is introduced after the basic lines

of the ethics are completed, and the *Summa* does not, in my judgment, overcome the dominance of eros as the central love.

3. *ST* I–II.65.5. Out of a desire to preserve God's immutability, however, Aquinas was quite hesitant to draw out the implications of a *mutual* friendship with God.

4. Karol Wojtyla, *Sources of Renewal* (San Francisco: Harper & Row, 1980), 54–55 (italics mine).

5. Karl Rahner, S.J., "Love as the Key Virtue," *Sacramentum Mundi* (New York: Herder and Herder, 1970), 6:338–39; Karl Rahner, S.J., *Foundations of Christian Faith* (New York: Seabury, 1978), 119–23. See also Richard McCormick, S.J., "Theology and Bioethics: Christian Foundations," *Theology and Bioethics*, ed. Earl Shelp (Boston: Reidel, 1985), 103–7.

6. Rahner, S.J., "Love as the Key Virtue," 6:341; Karl Rahner, S.J. "Existence: 'The Existential'," *Encyclopedia of Theology* (New York: Seabury, 1975), 494–95.

7. Bernard Lonergan, S.J., *Method in Theology* (New York: Herder and Herder, 1972), 120; also Gérard Gilleman, S.J., *The Primacy of Charity in Moral Theology* (Westminster, MD: Newman, 1959), xxiv.

8. Karl Rahner, S.J., "Thomas Aquinas on the Incomprehensibility of God," *The Journal of Religion* 58 (Supplement 1978): S114. Karl Rahner, S.J., in "Grace," *Encyclopedia of Theology*, 593, adds that this "occurs in a mutually conditioning relationship."

9. Karl Rahner, S.J., "Sin," *Encyclopedia of Theology*, 1589.

10. Rahner, "Grace," 588–92.

11. Karl Rahner, S.J., "Revelation," *Encyclopedia of Theology*, 1467.

12. Karl Rahner, S.J., "Man (Anthropology)," *Sacramentum Mundi* (New York: Herder & Herder, 1969), 3:370.

13. Lonergan, *Method in Theology*, 107, 120; Roger Haight, S.J., "Foundational Issues in Jesuit Spirituality," *Studies in the Spirituality of Jesuits* 19 (September 1987): 16.

14. Anders Nygren, *Agape and Eros* (New York: Harper & Row, 1969), 45, 70.

15. Gilbert Meilaender, *Friendship* (Notre Dame: Univ. of Notre Dame Press, 1981), 4–5, 28, 34.

16. Nygren, *Agape and Eros*, 150, 158.

17. *Sententiarum*, 3.27.2.1 (italics mine). See also *ST* I.19.2.

18. Lonergan, *Method in Theology*, 107. For Aquinas's contrary position, see Paul Wadell, C.P., *Friendship and the Moral Life* (Notre Dame: Univ. of Notre Dame Press, 1989), 124–27. Aquinas denies that grace and love are the same thing (*Sententiarum*, 3.27.2.4).

19. Nygren, *Agape and Eros*, 68, 80–81, 146, does say that *"Agape is the initiator of fellowship with God"* and that Jesus offers a *"new fellowship with God."* Nygren, however, has little to say about this fellowship. This is not strange because what he does say makes fellowship between God and human beings all but impossible. We are unequal and we are sinners (p. 92).

20. Gene Outka, *Agape* (New Haven: Yale Univ. Press, 1976), 34 (italics in original).

21. Germain Grisez, *Way of the Lord Jesus* (Chicago: Franciscan Herald, 1983), 460 (italics mine); also Patrick Byrne, *"Ressentiment* and the Preferential Option for the Poor," *Theological Studies* 54 (June 1993): 228.

22. For Aquinas, God is not said to love creatures for themselves as ends, but rather for God's own end, "which is *His own* goodness." Still, occasionally, Aquinas says

that God has friendship toward us, which implies that as friends we are loved for ourselves and not simply for God's self (*Sententiarum*, 3.27.2.1).

23. Third Eucharistic Prayer, *The Sacramentary*, 554–55.

24. Jan Aertsen, *Nature and Creature* (New York: Brill, 1988), 387.

25. Rahner, "Sin," 1589.

26. John Langan, S.J., "Beatitude and Moral Law in St. Thomas," *Journal of Religious Ethics* 5 (1977): 186.

27. Stephen Pope, "Proper and Improper Partiality and the Preferential Option for the Poor," *Theological Studies* 54 (June 1993): 257.

28. William Barry, S.J., "Jesuit Formation Today," *Studies in the Spirituality of Jesuits* 20 (November 1988): 6.

29. Walter Kern, "God-World Relationship," *Sacramentum Mundi* (New York: Herder & Herder, 1968), 2:405.

30. Donald Gelpi, "Two Spiritual Paths: Thematic Grace vs. Transmuting Grace," *Spirituality Today* 35 (Fall and Winter 1983): 253, 348–49.

31. "Opening Prayer for Fifth Sunday of Lent," *The Sacramentary*, 114 (italics mine).

Scripture Index

Author Index

Subject Index

Acceptance, 125, 127–28, 132, 224
Affected, being
    emotion, 12–13, 160
    God and, 123, 128
    love, 50, 53, 288
Affections. *See* Emotion
Affirmation, 49, 54–61. *See also* Trans-
    formation: beloved
    emotional, 14, 132
    of God, 130
    of independent other, 37, 125,
        251–53
    of self, 75
Agape. *See also* Primary Christian love:
    agape
    condemned, 109n. 51, 201–205
    contrasted with other loves, 159–
        60, 284–87
    directed to beloved's good, 109n.
        51, 171, 240–47
    emotion, 160–62, 193n. 21, 193n.
        40, 243
    episodic, 302
    faithful, 186–88
    God's love, 188
    impossible, 231
    manner of exercise, 173–75
    proportionate to value, 163–73
Aim of love, 162
Alienation, 125, 129, 308–309
Altruism, 184, 213, 236n. 60
Ambiguity, 119, 120
Anthropocentrism, xv n. 2, 115n. 159,
    158, 246
    fostered by theology, 94–95, 135–
        36, 230
    modified by theocentrism, 105–06

Apocatastasis, 261
Aseity, God's, 64, 89, 96, 122, 124,
    323
Association, voluntary. *See* Voluntary
    association
Atheism
    difference in action, 3, 4, 144, 230
    disappearance of Ground, 91
    gratitude and, 121, 230
Attractiveness: criterion for love, 162,
    177
Attributes of person, 171

Basic humanity, 162, 172, 177–78,
    265
Beneficence
    agape, 160, 162
    distinct from love, 35, 58, 162
    toward God, 131–32
Benefit
    basis of gratitude, 226
    distorting, 277n. 65
    for self, 164, 218, 229, 259. *See also*
        Self-interest
    indifference to, 254. *See also* Self-
        indifference
    philia and, 298
Benevolence
    agape, 160
    distinct from love, 35, 134, 230
    God's, 229–30
    subordinate to concupiscent love,
        207
Bestowal love, 165, 194n. 65, 244
    God's favor, 123, 165
Bestowal value, 18–21

339